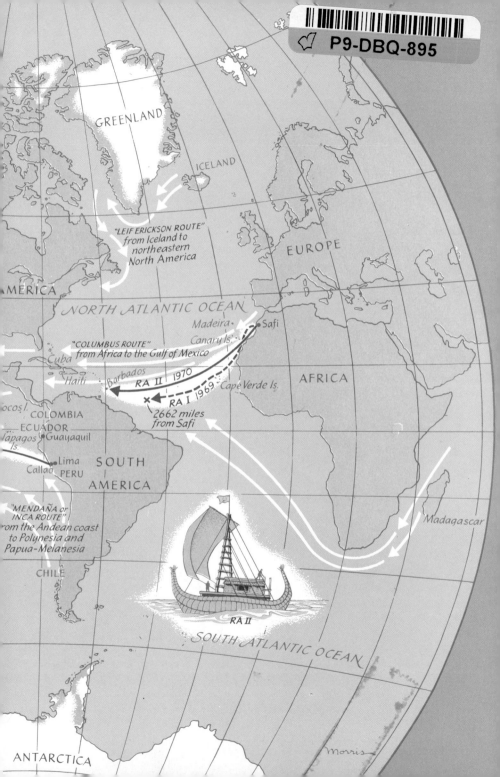

GREENLAND

ICELAND

EUROPE

"LEIF ERICKSON ROUTE"
from Iceland to
northeastern
North America

AMERICA

NORTH ATLANTIC OCEAN

Madeira
Canary Is.
Safi

"COLUMBUS ROUTE"
from Africa to the Gulf of Mexico

Cuba

Haiti
Barbados
RA II 1970
RA I 1969
Cape Verde Is.
AFRICA

ocos I.
COLOMBIA
ECUADOR
Galapagos Guayaquil
Is.
Lima
Callao PERU
SOUTH
AMERICA
×
2662 miles
from Safi

"MENDAÑA or
INCA ROUTE"
from the Andean coast
to Polynesia and
Papua-Melanesia

CHILE

Madagascar

RA II

SOUTH ATLANTIC OCEAN

ANTARCTICA

Morris

EARLY MAN AND THE OCEAN

THOR HEYERDAHL

EARLY MAN AND THE OCEAN

A SEARCH FOR THE BEGINNINGS OF NAVIGATION AND SEABORNE CIVILIZATIONS

DOUBLEDAY & COMPANY, INC., GARDEN CITY, NEW YORK
1979

First Published 1978

Illustration numbers 6 and 7 previously appeared in ZWISCHEN DEN KON-
TINENTEN © 1975 by Verlagsgruppe Bertelsmann. The remaining illustrations are new to this book.

PREFACE

THIS BOOK is not a travelogue of personal adventures. In this respect it is not a sequel to *Kon-Tiki, Aku-Aku, The Ra Expeditions,* or *Fatu-Hiva. Early Man and the Ocean* is an anthology of reports and speeches previously published independently, which I have here combined and edited to form a coherent book. The original idea of such a composition came from Dr. Karl Jettmar, Professor of Archaeology at the University of Heidelberg, and a German version edited by him was published in 1975 under the title *Zwischen den Kontinenten.* It was hoped that the book would give guidance to the many people who have followed the discussions about human migration routes and cultural origins that developed in the wake of the primitive vessels *Kon-Tiki* and *Ra* when they, contrary to expert opinion given in advance, managed to traverse the Pacific and the Atlantic oceans.

Most of the controversy has been based on the erroneous belief that the captain of the balsa raft *Kon-Tiki* and the papyrus ships *Ra I* and *Ra II* had made the claim that the Maori-Polynesians had descended from the Incas of Peru, and that the Incas, Aztecs, and Mayas had descended from the pyramid builders of ancient Egypt. Such theories are easy to refute, but have never been advanced either in my travel books or scientific volumes. Such tomes as *American Indians in the Pacific* (1952, 821 pages), *Reports of the Norwegian Archaeological Expedition to Easter Island and the East Pacific,* Vol. I (1961, 667 pages) and Vol. II (1965, 572 pages), and *The Art of Easter Island* (1975, 669 pages) are hardly known to the general public, and in our days of specialization very rarely read or quoted by the many scientists and pseudoscientists who have passed their opinions on to the public through modern mass media. Those volumes are always available to any who want to penetrate deeper into the library, museum, and field research underlying the more popular reports assembled here. These popular reports are taken from congress proceedings and periodicals not easily accessible to the layman or to the many scholars in related fields of science.

Early Man and the Ocean is edited to be easily readable for anyone interested in man's adventures in the past when the foundations of seafaring and the building of the great Mediterranean and New World civilizations were laid. An introduction has been added to each chapter to prepare the reader for the text which follows.

Thor Heyerdahl
August 7, 1976

To the countless challengers whose opposition made me an admirer of early man and a friend of the living sea. To the erudite experts on whose pioneering work this book entirely depends and who nevertheless left loopholes that made me turn to early man for lessons in fields where there are no surviving authorities.

The Pacific dogma prior to the Kon-Tiki *voyage:*

"Since the South American Indians had neither the vessels nor the navigating ability to cross the ocean space between their shores and the nearest Polynesian islands, they may be disregarded as the agents of supply." (Sir Peter Buck, leading scholar on Polynesia, in *An Introduction to Polynesian Anthropology,* Honolulu, 1945.)

The Atlantic dogma prior to the Ra *voyages:*

"On the Atlantic side the broad expanse of water made immigration impossible." (Franz Boas, leading scholar on the origin of American Indians, in "America and the Old World," *International Congress of Americanists,* Vol. 21, no. 2, 1925.)

CONTENTS

PREFACE   v

Part I: *Early Ships and the Sea*
   1. The Beginning of Navigation   3
   2. Paths Across the Oceans   27

Part II: *The Atlantic Problem*
   3. Isolationists versus Diffusionists   59
   4. The Bearded Gods Before Columbus   93
   5. Columbus and the Vikings   127

Part III: *The Pacific Problem*
   6. From Asia to Polynesia the Easy Way   151
   7. Incas Led the Europeans to Polynesia   185
   8. Balsa Raft Navigation   201
   9. Culture Plants and Early Navigators   229

Part IV: *Steppingstones from South America*
  10. The Pre-Spanish Use of the Galápagos   257
  11. The Coconuts of Cocos Island   275
  12. Easter Island Statues   289
  13. The World's Loneliest Meeting Place   319
  14. Review and Discussion   349

NOTES   399

BIBLIOGRAPHY   407

INDEX   421

LIST OF ILLUSTRATIONS

Reed ships from ancient Egyptian petroglyphs.
Reed ships from cave in Israel and from Cyprus cylinder seal.
Realistic reliefs of Egyptian papyrus and papyriform ships from Edfu
    and Sakara.
Building principles of reed ship.
Ra II, front and side view.
Map of globe from two angles.
Map of routes of modern raft voyages from South America.
Feasible sea routes to and from the Americas in early times.
A wheeled ceramic animal from Ur in Mesopotamia.
Ceramic animal (wheels lost) from the Mediterranean coast of southern
    Turkey.
Ceramic animal from Ibiza in the Baleares.
Ceramic animal with wheels from Tres Zapotes, Mexico.
Sakara pyramid in Egypt.
Drawing of Mexican pyramid of Mesopotamian type.
Peruvian pyramid, from Benzoni 1565.
Tahitian pyramid, from Wilson 1799.
Bearded men coming on rafts.
Olmec pottery head from Tres Zapotes on the Gulf of Mexico.
Olmec stone relief from La Venta on the Gulf of Mexico.
Olmec relief on stone mirror from Vera Cruz on the Gulf of Mexico.
Bearded face on a Peruvian jar, after Montell 1929.
Map of route used by the Incas to the nearest island in the Pacific.
Old drawing of balsa raft from Guayaquil.
Building principles of aboriginal balsa raft of northwestern South
    America.
Unornamented, utilitarian *guara* from southern Peru.
Guara navigation.
Archaeological sites in the Galápagos Islands.
Mythical Mochica reed boats from pre-Inca Peru.
The globe seen from the Antarctic.

PART I

EARLY SHIPS AND THE SEA

Chapter 1

The Beginning of Navigation

MAN HOISTED sail before he saddled a horse. He poled and paddled along rivers and navigated the open seas before he traveled on wheels along a road. Watercraft were the first of all vehicles. With them the Stone Age world began to shrink. By hoisting sail or merely traveling with the current, early man was able to settle the islands. Territories that could be reached overland only by generations of gradual transmigration for those who had to confront obstacles like swamps and lifeless tundra, naked mountains and impenetrable jungles, glaciers and deserts could be reached in weeks by casual drift or by navigation. Watercraft were man's first major tool for his conquest of the world.

The following chapter on early ships was originally published in *Dialogue* in 1972. It has been somewhat augmented, principally by a description of the durable reed rafts of the marsh Arabs studied in Iraq later the same year, and by subsequent findings during renewed field research in Egypt in 1976.

*   *   *

How early did man first venture into the ocean, and in what kind of craft? To what extent was he able to move freely on the high seas?

A couple of centuries ago, when sail still ruled the sea, it was usual to assume that the ancient civilized people were capable of almost unlimited movement. After all, the vessels of Magellan, Captain Cook, and many others had sailed around the world once or twice with only the wind to help them, so why not the ancient peoples? But when we invented the propeller and the jet, and the world grew smaller and smaller for rising generations, we began to acquire the idea that going back through the ages, it must have been larger and larger, until in the days before Columbus the world must have been endless and the oceans impassable.

In the first half of the present century, when steamships and airplanes replaced large and small sailing ships at sea, the attitude grew among modern anthropologists that until the ribbed and planked wooden hull was invented and acquired large dimension, man was restricted to voyages on inland and coastal waters. The possibility of transoceanic contact with America before the existence of the small but lofty caravels, like those of Columbus in 1492, was deemed impossible for practical maritime reasons.

The standard textbook idea of marine architecture was that in order to cross short stretches of water man first rode astride a log. To keep his feet dry, he next thought of hollowing it out with adz and fire, and as he ventured among bigger waves he added more and more side planks to keep the water from splashing in, until he eventually arrived at the hollow hull with waterproof deck high above the sea's surface, so that he could defy even the most violent movements of the waves. With ever bigger hulls, it has been assumed, he ventured ever farther into the open ocean. Hardly a textbook diverges from this version of how man built his first ships. Yet on closer examination this long-established dogma runs contrary to known facts.

It is obvious that man's first preoccupation in developing watercraft was to solve the problem of buoyancy. Throughout the world this aim was achieved as a result of two completely different principles. One consists of assembling a wash-through vessel from components which are themselves buoyant, until the resulting formation has sufficient buoyancy to carry the required crew and cargo. The second is the construction of a watertight hull which owes its buoyancy not to the material of which it is built but to the displacement of water by air.

A re-examination of the earliest boat illustrations in existence shows that ships developed out of the first of these two categories and not, as had commonly been assumed, out of the dugout canoe. This can be proved very easily, both in the Old World and the New. In America there is no other possibility. When the Europeans discovered America, deep sea navigation was already developed and intensively practiced on both the Atlantic and the Pacific sides of the New World. Yet not even the most developed aboriginal American civilizations had hit upon the idea of building ribbed ships with planks, although canoes were in com-

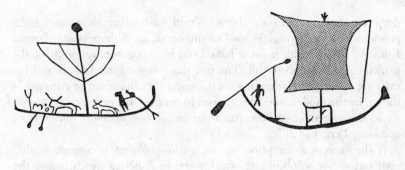

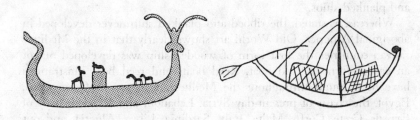

Reed ships from ancient Egyptian petroglyphs (after Resch 1967).

mon use. The sailing vessels of ancient America were flat and sturdy
rafts of balsa logs and boat-shaped reed rafts with elegantly upswept bow
and stern. Both carried tons of cargo on premeditated merchant voyages
between widely separated regions of the New World. Obviously then,

deep-sea navigation in the New World had either developed independently on the American side of the ocean, or if there was influence from the Old World, it must have been by navigators ignorant of the principles of the ribbed hull. The fact that seagoing reed boats and log rafts are as early as civilization itself among the aborigines of America is shown by the models and illustrations in ceramic art, on tapestry, and of wood uncovered in endless quantities in the oldest desert tombs from northern Peru to Chile.

If the current assumption among anthropologists is correct, neither civilization nor shipbuilding was known in America much before the first millennium B.C., a period when Mediterranean civilization had already started navigating the ocean beyond Gibraltar, both in reed boats and planked ships.

Whereas, as stated, the ribbed and planked ship never developed in aboriginal America, Old World art shows clearly that in the Mediterranean countries the first form of wooden ship was developed out of an earlier form of reed boat. Reed boats and reed boat illustrations have been found throughout the Mediterranean from Mesopotamia, Egypt, the coasts of present-day Syria, Lebanon, and Israel by way of Cyprus, Crete, Corfu, Malta, Italy, Sardinia, Libya, Algeria, and out through the Straits of Gibraltar to the Atlantic coast of Morocco. Recently a Phoenician jar, decorated with realistic reliefs of reed boats carrying a radiating sun on deck, was found by divers off the ancient Phoenician port of Cadiz on the Atlantic coast of Spain. Together with a small Egyptian bronze statuette found at the same Atlantic port, it is on exhibit in the Archaeological Museum of Cadiz. Such reed boats have been in sporadic use from Mesopotamia to Atlantic Morocco until the present century, while rock carvings and cliff paintings from Egypt and the Algerian Sahara show that they were already in use five, six, or perhaps seven thousand years ago.

The greatest number of early representations of such boats is found in the desert area of Egypt between the Nile Valley and the Red Sea. In a recent monograph on these Nubian rock carvings by Walther Resch, the numerous illustrations show that, apart from human and animal figures, reed boats are by far the dominant motif, and the reed boats are the only man-made product depicted, apart from weapons.[1] One is struck by the fact that the majority of these sickle-shaped vessels has a numerous crew, sometimes fifty men or more. In addition to the double

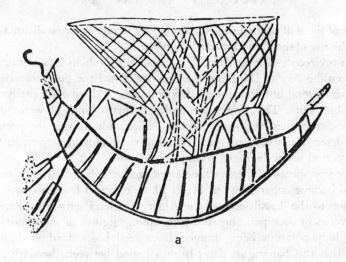

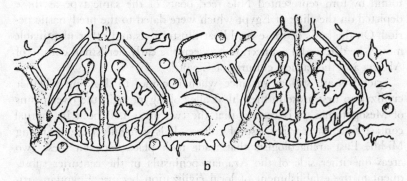

Reed ships from cave in Israel (a) and from Cyprus cylinder seal (b).

steering oar, some show forty or more rowing oars in the water, while a considerable number have mast and rigging and in many cases a large hoisted sail. The great dimensions of these vessels are indicated not only by the number of men and oars, but also by the fact that horned cattle and other large animals are dwarfed on their decks. It is not uncommon that one, or even two, cabins are shown on deck, one fore and one aft of the mast. The papyrus ship, *Ra II,* in which our inexperienced eight-man crew sailed across the Atlantic in 1970, was small compared with the larger of these illustrated vessels dating back to one or two millennia be-fore the rise of the First Dynasty in Egypt.

On my recent visit to Wadi Abu Subeira, a Nubian Desert canyon between the Aswan Dam and the Red Sea, I had the good fortune to discover several hitherto unrecorded examples of these early predynas-tic sailing ships. They were surrounded by petroglyphs of waterbuck, giraffes, crocodiles, and other animals which indicate that the present local desert was forest-covered, and the present canyon a river, in the early period when the rock carvings were made.

The vast spread of these sickle-shaped reed vessels at that same early period became apparent when Henri Lhote returned from his 1956 ex-pedition to the Tassili area of the Algerian Sahara with his amazing discoveries of rock paintings showing, among figures of men and ani-mals, hippopotamus being hunted from reed boats. Carbon datings show that this Sahara art dates from a period between the sixth and the second millennium B.C. Lhote stated that the various boat designs found by him represented Nile reed boats of the same type as those depicted on the cliffs of Egypt which were dated to the predynastic pe-riod. On the basis of these reed boat illustrations and other identifiable motifs, he deduced a connection between the early herdsman culture of Algeria and the earliest cultures of Egypt.[2]

Scientists are still at variance when it comes to deciding whether civilization first arose in the Nile Valley of Egypt or in the river plains of Mesopotamia. It is certain that the two areas had been in mutual contact since the earliest rise of culture. It is generally known among Middle East archaeologists that trade took place between these two areas on either side of the Arabian peninsula in the centuries subse-quent to the establishment of local civilization because Egyptian arti-facts have been found in Mesopotamian excavations and vice versa. In his study of the seafaring merchants of Ur, A. L. Oppenheim shows that the rich influx of ivory into southern Mesopotamia in the earliest cultural periods came from either Egypt or India with the Persian Gulf island of Bahrain as a central maritime marketplace for the Mesopotamian navigators.[3] As shown by S. R. Rao, Indus valley seals have been excavated archaeologically from inside areas of Mesopo-tamia ranging from Ur and Uruk near the Persian Gulf to Tell Brak in Syria near the Turkish border, and G. F. Dales deducts from recent excavations of elaborate ports constructed by the early Harappans of the Indus Valley that they were engaged in "highly organized sea trading ventures" to Mesopotamia and other countries to the west.[4] Imported ivory plaques carved with characteristic Egyptian motifs are so common among archaeological finds from ancient Mesopotamia that most museums in Iraq contain specimens and the National Museum in Baghdad has devoted an entire hall to these locally found Egyptian art objects. It is less known, however, that P. Amiet in his study of the first form of heiroglyphics in Mesopotamia discovered that the earliest precuneiform sign for "ship" was identical with the one representing "marine" in the script of ancient Egypt. As shown earlier by A. Falkenstein, this hieroglyphic sign for "ship" is very common in the earliest Sumerian texts of Mesopotamia, dating back to about 3000 B.C. It actually represents a sickle-shaped reed boat with crosswise lashings and with some peculiar S-shaped adornments both at bow and stern.[5] This goes to show that before the two respective continental civilizations took root in Mesopotamia and Egypt about 3000 B.C. these two areas on each side of the Arabian peninsula had already a most peculiar hieroglyphic sign in common, with the same basic meaning and with ornamental details so special that they are never repeated elsewhere in the world. The bow or stern section of the same type of ship is used as a separate hieroglyphic sign. Falkenstein shows that in this earliest Mesopotamian script the Sumerian sign for "lord" or "gentleman" (en) is represented by the mere stem of such a reed ship, presumably the usual place for its master.

From the hieroglyphic signs and from religious and mnemonic art it is clear that reed ships were an integral part of Mesopotamian culture prior to the local establishment of city states, and that this was probably the only watercraft known during the period of the earliest dynasties. Amiet in fact points out that the said hieroglyphic sign corresponds to a vessel so ancient that its special shape went out of use during the Early Dynasty and was thence preserved for religious use, although common forms of reed boats survived in former Sumerian territories until the present century.

The seagoing ships of ancient Ur and their valuable cargoes from foreign lands are constantly referred to in the earliest Sumerian clay tablets, and Oppenheim points out that these vessels "are exceedingly large," the Third Dynasty records giving them sizes of 300 gur, which equals 96,000 liters or almost 100 tons. In his thorough study of the watercraft of the early Babylonians also A. Salonen refers to tablets describing ships carrying over 50 tons of cargo and he, too, points out that shipbuilding in Mesopotamia clearly began with reed ships and that these later served as models or prototypes when the first plank-built vessels came into use.[6] It is perhaps difficult to visualize that people we are apt to consider as rather primitive could construct and operate what were truly large vessels, dwarfing our reed vessels *Ra I* and *Ra II*. However, it would have been even harder to believe that the same early people could have built such pyramids as those of Sakara in Egypt and of Ur and Uruk in Iraq had we only learned of their existence through written words and not actually seen them in enduring stone or brick.

Reed ships with the sun god, bird-men, and other deities on board and sometimes with deck structures, horned cattle, and other evidence of major dimensions are extremely common on the oldest Sumerian seals and occasionally occur as far up the twin rivers as the Hittite territory of southern Turkey. Large Assyrian reliefs from early Nineveh show realistic reed boats in maritime combat. Defeated mariners are thrown overboard to the crabs and fishes by double rows of boarding enemies. Reed boats and log rafts preceded wooden ships in Asia Minor just as in Egypt, and the same evidence is shown by the earliest ship illustrations on seals and petroglyphs from the early civilizations of Cyprus, Crete, and Malta.

Among these oldest known boat illustrations in the world there are none depicting a straight log-shaped dugout canoe. All the vessels are curved from bow to stern, and most are completely sickle-shaped, the stylized mode of rendering a reed boat. Whereas transition forms from dugout canoe to the earliest forms of wooden ships are absent in this and other early art, the evolution from the reed boats to the first wooden ships can be followed very clearly through the later and more sophisticated art of Pharaonic Egypt, and also through a direct study of the oldest known remains of framed wooden ships. In fact, throughout the inner Mediterranean where deep-sea navigation began, ancient art shows that all really early forms of seagoing ships were either built of reeds or in the shape of reed boats. Since the original vessels have decayed and disappeared everywhere except in the dry and perfectly sealed desert tombs of Egypt, it is there we must turn to find the explanation for the reed-boat shape maintained in the earliest wooden ships.

When the artist employed by the early pharaohs depicted legendary vessels assigned to the period of the early gods and first divine ancestors of man, these were invariably shown as sickle-shaped reed boats

constructed of papyrus stems lashed together and commonly terminating with a symbolic papyrus flower at each gracefully upcurved
end. Here, too, the sun-god, bird-headed deities, and other ancestral culture heroes of all kinds were invariably shown performing all their water
travel on papyrus vessels, never on wooden craft. The ancient artists
show only the later historic pharaohs using wooden boats side by side
with the older form of papyrus vessel, and by the second millennium B.C.
nearly all the larger ships appeared to be of sewn planks; only hunting
vessels and poor men's craft continued to be of bundled papyrus. The
tomb paintings of this period show harvesting and transporting bundles
of papyrus which are lashed together with coils of rope as in the days of
the gods. The striking observation is that all of these first wooden ships
imitate the shape of the papyrus boat in every detail, even to the high and
sweeping curves of bow and stern, terminating in the characteristic
beaker shape of the papyrus prototype. Infinite trouble was taken by the
carpenter, working in rigid timber, to copy from the ancestral papyrus
boats the extremely intricate curves which had resulted so naturally from
the flexible reeds.

The highly evolved shape of these pharaonic vessels, the original
ones of reeds as well as the wooden imitations, was adapted to navigation through surf and big seas. To maintain this complicated form was
quite superfluous, since pharaonic vessels were used mainly on the
Nile, where there are no waves but only ripples and where barges or
flat rafts would have been adequate for all purposes. This shape alone
is therefore sufficient to show that the prototype reed ship of the ancient Egyptians had been developed for use beyond the mouth of the
Nile.

This puzzling fact was dramatically brought into focus by the discovery, a few years ago, of the well-preserved cedar planks of the entire
vessel of Cheops, found in a slab-covered chamber at the foot of his
own pyramid. When Egypt's chief curator of archaeology, Ahmed
Joseph, succeeded in piecing all the huge planks together, by thread-
ing new ropes through the former lashing holes, the world was confronted with the oldest boat in existence.

Built some 2,700 years before Christ, it had an overall length of 143
feet and was so perfectly streamlined and elegant that the Vikings had
not built anything more graceful or more ship-shaped when, some
millennia later, they began to sail the high seas in smaller vessels with
similar lines. The most striking difference between the two seemingly

related types of ship was that the Viking hull was built to bear the brunt of the ocean rollers while Cheops' ship was built for pomp and ceremony on the placid Nile. Wear and tear on the wood where the former ropes had chafed furrows showed that Cheops' ship had been in proper use and was not a "solar ship" built for the pharaoh's funeral. Yet its perfect maritime lines were misleading: it would have collapsed on its first encounter with the high seas.

This paradox has much to tell us about marine history. The exquisite lines of Cheops' ship—but only the lines—were obviously specialized to perfection for true ocean voyaging. The transversal and longitudinal curvatures of the hull, with elegantly upthrust and extremely high bow and stern, had all the characteristic features found only in seagoing vessels designed to ride breakers and towering ocean waves. Yet Pharaoh Cheops, living on the calm shores of the Nile close on 5,000 years ago, had a boat sewn, slatted, and dovetailed together, ignorant of the necessity for internal ribs, and thus obtained a boat which could only stand up to the ripples of the river although built on architectonic lines subsequently never surpassed by seafaring nations. It was obvious that the masterly maritime lines of Cheops' ship had been created by shipbuilders with a long and thorough tradition of sailing on the ocean, and it is equally obvious that the lines followed in every detail the design of the earlier papyrus ships. All authorities agree that Cheops' ship is rigidly papyriform, even to the sharply incurved stern with the calyx shape of the papyrus flower at its tip.

To summarize, all available evidence shows that it was the papyrus ship which had developed all the seagoing ship's characteristic properties and which subsequently became the model for the wooden ship, not the other way around. The design of the papyrus ship was already developed when the First Dynasty began building pyramids along the Nile.

Practical evidence that the papyrus boat was originally designed and specifically rigged for ocean navigation was provided by my experiments which were organized in 1969 and 1970. Two papyrus boats were built and tested in the open Atlantic Ocean. Both were built according to the general outlines shown in ancient Egyptian art, and the shape of the papyrus hull, as well as the details of rigging, cabin, and steering oars, followed a working design by the leading authority on Egyptian ships, Björn Landström, being a synthesis of all the details he had observed during his extensive study of the topic. Since neither he

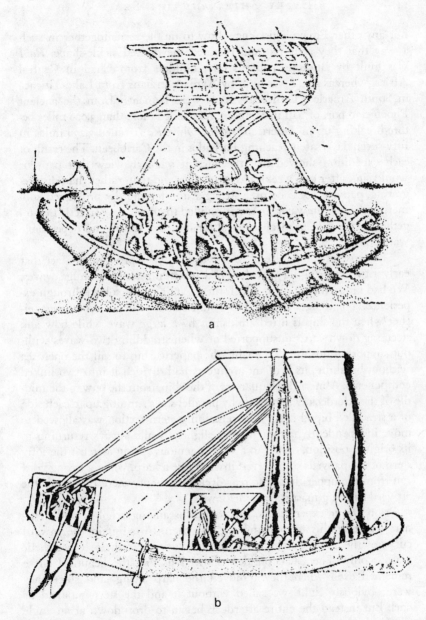

Egyptian reliefs of papyrus and papyriform ships from Edfu (a) and from Sakara (b).

nor any other Egyptologist knew how to tie the reeds together in such
a way that they acquired and retained the desired sickle-shape, *Ra I*
was built by Buduma papyrus boat builders from Chad in Central
Africa, whereas *Ra II* was built by Aymara Indians from Lake Titicaca
in South America. Both test vessels were launched from the ancient
Phoenician port of Saff in Morocco. *Ra I* sailed more than 3,000 miles before breaking up in American waters, while *Ra II* sailed 3,270 miles in
fifty-seven days, safely reaching Barbados in the Caribbean. The result of
each expedition showed that the current scholarly view that papyrus
would sink after two weeks was erroneous, and that, rather than disinte-
grating, papyrus reeds become stronger and tougher by prolonged submergence in ocean water. In fact, provided the reeds are correctly tied together, papyrus is an ideal material for building secure and dependable
watercraft.

The cause of the failure of *Ra I* was in itself a proof of the fact that
early Egyptian rigging was designed for riding surf and huge waves.
We had ignored a problem which the Egyptians had solved through experience. The danger to any ship of fair size is to break up athwart, either when the ship is lifted amidships by a large wave while bow and
stern sag downwards unsupported or when straddling two waves without support amidships. To enable the papyrus ship to sail the open sea
without breaking, its brilliant architects had divided it into two linked
components. Almost three-quarters of the ship, from the bow to the middle of the afterdeck, was held up by parallel stays running up to each side
of a straddled bipod mast. The remaining stern section was allowed to
move independently, although very slightly, while always returning to
its original position, owing to a very ingenious spring system: the lofty
stern of the papyrus ship curved inward like a harp, while a strong cord
ran from the upper tip to the rear deck just about where the last of the
aftward-running mast stays came down.

Prior to our experiments, the consensus among scholars and mariners was that this harp string aft was there to maintain the inward
curve of the stern, and that the inward curve was there for aesthetic
reasons only. The Chad builders showed us that the beautiful curve
remained even when they removed the harp string, and since they
were obviously right, we sailed without it and the stern retained its
curl. But instead the entire afterdeck began to drop down at an angle
until only the curly tail emerged above the water. Too late we had discovered what only the ancient Egyptians could have taught us: that

the harp string was not there to pull the curly tail down, but that the curly tail was there to keep the undulating afterdeck up. It was to function whenever the vessel was riding waves and swells, with the harp structure acting as a spring. This ingenious invention would never have been made for river navigation and would have served no function whatever on the calm Nile. This alone proved that the ancient Egyptians had evolved a specialized rigging to permit their flexible papyrus ships to sail rough seas.

Only those who have tried to build a boat of reeds and rope will realize how extremely ingenious the technique had to be to maintain, in turbulent seas, the boat form so gracefully reproduced on Egyptian walls. Our Chad builders solved the problem the obvious way; they lashed one bundle at the side of another in ever increasing numbers with interlocking chains of rope, like a thick flat raft with bundles in many layers and with bow and stern thinned out and bent up to imitate the profile of the Egyptian reed ship. As stated, on the sea this improvised stern sagged down, and as waves were thus free to thunder aboard from behind, the lashed-on cabin moved back and forth and chafed through interlocking chains of rope. The Egyptian frescoes and reliefs do not show such superimposed bundles or any interlocking ropes. They show one single, thick bundle, pointed and upcurved at each end, with lashings winding uninterruptedly from above deck to below the bottom. This would indicate that the ship was built like a single reed cylinder with upraised ends; a clear impossibility, however, because a cylindrical vessel would roll over like a barrel and also be without a deck. But the Egyptian ships are always depicted in profile, and it is most remarkable that in the modern world there is only one place where reed boats with this characteristic profile are still being built—South America.

The civilization that suddenly began building phyramids and worshiping the sun among the primitive fishermen on the coast of North Peru has left for posterity ceramic models of reed boats which show that a second reed bundle, hidden by the first when seen in profile, gave stability and deck space to the peculiar watercraft. Thus, when searching the world for builders for *Ra II,* we were to learn that the only surviving reed-boat builders still able to produce a vessel conforming to the long-lost Egyptian-Mesopotamian system were the Aymara, Uru, and Quechua Indians of South America. Their method of producing an unshakably compact, double-cylinder hull, with no knots on crisscross ropes, was first to place a slender papyrus roll in the open passageway between two much thicker rolls. All three of them were about thirty feet long, but the middle one was only two feet thick whereas each of the two outer bundles was eight feet thick. One long rope was now wound in a continuous spiral, lashing the thin roll to one of the thick ones, then another continuous spiral lashed the same thin roll to the thick roll on the other side. When these two independent spiral ropes were drawn tight by the united strength of many men, each of the big rolls was forced toward the small central roll until it was jammed between them and finally squeezed into them, forming a completely invisible core (as shown on page 17).

The resultant twin-bundled form had a lengthwise midline where the bundles met, which was not thick enough to hold the foot of a heavy mast. This type of vessel therefore required a bipod mast which straddled the two thick bundles in such a way that each leg had a solid foothold. This, in fact, was precisely the type of bipod mast used by all the South American Indians and also in ancient Egypt, and although pointless on a wooden ship it was traditionally maintained in them, too, until superseded by the single, central, modern mast in later pharaonic times. The original bipod mast, on which man's first sails were hoisted, was thus designed for a twin-bundled reed boat and not for a planked wooden ship.

The earliest known sail is the one depicted in ancient Egypt, of trapezoid shape, being much wider at the top than at the bottom. Having sailed on the Nile, I could never quite understand the generally accepted theory that the shape of this Egyptian sail was dictated by the banks of the Nile permitting very little wind close to the surface of the water. The logic is not clear, since the widest spread of the sail should then be at the base where the wind was supposed to be scarce. Furthermore, the Nile is so wide and its banks so low where most navigation takes place that they afford little or no shelter. Finally, if dictated by conditions on the Nile, why did this original trapezoid shape not persist locally until the present day? An alternative explanation offered itself immediately to the crew of *Ra* at sea: the papyrus ship was so sturdy that it could take a much larger sailspread than any wooden ship of similar size; yet being a compact raft-ship, the deck was so close to the surface of the sea that no sail could be wider than the vessel without being struck by the wave crests chasing along at the sides. To obtain the great spread of sail made possible by the craft's amazing

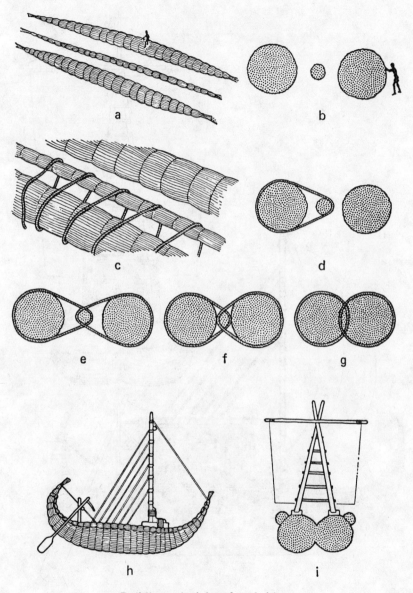

Building principles of reed ship.

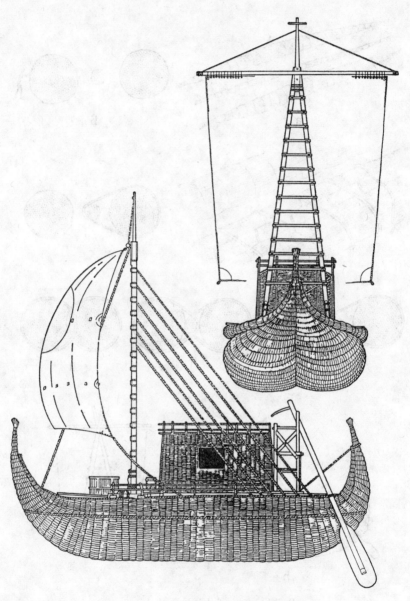

Ra II, front and side view.

stability, the width of the canvas was increased above the reach of the waves and a trapezoid shape was the automatic and inevitable result.

Since its early disappearance, the extraordinary steering mechanism consistently shown in ancient Egyptian art was tested and used for the first time on the *Ra* expeditions. Following the Egyptian design, we had two twenty-foot steering oars with huge blades made fast in a slanting position aft on either side of *Ra*'s peaked stern. The lower parts of the shafts were lashed to a cross log at deck level and the upper parts to an elevated crossbeam further away from the stern. Since each oar was lashed at two points, they could not swing freely like a normal steering oar, but only rotate around their own axes like a sort of long-shafted rudder. Each was in fact rotated by a small tiller at the upper end, and so that both rudder-oars could be operated simultaneously by one man, a thin transversal pole was hinged on with rope from one tiller to the other.

The vulnerability of these long-shafted and large-bladed oars, secured in two places, became obvious during the voyage of *Ra I*, when the shafts broke repeatedly and constantly had to be spliced. As the strong and flexible Lebanon cedar used by the Egyptians was not available to us, we ascribed these mishaps to the unsuitability of the wood we used, and on *Ra II* we used thicker and stronger oar shafts. We likewise increased the thickness of the double pairs of rope bindings, the one on the bridge and the ones at deck level, to resist the onslaught of the bigger waves. It was only when a single giant wave managed to snap one of the extremely thick rudder-oars on *Ra II* that experience taught us a practical lesson: as a safety measure we should have used a thinner rope to lash the oar to the cross beam at deck level than the one we used above the tiller; an exceptionally strong wave would then have broken the rope instead of the oar, which would merely swing out to the side and could be readily lashed on again.

Mentioning to Björn Landström on our return this practical solution to the only steering problem we had encountered, he immediately saw an explanation to a detail he had frequently observed in ancient Egyptian boat illustrations. In copying numerous designs he had been puzzled by the fact that rudder-oar shafts were generally shown with thinner rope or fewer loops at the lower lashing point than at the upper one. Before he learned about our definite need for two different thicknesses of lashings, the lower one serving as a kind of fuse, he had not suspected that this peculiar detail of the artist had any practical significance. This is indeed another convincing indication that the ancient Egyptians had sailed beyond the mouth of the Nile and into really rough seas.

A review of the evidence gained from predynastic boat designs incised on cliffs from Egypt to Algeria, from subsequent Mesopotamian and Mediterranean art, from the sequence of ships as recorded by the artists of the pharaohs, from the oldest buried vessels like the papyriform wooden ship of Cheops, and from discoveries made during experiments with papyrus boats in the open ocean, shows that the planked ship with hull was chronologically secondary to the reed boat in serving man in deep-sea navigation.

All available data indicate that it was somewhere around 3000 B.C. that the Middle East pioneers in maritime architecture took the revolutionary step of replacing compact papyrus bundles with a hollow wooden hull, imitating throughout a long transition period the characteristic lines of their previous reed ships. People with access to the easily split and incredibly durable Lebanon cedar, like the Hittites and the Phoenicians, were early to abandon papyrus reeds for boatbuilding, a material they received through overseas trade with Egypt. Next, the Egyptians themselves began importing cedar from Lebanon, building their own wooden pleasure and cargo vessels on the Nile. In this period trade between the local maritime nations became so important that the old port of Byblos in Lebanon had a special harbor set aside exclusively for trade with Egypt, the main cargoes being cedar for export and papyrus and Egyptian granite for import. The papyrus ships from Egypt, formerly sailing along Israel's coast and mentioned by the Hebrews in the Bible (Isaiah 18:2), were replaced by timbered ships, and illustrations of these replaced the former sickle-shaped reed boats with their bundles and transversal lashings in the boat designs incised on the walls of Israel's burial caves.

Pitch, tar, or bitumen was commonly used for waterproofing hulled vessels in ancient times. In Egypt, pitch was employed by the mother of Moses to cover the little reed craft in which she set her baby afloat on the Nile (Exodus 2: 1–3). The Bible has another ancient reference to a shipbuilding system which may represent a transition from the original compact bundle boat of reeds to the planked vessel with an open hull. The first shipbuilder in biblical records, Noah, received the following command, according to Genesis (6: 14–16): "Make yourself an ark with ribs of cypress; cover it with reeds and coat it inside and out with pitch." It is immaterial how we evaluate this early Hebrew statement; the fact remains that the early scribe who put this story on record knew that reed bundles coated with pitch could be used to cover the hull of a ribbed ship, and even one of formidable size. We may trust or believe the dimensions of Noah's reed ship, 450 feet long, 75 feet wide, and 45 feet deep, but the early concept of a true ship of impressive size is clear from the reference to "three decks, upper, middle, and lower."

The Hebrews were not the first to describe a primal deluge in which a single family survived by building a large watercraft. The early Sumerians left written tablets in the third millennium B.C. claiming that long before their time there had been civilization and cities. A great flood was decreed by the supreme god to wipe out mankind as a punishment, but Enki, the ocean god of the Sumerians (equivalent to the Greek god Poseidon), warned a pious god-fearing king named Ziusudra about the danger "and advised him to save himself by building a very large boat." Unfortunately the section of the text describing the manner of construction is destroyed but we learn that the deluge had raged over the surface of the earth for seven days and seven nights "and the huge boat had been tossed about on the great waters" until the sun god Utu shed light on heaven and earth and permitted Ziusudra to open a window of his huge ship and prostrate himself in gratitude, killing an ox and a sheep as offerings. It is interesting to note that whereas the Hebrews believed their Noah landed on Mount Ararat at the source of the rivers Euphrates and Tigris, the early Sumerians were convinced that Ziusudra landed with his big boat on the island of Bahrain (Dilmun). From here he, like the ocean god Enke himself, went to Ur in Mesopotamia and founded the Sumerian civilization.[7]

Small open boats known as *jillabie,* and round coracles called *guffa,* both types with reed-covered ribs plastered with pitch (bitumen) inside and out, like Noah's ship, are still in use on the Mesopotamian rivers. Ancient Sumerian models of pitch-covered *jillabies* are preserved in the Baghdad Museum. Thus boats with ribbed hulls covered with reeds possibly represented the early transition form from the original reed-bundle ship to the later plank-covered vessel. It would be hard to find a more logical evolution than to assume that the first ribbed hull was covered with the earliest-used boat building material —buoyant reeds, so plentiful in Egypt and Mesopotamia and so scarce in Lebanon, the area where wooden ships had their first known break-through.

Even the art of Cyprus and Crete reflects an early transition from lashed-together bundle boats to the first papyriform wooden ships, the forerunners of Greek and Roman vessels. European oak and pine grad-ually replaced the disappearing cedar in shipbuilding, and at last the seas were dominated by lofty wooden ships of all types, and yet not one with resemblance to the original papyrus prototype. By the time rigid iron sheets began to replace vulnerable planks in shipbuilding, there were hardly any reed-bundle boats left in salt water. The few ex-ceptions were rudimentary: the small *caballitos* of *totora* reeds off Huanchaco in northern Peru; the *madia* and the *shafat* of *khab* reeds off Lixus on the Atlantic coast of Morocco; the *jassoni* of Sardini, and the *papyrella* of Corfu, both of local reeds; and the large *gáré* of *berdi* reeds innermost in the Persian Gulf. Other ocean rafts of bundle-boat type still in use elsewhere are generally built from hollow canes and thus lack enduring buoyancy. True reed boats have otherwise survived into the present century only on inland waters, the largest by far on Lake Chad and Lake Titicaca, two inland seas on each side of the Atlantic, from which were brought the builders respectively of *Ra I* and *Ra II*.

Why did the popularity of the early reed ships decline so markedly once the wooden hull became known? A possible explanation may be the fact that, for reasons unknown to botanists, the papyrus disap-peared entirely from the lower reaches of the Nile. Today it is an ex-tinct plant species throughout Egypt, with the exception of a modern papyrus plantation recently started in Cairo for producing tourist sou-venirs. For the construction of *Ra I* and *Ra II* it was necessary to cut the large quantities of papyrus at the source of the Blue Nile in Ethiopia and transport the numerous bundles overland to the Red Sea.

However, no matter how perfectly they were built, reed ships could not compete with wooden vessels in durability. The rope lashings en-circling the bottom would gradually chafe off if a reed vessel were beached too often, and a couple of years would probably be a fair life-time for a major reed ship in frequent use. Undoubtedly the superior durability and speed of the wooden ship counted more in the long run than any of the virtues of the early type of bundle boat. Yet these were not negligible; the reed boat offered far greater security at sea and a superior carrying capacity.

A reed boat of the classic type securely lashed together, today surviving only on Lake Titicaca in the stormy altiplano of the Andes, is beyond any doubt the safest type of watercraft ever invented by maritime experts. Compact as a hard rubber ball and buoyant as a cork, it will ride the crest of the waves like a sea bird and survive any hurricane, because it has no hull to fill. The bundle body of the reed boat permits it to enter surf and shallows without need of bailing or fear of springing a leak. In stability and carrying capacity it exceeds any wooden hull of the same size. After two empiric experiments involving over 6,000 miles of ocean sailing by papyrus ship, the participants in the *Ra* expeditions, wise from the many blunders of uninitiated beginners, know that a reed boat correctly built and handled by an experienced crew can circumnavigate the world as easily as a caravel or any other wooden ship.

Eratosthenes, chief librarian of the huge Egyptian papyrus library in Alexandria on the Nile estuary, was able to report before the tens of thousands of irreplaceable papyrus manuscripts went up in flames that "papyrus ships, with the same sails and rigging as on the Nile" sailed as far as Ceylon and further on to the mouth of the Ganges River. The Roman historian Pliny later quoted that learned librarian in his geographical description of Ceylon, saying that while the papyrus boats took a full twenty days to sail from the Ganges to the island of Ceylon, the "modern" Roman ships made the journey in seven days.[8]

Reckoned in nautical distances this early record showed that the papyrus ship on such an ocean voyage averaged about seventy-five miles (nearly 140 kilometers) per day, a speed of more than three knots. This coincides well with the speed we maintained with *Ra I* and *Ra II* before the bundles got saturated and the increased submergence reduced our progress to not much over two knots.

The reeds for both *Ra I* and *Ra II* were cut during the month of December. There was no one to inform us that the season for cutting papyrus is essential for its buoyancy. The Ethiopians who harvested our papyrus at Lake Tana used their own reed boats for only a day's fishing trip or a few days' cargo transport, and, pulling their small vessels ashore to dry in the sun when not in use, they never took the problem of gradual water absorption into account. Owing to the error in tail construction of *Ra I*, much papyrus got loose from the bundles and numerous reeds were left in our wake, but they did not sink. *Ra II* absorbed water until complete saturation, yet it floated safely with deck at water level, carrying tons of superstructure, cargo, and crew ashore in tropical America on a trans-Atlantic voyage, starting from a former Phoenician port. The shortest distance from Africa to South America is only half of the 3,270 miles covered by *Ra II* starting so near Gibraltar. Still the fifty-seven days needed for the crossing could have been considerably reduced if the reed ship had kept up the speed it managed when dry, which at the start was between four and five knots.

Only subsequently to the two *Ra* voyages, in 1972, did I learn from marsh Arabs in southern Iraq, living where the Euphrates and Tigris meet, that reeds should be cut in August to retain their original buoyancy for a much longer time. Reed boats, still commonly in local use at the time of the First World War, were now very rare. In 1972 only plow-shaped one-man rafts of three bundles were seen, apart from the aforesaid *jillabie* and *guffa*, both still made with reed hulls thickly covered by bitumen. Such coated reed vessels would indeed float forever. Yet the floating reed islands on which many of the present marsh Arabs build their homes and permanently live show that even untreated reeds cut in the proper season have an incredibly long buoyancy. Near Basra, where a modern fiber board mill buys papyrus-like *berdi* reeds floated down the river by the marsh Arabs, I found in 1972 half a dozen colossal and solidly built reed rafts, termed *gáré*, tied up afloat like ships along the river bank. One of these measured 112 feet long, 16 feet wide and 10 feet deep, dwarfing *Ra II* with its overall length of 39 feet. These rafts sometimes had to wait as long as a year before it was the owner's turn to dispose of them to the mill, and yet they maintain their buoyancy. Some of them had a reed hut on deck where the owner lived and cooked his food by burning dry reeds on a base of clay. These enormous *gáré*, like the colossal *kaday*, or papyrus barges of Lake Chad, which sometimes carry forty tons of cattle and other cargo across the water, give us a valid image of the size of vessel the pyramid builders of Mesopotamia and Egypt were capable of constructing. We should not be surprised therefore that the early written records from Uruk speak of merchant vessels of 300 *gur*, or almost 100 tons.

Although the Mesopotamian *berdi* reeds, like Egyptian papyrus and Peruvian *totora*, are crisp and fragile when dry, soaked in water they become as tough and pliant as rope, and two men cannot pull a single reed apart. Compact reed bundles, tightly bound with spiral lashings, become as hard as rubber tires, and unbreakable as compared with timber. The excellent string and rope still made by the surviving reed-boat builders in these areas, either from the fibers of the reed itself or from the *dom* palm or some of the many other locally available fiber plants, is still not quite comparable to the truly exquisite hemp rope once painstakingly produced by their ancient, classical predecessors. This is amply manifested by the ropes and cables found in a good state of breaking in heavy seas, there is no corresponding restriction to the size of a wooden ship must necessarily be limited to reduce the danger of preservation in desert tombs in Egypt, Iraq, and Peru. Although the dimensions of a papyrus ship. Theoretically, a reed bundle vessel can be built the size of a modern ocean liner, provided the shipowner has unlimited access to reeds and manpower. The structures left ashore show that there was no lack of time and labor in the early empires of the Middle East, and reeds grew in overabundance in the river swamps of both ancient Mesopotamia and Egypt. Since reed boats perish, while stone and brick are durable, we are left with the actual Egyptian pyramids and Sumerian ziggurats, but the magnitude of the contemporary reed ships can only be judged from the artists' incisions on Egyptian rocks and Sumerian ceramic seals.

The quality of available reeds, the shape of the Egyptian, Mesopotamian, and Peruvian vessels with upswept bow and stern and highly maritime lines, with sprung stern and associated rigging designed for flexibility, and bipod mast which straddled twin reed rolls, the trapezoid sail tailored to avoid wave crests, and the steering mechanism with a "fuse" protecting it in rough seas prove that these highly developed reed boats, when built by experts, were originally designed for ocean voyaging and not for river transport. They were rigged and equipped for deep-sea navigation before their lines and rigging were copied in more durable vessels built of solid planks. The dugout canoe never developed into the true hull of a ribbed sailing ship. In Polynesia, and among the Indians in America, planks were sewn to the gunwales when logs were not available large enough to provide vessels of the desired size. But this evolution was a blind alley, since boats thus constructed still remained canoes. The mere principle of displacement of water by air, however, was borrowed from the canoe when the Mesopotamians built their first reed- and pitch-covered hull, and when the lines and rigging of the first deep-seagoing reed ships were copied in wood by Middle East boatbuilders about 3000 B.C. Thus the modern sailing ship, with its early Mediterranean ancestry, combines two pedigrees, beginning respectively with a hollow tree trunk and a bundle of floating reeds.

Chapter 2

Paths Across the Oceans

IN THE SPREAD of the human species complete freedom of movement never existed. The travels of early man were always guided and restricted by natural obstacles and by the presence of other men. Whether moving on foot or by primitive vehicle, man would be stopped or seriously impeded by forbidding mountain ranges with glaciers and precipices, swamps, deserts, impenetrable jungle, Arctic ice, ocean shores, and resistance from earlier settlers and hostile nations. The latter, in the form of existing communities, were no doubt the main obstacles to the freedom of human movement in all habitable areas, except in very early periods when primitive food gatherers were entering regions still dominated by birds and beasts alone.

To the pedestrian the ocean was indeed a formidable barrier. A coastline would interfere with any itinerary, divert the course of the migrant, and at the same time tend to set him exploring the coastline up or down. A lake and a wide river would have much the same guiding influence in leading man along the banks and shores on pioneering visits into the unknown. Running water, however, would be more than a passive guide; it would represent an all too obvious invitation for a free ride on any floating support back to familiar land or into *terra incognita*.

Rivers are known to have been man's first highways through landscapes covered by thick forests that hid unknown enemies and all the dangers of the original wilderness. Migrations penetrating the continents of Asia, Africa, Europe, and America are known to have taken full advantage of nature's inland waterways. Founders of civilizations have been lured along the rivers Indus, Euphrates, Tigris, Nile, Volga,

Danube, and Magdalena, to mention just a few of the more conspicuous cases. We notice the rivers no matter how slowly and smoothly
they may flow through the land. But we do not see the ocean currents
and are therefore apt to forget the greatest and mightiest of all streams;
they have banks of water and flow invisibly through the sea. The largest river with its source in Peru is not the Amazon, flowing eastward
through Brazil, but the Humboldt Current flowing westward through
the Pacific. The mightiest river of North Africa is not the Nile, but
the Canary Current with its delta between the Caribbean Islands, emp-
tying African sea water into the Mexican Gulf. The fixed itineraries of
these marine rivers span the oceans and form paths between the continents.

The following text is a reminder of the fact that the American continent is not surrounded by a dead sea; it lies in the heart of a living
ocean, streaming with its own system of arteries and veins. The present chapter is a combination of two papers. Basically it is the first part
of a speech on "Primitive Navigation" delivered before the Thirteenth
Pacific Science Congress in Vancouver in 1975, and published as Chapter 13 in the *Congress Proceedings* the following year. The second half
of that speech is here omitted, being the topic of Chapter 6, and instead this chapter is augmented by text from a previous paper on "Feasible Ocean Routes to and from the Americas in Pre-Columbian
times," written for the Thirty-fifth International Americanist Congress
in Mexico in 1962 and published in the *Actas y Memorias* of that
congress in 1964.

*   *   *

Science is like a growing tree; as it grows it acquires more and more
branches. The early scientist could understand the trunk, but none of us
living today can understand all the branches. We can only grasp the
fruits. There was a time when a scholar could be referred to as an anthropologist, and we would know what his field of activity was. Not so any
more. The science of anthropology has rapidly developed and expanded
to cover anything man is and does, and anything he was and did in any
part of the world down through the ages. Specialization has brought
the anthropologist who studies blood groups far away from the one
whose field is social science, and equally far from the work of the
philologist or the archaeologist.

Even the many subgroups of anthropology are beginning to lose internal contact. An archaeologist may be a leading authority on Minoan art from Crete and yet know no more than the average layman about Mochica pottery from Peru, or vice versa. However erudite, any modern anthropologist will have to ignore a major section of his own highly heterogeneous field to concentrate on one or more specialties. Certain topics and geographical regions are therefore bound to become better covered than others. It is only natural that ethnologists are attracted to regions like Africa, Greenland, or Brazil, where aboriginal kinship systems, arts, and crafts have survived until our own time, while archaeologists are more commonly drawn to countries like Egypt, Mesopotamia, Mexico, or Peru, where architecture, tombs, and potsherds invite them to reconstruct man's local activities in the past.

In view of its paramount importance to the understanding of cultural relations and interdependence, there is one section of anthropology that has so far not received adequate attention as compared with other aspects of human endeavors, namely primitive navigation.

The fact that it is primitive does not imply that the topic is so simple and uncomplicated that we can cope with it through intuition and by unqualified statements without adequate research of the type allotted to other aspects of primitive culture, of which we would never dare to write without source material or personal investigation.

The wake of a navigator is gone a moment after his vessel has passed, and modern scholars have nothing left to study at sea but the occasional wrecks of ships and cargo found in shallow waters on continental shelves. True enough, underwater archaeology is attracting an ever-increasing number of young scholars, but otherwise discussions on primitive navigation are generally based on a study of ancient models supplemented with boat designs from ancient petroglyphs, mural paintings, pottery decorations, or reliefs. The judgment of such important features as the seagoing qualities, carrying capacity, and voyaging range of prehistoric craft are therefore generally purely theoretical and often even quite unscientific.

Too often the pronouncement on whether a certain watercraft could carry man alive from one point to another has been based on preconceived theories as to whether cultural contact had taken place between these two areas. A perusal of existing literature will show that diffusionists generally attribute almost unrestricted abilities to any primitive craft that will satisfy a given migration hypothesis. The isolationists in contrast are likely to deem the same vessel not seaworthy on the assumption that the cultural parallels pointed out by the diffusionists are not based on overseas contact but due to independent evolution along parallel lines.

In other words, the verdict on certain primitive watercraft known to scholars only through models and iconographic art generally amounts to no more than indirect conclusions based on variations in interpretation of the genesis of cultural parallels ashore, which have nothing to do with the actual vessel under consideration. Much remains to be done before the subject of primitive navigation finds the place it deserves among the many other scientifically founded, and today truly advanced, branches of anthropology.

It is the more regrettable to note that what in reality amounts to no more than an expression of personal opinions is spread from anthropological literature into unrelated disciplines as if it represented scientific knowledge. A realistic understanding of the possible range of aboriginal explorers and drift voyagers is often required by scholars in other fields who have no personal foothold in anthropology. Thus, as will be shown later, botanists and zoologists working in the Pacific island area depend directly on the statements of anthropologists when it comes to their own interpretations of how certain plant and animal species could have obtained their pre-European distribution. The aboriginal flora and fauna of the Pacific island world contain a number of domesticated species with a problematical origin. Of these, many are known for botanical reasons to be quite incapable of propagating across an open ocean without human aid, yet they had reached some of the world's most distant islands prior to the arrival of Europeans. In searching for an explanation of such evidence, it seems a paradox that the botanist is accustomed to seek guidance from the anthropologist rather than vice versa, for the genetic findings of the biologist do indeed provide safer pointers to dispersal routes and distances necessarily traveled by the ancient conveyer than do any theoretical judgments on the possible range of ancient mariners. Since the subject of primitive navigation represents an obvious vacuum in the field of anthropology, assumptions concerning the possible range of prehistoric or protohistoric watercraft have more than once proved to be erroneous.

We of the twentieth century, regardless of profession, are so prejudiced in our ideas of what is needed to cross an ocean that we let ourselves be guided by dogma that runs contrary to known facts. It took the present writer three ocean crossings by raft and a considerable number of other empirical experiments to appreciate how far removed from reality are our modern concepts of what is needed for survival at sea, and how much empirical research has still to be done before the subject of primitive navigation becomes true science.

Four basic misconceptions must be cleared away before discussions on primitive seafaring possibilities become anywhere near realistic.

1. A watertight hull is not the only, nor is it the best, solution for security at sea.

2. It is wrong to believe that security in ocean travel invariably increases with the size of the vessel and the height of its deck above sea level.

3. The idea that it is easier and safer for primitive navigators to hug the continental coastline than to cross an open ocean is a very common illusion, contrary to facts.

4. The logical conclusion that the distance from A to B equals the distance from B to A is correct ashore, but wrong at sea.

To accept these seemingly heretical statements we shall examine them one by one, as they are fundamental for the understanding of, for instance, what might and what might not have happened in the Atlantic and the Pacific before the advent of the European caravels.

1. Primitive watercraft, as we have seen, can be divided into two categories built on fundamentally different principles; the vessels with watertight hull and those with wash-through bottom. Among the countless varieties of the former are, for example, the seagoing canoes of the Northwest Coast Indians and Polynesians, the junks and proas of Asia, or the open ships of the Phoenicians and the Vikings. The second class includes, among many others, the balsa log raft of South America, the reed boat formerly used in the same area as well as throughout the Middle East and the entire Mediterranean world, Easter Island, and aboriginal New Zealand, the *pahi* or raft-boats of Mangareva, the Marquesas, and the Leeward Islands, the four types of wash-through *waka* of the Morioris of the Chatham Islands, and the many types of Asiatic bamboo vessels. A vessel with a hull is vulnerable, since buoyancy does not derive from the building material but from the displacement of water by an adequate volume of enclosed air. If built of wood such watercraft are attacked by boring worms when in tropical waters for a long time. They run the risk of sinking if the hull is filled from above by breaking seas, or if the bottom is broken in

a storm or against uncharted reefs. In the second class with a wash-through body, the building material is self-buoyant, boring worms are no threat, and bailing is superfluous since any sea breaking on board will merely run through and leave the vessel on top of the waves as before. As stated, the shallow draft and compact body structure permit such vessels to voyage among reefs and shoals and to make crash landings on coasts which no hulled vessel could approach. These advantages alone explain why the mariners of the advanced civilizations in ancient Peru preferred their two types of wash-through raft-ships, although they were thoroughly familiar with the principles of the hull, which they used only for river traffic. The crash landing of the balsa raft *Kon-Tiki* on the windward side of the Tuamotu islands clearly showed the greater security of a vessel of this kind, and the writer has also enough experience of ocean travel by Polynesian canoe and open European lifeboat to be able to confirm that, in case of either a mid-ocean storm or coastal peril, he would unhesitantly prefer to be on board a wash-through type of craft.

2. Speaking of aboriginal watercraft, safety at sea does not increase with the size of the vessel; indeed, numerous experiments in the Pacific and the Atlantic oceans have convinced the writer and others of the fact that primitive vessels less than thirty feet in length have a greater chance of survival in stormy seas than similar vessels of larger dimensions. It is a great advantage to a vessel to be small enough to move freely between and over the swells, since a boat much over thirty feet long will either be forced to bury bow or stern into surrounding waves, or will bridge two waves simultaneously with the risk of breaking amidships. The same gale that may whip up rollers that might wreck an average-sized caravel will get no grip at all on a small raft moving over and between the waves.

3. The fear of any navigator in primitive craft is coastal water; security increases with distance from land. Whether in storm or normal weather, nowhere are the oceans more treacherous than near coasts and over shallows. Nowhere do the seas raise steeper and more dangerous waves than where ocean rollers meet the backwash from cliffs and as a result increase in chaotic interference with tides and deflected currents. In mid-ocean there are no rocks or reefs to interfere with the progress of either craft or currents; the swells are drawn long and regular, and the peril of wrecking is reduced to a relative minimum. The common statement that a certain itinerary is easier or less dangerous

for primitive navigators because it involves coastal rather than deep-sea navigation is thus highly heretical. The only real danger during the crossing of the Pacific on the *Kon-Tiki* raft was when we came within sight of reefs and land in Polynesian waters. In the two Atlantic crossings with the reed boats *Ra I* and *Ra II* the crew felt profound relief when, after sailing some six hundred miles along the threatening North African coast, land at last disappeared behind us and we headed into the smooth and regular swells of the open Atlantic.

4. One of the main differences in traveling by sea and traveling on land is that at sea the distance to be covered is very deceptive because it is not measurable on a map and is entirely dependent on the speed of the vehicle. For instance, the distance from Peru to the Tuamotu islands is 4,000 miles, but after traversing only a quarter of that distance, or about 1,000 miles of ocean surface, the *Kon-Tiki* raft had already reached the Tuamotu archipelago from Peru. The reason is, of course, that the ocean surface had displaced itself about 3,000 miles in the direction of Polynesia during the period of 101 days of the crossing. The raft had benefited from an invisible free lift from the Humboldt Current, running like a river from Peru through Polynesia. If another aboriginal type of vessel had been able to sail with straight course in the opposite direction at the very same speed, it would have had to move upstream and cross no less than 7,000 miles of running sea water to reach Peru from the Tuamotu archipelago. That is, about seven times the sailing distance and sailing time confronting the *Kon-Tiki,* although the distance would be exactly the same on a map. In addition, no sailing vessel can advance in a straight line directly into the wind, so in trying to force its way in the opposite direction to that taken by the *Kon-Tiki,* it would also have to tack against the powerful trade winds and thus add another couple of thousand miles to the straight 7,000-mile itinerary.

To get the clearest possible impression of how the surface distance to be traversed between two given coasts depends less on the mileage on a map than on the type of vessel used, we may consider the dead distance from Peru to the Marquesas Islands, which is approximately 4,000 miles. The average set of the local current is about 40 miles a day due westward. This means that if an aboriginal craft is propelled westward with a surface speed of 60 miles a day, it will actually make 60 plus 40 equals 100 miles a day and complete the voyage from Peru to the Marquesas in 40 days. Attempting to proceed in the very opposite direction, it will advance 60 minus 40 equals 20 miles per day, and thus need 200 days to get from the Marquesas to Peru. Suppose the craft can only make 40 miles a day; it will then move west with a progress of 40 plus 40 equals 80 miles a day and reach the Marquesas after 50 days, whereas, if it aims in the opposite direction it will make 40 minus 40 equals 0 miles and never get away from the Marquesas at all.

There is still another decisive factor in ocean travel, well known to all of us and yet for some inexplicable reason constantly overlooked in anthropological literature. With a world map in front of us it is easy to forget that our planet is represented in an utterly distorted manner, generally with the two polar points stretched out as long as the equator. If we roll such a Mercator's world map up to let east and west meet, we find our earth represented as a cylinder. And as a cylinder we commonly treat it in anthropological theories postulating transoceanic migrations. In the discussions on the movements of Polynesians or other Pacific peoples, it is invariably assumed that Mercator's projection is correct, and migration routes are proposed accordingly. The frequently suggested and equally often rebutted theories of prehistoric navigators having reached South America from tropical Asia have always assumed that the hypothetical migrants followed the equatorial belt, which indeed shows up on the map as the straightest and shortest line across the Pacific. Although the theory as such was never accepted, the concept of the equator as a straight line has survived. This illusion, born from the map makers' projection of a cylindrical world, was revived when some internationally renowned archaeologists more recently looked for ocean currents that might have carried prehistoric watercraft from Japan to Ecuador and thus might explain curious parallels in the very early ceramic art of these two areas. The equatorial route was again preferred because, it was argued, from Asia the Equatorial Counter Current "flows straight toward Ecuador" whereas the more northerly Japan Current "loops through the North Pacific" (*Newsweek*, February 19, 1962, p. 49). This common and widely used phrasing ignores the globular shape of our planet, since in reality the Japan Current is both the straighter and the shorter of the two routes, quite apart from its greatly superior strength. The Pacific Ocean is a complete hemisphere and it is entirely deceptive to look for a shortcut by way of the equator, which loops as much as any other great circle across the Pacific.

Indonesia and Peru form antipodes. The distance as the crow flies between the Pacific coast of Southeast Asia and South America is just as short by way of the North Pole as by way of the equator. If we bend a wire along a globe from Sumatra to Ecuador following the equator, we may hold both ends firm and twist the same wire upward to pass through the Aleutians or the Bering Sea as well without any adjustments.

When we bear in mind that the vast Pacific is not a level lake but a complete hemisphere with the same curves from north to south as from east to west, we get entirely different premises for a realistic approach to the problem of early migration routes in and around this gigantic body of water.

This brings us to a very important lesson we can harvest from history: the early establishment of the so-called caravel route in the Pacific. As we recall, the Asiatic coasts of the Pacific were known to the Europeans more than two centuries before the American coasts of the same ocean. Marco Polo reached the coasts of China and Indonesia in the latter part of the thirteenth century, whereas Balboa crossed the Panama isthmus to sight the same ocean from the opposite side in 1513. Yet, in spite of the early arrival of Europeans among the culture people of the Far East, with the Portuguese founding important trading ports on the Pacific shores of the Philippines and the Spaniards establishing themselves in other parts of Indonesia, not a single European vessel sailed into the open Pacific from that side. Winds and currents repelled every attempt, and the Asiatic civilizations with whom they were in contact had no information about foreign people living far out in the distant ocean. It was not until Columbus brought the Europeans to America that the geographical gates to the Pacific were flung wide open. The Spaniards had no sooner crossed the Panama isthmus and reached the Pacific coast of Peru when the Inca historians recounted that islands inhabited by different people were to be found two months' voyage westward from their own empire. As we shall see later, they gave correct sailing directions to some of them, including Easter Island, which the Mendaña expedition missed by sheer misfortune due to quarrels on board that led to a last-moment change of course. Nevertheless, it was directly due to the Inca reports that the Spanish caravels set out from Peru on the two successive voyages that discovered first Melanesia and then Polynesia.

The sailing ships of the early Europeans are generally considered to be superior to any aboriginal watercraft; certainly they are not inferior,

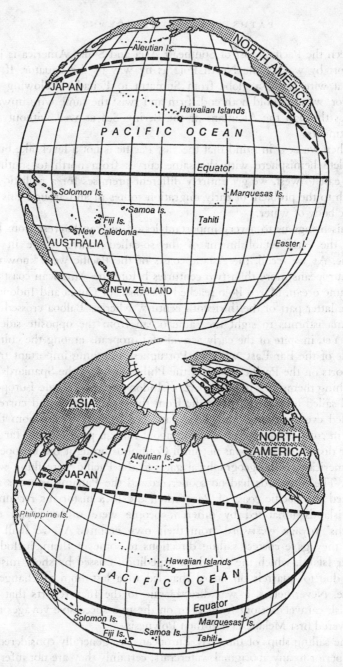

The Pacific hemisphere: two views showing the error in considering the equatorial line shorter than the extreme North Pacific route.

and thus their sailing capacities in the uncharted Pacific Ocean may be a good guide to us today in our evaluation of primitive navigation possibilities. We will learn that distance is not the decisive factor in oceanic explorations, but direction of combined wind and current.

The first Pacific island found by Europeans was Guam in the Marianas. Although one of the oceanic islands closest to the European colonists living in the Philippines and located nearest to the Asiatic mainland, it remained unknown until it was discovered in 1521 by Magellan, who came sailing from distant South America. In the following centuries the rest of Micronesia, including the Carolines, the Marshall, and the Gilbert Islands were discovered, all of them from America and most of them from Mexico, since the North Equatorial Current, accompanied by the strong trade winds, bears directly down upon Micronesia from that particular area.

The second discovery in the Pacific happened to be one of the groups in Melanesia, the Solomon Islands, which, as stated, were found by the Mendaña expedition on a direct voyage from Peru in 1567. Subsequent discoveries in Melanesia all resulted from voyages setting out in the same way from South America, the most important being that of Quiros, who left Peru in 1606 and reached the New Hebrides.

Polynesia, as stated, first became known in 1595 when Mendaña reached the Marquesas group on his second voyage from Peru. Next, the Tuamotu archipelago was first sighted by Quiros in 1606, also sailing from Peru, and in 1616 the Tonga Islands were found by Le Maire and Schouten coming from Chile. Easter Island was found by Roggeveen in 1722, he too coming from Chile. And following the same route from South America, Byron encountered the Cook Islands in 1765 and Wallis, following him, came upon Tahiti and the Society Islands in 1767.

Why did Europeans in Asia fail to discover any of these oceanic islands? Here again history is a very dependable guide. The European sailing vessels that crossed the entire Pacific from America were unable to sail back along the route they had come. Even when the vast Pacific expanse of island-studded ocean had been thrown open to voyagers from the American side, this same ocean world continued to be inaccessible for sailing vessels setting out from Asian ports.

In 1527, when the Spaniards had established important trading posts both in Mexico and in Indonesia, Mexico's conqueror, Cortez, decided to fit out a two-way expedition led by Saavedra, who was to sail from Mexico to the Philippines and back. Saavedra sailed from Zacatula in Mexico and reached Mindanao in the Philippines. Next year he set sail on the return voyage, but winds and currents forced him to abandon his attempts. The following year he tried again, this time by following the coast of New Guinea, hoping to get south of the contrary elements, but wind and current forced him back to Indonesia, where Saavedra died and the first attempts to return to America across the Pacific were abandoned. A number of caravels sailed with few problems from Mexico to the Philippines in the years that followed, but none of them were able to return the same way. To get back to Mexico it was necessary to circumnavigate the entire globe and return by way of the Atlantic.

Not until 1565 did Urdaneta succeed in discovering the only feasible return route for the sailing ships of that period. He steered northward along the coast of Japan and crossed the Pacific with the Japan Current and the westerly winds at his back in the extreme latitudes north of Hawaii. Even though the compass suggested that he was sailing in a northward curve, his itinerary was in reality just as straight toward tropical America as was the equatorial line. Urdaneta kept an exact log of his course, and from that time this became the so-called caravel route which Spanish and Portuguese ships followed for more than two centuries. This circular route went westward from Mexico to the Philippines in the tropical waters near the equator and back again across the extreme North Pacific in the empty ocean between Hawaii and the Aleutians. In fact, even the two Mendaña expeditions which discovered both Melanesia and Polynesia from Peru, i.e., south of the equator, had to sail northward high above Hawaii to catch westerly winds and currents permitting them to return to their starting point in South America.

In a study of primitive navigation it would be an oversight not to bear in mind our own early history in the Pacific. The constant rotation of the very ocean itself and the air above it in this complete hemisphere dominated all European discoveries and trade routes for five hundred years, from Marco Polo's travels in the 1270s to Captain Cook's voyages in the 1770s. The only explorer who, to a limited extent, managed to outflank this maritime circumvolution was Tasman, who in 1642 sailed due south from Indonesia instead of eastward, and by rounding the southern coast of Australia first discovered Tasmania south of the "roaring forties" and then New Zealand. Thereupon he tacked north to Tonga before he was trapped by the tropical conveyer which sent him back to Indonesia. Not until Captain Cook toward the end of the eighteenth century entered the then fairly well-known Pacific had modern sailing technique developed so far that it was possible to defy to a degree the rule of the elements. On his first voyage Cook, too, sailed the routine downwind itinerary from South America to Indonesia, but on his subsequent two voyages he followed Tasman's wake far south of Australia and then turned straight north across the tropical belt, whereby he also hit upon Hawaii, hitherto undiscovered by Europeans.

The period of 500 years in which all the intrepid European navigators were utterly incapable of forcing their ships from Asia into Oceania by way of Papua-Melanesia or Micronesia gives us a realistic picture of the restrictions imposed to an even higher degree on primitive explorers. It would be an impermissible oversight if we in our days of steamship travel neglect no less than half a millennium of our own recorded sailing history and proceed to postulate Pacific itineraries for prehistoric craft, itineraries already documented as impossible for historic sailing ships.

Furthermore, the unmistakable lesson from well-documented European history is supported by a long series of practical experiments with pre-European types of watercraft carried out in our own century. Since 1947, when the balsa raft *Kon-Tiki* was built according to Inca models, no less than thirteen manned rafts have left the Pacific coast of South America, and all of them have reached islands in Oceania. One raft has left Polynesia and two junks have left Asia, their crews intent on accomplishing crossings in the opposite direction; all of them had to give up. Their experiences and itineraries are as suggestive as the early European sailings.

The balsa raft *Kon-Tiki* sailed from central Peru to Raroia in eastern Polynesia in 1947.

The balsa raft *Seven Sisters* next carried William Willis from central Peru to Samoa in western Polynesia in 1954.

The balsa raft *La Cantuta I* was sailed from northern Peru to the Galápagos Islands by Eduard Ingris and his companions in 1955, whereupon the raft was rescued as it was unable to travel either east or west because it entered the area of the so-called Equatorial Counter Current.

The log raft *Tahiti Nui II* was sailed by Eric de Bisschop and crew from central Peru to Rakahanga in western Polynesia in 1958.

The balsa raft *La Cantuta II* brought Ingris with a new crew from central Peru to Matahiva in central Polynesia in 1959.

The balsa raft *Age Unlimited* was next sailed by the aging Willis all the way from central Peru by way of Samoa to Tully Beach in Australia in 1963–64.

Then the balsa raft *Tangaroa* carried Carlos Caravedo Arca and his companions from central Peru to Fakareva in central Polynesia in 1965.

The balsa raft *Pacifica* was launched by Vitale Alsar and his companions from the southern coast of Ecuador in 1966–67. They reached the Galápagos group and subsequently came so far north that they entered the area of the so-called Equatorial Counter Current which they tried to utilize for a return voyage to America. Although commonly believed to be an east-bound current, this is in reality nothing but a confused series of upwellings and whirls formed in the narrow belt of doldrums and calms between the two strong westward-moving currents above and below the equator. After struggling for 143 days in a futile attempt to get back to America this way, the crew was finally picked up by a rescue vessel.

Next the rubber raft *Celeusta* in 1969 drifted with Mario Valli from central Peru to Raroia, the same Polynesian atoll where *Kon-Tiki* had previously landed.

The balsa raft *La Balsa* was now launched by Vitale Alsar and his companions from the coast of Ecuador and in 161 days sailed all the way to Mooloolaba in Australia in 1970.

Three more balsa rafts, *La Aztlán, La Guayaquil,* and *La Mooloolaba,* manned by international crews, once more set sail from Ecuador under the leadership of the same Alsar and sailed in a joint flotilla through Polynesia and Melanesia, landing after 179 days at Bellina in Australia in 1973. After completing this third voyage, Vitale Alsar had traveled by South American balsa raft a total distance of 42,555 kilometers, or 2,555 kilometers more than the circumference of the earth at the equator.

In other words, thirteen manned rafts were set into the water along the Pacific coast of South America in the period from 1947 to 1973; two of them landed in the Galápagos Islands, the remaining eleven all reached Polynesia and five even reached Melanesia or the Australian continent beyond. Let us next consider the fate of primitive vessels launched this century with the intention of sailing in the opposite direction.

The first attempt was made by Eric de Bisschop prior to the Second World War. He intended to sail a Chinese junk from Indonesia to Polynesia to demonstrate the feasibility of the then current theory that this was the itinerary followed by the Asiatic ancestors of the Polynesians. He spent three years in his junk trying to benefit from the elusive Equatorial Counter Current, but did not manage even to enter Micronesia. He finally gave up his experiment and concluded, "the generally accepted theory of a peopling of Polynesia from Malaysia, or from any other centre in the west Pacific . . . is inconceivable!"[1]

He next built himself a Polynesian canoe in Hawaii and sailed from Polynesia to Indonesia in a few weeks. When the *Kon-Tiki* raft later showed how easily Polynesia could be reached from Peru, De Bisschop built a bamboo raft in Tahiti to see if the opposite voyage was equally feasible. He sailed south into the stormy latitude below the "forties" to get westerly winds, but having suffered from cold and violent seas for almost seven months he had to send an SOS when about a thousand miles short of Chile because his storm-ridden bamboo raft had now reached the birthplace of the Humboldt Current and threatened to drift back to Polynesia. Rescued and brought to South America, he now built the aforesaid log raft that brought his crew safely from Peru to western Polynesia, where he himself lost his life on the reef.

Certainly the most elaborate attempt to cross the Pacific from the Asiatic side by primitive vessel was the so-called "Projekt Pazifik," which was realized in 1974 after six years of preparation. Reviving the diffusionist theory of the Vienna School, Kuno Knöbl, a pupil of the noted anthropologist Heine-Geldern, built an authentic Asiatic junk, using as his model a ceramic vessel from the first century A.D., found near Canton in South China. The object of the experiment was to sail this Asiatic vessel from the China Sea to Ecuador in South America. The faithfully copied experimental junk, named *Tai Ki,* confirmed what we knew from five centuries of early European sailing; primitive navigation from Asia into the Pacific must follow the caravel route. *Tai Ki* could not resist the force of the contrary tropic winds and current and was dragged helplessly northward. On reaching 40° N, closer to the Aleutians than to Hawaii, the crew of the originally seaworthy but quickly worm-eaten and gradually collapsing junk sent out an

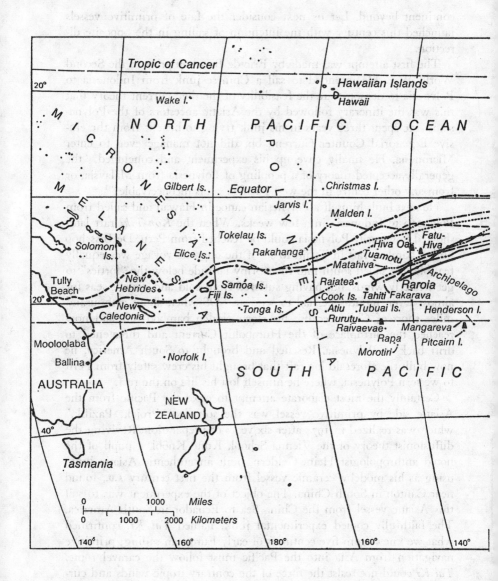

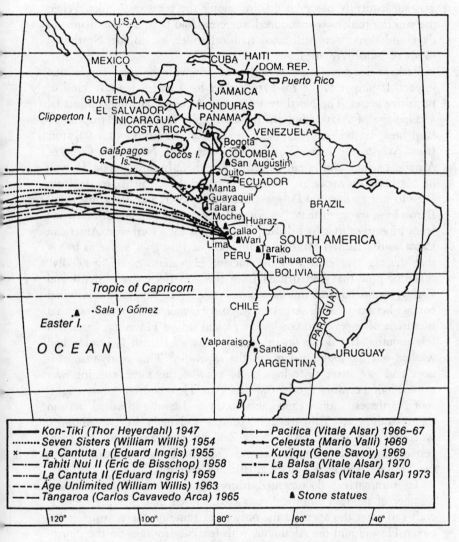

Raft voyages from South America into Oceania since 1947.

SOS and were picked up by aircraft, while the wreck of their vessel was subsequently observed drifting along the coast of Alaska. When the sinking junk was abandoned, the crew had been on board for 114 days and there were still 2,000 nautical miles left to the Northwest Coast of North America.

Perhaps this experiment was after all one with the greatest scientific impact. It pinpoints the road from Asia to America for any kind of primitive vessel. The Northwest Coast of America, i.e., the continental archipelago of Alaska and British Columbia, and not the tropical island area, is the only feasible gateway for pre-European navigators from Asia to the New World. From this same Northwest Coast of America, winds and ocean currents turn directly down upon Hawaii in northern Polynesia in the same way as the elements rotate from Peru to east and central Polynesia. Early explorers like Vancouver and Byron have recorded that they found large canoes in Hawaii fashioned from pine trees that had drifted down from the Northwest American Coast, and a Bishop Museum Handbook of 1915 goes so far as to say that the big war canoes of the ancient Hawaiians were "generally" made of pine that had drifted from the American coast. Sharp and Farley, on the basis of similarities in petroglyphs, suggested aboriginal contact between Northwest America and Hawaii, and pointed out that hundreds of logs of redwood were picked up on Hawaiian beaches a few months after floods on the Pacific coast of British Columbia had washed out the logging dams of the sawmills.[2] That ready-made canoes and not mere drift logs could survive the same crossing was proved half a century ago by Captain Voss. He procured a thirty-eight-foot Northwest Indian canoe at Vancouver Island and sailed it from there straight to Tongareva in central Polynesia in two months, whereupon he continued to New Zealand and westward. His converted Northwest Indian canoe, the *Tilikum,* is still on exhibition in the Thunderbird Park, Victoria, British Columbia.

To summarize: documented historical records and an extensive number of modern empirical tests have shown that primitive Asiatic craft can enter the open Pacific only in extreme northern latitudes between Hawaii and the Aleutians, with feasible landings on the Northwest American Coast archipelago. From here the road is open to the subtropical and tropical islands of the mid-Pacific.

We have hitherto been dealing with deliberate attempts at entering the open Pacific from east or west in early European sailing vessels or replicas of prehistoric craft. In recent years, however, much discussion has been centered on the question of whether Oceania was originally found by premeditated exploring expeditions similar to those of the early Europeans or by purely accidental drifts. From some quarters it has been maintained that gales blowing contrary to prevailing winds might have carried the Polynesian ancestry to their mid-Pacific islands. A computer simulation, testing these theories, was carried out by M. Levison, R. G. Ward, and J. W. Webb. The authors ran more than 100,000 simulated drifts and over 8,000 guided voyages from 62 starting points east and west of Polynesia through computers. The distant Asiatic coasts were then totally eliminated, since the chances of reaching Polynesia even from any of the nearer islands in the 4,000-mile-wide interadjacent ocean of Micronesia were found to be nil. In fact, it was found that the mere 400-mile expanse of open sea separating the Solomon Islands and the New Hebrides from Polynesia "presents a formidable barrier to eastward drift."[3]

Since drift voyages bringing people to Polynesia from either Micronesia or Melanesia were properly confuted, the computer simulation showed what historic voyages have already suggested, that within the Oceanic area accidental drifts resulting in island discoveries will follow the prevailing elements from east to west and not casual gales or irregularities. Archaeologists and linguists have already shown that the origins of all Polynesian outliers within Micronesia and Melanesia derive from voyagers arriving from Polynesia proper, and do not represent steppingstones of early migrants out of Indonesia or continental Asia. Also the computer study of Levison et al., in their own words, makes a *prima facie* case for such colonies being derived from direct drift voyages from Polynesia.

Even within Polynesia proper the possibility of encountering any island through drifts contrary to prevailing winds and currents is very small. Drift voyages from western Polynesia to any of the other Polynesian islands are thus most unlikely. The computer survey shows that there is "less than one in seven hundred chances of drifting from Samoa to the Cook or Society islands. There is no chance of reaching Hawaii, Easter Island, and New Zealand [by accidental drift] from other parts of Polynesia."[4] And "The greatest degree of penetration and coverage of Polynesia is achieved by entering at the Marquesas or Easter Island."[5] These are the two outposts of Polynesia nearest South America.

The possibility of drifts from the direction of South America is found, as could be expected, to be a different matter. Levison et al. write: "If navigators were to set off from the coast of Peru in the vicinity of Callao and keep a course as close to west as possible, the probability of their reaching Polynesia would be very high. Just over one-third of the craft in our experiment from off Callao landed on Polynesian islands, usually within three months of starting."[6]

Referring to the Inca type of balsa raft, Levison et al. say that their sophisticated system of steering with centerboards and their seaworthiness made them capable of sailing from South America to eastern Polynesia, yet at the same time these superior sailing qualities would have enabled them to regain the coast if trapped by the strong drifts some 300 miles off their shores. Summing up their findings, the authors conclude that it is highly improbable that men entered the Polynesian triangle from anywhere as a result of accidental drift voyages.

It should be borne in mind that the thirteen rafts leaving the coasts of Peru during recent decades all kept their sterns to the trade winds and were therefore not drift voyages in the sense of the word used by Levison et al. Pure drift voyages from South American waters, according to their computer simulation, would reach the Marquesas group which, together with Easter Island, would also offer the maximum possibility of coming upon the rest of the Polynesian islands subsequently.

There is one serious flaw in this otherwise important study. The authors did not run their tests far enough north to include the British Columbian archipelago. This is the more regrettable since it is the only area known to receive natural drifts from Southeast Asia and send them on directly into the Polynesian triangle. Levison et al. are aware of this deficiency, however, as they state that the limits of their study did not allow them to start voyages far enough north to simulate what they term the "driftwood voyages" from the Northwest American Coast. They do show a low probability route into Polynesia from Mexico, and add "The chances of reaching the Hawaiian group from further north on the Pacific coast are no doubt higher . . . if drifts were made from North America, the British Columbia area would be the most likely starting point."[7]

The British Columbia area, the only island area offering direct access to Polynesia both through drifts and guided voyages by primitive craft, is itself the only territory at the receiving end of similar voyages from Southeast Asia. In other words, the island-studded coast of British Columbia offers what Micronesia and Melanesia failed to represent, a feasible geographical steppingstone from the Philippine Sea to Polynesia. Early sailing expeditions and simulated drifts show that there is no alternative choice. Malay canoes and proas or Chinese and Japanese junks, whether guided or lost in drift, will be readily brought to British Columbia with the Japan Current and, if drifting on, in another few weeks find themselves transported to Hawaii. The forced itinerary of the experimental junk *Tai Ki* had been preceded this century by a quite considerable number of genuine Asiatic castaways carried to British Columbia, and some of them even further on down to reach Hawaii with crew still alive. Recorded evidence to this effect was presented at the 5th Pacific Science Congress by J. F. G. Stokes, and pointed out also by anthropologists like E. S. C. Handy and R. U. Sayce.[8]

The main object of the present analysis is to locate and extract feasible ocean routes which, from a purely practical point of view, could have brought aboriginal man to or from the Americas in pre-European craft. It is not here implied that the routes discussed have all been followed by pre-Columbian voyagers, although it is quite apparent that there would have been no effective barrier to early man along the suggested passages. The purpose of this survey is not to argue diffusion, but to analyze the practical problems involved for anyone who proposes transoceanic contacts between the Old World and the New by means of manned aboriginal craft.

The invisible rivers which float across all major oceans, stronger and larger than any river ashore, are held in constant motion by nothing less than the rotation of the earth itself. They flow from east to west in the tropical belt, and striking continents they turn, each in a wide loop, coming back east in colder latitudes as near as possible to the Arctic and Antarctic regions. These tropical currents do not move alone; they pull with them any floating thing, while above the sea the eternal trade winds blow with full strength in the same general direction, from east to west, the year around. Dwarfing the continental rivers as conveyer belts, they are even more one-way directed because of the permanent company of the extremely forceful easterly trade winds. Where visible coasts and premeditated decisions have not guided man in search of new land, the invisible marine conveyers have been ever present to lure him from one coast to the next with or without the traveler's own wish and awareness.

History and oceanography concur in pointing out three favorable ocean highways from the Old World to the New, two on the Atlantic side and one on the Pacific; and two main routes of departure, both on the Pacific side. The routes are so clearly defined that each may well be named after its historically recorded discoverer.

The *Leif Eirikson route* is the one least favored by the elements, but the one first used by Europeans because it offers steppingstones to America equaled only by the Aleutian chain on the Pacific side. If we ignore the absurdly magnified Arctic of Mercator's map and consult a globe, we find no ocean gap wider than the length of Lake Michigan on a route from Norway or Great Britain by way of the Shetlands, the Faeroes, Iceland, Greenland, and Baffin Island to Labrador and continental America. As we shall see in a subsequent chapter, during the period from A.D. 986 to about 1500 the Norsemen founded and maintained settlements with 280 farms, two episcopal residences, monasteries, and seventeen churches on the southwest coast of Greenland. Although maintaining their cumbersome contact with Iceland and Norway by open boat, and regularly supervised and taxed by the Vatican in Rome, these early European colonists lived for five centuries only 200 miles from the American coast, prior to the arrival of Columbus. Written records from the eleventh to the fourteenth century document at least five visits undertaken from Greenland to the New World just on the other side of the Davis Strait. As we shall see later, the fifteenth-century Norsemen were not the only Europeans active in this remote corner of the Atlantic. A papal letter in 1448 condemned the British pirates that raided the Christian Norse settlements and destroyed their churches in Greenland. Previously, in 1432, a treaty had been reached between the Norwegian and English kings in an effort to stop the English pirates from harassing the Norsemen in the Davis Strait, historic evidence to the effect that even unknown adventurers from the British Isles were familiar with the extreme northwest Atlantic shores prior to the historic voyage of Columbus.

The vague concepts prevalent in medieval Ireland concerning distant land in the North Atlantic may well date back to this period, or even earlier. There were numerous ties between medieval Norway and Ireland. About A.D. 840 Norwegian Vikings had founded the city of Dublin. Moreover, when Norwegian refugees fled to settle Iceland fol-

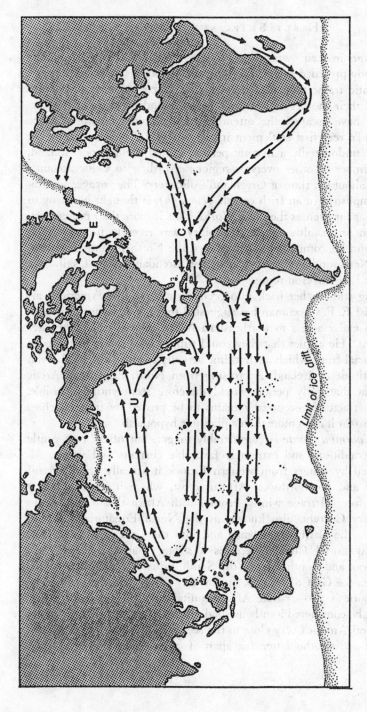

Sea routes to and from America as utilized by the early European voyagers. E: Leif Eirikson and the Norsemen; C: Columbus and medieval Europeans; M: Mendaña and the discoverers of Polynesia and Melanesia; S: Saavedra and subsequent caravel voyagers from Mexico to Indonesia; U: Urdaneta and return voyagers from Indonesia to America.

lowing wars in their own country in 872, they found that Irish monks
had already preceded them in settling that remote island. The regular
transatlantic traffic thereafter between the Norse colonists on Greenland and their mother countries of Norway and Iceland could therefore not have escaped the attention of Irish contemporaries since
Greenland's very first settlement in the year 985. The Irish monk St.
Brendan, undoubtedly a historic person, visited the Faeroes, Iceland,
and a number of other overseas regions according to Celtic accounts
recorded about the time of Greenland's discovery. The voyage, admira-
bly accomplished in an Irish coracle (*curragh*), is thought by many to
have got as far even as the New World. This is more than present evidence can prove, although its feasibility was recently proven by T.
Severin and his companions who crossed the North Atlantic from Ireland to Newfoundland in 1977, using St. Brendan's type of skin boat
along the Leif Eirikson route.

Moving still further back into prehistoric times, the American archaeologist E. F. Greenman has suggested that upper palaeolithic man
had even easier access to northeastern North America than the later
Norsemen.[9] He argues that they could simply have followed the edge
of the glacial front which at that time actually spanned the local ocean
at the latitude of Ireland. A crossing from North Europe by Arctic
hunters at that early period would therefore seem entirely feasible.
Whether it actually occurred remains to be proved by future archaeologists; so far it is no more than a plausible hypothesis.

The *Columbus route* is considerably longer, but offers very gentle
climatic conditions and extremely favorable currents and winds. Although fed by waters from western Europe it actually originates off
Gibraltar and the northwest African coast, where it joins company
with the forceful trade winds. From North Africa this route follows
the Canary Current, also known as the North Equatorial Current,
straight to the Caribbean Islands and into the Gulf of Mexico. The
North Equatorial Current receives a strong southern feeder from
Madagascar and South Africa, the South Equatorial Current, which
also enters the Gulf of Mexico, but by way of the Brazilian coast. Although born as two separate African units, these two ocean pathways
may well be considered jointly as subdivisions of a vast conveyer drawing Central America very close to the seemingly distant African continent, yet setting the latter far apart if approached from the New
World.

As far as we know from written records, Columbus is the first historic person to have benefited from this route. It is not entirely inconceivable, however, although in no way historically documented, that westbound Arabs, upon conquering the Berbers of Morocco and visiting the Guanches of the Canary Islands, sailed further on into the Atlantic in the sweep of the local conveyer belt. Several indications to this effect have been pointed out by various authors. Among these is a reference found in *The History of the Discovery and Conquest of the Canary Islands* translated into English by G. Glas in 1764 from an old Spanish manuscript found on the island of Palma. In the text appears the following quotation from "The Nubian Geographer's Third Climate" concerning remote Atlantic lands visited by roaming Arabs: "In this sea is also the island Saale, in which is found a kind of men like women, . . . their breath like the smoke of burning wood, . . . and the men are only distinguished from the women by the organs of generation: they have no beards, and are cloathed with the leaves of trees."[10]

This remarkable description merits attention, since the Guanches of the Canary Islands, like the Berbers of the African mainland, were as strongly bearded as the Arabs themselves, they dressed in sheepskins, and furthermore had been known to Semitic peoples since Phoenician times. But American Indians are beardless; this was in fact the physical trait that mostly surprised the Spaniards when they arrived, and tobacco smoking was practiced among Caribbean tribes, many of whom went about nude or dressed in skirts made from palm leaves in contrast to people known to the Arabs in the Old World.

Columbus, however, will forever remain unchallenged as the one who came back with ample proof of his discovery. He went across along the same general route twice more, and none can deprive him of the merit of having opened the door to America to men and women of all nations. In his wake swarmed an infinite number of large and small caravels, some so tiny and fragile that they would be justly ridiculed by the boatbuilders of the ancient Middle East. Once Columbus had discovered the path and set his example, hardly a craft could be found that would not be fit for a voyage along the Columbus route. In our own days there is an annual regatta of single-handed navigators, men and women, following precisely the Columbus route from the Canary Islands to the Caribbean. Beginners who boast of never having sailed before go across in tiny open rowboats, dinghies, canoes, and rafts of all kinds. The papyrus ship *Ra II* also sailed along the traditional Columbus route, manned by eight men, at least five of whom were notorious landlubbers, one to the extent that he had not previously known that sea water was salty.

In marked contrast, there is no favorable departure point for aboriginal Americans on the Atlantic side. The cold southbound Labrador Current dominates the temperate areas of North America, and the warm Gulf Stream originates among tropically acclimatized aborigines, poorly prepared for survival during the long northbound drift into the cold North Atlantic.

Turning next to the Pacific side, the conditions are still dictated by the rotation of the earth. The westward progress of wind and water along the Columbus route, interrupted by the collision with Central America, is immediately resumed on the Pacific shore, where the North and South Equatorial Currents push on with the same trade winds westward into and across the ocean.

We have seen that although European explorers first saw the Pacific from the Asiatic side, not one vessel managed to enter the newly discovered ocean from that direction. It was only when Columbus had brought Europeans to America that they then pushed on westward from the other shore into an ocean inaccessible in the past.

The *Mendaña route* could also with good reason be referred to as the *Inca route,* since we shall later return to the historic fact that it was Inca sailing directions that stimulated and guided Mendaña's exploring party. The Mendaña route is probably the one with most apparent consequences for anthropological investigations due to its short and powerful sweep, linking the world's most isolated and yet inhabited island groups to a New World coast abounding in buoyant watercraft. The strength of this route lies in the extremely powerful South Equatorial Current, also known as the Peru Current, which is fed by water sweeping northward along the South American coast from Chile and turning sharply west off the north coast of Peru in a wide flow straight into Polynesia and beyond. Very strong trade winds follow this current, the north edge of which touches the Galágapos Islands, while the southern edge touches Easter Island. The main flow embraces all inhabitable land in Polynesia except Hawaii, and all of Melanesia, before spreading out into a sort of delta where New Guinea and Australia interfere with its free passage.

Even Magellan drew full benefit from this conveyer when he discovered Guam in 1521. Yet for all practical purposes its grip peters out in Melanesia, with limited influence as far as the northeast coast of New Guinea and the southeastern islands of Micronesia. Nautically seen, the entire South Pacific island area lies right next to South America, and even though the Papua-Melanesians are undoubtedly of very early Asiatic stock, nothing lies between them and the New World that could prevent the sporadic influence of Andean culture.

We have seen that a return voyage across the same stretch of water was found impossible by the early Europeans who were forced to return to Peru by way of the high latitudes north of Hawaii. De Bisschop's experiment, when he struggled in vain for seven months in an effort to reach South America from Polynesia in primitive craft in the icy winds below the "roaring forties," and the failure of both Ingris and Vitale Alsar to return to America with the aid of the confused Equatorial Counter Current, clearly show that the South Pacific certainly offers no marine conveyer for aboriginal man.

The *Saavedra route* from Mexico to Indonesia runs parallel to the Mendaña route on the north side of the equatorial line. It spans the entire width of the tropical Pacific from America to Asia, and the speed of the current and the force of the trade winds are not inferior to those of the shorter South Equatorial. In fact, we have seen that Saavedra made full use of this marine conveyer on his one-way voyage from Zacatula in Mexico to Mindanao in 1527, forty years before Mendaña put to sea from Peru. Whereas Mendaña first ran into the closely packed islands of Melanesia and only subsequently found some of the widespread islands he had by-passed in Polynesia, Saavedra crossed the ocean in the empty belt south of Hawaii and north of Polynesia proper. For geographical reasons then, this route, although possessing a high potential for the transfer of aboriginal craft, offers less obvious opportunity for discovery and the spread of culture than does the Mendaña route in the island-studded latitude of Peru.

The much debated theories of very early overseas contact between Southeast Asiatic and Central American cultures, which have been propounded in recent years by a small group of prominent archaeologists, would be easier to defend if, chronology permitting, the transfer was seen as having followed the Saavedra route westward from Mexico rather than vice versa.

Micronesia lies in front of Asia, but was discovered by European voyagers from America. It would not be inappropriate therefore to

bear in mind the many cultural parallels between the vestiges of certain of the vanished Mexican civilizations and those of some of the
unidentified ancestors of the early Micronesian tribes, like the megalithic ruins on Kusaie and Ponape in the Carolines, and on Guam and
Tinian in the Marianas. They all lie athwart the Saavedra route.

The *Urdaneta route* is no more than an uninterrupted continuation
of the Saavedra route, beginning where the other ends, in the Philippine Sea. Here the warm water of the North Equatorial Current turns
north because it is blocked from further westward progress by Indonesia and the mainland behind. It passes Japan as the Japan or
Kuroshiwo Current and, moving south of the Aleutians in company
with prevailing westerly winds, reaches the west coast of North
America in a long sweep from Alaska to lower California. As we have
seen, it is the Saavedra and Urdaneta routes which combine to form
the once important caravel route followed by all Europeans crossing
the Pacific in the early days of sail.

The Urdaneta route is the only one that could have permitted early
Asiatics to reach aboriginal America by water. Perhaps its major importance, in an anthropological context, lies in the fact that it could have
brought Indonesians to temperate areas of America without wading
through the snow of the Arctic tundra. The striking physical analogy between the tropical Malays and aboriginal jungle people of Brazil is recognized by everybody as due to a once common cradle in Southeast Asia.
These correspondences have been shown to include such specific cultural
elements as the use of blowpipes with poisons similar to one another.
Such jungle equipment could not be obtained on the barren tundra. The
Arctic route is both long and improbable for tropic tribes, yet they could
have survived quite easily an involuntary passage along the Urdaneta
route, for aboriginal people were not less resistant to hardship and hun-
ger than the survivors of the many modern shipwrecks who have drifted
about for months and covered thousands of miles of ocean with no
other provisions than rain water and the birds and fish attracted to
their craft.

The Mendaña, the Saavedra, and the Urdaneta routes are the only
natural conveyers across the Pacific. Other than by using these marine
conveyers man would have had to confront the ocean as the obvious
obstacle to unsophisticated watercraft. The so-called Equatorial
Counter Current which figures so prominently on many maps as running in an eastward direction between the two wide westbound cur-

rents is no more than a narrow belt of eddies and upwellings occurring within latitudes of calms and confusing winds, the doldrums, dreaded in the days of sailing vessels. The Equatorial Counter Current is of little use to trans-Pacific voyagers as De Bisschop, Ingris, Vitale Alsar, and Kuno Knöbl have discovered; they all abandoned their attempts at maneuvering junks and rafts toward America along that narrow belt.

In outlining nature's own ocean highways to and from the Americas it is by no means the author's intention to rule out the possibility of other voyages by primitive mariners. Like present-day captains of small sailing vessels, aboriginal navigators had invented many types of craft capable of tacking into the wind and thus crossing contrary to the course of the marine conveyers in the calmer ocean regions between them. The balsa raft with correctly manipulated *guara* set as centerboards between the logs, is only one of the aboriginal sailing vessels that can effectively tack, and the double-bundled reed ship with its "negative keel" is another, and so is a Polynesian double canoe. But forced transoceanic crossings outside the natural ocean routes require supreme navigational skill, and would almost certainly not be undertaken without the advance knowledge that land lay ahead.

PART II

THE ATLANTIC PROBLEM

Chapter 3

Isolationists Versus
Diffusionists

APES NEVER reached the New World except by human transportation in post-Columbian time. The lack of the highest primates
among the indigenous fauna of America proves that *Homo Sapiens,*
their last offspring, necessarily must have reached the New World as
an immigrant. There is no background for the independent evolution
of the human species in the Americas.

The antiquity of the period when man entered the New World is
indicated by the large number of mutually unrelated languages spoken
locally when the first Europeans arrived. The multitude of different
tribes and nations preceding Columbus also showed a wide variety of
physical types and cultural levels. Some had never got beyond the most
primitive stage of unorganized food gathering, whereas others were
truly civilized in a way which in some aspects surpassed that of contemporary Europe. Did this complexity argue mixed origins or result
from untold generations of local evolution along different lines?

Until not very long ago it was generally assumed that man was
rather recent in America, having moved across from Asia in the last
millennia before the Christian era. Modern scholars have gradually
pushed the assumed date for this original settlement period back
through time, and now most anthropologists are willing to admit that
America was peopled by 30,000 B.C., others believe by 60,000 B.C. or still
earlier. At such early periods glacial conditions in Siberia and Alaska
extended so far as to permit Arctic hunters to cross into America in
the far north with little or no navigation. Since that early period until

the arrival of Europeans, most of the North American tribes continued as primitive food gatherers, and so did the bulk of the tropical American jungle dwellers, even the descendants of the first migrants who were pushed right down to the wintry latitudes of Tierra del Fuego. What was it that stimulated the sudden outburst among them of true culture at the highest level but restricted to a narrow belt from Mexico to Peru? This is where isolationists and diffusionists disagree. Was it an evolving process in that limited area or was it the product of contact with other cultures overseas?

The present chapter is based on a paper of the same name in the anthology *The Quest for America,* altered to avoid repetition elsewhere in this book.

*   *   *

Speculation regarding pre-Columbian contact between the Old World and the New has been endless. In scientific terms, it has gradually hardened into two opposed schools of thought, those of isolationism and diffusionism. The isolationists believe that the two great oceans surrounding the Americas completely isolated the New World from the Old World until A.D. 1492; they accept only that primitive food gatherers may have passed by foot from the Asiatic tundra to Alaska in the Arctic north. The diffusionists, by contrast, believe in a single common cradle of all civilizations; they postulate various hypothetical pre-Columbian voyages to aboriginal America from Asia, Europe, or Africa. Extremists in both schools have one marked characteristic in common: little or no appreciation of such oceanographic factors as prevailing winds and currents. To them the oceans are dead, immobile lakes. The difference between the two schools of thought is that the extreme isolationist believes that these dead expanses of water represent barriers to human movement in any direction, whereas the extreme diffusionist considers them rather as open "skating rinks" upon which aboriginal voyagers could travel in any direction they pleased. This disregard for geographical reality has frequently led diffusionists to postulate ill-founded migration theories which have had no other effect than to harden the attitude of the isolationists. At the same time, the dogmatic manner in which the isolationists have defended their case—solely by passing the burden of proof to the diffusionists—has caused equal resentment among the latter. Indeed, the isolationists have never attempted to adduce direct proof for their case, considering their position to be sufficiently vindicated by the absence of proof for the diffusionist position: lack of proof of contact they regard as proof of no contact.

It is generally agreed that there are many—and often remarkable—similarities between the civilizations of pre-Columbian America and those of the Mediterranean world. This observation was made and recorded by the Spanish conquistadors as they advanced into the astounding empires of Mexico and Peru. Indeed, the basis for the diffusionist attitude was laid by the first Spaniards in America. Many of the early chroniclers were convinced they had been preceded across the Atlantic by Semitic voyagers from the inner Mediterranean who had inspired the local savages with their beliefs, art, dress, and customs. The sea route used by Columbus was found so safe and simple by the emigrating crews of the endless train of flimsy watercraft which followed in his wake that they naturally suspected that others had taken the trip before them, for in the early days of sail the oceans were thought of as conveyers and the tundra as a barrier, and it was not until the days of modern ocean liners that voyagers, accustomed to mechanical propulsion, began to think that in earlier days the oceans surrounding the Americas had been impassable.

The isolationist view was born of the motor age and nourished by the growth of an ever more exact science of anthropology. It was recognized that a red skin does not betoken less intelligence and inventiveness than does a white; that the human brain works along very similar patterns wherever it is studied. To the isolationist, therefore, proof of contact could not be demonstrated merely by mustering cultural parallels between Mexico–Peru and Mesopotamia–Egypt, such as had been done since the discovery of America. Pyramids, paper manuscripts with hieroglyphics, hieratical dynasties claiming descent from the sun, and many other apparent analogies could all be of independent origin.

In the twentieth century the diffusionist view quickly began to lose ground, maintaining only a nest of resistance among German-speaking scholars who were popularly referred to as the Vienna School. The isolationist attitude was quick to gain impetus, in North America especially, just as it did for some time in local politics. Due to the high standards of American anthropology, its teachings could not readily be dismissed and it was not easy to contest the thesis that the identity or parallel occurrence of any tool, ornamental design, custom or other cultural trait was invalid as proof of human contact.

With the almost general acceptance of the logic of the independent invention alternative, a whole series of formerly convincing diffusionist arguments for global voyages lost impact. Whenever diffusionists emerged with a new case of Old and New World parallels to argue contact across the Pacific or the Atlantic, the argument was predestined to be labeled "not proven." A perusal of the diverse material produced to bolster the view that others besides pedestrians from Siberia reached pre-Columbian America fails to show a single piece of evidence accepted as conclusive by the isolationists. In those cases where they cannot for some reason counterpropose independent evolution, as with certain culture plants or artifacts too special for coincidence, isolationists have suggested post-Columbian introduction. If even this is found to be unacceptable, the last resort has been to propose that the seed of the plant or the prototype of the artifact could have been found by American Indians on the beach after it had made an unmanned drift across the ocean. It has been argued that the strictly American sweet potato had drifted from Peru to Polynesia caught in the roots of a fallen tree, and that the highly specialized Easter Island type of stone fishhook had drifted to the Santa Barbara region in an empty Polynesian canoe or was found by aboriginal American fishermen in the mouth of a fish which had snatched the line of a Polynesian fisherman.

In spite of the setbacks that the diffusionist movement suffered from the isolationist doctrines, attempts to muster arguments in favor of cultural contacts across the sea never quite disappeared, and in recent years they have even gained momentum, not least in America where resistance had for many years been strongest.

There can be but two reasons for this return swing of the pendulum toward diffusionism. Either the diffusionists' arguments are beginning to convince an increasing number of scholars, or the arguments of the isolationists are falling short of being regarded as conclusive. In a paper on "Theoretical Issues in the Trans-Pacific Diffusion Controversy." D. Fraser clearly demonstrates how the available evidence can be interpreted either way and that what stands as valid evidence of diffusion for one scholar is interpreted in precisely the opposite way by another.[1] He shows how the Asian game of *parchesi* and the closely analogous Mexican one of *patolli* are used by the diffusionist as well as the isolationist to bolster their respective cases. One camp argues that because of the similarity of these two games links must exist, and it proceeds to search for those links; the other camp claims that distance and other factors preclude a relationship, and that the existence of the game therefore demonstrates the validity of the independent invention doctrine. In the light of this example, one can see that the difference in opinion calls for cautious and fully unbiased attitudes from both sides and that the isolationist should divide his efforts equally between rebutting the diffusionist's case and searching for positive evidence in support of his own. Although it is often claimed that the burden of proof falls heaviest on the diffusionist, it certainly does not fall on him alone, and until either side has conclusively proved the validity of its case, controversy is bound to continue.

Why, asks the diffusionist, are the isolationists unable to show us a single geographical area in America where traces of independent evolution can be verified? And why was there no corresponding evolution among the aboriginal inhabitants of the climatically more stimulating areas that are now the United States, Chile, and Argentina? Here it is the isolationist who is lost for a satisfactory answer. For isolationist and diffusionist alike agree that America was first peopled by primitive food gatherers who filtered across from Arctic Siberia without agriculture, architecture, writing, or any of the other remarkable cultural attributes typical of the peoples discovered by the Spanish conquistadors in the Central American area. In the opinion of the diffusionist the vulnerability of the isolationist view lies in the noteworthy observation that in spite of intensive archaeological test digs and stratified excavations in all main culture centers from Mexico to Peru and Bolivia —that is, wherever high culture flourished in ancient America—no trace of gradual evolution from primitive society to civilization has ever been discovered anywhere. Wherever archaeologists have dug they have found that civilization appeared suddenly in America, in full bloom, superimposed upon a primitive, archaic society. The sudden flourishing of civilization begins at a peak and shows a decline rather than a progression through the centuries leading to the arrival of the first Europeans.

The Incas of Peru astonished the Spaniards with their high degree of culture, yet archaeology has shown that the Incas had borrowed most of their cultural elements from the earlier Tiahuanaco, Chavín, Nazca, and Mochica cultures, which in many respects had had an even more sophisticated and impressive civilization that suddenly appeared without traceable background on the coast of Ecuador and Peru and in the Andean highlands. Modern archaeology has established that contact took place between these early pre-Inca civilizations and the contemporaneous civilizations of Central America and Mexico. In Mexico, correspondingly, the great cultures of the Aztecs, Toltecs, and Mayas had drawn many basic lessons from the highly advanced civilization of the Olmecs, an unknown people who suddenly established one of Mexico's earliest civilizations—with writing, a calendar system, pyramid building, etc. fully developed—on the swampy and unfavorable jungle coast of the Gulf of Mexico, precisely where the marine conveyer from Africa ends. There is neither climate nor geographic support here for a sudden blossoming of an outstanding civilization.

With the controversy still unsettled, an ever-growing number of scholars, perhaps today even the majority, seems to have adopted a cautious middle course, not siding with either of the two extreme doctrines but admitting that ocean currents *may* have carried aboriginal craft with surviving crews to or from America, without this necessarily representing a population movement on a major scale. In the following pages, therefore, I will use the term diffusionist for one who generally favors human contact as an explanation wherever cultural parallels occur, and isolationist for one who dogmatically believes that the oceans surrounding the Americas were impassable for man before A.D. 1492.

The fanatical isolationists, although advocating as a basis for their thesis the uniform behavior of men of all breeds, have a totally different view when it comes to the assumed superiority of the medieval Europeans. A typical example of this inclination to regard 1492 as a turning point in anthropology, with a clear break in all former rules of human behavior, is found in a paper on "Diffusionism and Archaeology" by J. H. Rowe, published by *American Antiquity* in 1966. The author compiles a most impressive array of no less than sixty remarkable parallels between two restricted areas within the Old and the New Worlds. Rowe describes this assembly as "a substantial list of specific cultural features of limited distribution which were shared by cultures of the ancient Andean area and the ancient Mediterranean prior to the Middle Ages." His list ranges from reed boats to sandals of hide or coiled rope, of which he says, "Very specific resemblances in design and manufacture can be traced." One might think that this thought-provoking list had been compiled to bolster the case for diffusion. But this is not so by any means, as the author lets us know in no uncertain terms. He starts his paper by stating: "Doctrinaire diffusionism is a menace to the development of sound archaeological theory. . . . In the science-fiction world of the diffusionists . . . time, distance, and the difficulties of navigation are assumed to be irrelevant. Archaeology has too long and honourable a tradition to be surrendered without a protest to fantasies which require us to start with our conclusions and use them to deform the evidence."

But Rowe is indeed basing his entire argument on just such a method of starting with conclusions. In fact, he presents his list of parallels to argue that areas he tacitly assumes are too far apart for any pre-Columbian contact to have occurred—like the Andean area and the Mediterranean world—still possess an array of very specific culture features in common. Ergo, he concludes, even the most impressive array of parallelism can arise through independent evolution. In other words, he assumes as a basis for his entire argument that Peru and the Mediterranean world are too far apart for contact and uses this assumption to discredit cultural identities as evidence of diffusion.[2]

On what basis can it be regarded as axiomatic that Peru is "too far" from the Mediterranean world for contact to have taken place prior to 1492? In Columbus' own generation, with a crew of no more than normally endowed men, Francisco Pizarro traveled straight from the Mediterranean world to Peru by way of Central America. Like Columbus shortly before him, he managed the ocean voyage entirely without engine or navigational charts of the waters around the Americas. He then succeeded in traversing the jungle-covered Isthmus of Panama to the Pacific side, whence he sailed onward in new vessels, past the impenetrable coastal swamplands until he reached the favorable open terrain of Peru, where he established a settlement. His compatriot Cortez, on the other hand, had already landed on the jungle coast of the Gulf of Mexico, making his way up into the open Mexican high-plateau country far from his landing site and establishing a settlement there.

If the isolationist thesis solidifies into a dogma which in order merely to survive violates its own basic principles, then one need not be a diffusionist to react. We of European extraction are surely not so blinded by our own history that we consider ourselves a line of supermen, able to do four centuries ago what the great civilizations of Asia

Minor and North Africa could not have done earlier. It must not be forgotten that these people of antiquity had skills and capacities that far surpassed anything done in the same fields in Europe during the Middle Ages. The Egyptians and their neighbors in Mesopotamia and Phoenicia knew more about astronomy, the key to ocean navigation, than any Europeans contemporary with Columbus, Cortez, and Pizarro. And the Phoenicians, in collaboration with the Egyptians, were circumnavigating Africa at the time of the Pharaoh Necho, 2,000 years before Columbus set sail in an ocean that Europeans believed was filled with dragons and ended at the horizon in a precipice.

We marvel at the abilities of the ancients as embodied in their pyramids and obelisks, sophisticated mathematics and calendar systems, profound literature and philosophy, perfect mastery of maritime architecture, as evidenced by the functional form and complex rigging of their ships of planks and reeds 5,000 years ago, and their skill in exploration and colonization as revealed by the numerous archaeological vestiges of Phoenician settlement all the way down the Atlantic coast of Morocco dating back 3,000 years. But is it realistic to stand in awe of such achievements only to deny these ancients the ability to do what Pizarro did with a handful of men in a subsequent age beset by ignorance and superstition?

It is a long way from the eastern Mediterranean to the Gulf of Mexico, yet Columbus was born in Italy and sailed to America three times. At least twenty-seven centuries before Columbus, Phoenicians, sailing from the innermost corner of the Mediterranean, were engaged in large-scale exploration with colonization on the open Atlantic coasts of both Spain and Africa. Of course, one cannot imagine that the high cultures of Mexico and Peru were founded by ordinary marooned sailors shipwrecked or blown off course. A handful of uneducated eastern Mediterranean seamen, cast ashore among small, unorganized family groups of primitive people—and probably given the same friendly reception as Columbus—would hardly have been able to transmit their limited knowledge of their own civilization to the scattered native families who met them. The transmission of concepts such as hieroglyphic writing, the zero, or the techniques of mummification and trepanation, needs more than just a knowledge of their existence, or even a cursory knowledge of their working, on the part of the teacher. A group of ocean voyagers capable of founding a culture like that of the Olmecs must have been large enough to include representatives of the intellectual elite of its own homeland: something like a premeditated and fully equipped colonization voyage that perhaps went off course. Both archaeology and written history witness how large organized groups of colonists left the Mediterranean to found major settlements and trading posts along the coast of West Africa. The earliest written record is the stele in Carthage, which records how the Phoenician king Hanno, in about 450 B.C., sailed with sixty ships crowded with men and women to establish colonies all down the Atlantic coast of Morocco. And archaeology shows that Hanno was not a pioneer. When he arrived, other organized expeditions from the inner Mediterranean had long since founded the large megalithic city of Lixus far south of Gibraltar, just where the ocean current sweeps past directly toward the Gulf of Mexico.

The history of Lixus has vanished into the mists of time. The Romans called it "The Eternal City," because they considered it the early home of gods and said it was the burial place of Heracles. It was built by unknown sun worshipers who oriented the gigantic megalithic walls according to the sun. Its oldest known name in fact is "Sun City." Whoever founded and built Lixus, it is clear that astronomers, architects, masons, scribes, and expert potters were among them. Around 1200 B.C., just before Olmec culture suddenly began to flourish in America, organized colonists from the eastern Mediterranean, with ample knowledge of both Mesopotamian and Egyptian civilizations, had penetrated as far as the Atlantic area where eternal winds and currents constitute a marine conveyer to the Gulf of Mexico.

Nevertheless, such boatloads of colonists as might have been blown off course in this area could still not be the founders of the vast Inca, Mayan, and Aztec cultures. Traditional history, supported by archaeology, clearly shows that these great historic and proto-historic nations of the Andean area and Mexico were purely local products—amalgamations of indigenous peoples. These, however, owed their inspiration to more obscure predecessors. Thus in Mexico, for instance, culture seems to have sprung to a large extent from a very advanced coastal people, the Olmecs, whose early activity, as stated, began in a limited area around the Gulf of Mexico. These original inspirators could very well have come by the overseas route. This possibility is more apparent when it is borne in mind that all the pre-European civilizations under consideration were ruled by a hierarchy claiming descent from the sun. The Sumerians, Assyrians, Hittites, Phoenicians,

Egyptians, and Lixus people were all fanatic sun worshipers, just as were the Olmecs, the Mochica, and all their successors until Aztec, Maya, and Inca time in Mexico and Peru. They built astronomical observatories to study all solar movements, and would be more apt than any other people to steer due west to follow the path of the sun and visit its daily place of retreat. Due west of the Canary Islands is the Gulf of Mexico. On the voyages of the two reed ships *Ra* along the Columbus route, we had the setting sun before our bow every night.

One of the sixty parallels cited by Rowe as being shared by the ancient civilizations of Peru and the Mediterranean world was, in fact, the reed boat. He did not know when he compiled his list in 1966 that a Peruvian reed boat was to be sailed all the way from Peru to Panama only three years later. This experimental voyage, undertaken by untrained volunteers led by Gene Savoy, took two months, from April 15 to June 17. At about the same time, from May 25 to July 18, my own reed boat *Ra I* sailed from Africa into American waters. The next year *Ra II* repeated the trip all the way to reach land in less than two months. These three reed boat voyages, all within a period of sixteen months, thus combined to span the overseas distance between the Mediterranean world and Peru. Neither Gene Savoy and his men nor my own party would have had greater trouble crossing the Panama Isthmus on foot than had Pizarro and his men, and it is difficult to see why the reed boat and the fifty-nine other special culture traits of limited distribution on Rowe's list should have been separated by impassable barriers before the Spaniards hoisted sail, in 1492.

Why did the Spaniards move straight on past the Caribbean islands to settle in the highlands of Mexico and Peru? Were they unlike earlier breeds of men, or might other sailors before them have found geographical reasons to do the same? The swampy jungle country of the Isthmus area did not tempt Pizarro and his men to found a colony when he arrived there; instead, they pushed on across land and water until they reached the hospitable coastal terrain of Peru. Why should other people have acted differently if they preceded Pizarro across the Atlantic? By attributing motivations and accomplishments to Pizarro's little group of voyagers—and rejecting the very idea that other Mediterranean voyagers might independently have benefited from the same winds and currents and thus ended up with a similar itinerary—the isolationists betray the basic law of isolationism: that people are apt to duplicate each other's feats, given the same environmental conditions.

There is another snag in the reasoning of the doctrinaire isolationist. He will argue, and usually with good reason, that similarities in environmental conditions will stimulate similarities in cultural manifestations. Although there is obviously no fault in this thesis, it is not the only explanation of cultural similarities, and falls short of explaining the geographical pattern of culture in the New World. The Olmecs in the jungle of Mexico and the Lacandones who live in the same area today have had identical environmental conditions. Yet the Olmecs laid the foundation for mighty civilizations some 3,000 years ago, whereas the Lacandones today still live as primitive jungle dwellers. Archaeology has shown that the civilization of the early Olmecs was expansive and spread throughout Mexico and down through Central America where it lost identity in a continuous line of closely related jungle civilizations as far as the Andean slopes from Colombia to Bolivia. Outside this narrow and coherent line of contact or diffusion, in Venezuela, Guiana, and all of Brazil, lived numerous jungle tribes presumably with the same Siberian ancestry and with the same environmental conditions, yet nothing had stimulated them to abandon the primitive life of their forebears. Environmental conditions do not therefore seem to be the primary stimulator of aboriginal American civilizations.

What is more, hardly anywhere in America do we feel greater geographical contrasts than between two main source areas for American civilization; La Venta in Mexico and Tiahuanaco in South America. La Venta, with a hot, humid, and oppressive climate, lay in the lowlands on the Gulf of Mexico in a very swampy area then covered by dense, tropical rain forest. Tiahuanaco, with a cold and windy mountain climate, lay 12,500 feet above sea level on a treeless, barren plain between snow-covered ridges. The environmental contrast could hardly have been more extreme. Nevertheless, archaeology has shown that in just these two areas foundations were laid for two of the oldest civilizations of the New World. La Venta, on the coast where the Canary Current arrives from the Old World, has been pinpointed as the birthplace of the vigorous culture of sudden appearance that we have arbitrarily termed Olmec for the lack of any better name. Since emerging on the Atlantic side of Mexico shortly before 1000 B.C. the Olmecs spread their influence across the full width of Mexico to the Pacific coast and southward down through Guatemala. As stated, this vigorous mother culture inspired the subsequent great and diversified civilizations of the Mayas, Toltecs, Mixtecs, and Aztecs. Much about the same time an equally unidentified migrant people with a strikingly similar civilization settled the Tiahuanaco area on the south shore of Lake Titicaca, and through so far unidentified relationships with Chavín, Mochica, and other early local people, inspired the later Chimu, Nazca, and Inca civilizations which grew forth in South America.

It springs clearly to the eye that geographical proximity and not environmental similitude stimulated the rise and fall of the great pre-Columbian civilizations. Independently of environmental conditions they lay like pearls on a string down the narrow Central American bridge between La Venta and Tiahuanaco. Outside this coherent belt of aboriginal American civilization, whether in the Alaskan tundra, the Canadian forests, the plains of the present United States, the jungles of Brazil, the mountains of Chile, or the pampas of Argentina, the people of aboriginal America maintained the primitive life of their Stone Age ancestry, adapted to mere local survival. Were these people backward because of inferior abilities, or were they simply handicapped because they had lived outside a geographical nucleus receiving overseas stimuli?

The isolationist sees it as an insult to the intellect of the American Indian to look for outside inspiration behind the aboriginal American civilizations. But is it not more of an insult to the bulk of American Indians, who lived outside the high culture area and who had no civilization, to overlook the possibility that they simply may have lacked corresponding helpful influence? Can we Europeans say that we descend from independent inventors of civilization? Do we forget that Europe was still the domain of illiterate barbarians when the literate Olmecs erected masterpieces of sculpture with hieroglyphic inscriptions and complicated calendric dates? Indeed, the Spanish conquistadors brought to America a civilization acquired by their own European ancestry through cultural diffusion. European civilization came by way of the early Greeks and Romans, who in turn had received all the basic elements of their culture from Crete, Asia Minor, and Egypt.

Literacy and advanced culture was spread by ship to distant islands and continental corners of the Mediterranean in a period beginning shortly before 3000 B.C. and culminating with the Phoenicians establishing major trading posts on the Atlantic coasts of Spain and Morocco about 1200 B.C. The Phoenician merchant explorers who lived on the open shores of the Atlantic at that early time had progenitors in Asia Minor and passengers and crew from all over the Mediterranean world. Egyptian artifacts were carried past the Straits of Gibraltar, as testified by an Egyptian bronze figurine and an Egyptian effigy jar recently found by archaeologists in the Phoenician port of Cadiz on the Atlantic coast of Spain. Both objects are now in the Cadiz Archaeological Museum.

No sooner had Middle East civilization sailed out through the Straits of Gibraltar with large organized fleets of colonizers, than Olmec civilization began to flourish in the Gulf of Mexico at the other end of the Canary Current. Why this remarkable coincidence in time? If mankind had lived on this planet for millions of years and inside the Americas for scores of millennia, why did civilization coincide in its appearance at each end of the Canary Current?

The fundamental cultural material brought to America by Cortez and Pizarro, from the alphabet to the Christian cross, had originally come to them through teachers from the Middle East. If we of European blood have to live with this concession, why should it be humiliating for Montezuma and his Aztec nation to share a basic source of cultural inspiration with his conqueror Pizarro and the people of Spain?

Geographical considerations do not isolate the Olmec area from the Atlantic seaboard of the Old World. On the contrary, it is on the receiving end of the marine conveyer we have called the Columbus route. But if pre-Columbian voyagers had inspired or perhaps even founded the Olmec culture, why then, the isolationists ask, did neither the wheel nor any of the Old World culture plants reach aboriginal America? Certainly, they say, the New World would not have remained ignorant of such important cultural acquisitions if reached by civilized voyagers prior to Columbus.

The argument about the wheel has been repeated so often that it still occasionally emerges because of its frequent presence in old books. In the meantime, however, archaeology too has progressed and it has long since been discovered that the principle of the wheel was actually well known in aboriginal America, and precisely among the Olmecs. Since systematic excavations of Olmec sites started in the Vera Cruz area of the Gulf of Mexico a few decades ago, a great number of small ceramic animals running on wheels have been found in the funeral urns. Gradually finding their way to Mexican and foreign museums,

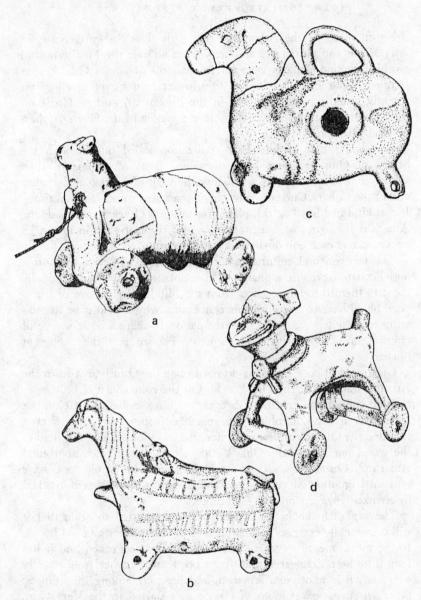

Wheeled pottery animals as funeral objects. (a) Sumerian from Ur in Mesopotamia; (b) Hittite from Antakia on the Mediterranean coast; (c) Phoenician from Ibiza in the Baleares; (d) Olmec from Tres Zapotes, Mexico.

they constitute one of the most characteristic artifacts left by the Olmec people. These funeral figurines are modeled in the form of either dogs or pumas with ceramic wheels attached to wooden axles revolving in holes through the feet of the animals. The original function of these wheeled figurines is obscure although most of them have vents for whistling. In concept, however, they concur entirely with the small ceramic animals similarly equipped with wheels on axles found in Sumerian, Hittite, and Phoenician burial sites from Ur in Mesopotamia to Ibiza in the western Mediterranean.

The fact that the wheel was known to the very founders of New World civilization is of course particularly significant. Why it subsequently failed to be adopted by American tribes as an aid to overland travel may well be speculated upon but has no bearing on the present problem. Any visitor to La Venta will realize that the swamps and jungles where the Olmecs made their first homes permitted no wheeled traffic and still today create major difficulties for modern road construction. Whatever the reason, irrespective of the terrain, the descendants of great people like the Mayas and the Incas still today ignore the the arrival of draught animals and the invention of the wheel. Thus, the Lacandones of Mexico and the Quechua of Peru continue to travel on foot, and transport burdens on their own shoulders or on llamas even where roads are available. Clearly enough, a favorite argument against contact across the ocean is rendered invalid the moment it has been found that the wheel was known, manufactured in miniature, and subsequently ignored by growing American generations.

The wheeled Olmec dog and the extremely realistic dog portraits modeled in ceramic by subsequent Mexican cultures before Columbus create another thorn in the side of the doctrinaire isolationist. What was the origin of these dogs? There are no wild progenitors in America of the domesticated dogs of aboriginal Mexico and Peru. The only dog that could have reached aboriginal America with pedestrians is the Siberian spitz of the husky type which followed Arctic man into Alaska and Greenland. The Olmec dogs and the *Canis ingae* known from the mummified dogs of ancient Peru differ markedly in breed from the Siberian spitz, but share their peculiar traits with breeds known from mummified dogs in Egypt and from extremely realistic Middle East art. The Mediterranean species spread westward with early voyagers from Mesopotamia to Morocco and the Canary Islands, but never reached Siberia in the remote east and could thus not have reached Mexico and

Peru by way of Alaska. Of all domesticated animals, the dog is the species most accustomed to accompanying early travelers by land and sea, and there was nothing to prevent it from reaching tropic America with voyagers following the Canary Current.

The argument that Old World culture plants never reached aboriginal America is relevant, but unconvincing as evidence against contact, since hungry navigators might well have finished their edible supplies at sea. Also, the tropical swamps of the Olmec area have never been, nor are they today, fit for the sowing of Mediterranean wheat or other crops commonly carried by Middle East sailors. The chances that culture plants from North African fields should take root in La Venta are extremely small. The validity of a negative evidence depends at any rate on the verification of a total absence in aboriginal America of any cultivated Old World species. If a single culture plant could be proved to have come across before Columbus, then what was a former indication of isolation now becomes a proof of contact. Naturally then, ethno-botany has become a key study in attempts at tracing early human movements, and botanists have often found themselves involuntarily caught in the anthropological controversy between isolationism and diffusionism.

The history of the common garden bean, *Phaseolus vulgaris,* clearly illustrates how preconceived opinions on aboriginal navigational possibilities have biased the reciprocal conclusions of botanists and anthropologists. In 1885, Körnicke pointed out that this important crop plant was formerly generally accepted as having been cultivated by the Greeks and Romans under the names of *Dolickos, Phaseolos,* etc. (Aristophanes and Hippocrates wrote about it in about 400 B.C.). When it was observed that the same bean had been cultivated among the aborigines of the New World, it was thought that it must have been introduced by the early Spaniards. This was accepted until Wittmack, in 1880, discovered the common bean at the prehistoric cemetery of Ancon on the coast of central Peru, where it had been buried as grave food. These burials long antedated the European discovery of America. *Phaseolus vulgaris* was later encountered in pre-Inca sites along the entire coast of Peru, and botanists were confronted with ample evidence of its pre-European cultivation in America. A theoretical introduction by the Spaniards thus became untenable as an explanation. At this time, however, pre-Columbian specimens of the bean in the Old World were no longer available. The theory was therefore reversed and the view taken that *Phaseolus* had originated in aboriginal America, from whence it had been carried to Europe by the Spaniards. A re-examination of this confused botanical issue by Hutchinson, Silow, and Stephens in 1947 convinced them, however, that *Phaseolus* was not indigenous to the New World and that its peregrinations represented a piece of botanical evidence for contact between the Old World and the New World before Columbus.[3] The same problem is also raised by a related bean, the jackbean, or swordbean, *Canavalia sp.* C. R. Stonor and E. Anderson have called attention to the following: "The sword bean (*Canavalia*), widely cultivated throughout the Pacific and always considered to be of Old World origin, is now known from prehistoric sites along the coasts of both South America and Mexico."[4] *Canavalia* beans excavated from the stratified deposits at Huaca Prieta on the Pacific coast of Peru dated from between 3000 and 1000 B.C. C. O. Sauer states that its archaeological distribution and relation to wild species now indicate the jackbean as a New World domesticate.[5]

The bottle gourd, *Lagenaria siceraria,* represents another piece of botanical contact evidence. This important culture plant was widely cultivated in Africa before Columbus. Although the gourd itself is of only moderate food value, its rind was fire-dried and used as a watertight container from Mesopotamia and Egypt to Morocco. When botanists came to study plants in the New World, they found it cultivated and used for the same purpose in all the American high-culture areas, including Mexico and Peru. It was supposed that, just like the bean, the Spaniards had brought it over; again, however, this theory was gradually abandoned when the bottle gourd was found by archaeologists in pre-Columbian culture sites in both Mexico and Peru. It was one of the most consistent culture elements within the American high-culture area. A second theory was then advanced: the bottle gourd could have floated across the Atlantic from Africa, been washed ashore in tropic America with live seeds, and grown. The Indians would have noticed that the rind, when dried over a fire, made an excellent container, and the original African use of the gourd would thus have been rediscovered. This of course is a deliberate attempt to dispose of a piece of undesirable evidence. The isolationists, with the intention of being cautious, are in effect throwing the baby out with the bath water. They are attempting to wipe away an important African fingerprint in America; solid genetic evidence. As anyone who has drifted across the oceans will be well aware, small edible objects—like gourds—would immediately become the prey of sharks and boring organisms such as the shipworm, *teredo,* during the four months needed for drifting alone across the Atlantic. To a raft voyager it sounds paradoxical to hear it said that of two African culture elements—the terrestrial gourd and the maritime craft—the gourd can drift successfully by sea to America, but not the manned watercraft!

The cotton plant, *Gossypium,* provides even more intriguing evidence. Wild cotton is short-linted, unspinnable, and unsuggestive of any practical use to man. Yet, when the Europeans came to America, they found the Indians all through the high-culture area from Mexico to Peru wearing sophisticated cotton clothes of outstanding quality. In fact, subsequent archaeological excavations in the mummy tombs of Peru have uncovered cotton cloth from the earliest pre-Inca period exhibiting a fineness of mesh and decorative patterns unsurpassed anywhere. Obviously then, the very founders of Peruvian civilization had somehow come into possession of a cultivated, long-linted species of cotton, as well as the spindle whorl and the loom. The progress from useless, short-linted cotton in the wild, via spindle whorl and loom, to finished cloth is long and not at all self-evident until it has already been completed. As shown by such a declared isolationist as Rowe in his list of Peru–Mediterranean parallels, the method and the results of cotton weaving in Peru are the same as those in the Old World. He shows that the vertical-frame loom with two warp beams used by the Incas was the same as that used in Egypt in the New Kingdom, probably introduced from Mesopotamia. He adds that the second of the two types of Peruvian looms, the horizontal loom staked out on the ground, as used in the Titicaca basin, was also the same as that of ancient Egypt. Many observers have noted remarkable similarities between the cloaks and loincloths produced on these looms in America and those produced likewise in the ancient Mediterranean area. Rowe, in particular, goes so far as to use the word "identical" in listing "A kind of woman's dress, consisting of a rectangular piece of cloth wrapped around the body under the arms and pinned on both shoulders, fastened at the waist with a girdle . . ."[6]

In 1947, Hutchinson, Silow and Stephens published the first study of the genetics of cotton from all over the world. They discovered that cotton could be divided into three groups according to the number and size of its chromosomes. All the cottons of the Old World, both wild and domestic species, have thirteen large chromosomes. In the New World, however, there is a remarkable difference between the wild and the cultivated cotton. All the wild cottons of America have thirteen small chromosomes, whereas the cultivated species—and there were three of them from Mexico to Peru—have twenty-six chromosomes, thirteen small and thirteen large. Since there was no large-chromosome cotton among the wild American species, and since the cultivated American species is clearly a hybrid, some unaccounted-for species must have been available to the early American cotton cultivators at the rise of local civilization, enabling them to produce what was obviously a man-made hybrid with long lint. Since it is the thirteen large, non-American chromosomes that have been added, the three botanists concluded that the Indians somehow obtained either the wild or the cultivated species from the Old World, and that the hybrid with spinnable lint developed and spread with high culture through Mexico and Peru.[7]

Wherever one finds aboriginal civilization in the New World, one also finds twenty-six-chromosome cultivated cotton, and it spread from the Pacific coast into Polynesia as American influence extended into this adjacent island area. From the westernmost limits of Polynesia all the way into Southeast Asia, however, cotton—wild or cultivated—was unknown. The Polynesian cotton abandoned to grow wild before the Europeans arrived, proved to be a wild descendant of the hybridized, artificially produced American cotton. There is no doubt that the Polynesian cotton had been brought by man from America because it is the cultivated and not the wild species. The question is, how did spinnable cotton come into existence in America?

The wild species with thirteen small chromosomes was native to the New World, and the botanical problem refers only to how the Indians of Mexico and Peru subsequently obtained the thirteen large chromosome species, typical of the Old World from Egypt to Pakistan but absent in America. There are only two possibilities: either the Old World cotton species—just at the time when civilization was developing in America—happened to drift safely across the ocean without being destroyed, or it was brought there intentionally—along with the gourd—by ancient voyagers. If the former alternative is the right one, we must postulate that Indians were standing on the beach when the seeds of the Old World cotton drifted ashore; they then recognized them for what they were, planted them, and hurried to find some wild

American cotton to cross with them. After successfully developing a hybrid with long lint, they next invented a ceramic spindle whorl identical to that of the Middle East with which to produce thread; with hundreds of yards of thread, they then invented the loom and started producing Mediterranean-type loincloths and cloaks—in the warmest parts of America where clothing was least required. If the Old World cotton arrived by boat, however, brought by people who had long known how to use it, then it would be only logical for its arrival to coincide with the coming into existence of Peruvian and Mexican civilization. It would be natural for the experienced cotton cultivators to cross their imported stock with a wild American species, thereby creating the twenty-six-chromosome species subsequently cultivated in vast fields from Mexico to Peru. It would be equally natural for them to make clay and stone spindle whorls of the same type as those used in the Old World, and the same type of loom on which to manufacture the type of clothing they had been wearing in the part of the world from whence they had come.

Cotton seeds may float undamaged for months in laboratory tanks, but try to float those seeds across the Atlantic Ocean past all the fish and into the hands of people who have never even seen a cotton field, much less a loom, and the experiment will hardly succeed. It seems as if some rather hasty theories on transoceanic diffusion are coming from isolationists who, trying to be cautious, grant any diffusion hypothesis so long as it does not involve a boat!

A similar case is presented by the plantain or banana (*Musa paradisiaca*) in America. This species has no wild relative in the New World, and for this reason ethnobotanists—inspired by anthropologists —have taken it for granted that its presence in sixteenth-century America must be due to post-Columbian introduction. Yet this assumption runs contrary to written record. Various sixteenth-century chroniclers considered the plantain native to America and described it as cultivated from Jalisco in Mexico to the southern coast of Brazil. The aboriginal Indians from Mexico to South America even had their own names for the plant. Inca Garcilasso, Guaman Poma, Father Acosta, and Father Montesinos all stated that the plantain was cultivated in Peru before the conquest. As the historian W. H. Prescott pointed out as early as 1847: "It is a mistake to suppose that this plant was not indigenous to South America. The banana-leaf has been frequently found in ancient Peruvian tombs."[8] In 1879, A. T. de

Rochebrune reported the discovery of both banana leaves and fruit in a tomb at the pre-Columbian burial site at Ancon on the Pacific coast of Peru, the fruit being seedless and therefore belonging to the cultivated species of *Musa paradisiaca*.[9] Historical and archaeological evidence thus led H. Harms in 1922 to include *Musa paradisiaca* in his list of plants identified in pre-Columbian Peruvian tombs.[10]

Since no one dared suggest that seedless bananas could have floated to America without human help, the growth of bananas in pre-Columbian America proved yet another genetic obstacle to the isolationist view. Undaunted, however, by the records of the early Spanish chroniclers, E. D. Merrill, chief isolationist spokesman among botanists, theorized in 1946 that the banana was perhaps introduced into the New World by the Portuguese via the Cape Verde Islands off Africa.[11] Supporters of this theory have tentatively credited Thomas de Berlanga, Bishop of Panama, with introducing the plant to the aborigines of America in 1516, when he is recorded as having planted some plantain roots on the island of Santo Domingo (Hispañola) 500 miles from the nearest mainland. However, the noted plant geographer C. O. Sauer showed the impracticability of such a theory: "The multiplication of the plantains is more difficult than that of a seed-bearing plant. The mature root-stocks need to be dug up, divided, preferably dried for a while, and then replanted. This species is an extraordinarily poor volunteer, and its spread must have been almost entirely by deliberate and rather careful planting."[12]

If the isolationist theory were correct and the plantain first appeared in the New World on the island of Hispañola in 1516, then it must have spread with a speed that would be miraculous even for a hardy weed, misleading the Spaniards into believing that it was indigenous to Indian settlements from Mexico to Peru, even in the most inaccessible parts of the continent. For example, when Orellana in 1540–41 crossed the Andes from the Pacific side and became the first European to sail down the Amazon to its mouth, he found bananas under cultivation all along the upper reaches of the river only twenty-four years after Bishop Berlanga planted his bananas on the island of Santo Domingo. If the bishop's rootstocks were the progenitors of all American bananas, then aboriginal cultivators must have quickly dug them up again and carried them by sea to Mexico and Panama, as well as by boat to the mouth of the Amazon (in itself an oversea journey exactly as long as the one from Africa to South America), before the same or other tribes paddled up the world's longest jungle river with a vast supply, and interested the tribes all the way to the upper reaches of the river in cultivating this unknown tuber. From the sources of the Amazon or from the Isthmus of Panama, the banana carriers then somehow managed within the same decades to get the bishop's rootstocks into the irrigated fields and sealed desert tombs of Pacific Coastal Peru, confusing such local authorities as Inca Garcilasso and his contemporaries into recording that the plantain was pre-European in Peru. In their attempts to explain away the important genetic evidence of the banana, the isolationists become extreme diffusionists in matters pertaining to New World traveling possibilities after 1516.

Admittedly the isolationists are often justified in their criticism of the diffusionists' disregard for chronology. It has happened that migration theories have been proposed which postulate the diffusion to America of cultural elements which had a wide distribution inside the New World long before their presence can be certified elsewhere. Too often the diffusionists have argued that the ideas behind the stone statues and megalithic masonry of aboriginal Peru derived from immigrants from Easter Island. In such cases the untenability of the proposal is shown by stratigraphy and carbon datings. Stone statues and megalithic walls were characteristic of the major American high cultures from Mexico through Central America, Colombia, Ecuador, Peru, and Bolivia. The Olmecs of Mexico and the Tiahuanacans of the Andes were specialists precisely in this kind of work long before man had yet settled Easter Island or any other part of Polynesia. An outside inspiration behind this kind of cultural achievement is therefore excluded by available chronological evidence on the Pacific side of America.

Turning to the Atlantic side we find no similar chronological discrepancy. Two widely separate dates are indicative of great events influencing people on both sides of this world ocean; i.e., the early parts respectively of the third and the first millennium B.C. Although the latter date may be more relevant to the present study, the former cannot be neglected because of its fundamental importance in Old World prehistory. As stated, shortly before 3000 B.C. the great civilizations of the Middle East came into full bloom. In Egypt the First Dynasty of the pharaohs began between 3200 and 3100 B.C., and in Mesopotamia the First Dynasty of the kingdom of Ur has been dated to a closely corresponding time. If the most recent archaeological datings are correct, Malta was settled by civilized mariners even before this period, and Crete shortly after. We cannot yet pinpoint with any degree of certainty the exact area or areas from where early ships began to crisscross the Mediterranean Sea. Since recent carbon datings have given an earlier period for the beginning of megalithic architecture on Malta than in Egypt, some scholars have begun to speculate as to whether the primary impulses behind Old World civilization did not move from west to east rather than from east to west through the Mediterranean basin. The Roman belief that Lixus on the open Atlantic coast and not Byblos in Phoenicia was the oldest city in the world gives support to this trend of thought. So does the Egyptian belief in Atlantis, recorded by the early Greeks, which claimed that the cradle of Mediterranean civilization lay outside the Straits of Gibraltar. Without resorting to speculations so far based on inadequate evidence, it remains a well-documented fact that navigators versed in megalithic architecture were active on both sides of Gibraltar prior to the dawn of written history. Shortly before 3000 B.C. exceptional cultural activity took place in the inner Mediterranean, with new dynasties suddenly coming into power and building up advanced local civilizations in Mesopotamia and in Egypt.

There is as yet only scant archaeological evidence of similar activities in the New World at that early period. It is therefore quite remarkable, at least, that the zero year in the ancient Mayan calendar is 3113 B.C. when translated into our own time reckoning. The Mayan calendar was so accurate that it was based on an astronomical year of 365-2420 days, which is only one day short in every 5,000 years, while our own modern calendar is based on a year of 365-2425 days, which is a day and a half too much in every 5,000 years. On the ancient Mexican burial pyramid at Palenque is left an inscription stating that 81 months make 2,392 days, an observation giving these early American astronomers a month of 29-53086 days, which deviates by only 24 seconds from the true length. Why, may we ask, did the early Mexicans begin their very exact time reckoning with the calendar year 4 *Ahau* 2 *Cumhu,* that is, August 12, 3113 B.C.? Some believe that the Indians snatched this date out of the air just to have some date for beginning their calendar. Others think they may have worked back to some specific astronomical conjunction occurring long before even Olmec civilization began. The fact that the date concurs so remarkably with important events in Egypt and Mesopotamia and great migrations in the Mediterranean world could indicate that the concurrence in time was something more than coincidental.

The period of about 1200 B.C. marks another milepost in Mediterranean prehistory. All authorities agree that some catastrophe of unusual magnitude caused dramatic depopulation and the collapse of great civilizations in the Mediterranean world. The Minoan civilization on Crete disappeared, and all areas of the Mycenaean world were profoundly affected. The unidentified people referred to by contemporary Egyptians as the "Sea Peoples" roamed the Mediterranean with great fleets and raided the coasts of Asia Minor and Egypt. Sudden famines hit the entire Middle East and the mighty coastal nations of the past— the Egyptians and the Hittites—lost their power overnight and never again rose to importance. Phoenician colonists left their former ports and sailed in large numbers out through Gibraltar to found important settlements on the coast of Spain and down along the Atlantic shores of Morocco.

In a recent study L. Pomerance analyzes the possible causes of this all-embracing turmoil which has puzzled historians and archaeologists so much, and has been ascribed tentatively to assaults by the "Sea People" or an extremely severe drought. Beginning with the archaeology of Crete, he shows that "about 1200 B.C. the dismal record of catastrophe is almost universal. Destruction, burning, abandonment, and refugee centres are listed almost without exception against all sites." He musters a variety of arguments to show that the final eruption and collapse of the neighboring island of Santorini (Thera) has been wrongly dated and must have taken place about 1200 B.C. The tidal waves from this geological disaster must have been enormous, and his thesis is that "the tsunamis [flood waves] from Santorini created a cataclysm for the populations and primitive economies of the Aegean and eastern Mediterranean shores about 1200 B.C." Further: "The wasteland horizon of the period around 1200 B.C. should then be reconsidered not only as the violent act of the human remnant of survival, the Sea Peoples, but as an effect of the final collapse of the caldera of Santorini. Within an incredibly short period of time there occurs the collapse of most major cultures, the sudden loss of crafts and skills known for centuries, . . . the interruption of international trade and connections. Only in this period do the cultural high-watermarks of the Bronze Age suddenly disappear. After 1200 B.C. life in the Aegean descends for 400 years into the Dark ages."[13]

Since Olmec culture began to bloom on the coast of Mexico immediately after this period of exceptional unrest both inside and outside the Straits of Gibraltar, there is nothing wrong with the chronology on the Atlantic side, whatever the real reason for this violent turmoil among Old World civilizations might have been.

The isolationists have been vindicated in their claim that one by one the diffusionist arguments are not conclusive. Yet since the Olmec and Mexican history of civilization began where so many Mediterranean cultures ended, by the running waters of the Canary Current, could it not be that some of the diffusionist parallels, although insufficient as proof of overseas voyages, still might be due to overseas voyages? The lack of proof is in itself not valid counterevidence.

It is true that parallels in customs and artifacts can be eliminated one by one as inconclusive as proof of contact. But this is not so with the spread of culture plants. And the reasoning also loses validity if all the cultural parallels are considered en bloc. The probability of independent invention may be roughly estimated in a very schematic way. One may postulate that if one per cent of the world's population had constructed astronomically oriented pyramids, then there would be a one per cent probability for people hitting upon the idea of building such structures. It would, of course, not be at all unreasonable if this one per cent happened to fall within the two separate areas of Mesopotamia–Egypt and Mexico–Peru. The same could be said if one per cent of the world's nations began to illustrate their deities as human beings with the heads of birds of prey. Such mythical bird-men could also be independently conceived. There is, however, only one per cent of one per cent's chance that both pyramids and bird-men should happen to be thought of in just the same two restricted areas. If this reasoning is extended and we include in the calculations the ceremonial burial of small ceramic animals on wheels, then the world distribution for this item is so restricted that even if considered as a separate case there would be far less than a one per cent chance of repetition. But considered together with pyramids and bird-men, the chances would be less than one per cent raised to the third power. Since a survey reveals well over a hundred cultural parallels between these two areas—of such a special character that they do not appear elsewhere unless clearly derived from these centers—then the improbability of independent evolution increases in a logarithmic curve into truly astonomical figures. Admitting then that the method of calculation is highly diagrammatic and approximative, and that a number of the cultural parallels listed are interdependent and contingent upon each other, there are still enough left to show that the isolationists have made a mistake in eliminating the multiple indications individually rather than confronting them collectively.

The facility with which an experienced papyrus ship crew could cross the Atlantic along the Columbus route induced me to compose a list of pertinent transatlantic culture parallels through extensive field and museum research in the areas under discussion. The list may contain elements of seemingly unreasonably wide distribution if we judge their global appearance in medieval times, but we should bear in mind that these were traits which had spread in antiquity from a concentrated source area within the Afro-Asiatic corner between the river Nile and the river Tigris. As we know, it was the Greeks and later the Romans of antiquity who spread such inventions as paper manufacture and the art of writing, even the Christian faith and new manners, from the Middle East to Europe, while the Berbers, Phoenicians, and afterwards the Arabs took care of an independent spread of culture from the same source area by way of coastal North Africa to the Atlantic shores and the Canary Islands. Most of this diffusion took centuries. The remaining step to Mexico would take weeks.

In extracting the characteristic culture traits shared by the pre-European civilizations of Asia Minor, Egypt, Cyprus, and Crete—traits considered as uniting them into one coherent culture area—it proved difficult to find any such common characteristic without the same trait also reappearing as typical of the pre-European civilizations of Mexico and Peru. It is, in fact, the very bulk of the cultural characteristics that spread from the Middle East toward Gibraltar in the cultural expansion period from about 3000 to 1200 B.C. which within that same period turned up in a related form at the American receiving end of the Canary Current. The following list of examples belong to this category:

1. A hierarchy based on sun worship and complex state administration under the leadership of an absolutist priest-king whose dynasty claimed descent from the sun.

2. Brother–sister marriages in royal families to preserve the solar blood line.

3. A fully developed system of script in a period when writing was still unknown among European nations.

4. Paper manufacture by soaking and beating intersecting layers of vegetable fibers, and the production of books filled with polychrome hieroglyphic inscriptions and formed as long wide bands that were folded or rolled up.

5. The organization of spectacular masses of people for the erection of colossal structures with no practical function.

6. A technique unknown today which permitted mathematically perfect cutting of colossal blocks of stone which, quite independent of either shape or size, were fitted together without cement but with joints so exact that a knife's edge could not be inserted between them.

7. Technical knowledge which permitted the long-range transportation of such gigantic blocks, weighing upward of a hundred tons, across many miles of rugged terrain, swamps, rivers, and lakes; and the ability to maneuver them on edge as towering monoliths or to lift them onto each other in perfect megalithic walls.

8. The raising of colossal stone statues carved in human form and serving as religious outdoor monuments.

9. The erection of mnemonic stele with images of people carved in relief and surrounded by incised hieroglyphic inscriptions. The repetition in both areas of the same relief motif showing a bearded man fighting a giant snake standing on its tail. (Hittite stele in Aleppo Museum and Olmec stele from La Venta now in the Villahermosa archaeological park.)

10. Stucco-covered rooms of religious edifices with walls and columns covered with polychrome fresco paintings of priest-kings and processions and with people depicted in profile and with all limbs visible. The recurrence within both areas of such a special fresco motif as a man with bird head standing on the back of a plumed serpent. (Common on walls in the Valley of Kings, Egypt, and recently discovered on the excavated temple walls at Cacaxtla, Mexico.)

11. The construction of pyramids of the Mesopotamian ziggurat type of stupendous dimensions and geometric perfection, which on both sides of the Atlantic are sometimes built from squared stone blocks and sometimes from sun-dried adobe bricks, always with a ground plan carefully oriented astronomically. These pyramids do in some cases exhibit additional parallels on both sides of the Atlantic: a ceremonial stairway leading up one or more of the pyramid's sides to a temple structure on the summit; a sealed and hidden doorway to a secret inner staircase leading to a burial chamber; a special hectagonal

cross section of the steep passageway containing the long and narrow staircase to the door of the burial chamber; the presence in this burial chamber of a stone sarcophagus, a ventilation system, and burial gifts; the knowledge of a technical–architectural solution which, in spite of the ignorance of the principle of the arch among these pre-European constructors, nevertheless enabled the wide ceiling of the burial chamber as well as the narrower one of the inner staircase to support the enormous weight of the entire pyramid.

12. A large walled temple yard adjacent to one side of the pyramid with tall stone columns of both round and square cross sections set in long parallel rows.

13. Megalithic sarcophagus covered by a stone lid which itself weighed several tons and was sometimes sculptured to show a human image.

14. The ability and practice of mummifying deceased persons of high rank by evisceration through the anus and use of certain resins, cotton padding, and wrappings.

15. A special mummy mask perforated at the edges so as to be tied on in front of the face outside the mummy cloth.

16. Great skill in the difficult magico-surgical trepanning of the skull bone of living persons, with a high percentage of survival among the patients.

17. Circumcision performed on young boys as a religious ritual.

18. The preservation of ancestral crania padded with clay and with inlaid eyes of marine shells.

19. The use of false beards as ceremonial attire of high priests.

20. The making of adobe bricks from a paste of selected soil mixed with straw and water and formed into rectangular blocks in a wooden mold, subsequently sun dried and used for the building of pyramids, temples, and houses with one or more floors.

21. The building of cities of adobe houses regulated into blocks that were separated by streets and public squares and equipped with water and sewage systems.

22. Long-distance supply of water for irrigation and public consumption through channels and elevated aqueducts, and the manufacture of uniform sections of pottery piping widened at one end to receive and enclose the narrow end of the next and higher pipe to form a continuous closed conduit.

23. Large-scale terrace agriculture with the use of animal manure

Pyramids of Mesopotamian type. (a) Egypt's oldest structure, at Sakara; (b) old illustration of Mexican pyramid in Museo Nacional, Mexico, D.F.; (c) Peruvian pyramid, from Benzoni 1565; (d) Tahitian pyramid, from Wilson 1799.

and artificial irrigation for the cultivation of food crops and cotton for clothing.

24. The harvesting of the lint obtainable not from the wild cotton but only from the artificially hybridized cultivated cotton; the spinning of these short fibers into yarn by twisting a stick threaded onto a specially shaped ceramic spinning whorl of identical size and form in both areas; the dyeing of the yarn; and the manufacture of the same two types of looms used to weave the yarn into polychrome fabric.

25. The similarity of cotton garments as pointed out by isolationists and diffusionists alike: the loincloth and cloak for men, and the dress with girdle and shoulder pin for women.

26. Identical types of leather and rope sandals.

27. The extremely important feather crown worn by warriors and men of rank. (Characteristic of Mexican and Peruvian nobles, feather crowns are assumed by many to be a strictly American custom; it is nevertheless a characteristic headwear of the ancient Middle East, as shown in reliefs of Hittite warriors, as well as Egyptian illustrations of their sea-roving enemies, the mysterious Mediterranean "Sea People.")

28. The complex organization and maintenance of standing armies, with the custom of giving the soldiers shields with painted symbols intended to identify their units, and the use of canvas tents in military camps.

29. The use of the sling as an important weapon, and corresponding types of both rope and band slings with the same kinds of cradle, slit, and finger hole.

30. Parallels and identities in tools and utensils, often pointed out in farming implements, in carpenters' and masons' tools, in the instruments of artists, in the hooks, nets, and weirs of the fishermen, in the merchants' balances, and in the drums and wind instrumets of musicians.

31. Long-range expeditions in search of special mollusks, highly valued for their red shells or for the red dye extracted from the snail.

32. Identical stages in the evolution of metallurgy. The same metals were sought, yet iron was ignored by the pre-European cultures here compared. Gold and silver were highly treasured, the ore was melted, hammered and molded in the same kind of pottery matrix to form figurines and jewelry sometimes with striking similarities. For the hardening of copper into bronze difficult prospecting was carried out often in remote areas, in search of the tin needed to produce the alloy.

33. Short-handled bronze mirrors, pincers, and small ornamental bells as major products marking entry into the Bronze Age.

34. Gold filigree work of outstanding quality. The minutely detailed articles of adornment produced by the American high cultures equaled the masterpieces of the ancient Middle East and, like the best of the fine-meshed textiles, surpassed anything in contemporary Europe.

35. Extremely sophisticated ceramic art repeated in the same specialized forms as polychrome funeral ware. The conventional tripod vase, considered so characteristic of the Middle East that it is identified as Phoenician when encountered archaeologically on the Atlantic coast of Morocco or the Canary Islands, is equally symptomatic of the American high-culture area from Mexico to Peru. Characteristic of both areas are also the polychrome effigy vessels in the form of heads and objects of various kinds. Reappearing on both sides of the Atlantic, and well known in each area, is the ceramic vase in the form of a human foot truncated above the ankle and wearing a sandal; the constantly repeated jars in the form of fish, birds, and quadrupeds, with spout and loop handle on their backs; the ring-shaped vase in the form of a coiled-up snake carrying miniature jars on its back; and the composite clusters of fruits and globular jars joined by cross tubes into one common long-necked spout.

36. The great importance of an abnormally flat ceramic figurine representing a naked female goddess. Its universal characteristic is that the body and limbs were flat as a plate, whereas the head was represented in the round. From the Middle East the Phoenicians brought this figurine westward through the Mediterranean as a representation of their principal goddess, Tanit, the Earth Mother. With identical properties the same little female figurine is perhaps the most characteristic example of early ceramic art all the way from Mexico to Peru.

37. Clay models of daily life. In both areas occur identical pottery figurines showing a kneeling woman grinding flour; a pregnant woman sitting in a straddling position with another holding her from behind and a third one in front receiving an emerging baby; and a ring of little figurines holding hands in a dance around a little central figure playing the flute.

38. Funeral ware in the shape of small animals rolling on wheels. Although it was widespread in the Middle East and brought westward

by the Phoenicians at least as far as Ibiza, the American distribution seems to be restricted to the early Olmec horizon in Mexico.

39. Marked importance of short-handled stamp seals as well as cylindrical seals of terra cotta, with surfaces incised with a variety of figurative or geometric motifs. Dipped in color the stamp seals were used for printing symbols and designs and the cylinder seals for rolling them in continuous bands. The same special motif is sometimes repeated within both areas.

40. The custom of carving wooden figurines and sometimes also big stone statues with deep concavities in place of eyes, which were subsequently inlaid with sea shells surrounding a black obsidian pupil.

41. A round disk with a centrally placed human head with its tongue out and with the periphery of the disk divided by markers into sixteen equal parts.

42. Great importance in religious art of mythical figures illustrated as human beings with bird heads, and the frequent representation of these bird-men as captains or passengers on reed vessels, or as seamen pulling reed boats through the water with long ropes.

43. The occurrence also in both areas of another mythical figure with human body and limbs but a feline head.

44. The same three animals as royal symbols: the snake, the bird of prey, and the feline. In both areas the snake is sometimes illustrated with projecting horns. The eagle of the Old World is substituted by the condor in the New World, and the lion of the Old World by the puma in the New.

45. The plumed serpent as a symbol of the supreme god and ancestor of the royal dynasty. (The snake with feather-covered body or wings reoccurs in religious art from Mesopotamia and Hittite Syria to Egypt, Mexico and Peru.)

46. The belt of certain deities and important personages represented as double-headed snakes, and the importance of double-headed birds and mammals in symbolic art.

47. The idea of sometimes illustrating supernatural beings with three-fingered hands.

48. The understanding of the zero concept and its application in mathematical calculations.

49. The importance of the first century of the third millennium B.C. as an ancestral beginning.

50. The selection of the first annual reappearance of the same stellar

constellation, the Pleiades, as the beginning of a new year even though it is not inspired by seasonal reasons because of differences in geographical latitudes.

51. The remarkably high standard of the calendar system based on the most exact astronomical knowledge. Whereas open countrysides like those of Mesopotamia or Egypt, with their extremely dry climate, would be ideal for uninterrupted observations of the stars, the Olmecs on the Gulf of Mexico could hardly see the sky for jungle trees and tropical clouds, and their local evolution of a calendar system would seem as anomalous as their choice of dry-land sandals and long gowns for life in a muddy jungle.

52. The custom of lashing the round and painted combat shields of the warriors in a continuous row along the gunwales of navigating ships. (Phoenician custom also illustrated in the Mayo frescoes at Chichén Itzá depicting the vessels arriving with a crew of yellow-haired men.)

53. The appearance on both sides of the Atlantic of the same favorite kind of watercraft: ocean-going reed ships with sickle-shaped, maritime lines, a composite bundle body ingeniously lashed together with a continuous spiral cord, and a canvas sail hoisted on a double-legged mast straddling the two main reed bundles.

According to legend and artistic representation on both sides of the Atlantic, reed ships were sometimes so large that a second deck was built above the first. We have seen that reed rafts of prodigious dimensions still float today on Lake Chad and at the mouths of the rivers Euphrates and Tigris, and similar sizes were required of their American counterparts which once floated the gigantic Olmec monoliths of La Venta down the Tonala River and those of Tiahuanaco across Lake Titicaca. More important, however, than dimensions was the knowledge of a technique by which the sickle-shaped reed ship could maintain its curvature at sea. No other technique than the one formerly used in the Middle East and today recalled only by the South American Indians on Lake Titicaca could satisfy this requirement. The papyrus ship *Ra II*, built in Africa by Lake Titicaca Indians, maintained its perfect lines without the loss of a reed when it was lifted out of the water in the New World. Only after years of storage in Oslo did the ropes slacken, and as soon as bow and stern sagged down the elegant lines disappeared. Neither learned scholars nor practical handicraftsmen were able to help us reconstruct the shape, and it was necessary to bring the original Aymara boatbuilders from Lake Titicaca to Oslo to reconstruct the reed vessel in the traditional manner, a fact clearly arguing against the likelihood of independent evolution.

The ocean-going reed ship is not the only one of the specialized culture traits common to the pre-European civilizations on both sides of the Atlantic which is difficult to explain by theories of independent invention. It is the one culture element, however, that could explain how the other transatlantic parallels were born.

Chapter 4

The Bearded Gods
Before Columbus

NOTHING CONCERNING the first European encounter with
America has puzzled the rest of the world more than the Aztec claim
that the Spaniards were not the first white and bearded people to have
reached them from across the Atlantic Ocean. Wherever the Spaniards
advanced, from Mexico and Central America to Peru, they were received
with open arms and given the name and the honors of a legendary fair
people with a high cultural standard who had been active in the same regions in the dim ancestral past. Impressive ruins and monuments left by
the bearers of lost civilizations were encountered by the conquistadors
wherever they traveled within the area, and invariably explained by the
local tribes as vestiges of the benevolent white and bearded migrants.
Such memories were vivid among entire nations and formed the basis
of all local history and religion. The arrival and activities of the white
and bearded teachers were described with hieroglyphics in pre-Columbian paper books and depicted on stone monuments and ceramic art.
The beards of the Spaniards especially, like those of their legendary
predecessors, made a strong impression on the Indians, who were
physically incapable of growing facial hair. World history was changed
by the surviving memories of these legendary travelers since Cortez
and Pizarro, each with a handful of men, were able to conquer the two
mightiest nations of the contemporary world—the vast Aztec and Inca
empires—without any form of military resistance.

Were these images of pre-Columbian visitors from overseas mere inventions by beardless Indians who had no better explanation of who

had founded their civilization, or did they derive from actual contact with earlier navigators from the Old World?

The present chapter was originally published in 1971 as part of the anthology *The Quest for America*.

*   *   *

It was my research in the Pacific that led to my curiosity as to whether or not men could have sailed across the Atlantic before Columbus. This seeming paradox arose from my readings into the existing literature on the obscure provenance of the Polynesians and their culture. Early writers, such as A. Fornander, S. P. Smith, W. J. Perry, and E. Best, writing around the beginning of this century, all strongly argued that there was ample evidence that Polynesia—and especially Easter Island—had been originally settled by migrants from Egypt, Mesopotamia, or some other center within the ancient high-culture area of the eastern Mediterranean. These early Polynesianists pointed out that striking similarities were concentrated within these two antipodal areas, such as fitted megalithic masonry, stepped temple pyramids, monolithic statues, mummification, trepanation, priest-kings, royal brother-sister marriage, a calendar system, genealogies, gods of solar lineage, and hieroglyphic tablets. It was invariably stated that the hypothetical migration from the eastern Mediterranean to Polynesia had crossed the Indian Ocean, the Malay Archipelago, Micronesia, or Australia with Melanesia, and finally all of Polynesia, settling ultimately on Easter Island. It is only on this last little island off the coast of South America that script and other important culure elements parallel to the eastern Mediterranean have been found. Since no traces could be located in the vast continental and oceanic territories purportedly traversed by these migrants, it was very easy for more cautious, subsequent scholars to dismiss these early diffusionist theories as geographically and chronologically untenable. Yet such early diffusionist discoveries as the fact that certain important gods and place names in ancient Egypt and Mesopotamia survive in Polynesia made a lasting impression on Polynesianist literature. For example, the sun and the sun god were known and worshiped as *Ra* in ancient Egypt, while *Ra* was the name of the sun on all the hundreds of islands of Polynesia. Another example is that consistent Polynesian traditions speak of *Uru* as an important tribal and place name in their original, extra-

Polynesian homeland, which was interpreted as a reference to the ancient Mesopotamian culture center of Ur. Although the early theories of direct migrations from Ur and Egypt were dismissed by most scholars, the idea that the ancient cultures of the eastern Mediterranean or Arabian worlds had had some indistinct connection with the origins of the Polynesian people has never completely lost its grip on the Polynesianist subconscious.

A glance at the globe will show that Easter Island is closer to Mesopotamia by way of America and the Atlantic than by way of the combined Pacific and Indian oceans. In the high-culture area from Mexico to Peru are to be found the aforementioned Mediterranean-Polynesian culture elements of which no traces exist along the semi-global Indo-Pacific route. In fact, the legendary Polynesian name *Uru* is also the name of the ancient and important tribe dwelling now on Peru's Lake Titicaca and assumed to have formerly inhabited the entire area from the megalithic ruins of Tiahuanaco down to the Pacific coast. At the time of the Spanish Conquest, the Uru were the principal reed boatbuilders on Lake Titicaca, living, in fact, on floating islands of totora reed. The very same reed, a characteristic South American species, had been brought by man to Easter Island and planted in the local fresh-water lakes for the purpose of building the same boats of the same material as those of the Uru Indians. And according to Easter Island tradition, the god who brought this exotic fresh-water reed to the island was called *Ure*.

Two of the world's major marine conveyers, what we earlier termed the Columbus route in the Atlantic and the Mendaña route in the Pacific, led straight from the Mediterranean world to Polynesia—with the Isthmus of Panama posing only modest terrestrial interference to downwind conveyer passengers. In fact, Mendaña, the first European to set foot in Polynesia, had himself sailed from the Mediterranean world and crossed the Isthmus of Panama on foot to reach Polynesia by way of Peru. As pointed out in the previous chapter, there is no logical reason to assume that an itinerary possible for a sixteenth-century European should have been impossible for the bearers of the great civilizations of antiquity.

Although it was not until years later that I discovered by experiment how easy it is to travel by aboriginal craft from Africa to America and from America to Polynesia, I began early in my research to suspect that the first bearers of culture had reached Easter Island

and the adjacent Polynesian groups from South America—irrespective of whether tropical America had received any inspiration from the ancient Mediterranean world. Like the great majority of investigators of Polynesian cultural origins, I observed that Polynesian culture was a composite: that more than one group of migrants had ended up on the islands of the extreme East Pacific. With a background including geographical training, and with the practical experience of aboriginal life in Polynesia, I had come to the conclusion that the Southeast Asiatic elements in these islands had come from the Philippine Sea via the Japan Current and Northwest America, only to arrive at islands many of which had long since been reached by pre-Inca voyagers from South America.

The racial composition of the Polynesians remained a puzzle, however, no matter to what shores of the Pacific their origins were ascribed. Although clearly of racially mixed stock, the Polynesians as a whole are among the tallest people in the world, they are frequently long-headed and have a skin hue often as light as that of southern Europeans. Physical anthropologists have noted that throughout Polynesia there runs moreover a strain of rather Europoid type, often referred to also as an Arabo-Semetic type, with strongly hooked nose, narrow lips, marked beard growth, and sometimes reddish-brown hair with wavy texture. Such types were observed by the first Europeans all the way from Easter Island to New Zealand and the Chatham Islands. This component type, often running through entire families, was recognized by the Polynesians themselves under the name *uru-keu,* and was said by them to be descended from an earlier population of blond and fair-skinned demi-gods who originally lived on these same islands. The physical features of the Polynesians, who inhabited the East Pacific, did not tally at all with those of the peoples in the West Pacific, and the Europoid component contrasted particularly, in the aforementioned characteristics, with the Papua-Melanesians, Negritos, Malays, and Indonesians inhabiting the area whence most modern scholars hypothesized the Polynesians had come. The physiological enigma of the Europoid component in Polynesia helped keep alive the seemingly wild theories concerning a Mediterranean element in the East Pacific.

At a superficial glance it would not seem that a departure point in America would solve this problem. The South American Indians had no Europoid aspects and tallied closely with the Malays to whom they were basically related through a common ancestral stock. Apart from their general agreement with the Polynesians in blood types and in nose form, the South American tribes differed as much from the islanders in the East Pacific as did the peoples of Southeast Asia and the West Pacific. Tall and red-haired persons with full beards were equally unknown on either side of Polynesia when the Europeans arrived. The short, round-headed yellow-brown peoples of Indonesia and South America were equally anatomically beardless. How, then, could the Polynesian islanders have obtained their deviant Europoid features?

On Easter Island, the Polynesian outpost farthest from Asia and closest to the New World, detailed traditions insist that the islanders' earliest ancestors came from a vast desert land to the east—that is, from the direction of South America—and reached the island by sailing for sixty days in the direction of the setting sun. The historically minded, clearly mixed Easter Islanders maintain that some of their earliest ancestors had white skins and red hair, whereas others were dark-skinned and black-haired. This was confirmed by the first Europeans to reach the island. When the Dutch under Roggeveen discovered the island in 1722, they recorded that among the first natives to come aboard their ship was "an entirely white man," and they recorded about the Easter Islanders in general, "one finds some among them of a darker shade, and others quite white, and no less also a few of a reddish tint as if somewhat severely burned by the sun."[1]

All the early visitors also noted that some of the Easter Islanders were not only very fair and tall, but had soft, reddish hair as well. Could such people really have come from the east, from South America, where the Quechua, Aymara, and Uru Indians have the same physical characteristics as the black-haired, yellow-brown, very small people of Southeast Asia? Could it be that the pre-Inca culture people of Peru had physical features different from those of the small, round-headed Indians living there in historic times?

It is remarkable that in the earliest traditions collected on Easter Island, the Easter Islanders claimed that the land sixty days to the east, from which their ancestors came, was called the "Burial Place." They added: "In this land, the climate was so intensely hot that people sometimes died from the effects of the heat, and at certain seasons, plants and growing things were scorched and shrivelled up by the burning sun."[2]

Westward from Easter Island, all the way to Southeast Asia, there is nothing that corresponds to this description, since all the coasts are verdant, if not covered by dense jungle. But to the east, in the direction and at the distance recalled by the Easter Islanders, lies the desert coast of Peru and northern Chile, and nowhere in the Pacific does there exist a territory more in keeping with the Easter Islanders' description —regarding both climate and name. In the coastal areas of Peru, particularly, a slight seasonal humidity permits the appearance of a sparse vegetation which shrivels up in the burning sun of the cloudless months. Also, all along this South American desert coast are abundant, almost contiguous necropolises, many of which grew to fill vast areas as a result of the accumulation of human remains and funeral objects that were preserved almost indefinitely in a climate without rain. In fact, that climate and these burial grounds provide us with the possibility of studying human remains from early periods, whereas organic remains rapidly decayed in adjacent territories with wetter climates, such as Central America, Mexico, and the Pacific island world.

This means that modern archaeologists have direct evidence of the remarkable fact that true mummification was practiced by the very founders of the earliest pre-Inca civilization in Peru. In fact, true mummification—with evisceration through the anus and rubbing with resinous and oily preservatives—was common both to Peru and adjacent Polynesia, while it was totally unknown in Indonesia. But whereas hundreds of actual mummies are still available from the desert region of Peru, we have mainly the written records of early voyagers to attest to the wide distribution of the practice of mummifying royal persons throughout the far-flung islands of Polynesia—from Easter Island in the east to Hawaii in the north and to New Zealand in the southwest. The very widespread occurrence of this elaborate practice in a tropical island area whose damp climate prevents lasting success shows that it must have spread from a common cultural source outside the island area with climatic conditions more suitable for successful mummification. Since mummification cannot have reached the islands from Southeast Asia where it was non-existent, it is all the more noteworthy that two royal mummy bundles strikingly similar to those of pre-Inca Tiahuanaco and woven from unidentified, non-Polynesian fibers, have been discovered in a cave in Hawaii. Representing an admitted enigma to local scholars, they were stored away in the Bishop Museum of Honolulu. Even the human mask decorating the upper end of this Hawaiian mummy bundle recalls the presence of mummy masks on similar mummy bundles from ancient Peru and the highlands of Mexico.

In the tropical rain forests of Central America and lowland Mexico, no human remains of corresponding antiquity have withstood the humid climate, although mummy masks are common. The jade mummy mask and decayed bits of red cloth wrapping attached to the eroded bones found in the colossal stone-lidded sarcophagus inside the Mexican burial pyramid at Palenque testify to desperate attempts at mummification.

Do the pre-Inca mummies of Peru exhibit the same homogeneous characteristics of very short stature, marked round-headedness, and stiff black hair as do the Indians inhabiting that area today? Or was there, in pre-Spanish times, a more heterogeneous population in Peru that included tall and fair ethnic types like the puzzling *Uru-keu* strain of neighboring Polynesia?

When large-scale excavations of Peruvian necropolises in the middle of the nineteenth century began to provide science with abundant mummy heads for study, European anthropologists were startled to find that some of the heads—both in cranial shape and in hair color and texture—displayed physical traits thought to be alien to the aboriginal inhabitants of the Americas. D. Wilson had found in 1862 that hair examined by him from Indian graves elsewhere "retains its black color and coarse texture, unchanged alike by time and inhumation." From the ancient Peruvian cemeteries of Atacama, nevertheless, he described some mummies with brown, soft, wavy hair, stating that these "reveal important variations from one of the most persistent and universal characteristics of the modern American races." He even speaks of "essential diversity in cranial conformation."

Wilson was especially struck by the contents of one grave at Chacota Bay on the Pacific coast below Tiahuanaco. Here lay the mummies of a man, a woman, and a child—evidently persons of high rank. Their funerary effects included some perfectly preserved, brightly colored bags containing locks of human hair, probably from members of the same family. Of the male mummy, Wilson says: "The hair has undergone little or no change and differs essentially from that most characteristic feature of the Indian of the northern continent. It is brown in color and as fine in texture as the most delicate Anglo-Saxon's hair." He continues: "The body of the female from the same tomb presents in general similar characteristics. The hair is shorter and somewhat coarser but fine when compared with that of the northern Indians. It is of light brown color, smooth, and neatly braided. . . ."

The scalp of the infant, he writes, "is thickly covered with very fine, dark brown hair." Most remarkable is Wilson's description of the various individual hair samples found in the colored bags: "All the hair is of fine texture, of various shades, from fine light brown to black, and to all appearance has undergone no change." Wilson observed other hair samples that were "not only brown but remarkably fine, waved in short undulations, with a tendency to curl."

Wilson was one of the first scholars to suspect, on the basis of these and similar observations, that Peru had supported a mixed population in pre-Spanish times. He stressed that the features of the well-preserved mummies from the coast of Peru disproved the assumed unity of physical type throughout the western hemisphere in pre-European times.[3]

In 1925 the noted archaeologists J. C. Tello and S. K. Lothrop discovered two major necropolises on the Paracas peninsula of the south central coast of Peru, where several hundred carefully wrapped mummies of important personages were preserved in burial caverns and stone-walled tombs that have later been carbon-14 dated to the centuries around 300 B.C. It is interesting to note that in the vicinity of these human remains, and dating from the same period, large quantities of hardwood *guara,* a kind of centerboard used in the navigation of sail-carrying rafts, are constantly being found, attesting to extensive maritime activity in early pre-Inca times. When the colorful, exquisitely designed and woven cotton funeral garments were removed from the more than 2,000-year-old Paracas mummies, it was discovered that the physical attributes of the bodies differed markedly from those of any known South American Indians. The physical anthropologist T. D. Stewart, analyzing in 1943 the skeletal remains of these pre-Inca mummies, found a considerable discrepancy in body heights between the Paracas mummies and skeletal remains from known Peruvian Indians —the Paracas individuals being of notably taller stature. As it had previously been taken for granted that pre-Inca peoples were of the same ethnic stock as the historically known Indians of Peru, Stewart's discovery came as quite a surprise. And, at a loss for an anatomical explanation, he speculated, "this may be a selected group of large males and not typical of the population as a whole".[4] Apart from the fact that mummification according to physical stature is unknown anywhere, this theory assumes that hundreds of tall individuals were available as candidates. Moreover, the elaborate burial and careful preparation of these bodies show that the mummies had not been mere fishermen or peasants, but were exclusively persons of high rank.

Stewart also found that the skull shape of the Paracas mummies was different from that of known Indians in that it exhibited a marked narrowness of the facial features. Failing again to find an anatomical explanation for this difference, he suggested that the facial features might have been altered as a secondary result of the practice in Paracas of artificial deformation of the upper skull. This explanation seems less than plausible in view of the fact that corresponding deformation of the upper skull was widely practiced on infants both in the Americas and in the Old World—without resulting in narrower facial features.

To avoid deriving erroneous conclusions based on upper-skull deformation, Stewart refrained from hypothesizing on the natural cephalic index of the Paracas mummies, which, like their facial form, differed from that of of the round-headed American Indian norm. A year after Stewart's Paracas studies, however, A. L. Kroeber, reporting on pre-Inca crania from farther north on the same coast, stated that the majority of undeformed Early Chimu skulls were long.[5] Thus, these early culture-people who built the great pre-Inca pyramids of Peru were not identical with their historic successors, all of whom are round-headed, like the people of Indonesia. Moreover, according to a special study by A. Chervin, excavations at the principal pre-Inca site of Tiahuanaco show that there was a marked mixture of cranial types also in this germinal center of South American civilization. The Tiahuanaco cranial indices varied from 71.97 to 93.79—that is, from extreme long-headedness to ultra round-headedness.[6] Thus, prior to Inca times, people with utterly different cranial forms co-existed in the principal culture centers of the slopes of South America.

While Stewart examined the anomalous skeletal remains of the red-haired Paracas mummies, a hair analysis on pieces of scalp from ten of them was simultaneously conducted by M. Trotter. She reported that, although the dominant hair color was "rusty brown," some scalps were "interspersed with very light, yellow hairs." She found the hair of two of the scalps to be "quite definitely wavy."

Trotter pointed out that the extent of waviness or curliness of human hair depends on its degree of ovalness in cross section. The straight, Mongoloid hair of the present American Indians is uniformly circular in cross section, while that of Europeans is commonly oval. The Paracas mummy hair did not follow this established pattern: "The cross-section form shows so much divergency between the different mummies that they cover all divisions of hair form."

Finally, the dimensions of the cross section supplement the form and the hair color in determining human hair types. The cross section of the Mongoloid and American Indian hair is very large compared with that of the hair of most Europeans. Trotter found the Paracas mummies to divert markedly from the expected norm also in this respect: "The size of the hair was much smaller than has been found for other Indians . . ." In fact, in spite of great variations between the individual scalps, she found the average mean of all samples to be about thirty per cent less than what should be expected had these mummies conformed with standard American Indian types. She was so puzzled by her observations, which clashed with the uniformly accepted view in current anthropology, that she found no other explanation than to use the method resorted to by Stewart in his analysis of the skulls and long bones: to suggest that perhaps these mummies told us nothing as they may misrepresent the people mummified. Perhaps the hair of gray-haired Indians had turned yellow in the tomb and that of black-haired Indians faded to red, while cross-section area and shape had altered due to dehydration.[7]

In response to my inquiries, Trotter in 1951 took up the problem once more in collaboration with O. H. Higgins of the hair and fiber section of the FBI. She now came to the conclusion that there were two errors in her publication of 1943; firstly to refer to the persons embalmed at Paracas as "Indians," and secondly to suggest that the hair might have faded. Existing evidence "would not deny that the original colour was a reddish brown and that the original texture was fine."[8]

It would seem too much of a coincidence if selective burial, cranial deformation, and post-mortem changes had made these mummies a contrast to the common Indian, that each particular departure from the norm invariably caused them to resemble the European-like culture-bringers so vividly described to the arriving Europeans by the Aztec and Inca nations. In full apprehension of the fact that science could never get a more direct opportunity to learn about the physical appearance of the founders of pre-Columbian high-cultures than through a study of these mummies of the actual individuals in question, I also consulted a leading British authority on the matter, W. R. Dawson, known for his studies of mummies from both Egypt and Peru. He wrote as follows: "My opinion is that hair does not undergo any marked changes post-mortem. The hair of a wavy or curly individual remains curly or wavy, and that of a straight-haired person remains straight. In mummies and desiccated bodies, the hair has a tendency to be crisp and brittle, but this is the natural result of the drying-up of the sebaceous glands . . . It seems to be very unlikely that any change in color would take place in a body which has never been exposed to the light . . . To sum up, then, all the evidence I have indicates that the nature of hair does not alter after death except in becoming dry and brittle."[9]

Red-haired mummies have also been found in the Canary Islands, but the hair color has never been questioned because European discoverers had observed that many of the aboriginal Guanches were fair-skinned with reddish-brown hair. Egyptian mummies are as black-haired as were the early Egyptian people, with a marked exception in the well-preserved mummy of Pharaoh Rameses II, which has blond hair, but we know that the pharaoh was in fact blond, as can be verified by the contemporary polychrome frescoes of the temple walls at Karnak, which depict him with yellow hair. In view of this, it seems unreasonable to propose that the Peruvian mummies analyzed misrepresent the ethnic stock from which they derived. If this is so, nothing has been learned from the discovery of the Paracas mummies and, for those who wanted to know what these early people looked like, nothing is to be gained by studying their remains. If, on the other hand, we assume that these mummies are what they appear to be—embalmed individuals with non-Mongoloid and clearly Caucasoid traits—then we have found in pre-Inca Peru what we were looking for: a natural source of the *uru-keu* strain on the adjacent islands of Polynesia, and an explanation of the blond ancestors of the Easter Islanders, cited by them as having come from a desert land to the east known as the "Burial Place."

We do not have to go to Europe or Asia Minor, on the opposite side of the world, to search for a source of the Caucasoid element in Polynesia; there is ample archaeological evidence that such a physical type was present on the nearest coast east of Polynesia centuries before these islands were settled. Could the Canary Current have brought Old World people to the New World, who then made their way across tropical America, leaving their mummies and eastern Mediterranean culture elements in their wake?

One need not delve deeply into the literature on Peru before discovering that local records are filled with tales of white, bearded migrants, who first appeared from an unspecified region and departed into the Pacific long before the Spaniards arrived. When Francisco Pizarro discovered Peru, his cousin the chronicler Pedro Pizarro, who accompanied him, recorded for posterity that some members of the local ruling classes were "whiter than Spaniards" and that he saw among the Indians some who were both white-skinned and blond. Pizarro added that the latter were, according to the Incas, descendants of their gods, the Viracochas.[10] In fact, no sooner had the Spaniards landed on the coast than Inca messengers, running in relay, brought word to the emperor in the highlands that the Viracochas—or "seafoam" people—had returned, as they had promised they would do, according to firm Inca tradition. The people of Peru had no beards, but they had a word for beard (*sonkhasapa*) as well as a word for the white foreigner (*viracocha*), which is still frequently applied by them to Europeans today. Because of their white skin and beards, Pizarro and a handful of men were allowed to march unmolested through the fortified mountain valleys of Peru and conquer the largest contemporary empire in the world, the vast army of which stood by in awed reverence of these returning Viracochas whose ancestors had played such an important role in Inca traditional history.

The false Viracochas under Pizarro took full advantage of the Inca mistake concerning their identity. They strangled the emperor with impunity in front of his own army and entered Cuzco's sacred temple, where they found realistic images in gold and marble of the ruler of the original Viracochas, Con-Tic Viracocha, whom the Incas venerated as a divine person. The Spaniards melted down the gold image and smashed the marble statue to pieces, leaving only a written record in which they described the image as being "both as to the hair, complexion, features, raiment, and sandals, just as painters represent the apostle St. Bartholomew."[11]

The conquistadors continued southward along the high Andean plateau, looting and pillaging their way from Cuzco to the vast Inca temple at Cacha, devoted to the worship of Viracocha. Within this architectural materpiece they found a huge stone statue, again of the divine priest-king Con-Tici Viracocha himself, represented as a long-robed man of regal bearing with a long beard. A contemporary, Inca Garcilasso, chronicling the encounter, wrote: "The Spaniards, after seeing this temple and the statue with the form that has been described, wanted to make out that St. Bartholomew might have traveled as far as Peru to preach to the Gentiles, and that the Indians had made this statue in memory of the event."[12] Indeed, the Spaniards were so impressed by this bearded statue and Inca accounts of the wandering foreigner who had visited Peru with his white and bearded entourage some time in the distant past that the statue and the temple escaped destruction for many years. And the Spanish-Indian Mestizos of Cuzco formed a brotherhood, adopting this statue of "St. Bartholomew" as their guardian. Ultimately, however, the Spaniards realized their mistake, and the huge temple was destroyed; the bearded statue, first disfigured, was later carried off and broken into pieces.[13]

Advancing through the vast Inca empire, the Spaniards came upon huge megalithic sites of pre-Inca origin, which had been abandoned centuries before Columbus and now lay in ruins. One of the most spectacular examples of megalithic architecture in the New World was found at Vinaque, between Cuzco and the ocean. The contemporary Spanish chronicler, Cieza de León, writing in 1553, reported: "When the Indians are asked who built these ancient monuments, they reply that a bearded and white people like ourselves were the builders, who came to these parts many ages before the Yncas began to reign, and formed a settlement here."[14] How firmly rooted these traditional memories were is best illustrated by the fact that the Peruvian archaeologist Dr. L. Valcárcel, arriving to study the Vinaque ruins 400 years after Cieza de León, was given the same information: that these structures had been built by a foreign people "white like Europeans."[15]

Proceeding southward to Lake Titicaca, the Spaniards entered the hub of former Viracocha activity. Throughout the Inca empire, traditional histories have agreed in placing the center of Viracocha habitation on the island of Titicaca in the lake of the same name, and in the neighboring city of Tiahuanaco, with its vast stone-dressed pyramid, megalithic walls, and monolithic statues. Cieza de León writes: "Before the Yncas conquered the country, many of the Indians declare that there were two great lords in the Collao, the one called Sapana and the other Cari who conquered many *Pucaras* which are their fortresses. They add that one of these chiefs entered the large island in the lake of Titicaca, and found there a white people who had beards; that they fought with them in such a manner that all were killed . . ."

He returns to the same topic in his second part: "They also relate what I have written in the first part, namely that there were people with beards, in the Island of Titicaca in past ages, white like ourselves; that, coming from the valley of Coquimbo, their captain, who was named Cari, arrived at the place where Chucuito now stands, whence after having founded some new settlements, he passed over with his people to the island. He made such war upon the inhabitants that he killed them all."[16]

In a special chapter on what he calls the ancient buildings of Tiahuanaco, Cieza de León has this to say: "I asked the natives, in presence of Juan de Vargas, whether these edifices were built in the time of the Yncas, and they laughed at the query, affirming that they were made before the Yncas ever reigned . . . From this, and from the fact that they also speak of bearded men on the island of Titicaca, and of others who built the edifice of Vinaque, it may, perhaps, be inferred that, before the Yncas reigned, there was an intelligent race who came from some unknown part, and who did these things. Being few, and the natives many, they may all have been killed in the wars."[17]

When A. F. Bandelier arrived to excavate among the ruins of the island of Titicaca 350 years later, this version of local history still persisted. He was told that in very ancient times the island was inhabited by gentlemen of unknown provenance similar to Europeans; they had cohabited with the local native women and the resulting children became the Incas, who "drove out the gentlemen and held the island thereafter."[18]

All the chroniclers accompanying the conquistadors or visiting Peru immediately after the conquest included references to the pre-Inca Viracochas in their reports. These reports, while differing in minor details as a result of having been gathered from informants in widely scattered parts of the vast Inca empire, nevertheless agree in all essentials. The Spaniards' informants included professional Inca historians, who passed on their history from generation to generation, sometimes aided by a system of knotted string—*quipu*—or painted boards. Common to all accounts of how culture reached Peru is the admission that the Incas lived more or less as savages till a light-skinned, bearded foreigner and his entourage came to their country, taught them the ways of civilization, and departed.

Inca Garcilasso provides the following striking account, in which he interviews his royal Inca uncle about the earliest history of Peru: "Nephew, I will tell you what you ask with great pleasure, and you should preserve what I have to say in your heart . . . Know, then, that in ancient times, all this region which you see was covered with forests and thickets, and the people lived like wild beasts, without religion, or government, or town, or houses, without cultivating the land, or clothing their bodies, for they knew not how to weave cotton nor wool to make clothes. They lived two or three together in caves, or clefts in the rocks, or in caverns underground. They ate the herbs of the field and roots or fruit like wild animals, and also human flesh. They covered their bodies with leaves and the bark of trees, or with the skins of animals. In fine, they lived like deer or other game, and even in their intercourse with women, they were like brutes; for they knew nothing of living with separate wives."[19]

Cieza de León, writing of the period "before the Incas reigned in these kingdoms, or had even been heard of," says the period of barbarism ended with the appearance of the personification of the sun on the island of Titicaca: "afterwards, they say, that there came [to Cuzco] from a southern direction a white man of great stature, who, by his aspect and presence, called forth great veneration and obedience . . . In many places he gave orders to men how they should live and he spoke lovingly to them and with much gentleness, admonishing them that they should do good, and no evil or injury one to another, and that they should be loving and charitable to all. In most parts he is generally called *Ticiviracocha,* but in the province of the Collao they call him *Tuapaka* and in other places *Arunaua.* In many parts they built temples in which they put blocks of stone in likeness of him . . ."[20]

The chronicler Betanzos, who took part in the discovery of Peru, recorded: "When I asked the Indians what shape this Viracocha had when their ancestors had thus seen him, they said that according to the information they possessed, he was a tall man with a white vestment that reached to his feet, and that his vestment had a girdle; and that he carried his hair short with a tonsure on the head in the manner of a priest; and that he walked solemnly, and that he carried in his hands a certain thing which today seems to remind them of the breviary that the priests carry in their hands."[21]

There is no clear information, however, as to where Con-Tici

Viracocha came from. The chronicler Andagoya, who also took part in the conquest, wrote: "There is no record of whence he came, except that Viracocha, in the language of the people, means "Foam of the Sea." He was a white and bearded man like a Spaniard. The natives of Cuzco, seeing his great valour, took it for something divine and received him as their chief . . ."[22]

The chronicler Zárate cites Lake Titicaca as a possible beginning point for Viracocha and writes: "Some mean to say that he was called Inga Viracocha, which is 'froth or grease of the sea,' since, not knowing where the land lay whence he came, (they) believed him to have been formed out of that lagoon."[23] Gómara, however, wrote: "Some aged Indians also say that he was called Viracocha, which is to say 'grease of the sea,' and that he brought his people by sea."[24]

The very name Con-Tici Viracocha is a composite of three names for the same white and bearded deity. In pre-Inca times, he was known on the coast of Peru as Con and in the highlands as Tici or Ticci, but when Inca rule and language (Quechua) spread to encompass the entire territory, the Incas recognized that the names Con and Ticci referred to the same deity as the one they themselves called Viracocha. They therefore grouped the three names together, to the satisfaction of all the people of their empire.

Legends among the Chimu Indians of the north coast of Peru relate the interesting tale of this deity's having arrived by sea along the coast from even farther north. Whereas most of the highland legends have him appearing suddenly at Lake Titicaca, as a personification of the sun, less reverent legends on the coast directly below Titicaca speak of a white-skinned, blond Viracocha who came sailing from the north and paused briefly among the coastal Indians before ascending to Lake Titicaca, where he established a hegemony through fraud, by introducing his fair-haired children to the Indians as supernatural offspring of the sun.

The human aspect of Viracocha is also revealed in a highland legend that says that Viracocha "was very shrewd and wise and said he was a child of the sun."[25] All the highland traditions agree that his first place of residence was on Titicaca Island, before he set forth with a fleet of reed boats to a site on the south shore of the lake, where he built the megalithic city of Tiahuanaco. He and his white and bearded followers were expressly referred to as *mitimas,* the Inca word for colonists or settlers. They introduced cultivated crops and taught the Indians how to grow them in irrigated terraces; they showed the Indians how to build stone houses and live in organized communities with law and order; they introduced cotton clothing, sun worship, and megalithic carving; they built step pyramids and erected monolithic statues which were said to honor the ancestors of each individual tribe over which they claimed dominion.

From Tiahuanaco, according to legend, Viracocha sent his white and bearded messengers into all parts of Peru to teach people that he was their god and creator. However, dissatisfied at length with the bad conduct and hostility of the local Indians, Viracocha, sun king of Tiahuanaco, which had become the religious and cultural center of the pre-Inca empire, decided to leave. Throughout the vast Inca empire, the Indians recalled until the Spaniards arrived the routes followed by Viracocha and his two principal disciples as they departed. On Viracocha's instructions, one disciple followed the inland mountain range northward from Lake Titicaca, preaching as he went, while the other, in the same manner, followed the lowland coast. Con-Tici Viracocha himself took the middle route northward by way of Cacha, where the statue like St. Bartholomew was made in his honor, and Cuzco, whose megalithic walls he is credited with having built. Having told the Indians of Cuzco how to behave after his departure, he descended to the Pacific coast and gathered with his Viracocha followers near the port of Manta in Ecuador, from whence these sun worshipers sailed westward into the Pacific, departing from almost the exact point where the equator crosses the South American continent.

As we have seen, the Indians of Peru's north coast relate that the pan-Peruvian culture bringer disappeared westward, that is, toward Polynesia, although he had originally come from the north. North of the Inca empire, on the mountain plateau of Colombia, the Chibchas, another astonishingly advanced people, had distinguished themselves by a high degree of civilization by the time Europeans arrived. The traditional history of the Chibchas attributed their cultural attainments to the teaching of a foreign migrant, generally known to them as Bochica or Xue. He, too, was remembered as a white man dressed in long, flowing robes and with a beard that fell to his waist. He taught the savage Chibchas to build, to sow, and to live in village communities with organized government and laws. He ruled for many years, then departed, appointing a successor, whom he urged to govern justly. Bochica was also known as Sua, the local word for sun, and when the

Spaniards arrived they were taken to be his envoys and were called Sua, or Gagua, which also meant sun.

According to tradition, Bochica, alias Sua, had come from the east. East of Chibcha territory, in Venezuela and adjacent parts, we once again encounter memories of the migrant culture hero. He is referred to by various names, such as Tsuma or Zume, and he is always credited with introducing the people to agriculture and other benefits. According to one legend, he was accustomed to gathering the people around a lofty rock while he stood above them on its summit delivering his instructions and his laws. He lived a certain length of time with the people and then left them. In some areas, legend has him leaving of his own accord; in others, he is driven away by his stiff-necked and unwilling audience, which had become tired of his advice.

Immediately north of Colombia and Venezuela, the Cuna Indians of Panama, who practiced writing on wooden tablets, had a tradition that after a devastating flood, "there appeared a great personage who . . . taught people how to behave, what to name things, and how to use them. He was followed by a number of disciples who spread his teachings . . ."[26]

North of Panama, in Mexico, the highly advanced civilization of the Aztecs was flourishing when the Spaniards arrived. The vast military empire of the Aztecs—like that of the Incas—was far larger than Spain or any other contemporary European nation. Yet, when Hernando Cortez landed in Mexico in 1519, his small band marched unmolested through the jungle and up to the Aztec capital in the distant highlands, where they subdued the mighty Emperor and subjugated his nation with the same surprising ease as Pizarro when he reached the Inca empire a few years later. These events were due neither to Spanish military supremacy nor to Indian incompetence, but simply to religious confusion on the part of the Indians as to the nature of these "returning" white and bearded strangers. All the way from Anahuac in Texas to the borders of Yucatán, the Aztecs spoke of a white and bearded Quetzalcoatl, as the Incas spoke of Viracocha. And from the moment of their arrival on the beach in Mexico, the white and bearded Spaniards were regarded by the Aztecs as the returning people of Quetzalcoatl.

In his *Carta Segunda* of 1520, Cortez personally recorded the speech delivered to him by the Aztec emperor, Montezuma, after the Aztecs had anointed the Spaniards with blood from a human sacrifice: "We

have known for a long time, by the writings handed down by our forefathers, that neither I nor any who inhabit this land are natives of it,
but foreigners who came here from remote parts. We also know that
we were led here by a ruler, whose subjects we all were, who returned
to his country, and after a long time came here again and wished to
take his people away. But they had married wives and built houses,
and they would neither go with him nor recognize him as their king;
therefore he went back. We have ever believed that those who were of
his lineage would some time come and claim this land as his, and us as
his vassals. From the direction whence you come, which is where the
sun rises, and from what you tell me of this great lord who sent you,
we believe and think it certain that he is our natural ruler, especially
since you say that for a long time he has known about us. Therefore
you may feel certain that we shall obey you, and shall respect you as
holding the place of that great lord, and in all the land I rule, you may
give what orders you wish, and they shall be obeyed, and everything
we have shall be put at your service. And since you are thus in your
own heritage and your own house, take your ease and rest from the fa-
tigue of the journey and the wars you have had on the way."

In his study of aboriginal American religions Brinton comments:
"Such was the extraordinary address with which the Spaniard, with
his handful of men, was received by the most powerful war chief of
the American continent. It confessed complete submission, without a
struggle. But it was the expression of a general sentiment. When the
Spanish ships for the first time reached the Mexican shores the natives
kissed their sides and hailed the white and bearded strangers from the
east as gods, sons and brothers of Quetzalcoatl, coming back from their
celestial home to claim their own on earth and bring again the days of
Paradise; a hope, dryly observes Father Mendieta, which the poor Indians soon gave up when they came to feel the acts of their visitors."

Originally, Quetzalcoatl, as well as Viracocha, seems to have been
the hereditary name, or rather title, of a hierarchical sequence of priest-
kings, who worshiped—and claimed descent from—a supreme sun god
of the same name. Only with time were all Quetzalcoatls, like all
Viracochas, amalgamated into one, single historic deity—god and creator, as well as human culture hero and mortal benefactor.

The name Quetzalcoatl is a composite, often translated freely as
Plumed Serpent—*quetzal* (*trogon splendens*) being the favorite bird
of the Aztecs, and *coatl*, the serpent, being the sacred symbol of light

and divinity both in Mexico and Peru. Quetzalcoatl was the supreme god of the Aztecs as Viracocha was of the Incas. Yet, as Brinton writes: ". . . it was not Quetzalcoatl the god, the mysterious creator of the visible world, on whom the thought of the Aztec race delighted to dwell, but on Quetzalcoatl, high priest in the glorious city of Tollan (Tula), the teacher of the arts, the wise law-giver, the virtuous prince, the master builder, and the merciful judge."

He forbade the sacrifice of human beings and animals; teaching that bread, flowers, and incense were all that the gods demanded. And he prohibited wars, fighting, robbery, and other forms of violence to such an extent that he was held in affectionate veneration, not only by his own people but by distant natives as well, who made pilgrimages to his capital. The fact that the Aztecs, who excelled in human sacrifice at their pyramids and temples, still recollected a benevolent pacifist culture bringer whose teachings closely paralleled the biblical commandments so impressed the Spanish friars that they identified Quetzalcoatl with the Apostle Thomas—an exact analogy to the confusion in Peru of Viracocha with St. Bartholomew. Brinton shows that the deity Quetzalcoatl in his earthly male manifestation was also known as Tonaca tecutli, i.e., Chief Tonaca. This is remarkable since a similar appellation, Tonapa, happens to be one of the names for the corresponding migrant white and bearded Viracochas in Peru. Fray Alonzo Ramos claims that Tonapa was the legendary white man murdered on Titicaca Island, whereas the Quechua Indian chronicler Pachacuti identifies Tonapa with the migrant culture hero also variously known as Viracocha with the suffix Ra, Pacha, or Ccan, and claims he descended along the river Chacamarca to leave into the Pacific.

The essence of the Quetzalcoatl tradition is that he was a white man, tall of stature, with a flowing beard, which, according to some chroniclers, was reddish in color. He wore a strange dress, unlike the attire of the Indians who received him; the historian Veytia recorded that he was "clothed in a long white robe strewn with red crosses, and carried a staff in his hand." He was accompanied in his travels by builders, painters, astronomers, and craftsmen; he made roads, civilized the people, and passed thus from place to place until, in the end, he disappeared. According to some traditions, he died on the coast of the Gulf of Mexico and was buried there at the seashore by his followers after they had burned his body and all his treasures. Other traditions, however, insisted that Quetzalcoatl and his entourage embarked on a magic raft of serpents and thus sailed away after promising solemnly to return and take possession of the land.

The neighbors of the Aztecs were the Mayas of the tropical lowlands of the Yucatán peninsula, which juts into the Gulf of Mexico. Juan de Grijalva, passing from Cuba to the Yucatán peninsula a year before Cortez landed on the shore of the Gulf of Mexico, got the same amazingly respectful reception from the otherwise warlike Indians as that accorded Cortez and Pizarro. The great Maya civilization had collapsed before the Spaniards arrived, but the scattered remnants of the people still possessed detailed traditions as to the origins of the culture that had flourished under their ancestors. They spoke of two distinct culture heroes, *Itzamná* and *Kukulcan*—both bearded, although arriving at different times and from opposite directions, leading the Mayas' ancestors to Yucatán.

Brinton says of the descendants of the Mayas: "They did not pretend to be autochthonous, but claimed that their ancestors came from distant regions in two bands. The largest and most ancient immigration was from the east, across, or rather through, the ocean—for the gods had opened twelve paths through it—and this was conducted by the mythical civilizer Itzamná. The second band, less in number and later in time, came in from the west, and with them was Kukulcan. The former was called the Great Arrival; the latter, the Lesser Arrival. . . . To this ancient leader Itzamná, the nation alluded as their guide, instructor, and civilizer. It was he who gave names to all the rivers and divisions of land; he was the first priest and taught them the proper rites wherewith to please the gods and appease their ill-will; he was the patron of the healers and diviners and had disclosed to them the mysterious virtues of plants. . . . It was Itzamná who first invented the characters or letters in which the Mayas wrote their numerous books, and with which they carved in such profusion on the stone and wood of their edifices. He also devised their calendar, one more perfect even than that of the Mexicans, though in a general way similar to it. Thus Itzamná, regarded as a ruler, priest, and teacher, was, no doubt, spoken of as an historical personage, and is so put down by various historians, even to the most recent. After the Great Arrival came the Lesser: the second important hero-myth of the Mayas was that of Kukulcan. This is in no way connected with that of Itzamná, and is probably later in date, and less national in character. . . . The natives affirmed, says Las Casas, that in ancient times there came to that land twenty men, the chief of whom was called 'Cocolcan' . . . They wore flowing robes and sandals on their feet, they had long beards, and their heads were bare, they ordered that the people should confess and fast . . ."

Kukulcan was remembered as a great architect and pyramid builder who founded the city of Mayapan and caused various important edifices to be built at Chichén Itzá. He taught the people to refrain from using arms—even for hunting—and under his beneficent rule the nation enjoyed peace, prosperity, and abundant harvests.

The mere idea that the cruel and bellicose Mayas had invented such a peace-loving doctrine as that of Kukulcan, the immigrant priest-king, is as surprising as the insistence on the part of these beardless natives on the flowing beards, fair skin, and long robes of this cultured wanderer and his followers. Nevertheless, his humanitarian teaching and cultural activities coincide completely with those of Quetzalcoatl. Moreover, while Aztec tradition has Quetzalcoatl disappearing eastward from Mexico in the direction of Yucatán, Maya tradition has Kukulcan coming to Yucatán from the west, from the direction of Mexico, and the two may thus be the same personage. Brinton points out that one of the Maya chronicles opens with a distinct reference to Tula and Nonoal—names inseparable from the Quetzalcoatl tradition —and he concludes: "The probability seems to be that Kukulcan was an original Maya divinity, one of their hero-gods, whose myth had in it so many similarities to that of Quetzalcoatl that the priests of the two nations came to regard the one as the same as the other." In fact the word *Kukulcan* is simply a translation of *Quetzalcoatl*. *Kukul* is the Maya word for the quetzal bird, and *can* is a serpent.

Eventually, as in Mexico and Peru, the white and bearded priest-king also left Yucatán. According to Brinton, "He gathered the chiefs together and expounded to them his laws. From among them, he chose as his successor a member of the ancient and wealthy family of the Cocoms. His arrangements completed, he is said, by some, to have journeyed westward, to Mexico, or to some spot towards the sun-setting."

A westward migrant from Yucatán would necessarily enter the habitat of the Tzendals in the Tabasco and Chiapas jungles of Mexico. Tzendal legend, centering upon their culture hero Votan, who came from the direction of Yucatán, was originally recorded in the Tzendal language as dictated by a Tzendal native. Referring to this manuscript,

Brinton says: "Few of our hero-myths have given occasion for wilder speculation than that of Votan . . . At some indefinitely remote epoch, Votan came from the far East. He was sent by God to divide out and assign to the different races of men the earth on which they dwell, and to give to each its own language. The land whence he came was vaguely called *ualum uotan,* the land of Votan. His message was especially to the Tzendals. Previous to his arrival, they were ignorant, barbarous, and without fixed habitations. He collected them into villages, taught them how to cultivate the maize and cotton, and invented the hieroglyphic signs, which they learned to carve on the walls of their temples. It is even said that he wrote his own history in them. He instructed civil laws for their government, and imparted to them the proper ceremonials of religious worship. . . . They especially remembered him as the inventor of their calendar."

Also remembered as a city builder, he was spoken of as the founder of Palenque with its great stone pyramids, two of which contained burial chambers like those of ancient Egypt. The Tzendal text continues: "Votan brought with him, according to one statement, or, according to another, was followed from his native land by certain attendants or subordinates, called in the myth *tzequil,* petticoated, from the long and flowing robes they wore. These aided him in the work of civilisation . . . When at last the time came for his final departure, he did not pass through the valley of death, as must all mortals, but he penetrated through a cave into the underworld, and found his way to 'the root of heaven.' "

With this reference to his descent into the underworld the people of Chiapas close their account of him. Yet, from the high plateau of Chiapas we do not have to go farther down into the underworld than the coastal lowlands of the Zoques before Votan reappears, this time with the name of Condoy. Brinton says: "The Zoques, whose mythology we unfortunately know little or nothing about, adjoined the Tzendals, and were in constant intercourse with them. We have but faint traces of the early mythology of these tribes; but they preserved some legends which showed that they also partook of the belief, so general among their neighbours, of a beneficent culture-god. This myth relates that their first father, who was also their Supreme God, came forth from a cave in a lofty mountain in their country, to govern and direct them . . . They did not believe that he had died, but that after a certain length of time, he, with his servants and captives, all laden with bright, gleaming gold, retired into the cave and closed its mouth, not to remain there, but to reappear at some other part of the world and confer similar favours on other nations. The name, or one of the names, of this benefactor was Condoy . . ."

South of the Mayas, Tzendals, and Zoques lived the Kiches of Guatemala, whose culture shows a root relationship to that of the Mayas. Their traditions have been preserved for posterity by a rescript of their original national book, the *Popul Vuh*. From this aboriginal source, we learn that the inhabitants were well acquainted with the "wanderer," who seems to have passed through their territory more than once. Known in Guatemala under various names, one of which was Gucumatz, he educated and civilized the local savages, teaching them to develop their own civilization. Brinton concludes: "But, like Viracocha, Quetzalcoatl, and others of those worthies, the story goes that they treated him with scant courtesy, and in anger at their ingratitude, he left them forever, in order to seek a nobler people."[27]

The Spaniards thus encountered the same tradition of white and bearded culture bearers throughout middle America, from the Mexican highlands southward to the mountain plateaus of Peru and Bolivia—that is, precisely where they encountered spectacular ruins of lost civilizations. Yet many modern commentators, accustomed to train, car, and air travel, find it difficult to imagine that any "wanderer" can have covered such vast areas in pre-Columbian times. They forget that the medieval Spaniards had no access to trains, cars, or airplanes either. Yet, within a mere two decades of their first landing in Mexico, the relatively few Spaniards had explored the New World territory from the Atlantic to the Pacific, from Kansas to Argentina. Within the same few years, Caboza de Vaca and three companions were shipwrecked in the surf of the Florida coast and for eight years (1528–36) walked—unarmed, barefoot, and almost naked—through unmapped swamps, deserts, and mountains, from one Indian tribe to the next, right across the continent to the Gulf of California, where they finally reached the newly established Spanish settlements. Before the same two decades were over, Orellana, sailing from Spain, had crossed the Panama Isthmus and climbed the Andes from the Pacific side, from whence he descended to the sources of the Amazon, following the river across the continent to its mouth in the Atlantic Ocean before returning home to Spain. To believe that a few Spaniards could in two decades walk so far across mountains and jungles and yet to think that the founders of the pre-Columbian empires could not have traversed them in two centuries or even two millennia, is grossly to underestimate the latter's capabilities. It is to defy the thesis of the uniformity of human behavior.

Throughout the years, desperate attempts have been made to account for the seemingly paradoxical presence of white-skinned, bearded men dressed in long robes in the traditions of brown-skinned, beardless Indians all the way from Mexico to Peru, none of whom were dressed in such a manner. Brinton and others have theorized that the flowing beards and loose robes might have been allegorical references among sun worshipers to the sun god surrounded with rays. It has also been suggested that these traditions were perhaps not truly pre-Columbian, that they might have been inspired by the arrival of the Spaniards.

Either of these suggestions clearly reflects the European underestimation of the intellect and historical mindedness of the people behind the advanced civilizations on the other side of the Atlantic, and the unfounded conviction that nobody resembling ourselves could have come to America before us. It suffices to recollect that the stories about early people resembling the Spaniards were not only recited to the Spaniards verbally on their arrival, they were already recorded in the written history of the New World, as the Aztec emperor emphasized in his speech of welcome to Cortez. With the progress of modern archaeology the claims of the historic Indians have been verified, since highly realistic sculptures and colored illustrations have been found in tombs and ancient temples, some of which not only antedate Spanish arrival, but in a great many cases even antedate the living Aztec and Inca cultures which the Spaniards encountered. They were in fact vividly illustrated in the realistic art of the Olmecs, the Mochicas, and the other very early peoples who had founded the various civilizations from Mexico to Peru. To ignore this early documentation which confirms the oral and written history of the people who received the Spaniards is as unwarranted as the attempts to hypothesize that the pre-Inca mummies are tall because of selective burials, have Europoid head shape because of childhood deformation, and have reddish and blond hair with a cross section like European hair because of post-mortem changes.

Pre-Columbian art supports post-Columbian memories and the appearance of the mummies. We have seen that when the Spaniards entered the main temples of the Incas in Peru they found gold and stone statues of the pre-Inca culture hero, Viracocha, bearing a confusing resemblance to depictions of one of their own apostles, with his beard and his robe and sandals of east-Mediterranean style.

The majority of the many statues found by the Spaniards among the ruins of Tiahuanaco, said to represent the progenitors of the various tribes in the realm of Con-Tici Viracocha, were destroyed as heathen relics by the Catholic conquistadors. But a few were hidden by the Indians and thus escaped destruction. In 1932, while the American archaeologist W. C. Bennett was carrying out excavations in Tiahuanaco, he unearthed a complete statue representing Con-Tici Viracocha, with beard and long, girdled robe. The flowing garment was decorated with a horned serpent and two pumas, symbols of the supreme god in both Mexico and Peru. Bennett shows that this statue was almost identical to another bearded statue found on the shore of Lake Titicaca, on the peninsula close to Titicaca Island, where Viracocha landed when he left his refuge to make his way to Tiahuanaco.[28] Other bearded statues, similarly of pre-Inca origin, have been found at various archaeological sites around Lake Titicaca.[29] Stone suitable for sculpture was almost non-existent on the Pacific desert coast of Peru, but there, among the Chimu and Nazca cultures, illustrations of the early culture hero were either molded in or painted on ceramic, showing him with mustache and chin beard. These representations of Viracocha, originally known locally as Con, are especially common in the north coast of Peru, where legend has it that the bearded god, arriving from the north, ascended the area subsequently ruled by the Incas. The ceramic vessels date from the Early Chimu or Mochicas, the earliest founders of local civilization and builders of the finest pyramids in Peru. They all depict a person wearing such an un-American attire as a turban and full-length robe, with a most realistic mustache and long, pointed beard reaching down to his chest.

Ceramic heads and figurines realistically depicting the same bearded personage are common northward from the coast of Peru through Ecuador and Colombia, and they reappear sporadically up through the Isthmus into Mexico. In fact, highly realistic illustrations of the bearded and often almost Arabo-Semitic ethnic type are extremely common all the way across Mexico, from Guerrero into Yucatán, from the Mexican high plateau and the northern jungles of Vera Cruz to

Chiapas, and from there into Guatemala and El Salvador. He is depicted in freestanding statues, in carved reliefs on flat stone stelae, molded in clay, shaped in gold, painted on ceramic vessels and stucco walls, and in the picture writings of pre-Columbian paper folding books. His beard could be long or short; black or brown; trimmed or natural; pointed, round, or even forked and curled as commonly seen in art from ancient Mesopotamia. In some instances, the Maya priests and other important personages, who could not grow beards themselves, would wear false beards in imitation of the divine founders of their religion.

As we have seen, modern archaeology has come to the conclusion that one of the oldest civilizations in Mexico, which inspired and gave rise to subsequent civilizations, originated in the tropical jungle lowlands on the Gulf Coast of Mexico. This, as we have shown earlier, is precisely where the strong current comes in from across the Atlantic and where, in fact, the Spaniards themselves landed under Cortez. Here, on the coast, in a highly unfavorable climate, archaeology has revealed that American civilization began with the sudden appearance of an unknown people which modern science has merely assigned a name to: the Olmecs.

Lacking suitable stone in the deep soil of their jungle habitat, the Olmecs traveled far and wide to fetch stones weighing up to twenty-five tons and drag them back over fifty miles through swamps and jungles to their temple sites. With unsurpassed skill they sculptured human heads and full figures—in the round and relief—so realistically that we today have a very good indication of what the "Olmecs" looked like.

To judge from their art, the Olmecs comprised two contrasting ethnic types: one was remarkably Negroid, with thick lips, flat broad nose, and a round face bearing a naïve, unsophisticated, and rather sullen expression. This type has been popularly referred to among archaeologists as "baby face." The other Olmec type is completely different, sometimes representing a strikingly Semitic type, with sharp profile, a prominent hooked nose, narrow face, thin lips, and a pronounced beard sometimes in the shape of a square or pointed goatee, but occasionally so long that this type has been jokingly referred to among archaeologists as "Uncle Sam."

Neither of these two contrasting Olmec types—the Negroid and the Semitic—resemble any ethnic group known to have come across the

Bering Straits. Instead they represent to a remarkable degree the two physical types behind the pre-European civilizations in the Afro-Asiatic part of the Mediterranean region. Their appearance as self-portraits, carved by the founders of the New World civilization and left by them in the tropic jungle coast just where nature's own conveyer brings in the ocean surface from North Africa, has fired the imagination of the diffusionist and the enthusiastic layman, but has always remained without comment from the isolationist. As in the days of the early Spanish friars, so in modern times have religious sects concluded that biblical and Mormon personages—even the entire Lost Tribe of Israel —once reached the Gulf of Mexico. Such claims have confused and hampered the diffusionist cause. More than any other factor, they have frightened many serious students into joining the seemingly more cautious isolationist group. But is it in fact more cautious to close one's eyes and stand aside from such problematical evidence as the Olmec portraits and the fundamental claims of all civilized nations in aboriginal America? Is it not incautious to ignore the obvious possibility that civilized man before 1492 might have done what the European heirs of his civilization did thousands of times in the decades that followed? Can any reasonable scholar ignore the fact that highly civilized colonizers from the Afro-Asiatic corner of the Mediterranean were literally sailing in the same Atlantic water as that which uninterruptedly washed the shores of the Gulf of Mexico when the Olmecs founded American civilization? As today, so also in the days of these early sun worshipers, the Moroccan sun becomes the Mexican sun in a matter of hours, and Moroccan water becomes Mexican water in a matter of weeks.

The fact that the ocean meant something very specific to the most pronounced inland civilizations of Mexico as well can be judged from the fact that highland Aztecs shared the lowland Mayas' account of the founders of their cultures having come from over the Atlantic. In fact, in the very heart of Mexico, at the important cult site of Teotihuacan, some 7,000 feet (2,250 m.) above sea level, the pyramid of Quetzalcoatl, commemorating this Mexican culture bringer, shows him symbolically swimming as a plumed serpent among hundreds of large conches and other marine shells which, carved in high relief and painted with realistic colors, cover every side of the pyramid from its base up. Recently an important hilltop temple was located and excavated at Cacaxtla, some ninety miles from Mexico City. The stucco-

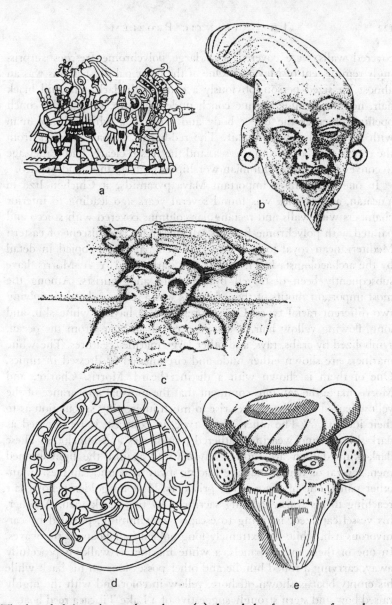

The bearded American culture hero. (a): bearded raft voyagers from the
Aztec Codex Nuttall; (b): Olmec pottery head from Tres Zapotes on the
Gulf of Mexico; (c): the "Uncle Sam" type of Olmec stone relief from La
Venta on the Gulf of Mexico; (d): Olmec relief on stone mirror from
Vera Cruz on the Gulf of Mexico; (e): typical pre-Inca ceramic portrait
of the bearded Mochica culture bringer, after Montell 1929.

covered walls were covered with large polychrome frescoes surprisingly reminiscent of Maya art. One of the principal illustrations was an almost life-sized person, obviously a deity, with dark skin and black hair, holding a huge marine conch under his arm. Out of the conch opening emerges the upper body and arms of a white-skinned man with long reddish-brown hair. The red-haired human emerges from the conch as if born from the sea, and the fresco clearly had a message to convey to the pre-Columbian worshipers high up in inland Mexico.

In one of the most important Maya pyramids, at Chichén Itzá in Yucatán, an entrance was found several years ago leading to interior chambers with walls and rectangular columns covered with stucco and painted with polychrome frescoes, all strikingly reminiscent of eastern Mediterranean royal tombs. These colored paintings, copied in detail by the archaeologists E. H. Morris. J. Charlot, and A. A. Morris, have subsequently been destroyed by humidity and tourists. Among the most important motifs of these frescoes was a seashore battle involving two different racial types. One, represented as having white skin and long, flowing yellow hair, is shown arriving in boats from the ocean, symbolized by crabs, rays, and other large marine creatures. The white mariners are shown either nude and circumcised or dressed in tunics. One of them is shown with a distinct beard. Morris, Charlot, and Morris make the cautious comment that the unusual appearance of the yellow-haired mariners "gives rise to much interesting speculation as to their identity."[30] The other ethnic type, in contrast, is represented as dark-skinned and wearing feathered headdresses and loincloths. These dark-skinned men are shown waging war against the light-skinned men, several of whom they are leading away as bound captives. In another panel, one of these white prisoners, his long golden-yellow hair reaching to his waist, is being sacrificed by two black men. Another, his vessel capsized, is trying to escape by swimming, pursued by carnivorous fish, while his extremely long golden hair floats in the waves. In one of these mural panels, a white mariner is walking peacefully away, carrying a rolled bundle and other possessions on his back while his empty boat is shown offshore, yellow in color and with the highly raised bow and stern strongly suggestive of a Lake Titicaca reed boat.

Reed boats have been recorded in post-Columbian times in eight different Mexican states, although they are not reported from modern Yucatán. The vessel depicted on the Maya pyramid recalls the reed boats used at Lixus on the Atlantic coast of Morocco whence the ocean current sets out to reach the Mexican shore. Similar mural paintings in ancient Egyptian tombs show reed boats sometimes involved in battles on the Nile. A relief in ancient Nineveh shows Mesopotamians using reed boats in a battle on the sea; bearded men with very long flowing hair are also shown, swimming for their lives in an ocean which, as in the Chichén Itzá mural, is symbolized by large crabs and marine creatures. In the Nineveh relief some of the reed boats are depicted as escaping across the sea, crowded with men and women with their arms raised in prayer to the sun.

Battles and escapes have possibly brought as many mariners to grips with unknown seas and currents as have famines, fogs, and offshore gales. What happened to the fleeing sun worshipers in the Nineveh relief happened to countless other mariners in Asia Minor and Africa from the very dawn of civilization. Basic similarities of human nature make history repeat itself. Thus we shall never know whether it was war, accidental drift, or planned exploration that brought tall, blond, and bearded men across the open sea from Africa to the Canary Islands long before Europeans arrived there. We know from written accounts of the discovery of the Canary Islands a few generations before Columbus that these remote Atlantic islands were inhabited by an ethnically mixed population called Guanches. Some of these aboriginal Canary Islanders were small, swarthy, and Negroid, whereas others were tall, white-skinned, and blond. An early water color by Torriani from 1590, showing six aboriginal Gaunches, depicts them with extremely white skin and with yellow hair and beard. Their beards are shown either extremely long and uncut or trimmed and pointed, whereas their long yellow hair flows far down their backs—just like the extremely long hair of the blond mariners in the frescoes of the Maya pyramid at Yucatán.

Cultural vestiges—including the art of trepanning and pottery stamps—clearly link the Guanches with the ancient Afro-Asiatic civilizations that extended from Mesopotamia to the Atlantic coast of Morocco. The Berbers of Morocco are also a people of composite ethnic origins, like the Guanches and like the Olmecs. The Berbers, who inhabited Morocco and adjacent parts of North Africa before the Arab invasion, comprised a clearly Negroid element side by side with a tall, blond, and blue-eyed type, and both components are still to be recognized in isolated communities from the Atlas mountains to the Atlantic coast.

Blond people are often erroneously associated only with northern Europe where they dominate the present population. Yet modern anthropology agrees with the Norse sagas in recognizing that the early Norsemen came from the Caucasian plains bordering on Asia Minor. Blond and especially red-haired people are well known from this area. Nowhere on the continent is red hair more common than in Lebanon, the home of the ancient Phoenicians. Even early Egypt was familiar with Mediterranean people who had red as well as blond hair. Pharaoh Rameses II was blond, and the daughter-in-law of Pharaoh Cheops was found pictured with yellow hair and blue eyes when her tomb was first opened at the foot of the pyramid of her husband, Pharaoh Chephren. Individuals with brown hair and some even with blond hair are depicted among both gods and simple reed-boat mariners on the walls of early Egyptian tombs, just as in Mexican frescoes. Such seemingly "Nordic" features were therefore undoubtedly at home in the Mediterranean world long before they reached Scandinavia.

Who were the blond seamen who settled the Canary Islands prior to the arrival of Europeans? How did they cross from Morocco in the midst of the strong westbound current and yet were ignorant of any kind of boat when the Europeans came? The Phoenicians, with home ports in Asia Minor and North Africa, had established themselves on the Canary Islands centuries before the birth of Christ. They used these islands as staging areas on sailings to their purple-dye manufacturing colonies of which vestiges have been found as far beyond Morocco as the coast of present-day Senegal.

It has been frequently suggested—rightly or wrongly—that the bearded Phoenicians were also light-skinned and blond. If this is true, there is no problem in explaining the presence of the light-skinned, blond Guanches on the Canary Islands. If it is not true, then some other early Afro-Asiatic mariners—fair-skinned, blond, and bearded like the legendary heroes of aboriginal Mexico and Peru—must have ventured into the Canary Current together with Negroid people and together formed the Guanche nation.

Not only does Guanche water become Olmec water in a few weeks, but Peruvian water also becomes Easter Island water in as short a time. I have personally traversed both stretches by reed boat and raft during a single lifetime. The conveyer-belts that today roll westward with the sun did so in Guanche and Olmec times as well, and it would be imprudent to assume that boats could not have crossed the oceans until A.D. 1492 nor rafts until our own generation.

Chapter 5

Columbus and the Vikings

NORWAY IS indebted to descendants of refugees who fled to Iceland over a millennium ago for the written sagas preserving the nation's earliest memories. The Norse sagas were carefully handwritten on parchment and in Latin characters after the official introduction of Christianity to Iceland in the year 1000, and became the background of Scandinavian literature in the centuries preceding the voyages of Columbus. With the introduction of the Latin characters the original Norse script, the *rune,* was abandoned and forgotten. The *Ynglinge Saga,* referring to the very beginning of Norse history and the original settling of Scandinavia, was put on record by the learned Icelandic scribe, Snorre Sturlasson.[1] With a remarkable knowledge of geography, this record of the origins and migrations of the first Scandinavian kings places the primeval ancestral home of these demi-gods on the border between Asia and Europe along the eastern shores of the Black Sea. In the Caucasian territory extending from the Russian river Don into northeastern Turkey, we are told, lived the ancient Norsemen under the rule of the Ynglinge dynasty. At that time, the saga goes on, ravaging Roman armies were advancing everywhere and escape was the only way of survival. Snorre's record goes into a detailed geographcial account of the early migration through Europe, passing from Saxony (Saksland) into Denmark, Sweden, and Norway. According to the old saga, the idea of writing in *rune* was brought along with these first migrants from the Black Sea.

With such a geographical background it is easy to understand how the Vikings, upon their later acceptance of Christianity, had no difficulty in finding their way to the Holy Land, which they repeatedly visited with great fleets both by sailing down the Russian rivers to the Black Sea and by rounding Spain and entering the Straits of Gibraltar. The Vikings entered the Straits of Gibraltar from the Atlantic side about two millennia after the Phoenicians had moved out through the same straits in the opposite direction. Although these two people had more in common than mere seafaring skill, and although their open ships with carved figureheads on the bow, square sail and shields along the gunwales were similar enough to be indistinguishable when reproduced in art, the Vikings could never have done what the Phoenicians might have managed: they could never have entered the Canary Current in a period early enough to have influenced aboriginal Olmec culture. Chronology alone suffices to show that they could certainly not have been the bearded, blond benefactors recorded and depicted by the pre-Columbian Middle American civilizations.

The present chapter was written as a speech delivered at the Norwegian-American sesquicentennial celebrations in Minneapolis, Minnesota, on October 12, 1975. Following a recommendation from Senator Hubert H. Humphrey it was unanimously accepted by the United States Senate for publication in full in the *Congressional Record* of October 30, 1975.

*   *   *

There are those who try to belittle the accomplishments of Christopher Columbus by claiming that he was not the first to set foot ashore in the New World. Yet the accomplishments of Columbus and their revolutionary impact on the whole world stand on their own merits no matter how many others have subsequently or had previously walked on American soil.

Let us agree, however, that others had arrived in the New World before Columbus. The Aztecs, the Incas, and hundreds of other nations and tribes were there when the first Europeans landed. Pyramids, cities with streets, monuments, and lofty palaces had been built in America even before the time of Christ. The landscape in certain temperate zones was dotted with architectural structures and ruins, crisscrossed by paved roads and abounded in areas cleared for cotton cultivation and food crops. In Mexico literate Mayas and Aztecs had recorded their own local history with hieroglyphics in paper books generations before Columbus' birth. The local emperors of Mexico and

Peru could muster armies larger than those of any contemporary king in Europe, and the science of astronomy and medicine as well as certain arts and crafts had reached levels unsurpassed and not even equaled in the Old World.

Nothing of this, however, belittles the subsequent attainments of Columbus. His place in history does not diminish by the fact that there was no untrodden path in the New World by the time he arrived from Europe.

We shall never know the name of the first traveler to reach America, for the art of writing was still unknown in the world when he and his food-gathering Stone Age family crossed from Asia into Alaska somewhere in the Arctic north. This unrecorded primary discovery took place at least thirty thousand years before the Christian era, if not much earlier. It was millennia later, and still several centuries before Columbus, that the remarkable cultures suddenly began to flourish in the restricted but continuous belt from Mexico to Peru. The people of Mexico now began to carve monuments and record texts in memory of the important ocean voyager, Quetzalcoatl. This white and bearded founder of the Mexican hierarchy, according to the hieroglyphic texts, had come across the Atlantic, as the Spaniards subsequently did.

Although the earlier arrival of Quetzalcoatl and his traveling party was cited by the Aztec king Montezuma to the Spanish conquistadors the very day they reached his court, yet Quetzalcoatl was never considered by Europeans as a rival to Columbus. His story was not recorded in immediately readable Latin letters, but in pagan Aztec codices, and the bulk of these were carefully collected and burned as the work of the devil by European priests who followed the conquistadors.

It was different with the later records of Leif Eirikson, the son of Eirik the Red from Brattalid on Greenland. The written sources never gave him credit for any cultural impact or lasting influence ashore, such as was the case with Quetzalcoatl. He was never said to have achieved anything beyond brief reconnaissance walks from a cabin he and his men built near the coast. However, his saga was written in Latin characters by Christian Norse colonists in Iceland and Greenland, and thus carried more weight to the European mind than the hieroglyphics of the Aztecs. Being a European and a clearly defined historic person, it was Leif Eirikson and not Quetzalcoatl who quite innocently came to appear to many as a sort of rival to Christopher Columbus.

Nobody can of course ever take from either Leif Eirikson or Christopher Columbus the credit for what they accomplished. Their deeds were of a completely different nature. There was never any competition or historic discrepancy between them, and there is no need, nor any reason for, a degradation of the one to appreciate fully the accomplishment of the other. Let us try for a moment to disentangle the reasons for this purely artificial rivalry and give each of these historic persons the credit he deserves: Leif Eirikson as the first European known with certainty to have set foot ashore in the Arctic and sub-Arctic regions of the New World, and Christopher Columbus as the person whose discovery of the tropic region flung the door wide open for the European conquest of America and the birth of all American nations. It would be as unfair to discredit Leif Eirikson's discovery as being a pagan Viking fairy tale as it would be to deny that the voyages of Columbus changed the world more than any other event in post-Christian times.

When we look at these two early seafarers, let us try to see each one in his true historic light. Since there was never any rivalry or competition between them, why should we now, for nationalistic or religious reasons, regard their voyages as something comparable to Amundsen's and Scott's race for the South Pole? The fact that we are apt to compare the two navigators as if they were competitors leaves us with a distorted view unfavorable to Leif Eirikson. He stands out as a fierce, pagan Viking in an open boat, compared to the splendor of Columbus and his graceful caravels. We do not get this picture if we view them independently and remember that almost half a millennium separated the two expeditions. That is the time span equal to the one which separates the caravels of Columbus from twentieth-century ocean liners. With this enormous time span taken into account, the Norse voyagers compare very favorably with the tenth-century Spaniards in level of culture. Perhaps the difficulty in some quarters to appreciate Leif Eirikson and his deeds properly stems from the common picture of him as a barbarian with horned helmet and broad sword, who sailed the ocean to rob and plunder Christians, whereas Columbus sailed under the symbol of the Holy Cross with the purpose, apart from searching for gold and glory, of taking the Christian faith to savages across the sea. This contrast is unfair, fictitious, and wholly erroneous. Leif Eirikson, although embarking earlier, took a Catholic priest on board his ship, and the express purpose of his transatlantic crossing was to bring Christianity to the pagan settlements on Greenland.

Let us try to revive a fragment of early Norwegian history relevant to the understanding of Leif Eirikson and his peaceful mission. It is as wrong to believe that all Norwegians in medieval times were Vikings as it would be to think that all eighteenth-century Englishmen were buccaneers or all Romans were expeditionary soldiers. Most of the population of medieval Norway were farmers, fishermen, or merchants and many were very able artists and craftsmen. In this respect there was no distinction between the people of Norway and the rest of contemporary Europe. Vikings, in the true sense of the old word, were those expeditionary groups which harassed foreign lands through their seaborne raids, sparing no accessible land from Russia in the east to Ireland in the west, from Scotland in the north to Sicily and the Moslem world. None today would wish to defend their cruel raids, yet whenever strong enough to proceed victoriously, other Europeans, from the Roman legions to the Spanish conquistadors, were just as merciless in their advances into foreign lands as were the Vikings. The term Viking, however, has gradually come to cover all the medieval people who lived in the northern countries harbouring the Viking ships, and this rather dubious term is sometimes bestowed upon some of those living today.

The British historian David Wilson wrote: "Though from a British point of view it was the seaward ventures of the Vikings that are most impressive, the links that they established overland to the East were no less important. It was they who dominated the great trade routes across the area we know today as Poland and western Russia, southward to Byzantium and eastward to the Volga and to Persia. And even if the Vikings were not always involved themselves, trading links were also established with China by way of the famous silk road across Central Asia; . . . The Vikings were thus great travelers and they performed outstanding feats of navigation; their cities were great centers of trade; their art was original, creative, and influential; they boasted a fine literature and a developed culture."

He has also this to say: "Their devastating raids of the eighth and ninth centuries gave the Vikings an enduring reputation for piracy and destructiveness—and yet their culture was in many ways as sophisticated as the cultures of the lands which they ravaged . . . And, in the end, they did not destroy western civilization, but enriched it. Parts of their legal system, their tradition of individual freedom, their zest for exploration, and the great Icelandic sagas which reflect their heroic era—these have all become part of our northern European heritage."[2]

So concludes the judgment of a British historian. Nobody knows the earliest homeland of the Viking ancestry. Certainly, they were at one time immigrants into their Scandinavian home. Most scholars seem to believe they came overland or that they sailed up the great Russian rivers from somewhere in Caucasia. This is strongly supported by Snorre's written records from the early thirteenth century, which claim that the early home of the first remembered Norse king was in the Black Sea area east of the river Don. From here it was an easy river journey with very little overland portage to reach the Baltic Sea and Scandinavia. For sure, once Christianized, it took the Norwegian Vikings no time at all to find their way in the opposite direction to reach the Holy Land by way of the Black Sea and the Straits of Bosporus. According to Snorre, the early Viking king who led his people northward from the Black Sea was Odin, who was later celebrated as a Viking god upon his death. His reign had extended into Turkey until the time when, again according to Snorre, the Roman emperors advanced far and wide and conquered all nations. For this reason the great progenitor of all Viking kings migrated northward with his people and settled first Denmark, then Sweden, and finally Norway. Snorre names thirty kings and records their adventures before he reaches the generation of Harold Fairhair who assembled all of Norway into one kingdom. Here we are on firm historic ground, for this happened in the year 872 in the midst of the most vigorous part of the Viking era. The victory of Harold Fairhair over the many independent regional kings and chieftains caused considerable unrest in the country, and many mighty men fled with their families and followers to settle islands already discovered far out in the ocean, islands hitherto used by Norwegians only as temporary hideouts during Viking expeditions. Among those who fled to settle on the distant shores of Iceland was Eirik the Red, who was born near Stavanger and whose wife, Tjodhild, gave birth to Leif Eirikson. Eirik the Red became Greenland's discoverer roughly a decade after his flight from Norway. With the mind of a true real estate agent, it was he who named his new discovery Greenland, as he had circumnavigated the inhospitable southern cape and found large unfrozen grassland fit for cattle ranging at the foot of the lofty glaciers on the west side facing the Davis Strait.

Upon his return to Iceland Eirik the Red organized and led one of the most intrepid Arctic expeditions ever put on record. The details of his maritime enterprise were written down by Are Frode, recording the memories of an uncle who had his information directly from one of Eirik's own companions. Thirty-five cargo vessels, broader and sturdier than the fast and slender Viking ships, took part in this planned migration westward across the open Atlantic. On board were entire families, several hundred men, women, and children, with all their earthly possessions including horses, cattle, sheep, pigs, and dogs. Only fourteen of these open ships with voluntary emigrants managed to round the stormy south cape of Greenland and land safely on the more friendly west coast. Here they built the settlement, the remains of which still exist, and laid the foundation for what were to become generations of descendants who lived and died with Eskimos as neighbors on the same large island, and with American Indians only a few hundred miles away on the opposite side of the Davis Strait.

While young Leif Eirikson grew up peacefully on his father's farm, Brattalid, in West Greenland, a young Norwegian prince was roaming Europe as a regular Viking. His name was Olav Trygvason. Prince Olav was born in Norway but grew up at the court of King Valdermar in Russia. His Viking adventures brought him from the Baltic countries to parts of Germany, England, Scotland, Ireland, and France, but as he anchored his fleet off the Scilly Islands in the Atlantic Ocean west of Cornwall, he suddenly came to change his pattern of life. Christianity was on its slow progress up through Europe and had already reached these islands. The Viking prince was so impressed at his confrontation with a local Christian hermit that he soon let himself be baptized with all his men. As they embarked for the home voyage after an extended sojourn, they took priests and learned men with them. In Norway an armed mission sent by the Danish king had already tried to enforce Christianity with limited success. As Olav now returned from his Viking adventures and became the king of Norway, he declared in an address to all his people that Christianity should be the only legal religion in the country. He traveled throughout his kingdom to ensure personally that all his subjects were properly baptized, and he let churches be built where there had previously been dragon-headed temples in honor of Tor and Odin. He was so keen in his missionary activity that he even embarked with his fleet to sail to the Norwegian settlements on the Orkney Islands north of Scotland to introduce Christianity there. He sent a German priest, Tangbrand, to bring Christianity to Iceland, but the temperamental foreigner was soon driven out, and King Olav next sent a whole party of ordained priests there under the leadership of Father Tormod. The Norse colony on Iceland finally agreed to introduce Christianity by law, and in the year 1000 everybody on the island was baptized.

By this time Eirik the Red and his large group of emigrants had already left Iceland and settled in Greenland on the other side of the Atlantic. It displeased King Olav that the Norse colony on distant Greenland remained pagan when all his subjects in the lands around the North Sea had adopted the Christian faith. His chance to Christianize Greenland soon came however. The Greenland colony took up fairly regular trade relations with Bergen and other ports in Norway, and one of the first navigators to bring a Greenland merchant ship to Norway was Leif, the son of Greenland's discoverer, Eirik the Red. Leif Eirikson sailed to Norway's capital, Nidaros, the present city of Trondheim, one summer shortly before the end of the reign of King Olav Trygvason. The Flatöy book, written two centuries before Columbus, has this to report: "Leif put in at Nidaros with his ship, and set out at once to visit the King. King Olav expounded the faith to him, as he did to other heathen men who came to visit him. It proved easy for the King to persuade Leif, and he was accordingly baptized, together with all of his shipmates. Leif remained throughout the winter with the King, by whom he was well entertained."[3] Further details are preserved in the ancient Hauk manuscript from the same early pre-Columbian period: "Upon one occasion the King came to speech with Leif, and asked him, 'Is it thy purpose to sail to Greenland in the summer?' 'It is my purpose,' said Leif, 'if it be your will.' 'I believe it will be well,' answered the king, 'and thither thou shalt go upon my errand, to proclaim Christianity there.'"

In the spring Leif set sail for his return voyage across the Atlantic, and in his company on board the ship was a Catholic priest as well as a number of religious teachers. Leif Eirikson departed shortly before King Olav's death, which was in the year 1000. On his return to Greenland Leif fulfilled his noble mission, so eloquently recorded in the same pre-Columbian manuscript: "He soon proclaimed Christianity throughout the land, and the Catholic faith, and announced

King Olav Trygvason's message to the people, telling them how much excellence and how great glory accompanied this faith. Erick [the Red] was slow in forming the determination to foresake his old belief, but Tjodhild [Leif's mother] embraced the faith promptly, and caused a church to be built at some distance from the house. This building was called Tjodhild's church, and there she and those persons who had accepted Christianity, and they were many, were wont to offer their prayers. Tjodhild would not have intercourse with Erick after that she had received the faith, whereat he was sorely vexed."[4]

According to the pre-Columbian records of Snorre, it was on this return voyage from Norway to Greenland that Leif accidentally came upon the section of the New World which he explored and to which he gave the name Vinland. Other and even earlier manuscripts seem to indicate that he first returned to his father's farm on Greenland and next set out to look for a flat and wooded land that Bjarne Herjolfsson had sighted from his ship when far out in the Davis Strait. At any rate, all the many early pre-Columbian manuscripts referring to Leif Eirikson's discovery of the New World agree on giving him credit for having made the first actual landing. And he went ashore with the same religious faith as Columbus did later.

We need not here repeat all the extensive details put on record by pre-Columbian scribes in Greenland and Iceland shortly after the actual event. Leif's expedition, as we know, called at three different parts of the newly discovered coast on the other side of the Davis Strait. He named his discoveries Helluland, Markland, and Vinland, and described the geographical features of their coasts in specific detail. In itself, Leif's discoveries had no profound effect on the outside world beyond enriching the otherwise rather drab lives in the nearby barren Greenland settlements. We have to look at his enterprise in the wider context of this entire Greenland venture to understand that his findings possibly had a greater influence on world history than is generally admitted. According to the records, Leif and his companions first built themselves some huts ashore while exploring the new land, then they built a big house where they spent the winter before sailing back northeast to their families on Greenland. The impact upon Leif's compatriots of this new source of timber, precious furs, and other valuable material from the newly discovered forest region is obvious, and clearly documented in the contemporary literature.

No sooner had Leif returned to Greenland with his cargo of wood

and berries before his brother, Thorvald Eirikson, set sail for the
newly discovered land, but his expedition was unsuccessful. After
killing a number of primitive natives he lost his own life and was
buried in the New World. An attempt to recover his body by a third
brother, Thorstein, failed completely, but soon afterward a number of
independent vessels managed to sail across the Davis Strait and southward as far as Leif's Vinland house, some taking women with them.
The most remarkable details are on record about Thorfinn Karlsefne,
who settled in the new land with sixty men and five women, bringing
with them cattle and other domesticated animals in a determined attempt at establishing a permanent settlement. Primitive aborigines
soon approached the new settlers, speaking an unintelligible language,
but demonstrating friendship by bringing packs of furs from squirrels,
sables, and other animals unknown on Greenland, which were offered
for barter against milk and red cloth.

These aborigines, termed "Skrellings" by the Norse colonists, first
ran away at the sight of a big bellowing Viking bull. The Norse
colony set up a strong palisade around their settlement, and Gudrid,
Karlsefne's wife, gave birth to a male child baptized with the name
Snorri, the first person of European descent to be born in the New
World. The friendly trade relations with the aborigines ended in a regular war on one occasion when so many of them came swarming up
the coast from the south that, according to the records, the canoes
seemed to fill the whole bay. Although the Skrellings are recorded to
have had only slings and stone axes while the Vikings had swords and
iron axes, so superior were they in numbers that the Norsemen had to
escape into the forest for a while and suffer the scorn of their women.
Two of Karlsefne's men fell, together with a great number of the natives. The saga left no doubt about the misfortunes of the outnum-
bered Vikings, and the Hauk text goes on: "It now seemed clear to
Karlsefne and his people, that although the country thereabouts was
attractive, their life would be one of constant dread and turmoil by
reason of the inhabitants of the land, so they forthwith prepared to
leave, and determined to return to their own country."[5] Prior to departure they captured two young native lads, whom they baptized.
These boys were brought along and taught to speak Norwegian, giving the Greenlanders more information about the aborigines of the
land that had been discovered. Undoubtedly, this recorded baptism
meant the first conversion to Christianity of any natives of the New

World. Snorri, Karlsefne's son, was three years old when the un-successful colonists returned to Greenland.

The detailed records of this fruitless attempt at colonization are im-portant, for they clearly show why the westward expansion from Nor-way by way of Iceland stopped in Greenland, with the forests of America only a couple of days' further sailing across the Davis Strait. Other equally unsuccessful attempts at settling the newly discovered territories followed, among them the ill-fated expedition by Fröydis, an illegitimate daughter of Eirik the Red. But the sailings across the Davis Strait soon changed character and ended up as trade missions by merchants who preferred to retain their safe home base on Greenland.

The extensive remains of four hundred years of uninterrupted Norse settlement in Greenland were never lost even though the people left the area about the year 1500. Danish archaeologists have had a rich field to work in and have done an excellent job in excavating the pre-Columbian Norse houses that once were scattered over two large sepa-rate areas. The traces of the Norse dwellings on the American shore were lost and forgotten, however, until the enterprising Norwegian explorer, Helge Ingstad, guided by the descriptions of the old Green-land and Icelandic sagas, managed to locate the now famous Viking site at L'Anse aux Meadows near the north tip of Newfoundland. His Norwegian archaeologist wife, Anne Stine, subsequently assisted by other Scandinavian and American scholars, in the early 1960s exca-vated the hitherto almost invisible house foundations. They found Norse artifacts including a typical Viking bronze pin, a soapstone spin-ning whorl of identifiable Norse type, the remains of iron nails, and a Nordic-type iron smithy. What is more, inside the houses of charac-teristic Nordic form, carbon was still present in the stone-lined hearths, thus making possible a whole series of radiocarbon datings, all coming out to about A.D. 1000, and perfectly corroborating the dates of Leif Eirikson, Karlsefne, and the other early voyagers from recorded his-tory. There is not one professional archaeologist who would doubt that the Ingstads have found an early Viking site in America. What can be questioned is whether or not this is the site of Leif Eirikson's house. A strong argument in its favor lies in the fact that Ingstad found the site simply by following the exact geographical descriptions in the Leif Eirikson saga.

The brief foothold of the Greenland Norsemen on American shores was clearly followed by a long period of occasional trade. No other land was as close to the Greenland settlers as was America, and the short trade route across the Davis Strait permitted a constant flow of precious timber and costly furs and ivory to increase the living standards of the Greenland colony through regular shipments to merchant centers in Norway. As we shall see, by specific order of the pope, the Greenland colonists were obliged to pay a crusader's tax in *naturalia,* which the Church collected as the Greenland ships landed in Norway. Among the trade items arriving from Greenland and listed by Archbishop Erik Valdendorf were the skins of black bear, beaver, otter, ermine, sable, wolverene, and lynx, all of which are North American animals non-existent on Greenland. The American historian J. R. Enterline also shows that the white gerfalcons so extremely popular among royal hunters throughout medieval Europe could also have been provided only by the Greenland traders, since these birds existed only in Greenland and the American Arctic.[6]

By raising livestock, by hunting, fishing and trade, the Greenland colony founded by Eirik the Red prospered and grew, as is clearly documented both by archaeology and early written records. The Catholic Church, introduced by Leif Eirikson in the year 1000, grew to become a real power and major landowner in Greenland in the period from the twelfth to the fourteenth century. It may surprise many to learn that in this pre-Columbian period seventeen churches were erected on the west coast, literally facing America across the straits. There was even an episcopal residence, a cathedral, and two monasteries, one for nuns dedicated to St. Benedict and one for monks dedicated to St. Augustin and St. Olav. It should not be forgotten that St. Olav was the Norwegian King Olav Haraldson, the successor of Olav Trygvason who had sent Leif Eirikson on his historic mission. The king's efforts to serve the Roman Catholic Church so pleased the pope that this eleventh-century Norwegian monarch was canonized as a saint, an honor not even bestowed upon King Ferdinand or Queen Isabella.

I stress these points because it is most important to see the intimate link between Norway with its colonies and the Roman Catholic Church in the period under discussion, for this strong link must inevitably have had a bearing on subsequent events of much more global concern. It is doubtful whether the Roman Church had a stronger grip on any nation than on that of King Olav the Holy and his successors right up to the time of the Lutheran Reformation. The schism did not occur until the sixteenth century, about one generation after the time of Christopher Columbus.

The intimate contact between Columbus and the Vatican is well known. Not so, perhaps, the close relations between the more distant Norsemen and the Vatican up to and including the entire Columbian period. Direct Norwegian contact with the Roman world goes back into early history, first by way of Russia and the Bosporus; much later, well after Norwegian colonists in about A.D. 840 had founded the city of Dublin in Ireland, they also entered the Mediterranean through the Straits of Gibraltar at the opposite extreme. By the beginning of the twelfth century it was so common for Vikings to visit the Mediterranean that the Norwegian king Sigurd Magnusson, while entering Gibraltar with sixty ships, had to fight another hostile Viking fleet on its way out.

No sooner had Christianity reached Norway before Norwegian kings and nobles began regular pilgrimages to Rome and the Holy Land. For instance Holy Olav's royal bard, Sigvat Skald, was homeward bound from Rome after a visit to the Holy Land when he learned of the king's fall, and Tore Hund, the king's vassal, actually died in the Holy Land. King Olav's brother and later successor to the Norwegian throne, Harald Hardråde, spent many years in the Mediterranean serving the East Roman emperor as commander of mixed Norwegian and Latin forces. With his Christian fleet he raided Moslem strongholds on the islands and all along the North African coast. The rich spoils, including all the gold paid by the monarch for this service to Christianity, Harald and his Norwegian Vikings brought to Jerusalem and left there as gifts to the Church. It can well be understood why the Lord's Prayer can still be found written in the old Norwegian tongue side by side with Hebrew, Latin, Aramaic, and other biblical languages in the oldest section of the temple on the Mount of Olives, for in the battles to protect Christian interests in the Holy Land, Norway was among the keenest participants. Snorre described how King Harald brought his whole army to the Holy Land and proceeded to Jerusalem, conquering cities and forts. The text ends: ". . . this land came unburned and unravaged under Harald's power. Then he went on to the river Jordan and there he had a bath, such as was the custom among other pilgrims. Harald gave great gifts to the tomb of the Lord and to the holy cross and to other sanctuaries in the

Holy Land. He protected the road all the way to Jordan and killed robbers and other bandits."[7]

The next Norwegian king to take up the fight against Moslem expansion was Sigurd Magnusson. King Sigurd left Norway with sixty Viking ships and passed the winter peacefully as guest of the English king Henry I. Then he sailed on to begin his struggle for the Catholic Church, first fighting the Mohammedan intruders in Portugal and Spain, killing all those who refused to be baptized, and then extending his activities to Morocco and the Balearic islands. Sicily was already conquered by his Norwegian predecessors who had installed their own Christian duke to rule the island. King Sigurd was so well received by his compatriots on Sicily that he promoted Duke Rodgeir to the rank of king, whereupon King Rodgeir conquered a large part of the Italian peninsula, and his royal family of Viking descent intermarried directly with the emperor in Rome. Sigurd had an equally friendly reception from King Baldwin in Jerusalem. Baldwin and the patriarch gave Sigurd several very sacred relics on the condition that the king should continue his fight for Christianity and also establish an archbishopric in Norway. Sigurd fulfilled both promises. His most spectacular deed was to conquer in the year 1110 the hitherto invincible fortress city of Sidon in Lebanon which for ages had harassed Christian pilgrims. At this important archaeological site there is still an inscription commemorating the Norwegian victory. King Sigurd left all his ships and most of his men in the Mediterranean for continued service and returned to Norway by horse. Christian Europe gave him a great welcome, and warm friendship was established between the king and the two Roman emperors in Constantinople and Rome.

Next Earl Ragnvald and Erling Skakke, accompanied by Bishop Wiljalm, followed Sigurd's route from Norway through Gibraltar with fifteen longships and many men, also harassing the Mohammedan parts of Portugal and Spain before they too completed their pilgrimage to the Holy Land and the Jordan river.

To fulfill the agreement reached between the Norwegian king and the papal envoy in Jerusalem, Pope Anastasius IV sent Cardinal Nicolas from Rome to Norway in 1153. The cardinal and Sigurd agreed on ordaining Jon Birgerson as archbishop. Never had any foreigner been received with such enthusiasm in Norway as Cardinal Nicolas, according to Snorre, and the cardinal returned to the Vatican with large quantities of friendship gifts. He no sooner reached Rome than Pope Anastasius died and he himself was elected as the new pope. Cardinal Nicolas now became Pope Adrian IV. Snorre, himself an Icelander, wrote: "It is said by those who came to Rome in his time that he never had such important matters to discuss with other men that he did not always first receive the Norwegians when they wanted to speak with him."[8]

Shortly afterward, in 1163, the Vatican sent the legate Stefanus from Rome as a papal ambassador to Bergen, the main port of call for Greenland ships, where he first held meetings with the Iceland bishop, Brand, and the second Norwegian archbishop, Öystein. They all afterward, in the company of the five Norwegian bishops and a large number of priests, conducted the coronation ceremony of the next Norwegian king, the eight-year-old Magnus Erlingson. The Norwegian historian, Alexander Bugge, describes the Catholic Church as the greatest power in Norway at this time.

With these strong ties between Rome and Norway in the twelfth century, let us see where the Greenland colony comes into the contemporary picture. We have seen that King Olav sent a Catholic priest to Greenland with Leif Eirikson before he discovered Vinland in the year 1000. By 1112 Greenland had already received its first visiting bishop. By then the discovery of a new world west of Greenland was already so well known to the Church that the Iceland annals record that Bishop Erik Gnupsson, upon his visit to the Greenland parish, sailed on from there expressly to visit Leif Eirikson's discovery, Vinland. Shortly after his visit, the colony of Greenland sent shiploads of walrus tusks, furs, and a live polar bear to King Sigurd of Norway, with a request for a permanent bishop on Greenland. The king immediately granted the request and from 1126 the Greenland colony had their own resident bishop. Not long after, they even had two, since the Norse farms and churches on west Greenland were spread over vast distances. The Vatican was of course fully aware of their Christian Greenland parishes. Yet the geographical isolation of the Norse colonies on Greenland from the rest of the Catholic world on the European side of the Atlantic ocean could not prevent certain ritual problems from arising.

The papal decree forbade Christian marriages closer than seven generations apart, but the Greenland colony was so young and small that closer intermarriage was hard to avoid. Envoys from Norway therefore went expressly to Rome to ask Pope Alexander III for a dispensation.

It was explained that twelve days of rough sailing were needed if the Greenland men had to go abroad in search of Christian wives. Pope Alexander consented to let the Norwegian archbishop give permission for marriage as close as the fifth generation in special cases.

The sacraments requiring bread and wine caused further problems in an Arctic area where neither grain nor grapes grew. The Greenland parish therefore next sent a request to Rome for permission to substitute meat or other available food for bread, and beer or fermented crowberry juice for wine. But Pope Gregorius personally interfered, with a letter to the Norwegian archbishop in 1237, in which he insisted that his Greenland parish should at least maintain the use of bread in the sacraments.

Later, in 1276, Pope John XXI refused a request from the Norwegian archbishop who was trying to release himself from his recently imposed duty of personally sailing to Greenland to collect the crusader's tax from the bishops on that side of the Atlantic. But not until 1279 did Pope Nicholas III allow the Norwegian archbishop to send an attorney in his own place on the long and hazardous voyage. Three years later the attorney was back in Norway, and the archbishop again wrote the Pope that the Greenland parish was poor except in skins and walrus tusks, which had scant value as crusader's tax. The pope, however, did not yield on the tax imposed on Greenland, and in a letter of 1282 he insisted that this Norwegian colony on the other side of the Atlantic should continue to pay the crusader's tax, but in *naturalia,* which the Church then could sell in Norway.

The Vatican never abandoned its interests in the Arctic colony in Greenland so long as people were still living there. And Norsemen were living on Greenland until shortly after Columbus set sail for America. Around the year 1500 there were still some settlers left, but the colony was then in rapid decline. Early in the sixteenth century the last of the many farms was deserted and the colony, formerly so prosperous, became ruinous. Nobody has ever discovered why. Pests, famines, climatic changes, attempts to move to richer pastures in American Indian territories are among the many possibilities suggested. Among the more plausible views is that the peaceful Greenland descendants of the once fierce Vikings might well have been completely exterminated by the English pirates who were known to harass the unprotected Greenland colony at that time. In England the existence of the Greenland settlement was so well known that in 1432 a treaty was reached between the Norwegian and English kings in an effort to stop the English pirates from raiding the remote Christian Norwegian colony.

The unfortunate arrival of European pirates in the Davis Strait between Greenland and America in the decades prior to Columbus' voyage shows that knowledge of settlements there had already spread to common people other than in Norway and the Vatican. Literate Europeans had had access to this geographical information for four hundred years; even the discovery of Vinland had been preserved in written records since about the year 1070 by the German historian Adam of Bremen in his *Geography of the Northern Lands*. The gradual entry into the limelight of the isolated Greenland colony brought it more problems than blessings, as is shown in a papal letter to the two bishops of Iceland. In this letter of 1448 Pope Nicholas V refers to piratical raids on Greenland as follows: "From the nearby pagan coasts came thirty years ago a fleet of barbarians which attacked the local people in a cruel assault, and thus fire and sword destroyed their native country with its sacred buildings, with the result that only nine churches remained since they are said to be most remote and least accessible because of steep cliffs. The pitiful inhabitants of both sexes, particularly those who were considered strong and fit enough to assume the unremitting burdens of slavery, the tyrants carried away as prisoners to their own country. But, as is also added in the accusations, in the course of time most of them have come back from their aforesaid captivity to their own homes, and have here and there repaired the ruins of their houses. Therefore, they are now longing to re-establish and extend the divine services."[9]

In spite of its distance, the Christian world kept track of the Greenland parish as long as it lasted. As the fifteenth century drew to its end the Vatican had learned that the survivors on Greenland were now so poor that they subsisted mainly on milk and dried fish. This statement in a last papal letter concerning Greenland was written in 1492, the very year when Columbus set sail for America. The transatlantic voyages of the Norsemen were accordingly not yet forgotten in the Mediterranean world when Columbus embarked on his historic enterprise.

Is there any connection? Or was Columbus ignorant of the regular sailings of Norwegian and Icelandic farmers, merchants, priests, monks, nuns, and bishops, as well as occasional English pirates, across the northern section of the ocean he himself was planning to cross?

Columbus was more than an intrepid and courageous sailor. Above all, he was a brilliant organizer, and, far from being an imprudent and neglectful adventurer, he was for his time a very learned geographer. He was very close to the Catholic Church, and he was certainly thoroughly familiar with everything the Vatican knew about its own Christian parishes in Europe and overseas. There is some stress in every biography of Columbus on how careful was his research before he embarked on his ocean crossing, gathering information on currents, drifts, castaways, and discoveries during his early travels along the Atlantic coasts of Europe and Africa. It is not generally accepted that he went to Iceland, although his son claims in writing that he did so, but it is at least historically documented that he maintained contact with some of the most learned men in England and in Rome to gain geographical information useful for his calculations in a period when England and Rome were involved in diplomatic and religious communication with Norway concerning the fate of the dwindling Greenland colony. He could not have avoided learning of its existence.

Only when we accept that Columbus was no more ignorant of the exact position of Greenland than was the sovereign of his own church or the English pirates does his premeditated discovery of tropical America become meaningful and meritorious for truly intelligent planning and calculation. Columbus did not imitate the Norsemen either in sailing directions or in discovery, but he set out on a wholly independent mission based entirely on his own very remarkable calculations.

Columbus contested the religious teachings of his time on one point: he was convinced that the world was a globe. Although the church in the fifteenth century still tried to preserve the concept of a flat earth, its spherical form had been recognized since the time of the early Greek astronomers, who had come amazingly close to an exact calculation of the earth's circumference as about 24,000 miles. The classical Greek results, based on astronomical observations, were well known to scholars in Columbus' time, but although Columbus on the one hand accepted Ptolemy's view of a spherical earth he doubted on the other hand the astronomical calculations of its size. Columbus was no astronomer and therefore must have had some particular geographical reason for his firm conviction that the earth was only a fifth of the size so closely calculated by the ancient Greeks. His enormous miscalculation, which, after all, led him directly to success, can only be explained by his knowledge of the Norse discoveries and his direct use of their longitude as a base and pivot for his own calculations. In other words, unless the Norse discoveries are taken into account, we shall never understand the greatness of Columbus and the reason for his success.

European expansion overseas prior to Columbus had first gone westward to Greenland and next eastward to Asia, leaving colonists in both areas that maintained commercial and religious relations with Europe. Like all his contemporaries, Columbus believed in the existence of one big world ocean, and one only. Accordingly, on the other side of this one and same ocean they visualized Greenland to the north and India to the south. Marco Polo, who like Columbus came from northern Italy but lived two centuries before him, had explored the coasts of distant Asia. Subsequently, with important Spanish and Portuguese trading posts in Indonesia, the Europeans of Columbus' time were very familiar with the fact that Asia extended into sub-Arctic regions in a northeasterly direction. Since Greenland and Asia were both believed to be on the other side of the same ocean, it would follow logically that one represented the northern extremity of the other, particularly since Marco Polo's Asia ran on uninterruptedly northeastward on the very same course as the one reappearing in Leif Eirikson's coasts in the sub-Arctic. It would seem highly logical to assume that the two coastlines would meet.

Columbus reached America on the very day and in the very place he had expected to reach Asia. Since the Pacific alone spans half the globe, he had sailed one fifth of the distance to India, yet he reached land exactly as he had anticipated. In spite of his three successful voyages across the Atlantic, Columbus died with the conviction that he had crossed the one and only world ocean and reached India. Because of this confusion the Caribbean Islands are still known as the West Indies and the American aborigines, termed Skrellings by the Norwegians, have forever become Indians although India lies as far away from them as possible, on the very antipode.

What could make Columbus so sure of finding land exactly where he found America? Only a firm conviction that Asia was a continuation of the North Atlantic area where there were settlements of Norsemen. Only the image of Marco Polo's Asia as a southwestward extension of Leif Eirikson's Vinland would give Columbus the vision of the tiny world which he had when he first sailed into the Atlantic and which he retained until the day of his death. And only if he knew the distance and direction to the northwestern corner of the Atlantic as well as did the merchant sailors from Norway or the pirates from England, would he be able to project the longitude of the mainland on the other side of the Atlantic as correctly as he did before his voyage.

Columbus' later traveling companion, the famous chronicler Las Casas, stressed that before his departure Columbus was as sure of the position of the lands he was heading for as if he had them "in his room." Moreover, some of the sailors from the first voyage testified that Columbus had assured them beforehand that after sailing only 800 Spanish miles they could expect to find land, which they did. Columbus consistently followed the 28th northern parallel, the latitude of Florida, which would have brought him far north of any landfall in India or Indonesia. Yet he was so sure of this course that he bluntly refused to turn south-southwest as demanded by despairing officers and crew who claimed to have detected indications of land in that direction. As shown by Columbus' own journal, against the increasing threat of mutiny, and by keeping a double log to cheat his own companions into believing they were not so far from home, he insisted that no other course would bring them to firm land as fast as the one he was making them steer. A brief deviation to avoid open revolt led by his second in command showed Columbus to be right. And on October 11, 1492, when his exhausted crew began to abandon all hope, and the coast of India was still four times as far away as the distance covered, Columbus declared that land would be discovered the next day. Land was discovered the next day: an island lying in front of Florida with the myriad islands and the continent of the Skrellings blocking further passage close behind it.

Columbus had something to sell when he talked their Catholic Majesties in Spain into financing this costly enterprise. The idea that the world was round was age-old and would have been accepted or rejected by the advisers of the Spanish court prior to Columbus' visit. He had to offer more than that to get from the war-ridden rulers of Spain what they would never have offered a foreign sailor from Genoa if he came without some trump card. What he asked for and received were three fully equipped ships, 120 crewmen including noblemen, civil servants, and soldiers, a cash payment of 2,000,000 *maravedis*, status as a Spanish noble, the rank of Grand Admiral of the Ocean Sea, the power of viceroy and irremovable governor of all the islands and firm land he himself and anybody else in the future would discover and conquer in the ocean, and the assurance that all these honors were to be inherited by his first-born son, from generation to generation. This tremendous price, listed in Columbus' own speech dictated *"In Nomine Domini Nostri Jhesu Christi"* for presentation to King Ferdinand and Queen Isabella of Spain, shows best of all that the foreigner from Genoa had more to sell than eloquence.

What Columbus sold could have been sold by any other explorer of his time, but he did it, and we all know the story of Columbus' egg. It was not a lucky strike, but an inquisitive mind, conscientious preparation, and logical calculations that crowned Columbus' great enterprise with success. Those who try to belittle the importance of the early Norwegian discoveries to the subsequent outcome of Columbus' endeavors inadvertently render him an ill and unfair service. If he did not know about the southwestward-running coast of Vinland, he would have been an irresponsible leader who equipped his vessels with only one fifth of the provisions needed and who lured his men to certain death by falsifying his log to keep them deceived. Columbus, however, died in the honest belief that India was exactly as close to Europe as he had predicted. It is most remarkable and thought-compelling that this firm belief made him modify his view that the world was round before he died. Since he knew that the journey to India was much longer for those who sailed in the opposite direction around the southern hemisphere, he came to a strange conclusion as to the earth's shape after his third and final voyage to America. He wrote: "I find that it is not as round as it is described, but is shaped like a pear, which is round everywhere except near the stalk where it projects strongly; or it is like a very round ball with something like a woman's nipple in one place, and this projecting part is highest and the one nearest heaven."[10]

Columbus has been scorned for this seemingly absurd idea, coming from one who is commonly celebrated for showing through action that the earth is spherical. His conclusion was quite meaningful, even logical, if we bear in mind that he thought the Viking settlements represented the northern part of Asia. Columbus believed he had come all the way to the spice islands, east of India, by sailing a shorter way across the "upper" northern part of a pear-shaped world than what was otherwise needed to reach these far islands for those who had gone there by way of the "lower" southern hemisphere.

Only when we give the Norse discoverers of Greenland and North America the credit they deserve does Columbus emerge in proper perspective, not as a reckless navigator who accidentally happened to hit upon America because it blocked his progress to India, but because he had combined creative imagination with keen scholarship and available information to plan a search for a coast which was found where it was supposed to be.

PART III

THE PACIFIC
PROBLEM

Chapter 6

From Asia to Polynesia the Easy Way

THE MAGNITUDE of the Pacific problem derives from the magnitude of the Pacific Ocean. This ocean alone covers half the earth's surface; its equatorial coasts in Asia and America represent exact antipodes. In remote geological periods two types of tiny islands rose to the surface of this marine hemisphere, one type grew up as steaming lava from submarine volcanoes, whereas the other was slowly constructed by coral polyps which built their colonies on crater rims that had not by themselves quite risen to the surface. If New Zealand be excluded, the combined surface areas of the oceanic islands of the Pacific would not cover an area half as large as the state of New York. Since the ocean housing them equals all the world's continents and other oceans put together, the distance between each speck of land necessarily becomes enormous. The fact that Stone Age people had built their homes on all these islands before they were found by Europeans is an amazing feat that dwarfs the European discovery of the American continent on the other side of the narrow Atlantic.

East of Asia and north of the equatorial line lies the Micronesian part of the Pacific Ocean, an area in itself equaling the total width of the Atlantic and hiding from the outside world tiny isles most of which are coral atolls barely rising above the waves and invisible until one is extremely close inshore. Their combined surfaces total 1,335 square miles, or less than Long Island off New York. We have seen that even the tallest volcanic islands nearest Asia were discovered by Europeans coming from America. Many were in fact not known to the outside world until well into the nineteenth century.

South of Micronesia lies Papua-Melanesia, a correspondingly wide ocean area beginning where the Indonesian archipelago ends and stretching 4,000 miles from western New Guinea to eastern Fiji. Large, high islands of continental type form an almost uninterrupted bridge eastward in this region, leaving only Fiji as an oceanic group distinctly separated from the rest.

East of both Micronesia and Papua-Melanesia, in the nearest half of the Pacific to America, lies Polynesia. The widely separated Polynesian islands and atolls are tiny and scattered within a triangle formed by Hawaii in the north, New Zealand in the south, and Easter Island in the east. There is no inhabitable land separating Polynesia from America.

The problem of how Stone Age people had managed to settle the semi-continental territories of Papua-Melanesia never created much dispute among scientists, even though archaeology showed that man's occupancy of this area goes back into extremely early periods. It was quite apparent that the dark-skinned, negroid peoples of Papua-Melanesia, like the primitive aborigines of Australia and Tasmania, could have come—almost on foot—out of South Asia and Indonesia in a geological period when even less water separated these closely packed land masses than is the case today. Except perhaps for Fiji, no navigational problem was involved.

The problem of how Micronesia was settled by primitive tribes in much later times is very often passed over lightly by scholars, who are satisfied by the observation that the Micronesian tribes seem to be a mixture of an unidentified people with subsequent intruders from Melanesia in the south and Polynesia in the east. Winds and currents would favor overseas drifts from these adjacent island areas.

The problem of how Polynesia was settled has caused more controversy, however, than any other puzzle in the history of the anthropological sciences. A vast number of mutually antagonistic theories have been advanced by scholars in different fields, and still more by pseudo-scientists and popular writers. These conflicting theories have only two basic conclusions in common: Polynesia was the last major area on earth to be settled, and man out of Asia had a major part in the migrations that gradually peopled the entire Pacific hemisphere, including distant Polynesia. In other words, we have all been searching for—and postulating—hypothetical sailing routes from Asia that could somehow have bypassed or crossed the 4,000-mile-wide racial and cultural buffer territory of Micronesia and Papua-Melanesia to allow Polynesians to settle in recent centuries on the isolated islands beyond them.

The migration route from Asia to Polynesia here proposed is the one I advanced as early as 1941 in a paper on Polynesian origins published in *International Science* in New York. Little attention was paid to this publication because of the global spread of World War II, and when I returned to America in 1946 to sail the *Kon-Tiki* balsa raft from Peru the following year, the Asiatic component in the proposed migration theory was completely overwhelmed by the attention given to the raft enterprise and its unexpected appeal to the general public through book and film. Scholars and popular writers everywhere accused me of ignoring Asia in an attempt to demonstrate that South America was the sole contributor to the settling of Polynesia. All attempts to contradict this accusation and clarify my own point of view were of little avail. In a book published in 1952, *American Indians in the Pacific,* I made a new effort to put right this seemingly universal misapprehension by devoting the first 178 pages entirely to an analysis of the most feasible route for the Asiatic component in the admittedly mixed Polynesia island population. Under the section heading "With the New World as Maori-Polynesian stepping-stone a new route but not a new source is proposed" the following explanation was presented: "It is not my intention to deny that the Polynesians, to a certain degree, have distant relatives among the Malay people. I only doubt whether any Polynesian ancestors ever dwelt on the Malay islands. I fail to see why we, when discussing Malay-Polynesian relations, should always regard the Polynesians as migrants to Polynesia and the Malays as stationary in the Malay archipelago. We know well enough that the Malays are not autochthonous of their present archipelago, but emigrants from the continent beyond. It is therefore very possible, in fact highly probable, that the present Malays, as much as the Polynesians, have moved in the long ages that have passed since their parental stocks were in contact. If so, the Indonesian archipelago cannot, any more than can the Polynesian islands, be the geographical area where the old ancestral lines of these two peoples converge. Like the Polynesian, the Malay line goes back to continental Asia. It is indeed the Malay *people* and not their archipelago that possesses rudimentary evidence of early contact with a palaeo-Polynesia stock.

"The Polynesian ancestors left the coastal area of Eastern Asia as a neolithic people before the high local civilizations developed. So did the Malays, and so did all the American Indians. We do not have to diverge from any of the known facts and established principles of Polynesian anthropology if we suggest that the Polynesian ancestors left East Asia on their prolonged neolithic migration to Polynesia, not necessarily by sailing slowly or quickly through the Micronesian ocean, but by following the Asiatic coast—or the eastbound Kuroshiwo Current—from the mainland of Southeast Asia—or even the Philippines—to a temporary abode and final embarkation place in the higher latitudes of the Pacific."[1]

The route then proposed from Southeast Asia is the one dealt with in the present chapter, and was also the main topic of a lecture, *Sea Routes to Polynesia,* delivered at the University Museum of the University of Pennsylvania in April 1961 and subsequently published in the Museum Bulletin. The same route from Asia was also the special theme of the speech on *Primitive Navigation* presented before the Thirteenth Pacific Science Congress in Vancouver, British Columbia, in August 1975, later published by the Congress and most recently repeated in the *Encyclopaedia Britannica Yearbook for Science and the Future* for 1976. This chapter is a blend of these previous publications.

*   *   *

Two hundred years ago it was a common presumption that the Polynesian tribes on the isolated islands in the East Pacific were American Indians carried there, like all the early Europeans, by the prevailing easterly winds and currents. We have seen that for five hundred years, from the time of Marco Polo to the time of Captain Cook, it had been impossible for any European ship to force its way from Asia or the subsequent colonies in Indonesia to any part of Polynesia. All the voyages in the Polynesian part of the ocean, without exception, followed a course from America towards Asia, and to return from Asia it was necessary to sail from Indonesian waters along Japan to the high latitudes between the Aleutian Islands and Hawaii.

Crisscrossing the Pacific Ocean, Captain Cook was the first to detect that a few Polynesian words were related to corresponding terms in the Malay languages. At the same time Cook, like his contemporaries Vancouver and Dixon, noted that in physical features and cultural characteristics the Polynesian islanders showed remarkable similarities not to the Malays, but to the maritime Indians of the continental archipelago along the Northwest American Coast. Eighteenth-century observers began to speculate about oversea connections between these three island people living in separate areas of the same ocean. The nineteenth-century ethnologists noted that more than vague linguistic evidence linked Polynesia to the Old World: the Polynesian islanders possessed pigs, chickens, breadfruit, bananas, sugar cane, yams, taro, as well as the custom of lashing an outrigger to the side of their canoes—all of which were unquestionably Asiatic culture elements.

The tide of opinion turned. Ethnographically, the problem of Polynesian origins now seemed an easy one. It was merely to search for the area inside the Malay archipelago from where the Polynesian ancestry had come island-hopping to their present habitat. The island-hopping theory got broad support from armchair observers who had never known the vast Pacific hemisphere except from island-studded maps on which necessarily exaggerated dots and printed island names seem to form a continuous carpet from Indonesia almost to Easter Island. Those who knew this watery half of the globe for what it was were not so easily convinced. The geographers pointed to the fact, here discussed in Chapter 2, that the island area of the Pacific was in the main sweep of the constantly rotating elements which had been so decisive in setting all the early European explorers on their compulsory sailing routes. The geographers also realized that the compressed maps they had produced to get all information on the Pacific hemisphere represented on a tiny sheet of paper would necessarily be deceptive and invite island-hopping theories. In his treatise on *The Geography of the Pacific,* H. E. Gregory wisely points out: "But the oceanic islands offered no facilities for migration. They mark out no route from anywhere to anywhere. They are small, wide spaced, irregularly distributed, and for plants and man to reach them involves exceptional conditions."[2]

The difficulties for the ethnologists who advocated the island-hopping solution were further aggravated when the archaeologists failed to find any traces of a former Polynesian abode anywhere in the Malay archipelago or the West Pacific from whence they were supposed to have come, and when the physical anthropologists began looking beyond the Malay habitat for people whose body build and physiognomy could better compare with the characteristics of the tall and sharp-featured Polynesians than could the physical traits of the small and flat-faced Malays. Before the end of the nineteenth century, therefore, the Polynesian problem arose, and scholars from all fields now began to clash and disagree in proposals and theories. Almost every country on the continents behind Indonesia, from China and Indo-China to India, Mesopotamia, Egypt, and even Scandinavia, has been seriously proposed as the possible homeland of the Polynesian ancestry. What made the problem the more complicated was that most observers came to the conclusion that more than one migration had reached Polynesia, and that racially as well as culturally Polynesia was a melting pot.

After a century of philological research the linguistic evidence remained valid and yet proved to lead nowhere. It was early discovered that the structures of the Polynesian and Malay languages were quite different, that less than one per cent of the vocabularies of the two people had related or similar roots, and that there was a marked absence in Polynesian of true Malay words or of Sanskrit terms which had entered the Indonesian speech at a very early period. Furthermore, terms with possible root relationship to Polynesian had such a diffuse and sporadic distribution inside the Malay archipelago that no one island could be suggested as the place of ancestral contact. As a result two distinct linguistic schools developed. Some began to look for a possible common Malayo-Polynesian mother tongue somewhere in continental Asia whence the Malays and Polynesians could have spread independently; during ages of island isolation these two peoples would have maintained more of the once common mother tongue than would the continental relatives, far more subject to conquest and racial and linguistic intermixture. Others took a different approach and suggested that the Polynesian language had not developed in Asia or Indonesia at all, but in Oceania, somewhere in the archipelagoes marginal to present Polynesia. From here the Polynesians were assumed to have spread eastward, with a common tongue, to all their widely separated groups and islands in the East Pacific, and from the same Oceanic evolution center some sporadic terms also diffused in the opposite direction into the Malay domain. The linguists have thus ended up by bringing us no closer to a solution of the complex problem than to present two opposing hypotheses, neither of which favors a former Polynesian homeland in Indonesia.

Although language offers no immediate clue there are other channels of approach to evade the stalemate in the Malayo-Polynesian problem. Physical anthropology is generally considered a safer indication of racial kinship than linguistics, as speech material can diffuse independently of human relationships. The prominent American physical anthropologist L. R. Sullivan conducted the first systematic comparisons of Polynesian and Malay somatology half a century ago. He found the Polynesian and Malay physical types to be markedly separated in degree of pigmentation, beard and body hair development, thickness of lips and eye form, and claimed that the Indonesians were the direct antithesis of the Polynesians in body height, head form, face form, and nose form. His conclusion was that a close physical relationship was excluded since there was a "great divergence in nearly every trait studied."[3]

Sullivan's disclosures have never been opposed by subsequent physical anthropologists, but have been reinforced by modern studies of blood groups. Scientists with the Commonwealth Serum Laboratories in Melbourne, Australia, especially R. T. Simmons, J. J. Graydon, and their associates, initiated a most thorough investigation of blood gene frequencies throughout the Pacific and found that the Polynesians deviated markedly from all the peoples of Southeast Asia and the West Pacific in blood types. Dominant genes, like blood group B, which according to Mendel's law of inheritance cannot totally disappear from a family where it has once been present, are conspicuous through their absence among all pure-blooded Polynesian tribes, although they reach the world maximum in South Asia with Indonesia, Melanesia, and Micronesia. The blood group studies of A-B-O, M-N-S, Rh, P, Le^a, Fy^a, and K genes disclosed that there was a marked transition line separating the Polynesians from all their neighbors to the west whereas they followed instead the blood types of the aboriginal American Indians.[4]

The fact that for blood genetic reasons the Polynesians could not have descended from the present population of Southeast Asia, nor could have changed their blood character by mixture with the intermittent Melanesian or Micronesian islanders, created a new dilemma. It had so far been commonly assumed that the island-hopping Polynesian ancestry must have sailed very fast, almost non-stop, through the 4,000-mile-wide Melanesian-Micronesian buffer territory to avoid losing their fair skin and European-like countenances by mixing with people who were even darker and far more negroid than the Malays. The blood groups, however, excluded such a fast transit, which gave no time for the very fundamental change from Indonesian to Polynesian blood gene frequencies. The most ardent defenders of the eastward-from-Indonesia theory now proposed the exactly opposite solution, suggesting that the Polynesian ancestry had not moved at all rapidly through Micronesia, but so very slowly that the Polynesian blood groups and other physical characteristics had had ample time to change en route through "micro-evolution." According to this hypothesis, a few men and women all of whom happened to lack the locally dominant B factor had left their relatives with B genes behind somewhere in the Asiatic area and settled an uninhabited atoll in Micronesia. Next, only those among their descendants again who lacked the B factor could have happened to push on to the next island. If only a small group of those lacking B always by chance embarked and left their relatives with B behind, "micro-evolution" among choice individuals might in the end result in the final island-hoppers reaching Polynesia and spreading over that area almost without the B gene so characteristic of their South Asiatic ancestors.

The weaknesses of this proposal are many. Firstly, there is no evidence of such a gradual drop in the B gene frequency as we move from west to east through the Micronesian or Melanesian domain. The disappearance of the B factor is sharp and sudden just where the other islands end and Polynesia begins. Secondly, it would be a bit too much of a chance that only couples lacking the B gene each time decided to move on eastward into the unknown; and it would be out of the question that a completely parallel "micro-evolution" also took place with the M-N-S, Rhesus, and all the other blood groups and physical features which combine to form the Polynesian type and set it so markedly apart from the peoples of the West Pacific.

The moment we venture back into the risky speculations about long-lasting Polynesian sojourns in Micronesia or Melanesia we are again trapped where the problems started, and we are furthermore in direct trouble with archaeology. The Micronesian atolls are small; the dry and open coral ground hides nothing, and yet there are no traces of former Polynesian occupation. The southeastern atolls of Kapingamarangi and Nukuoro are exceptions, but linguists and ethnologists have jointly demonstrated that these two atolls have been settled by genuine Polynesian voyagers who came down wind from Samoa in recent centuries. The complete failure to find any vestiges of Polynesian passage through the Micronesian area has caused some investigators to discard these open atolls in favor of the large, jungle-covered mountain islands of Melanesia as theoretical steppingstones to Polynesia. But there was never any possibility for protracted Polynesian "micro-evolution" in the midst of the old and densely crowded negroid population of this 4,000-mile-wide and hostile territory.

Traces of recent Polynesian colonies have been found on several of the easterly exposed shores of Melanesia as well as on the eastern headland of New Guinea, but as with the two outliers in Micronesia already mentioned, these displaced Polynesian colonies have always proved to be the result of fairly recent downwind voyages directly from Samoa or Tonga in Polynesia proper.[5]

Sir Peter Buck, the most noted supporter of the eastward-from-Indonesia theory, was so firmly opposed to any Polynesian trespassing of Melanesia that he argued: "Strong support in favor of the Micronesian route lies in the positive evidence against the route through Melanesia." He had, in fact, no other argument in favor of the Micronesian route, and in discarding the Melanesian route he also surrendered the long coveted botanical arguments for a Polynesian homeland in Indonesia. On the dry and sandy atolls of Micronesia only coconuts and dry-land taro grew, two plants which were at home also in aboriginal America, whereas the other, more demanding Oceanic food plants were absent from this entire area. Buck was fully aware of this pitfall, and took the consequences when he wrote: "The Micronesian route, therefore, could not have been taken by the plants . . . though the Polynesians traveled into central Polynesia by the Micronesian route, such important food plants as the breadfruit, banana, yam, and finer taro were carried from Indonesia to New Guinea and relayed by Melanesians to their eastern outpost at Fiji."

It was to Buck's credit to have shown that these important food plants were not brought by the original Polynesian migrants but were acquired through marginal contact between Polynesia and Melanesia once the well-known and long-lasting trade relations started between Samoa–Tonga on the Polynesian side and Fiji on the nearest outpost of Melanesia. In the same way he disposed of the domesticated animals originally seen by many as evidence of Polynesian origins in Indonesia: "Coral atolls thus formed a barrier to the spread of domesticated animals. They must have been relayed along the Melanesian route and passed from Fiji to Samoa."

Buck shows, in fact, that Samoan tradition expressly states that the pig, unknown to their forefathers, was first known when a voyager from Samoa visited Fiji and came back with some piglets. He asserts: "The importance of Fiji as a trade center cannot be overestimated. The western triangle of Samoa, Tonga, and Fiji became an important area for exchange and diffusion . . . The cultural changes that took place in the western triangle were initiated primarily by exchange and barter for food plants and domesticated animals . . . The plants and animals were carried to central Polynesia, but the Fijian customs remained in the west."[6]

The animals that spread to Polynesia from Fiji were the pig and the chicken. We will later see that the only remaining Polynesian animal, the dog, was unknown in Melanesia and Micronesia but concurs with aboriginal American breeds. It is therefore significant to note that the dog was known to the New Zealand Maori, but not the pig and the chicken. We shall also see that the dog is mentioned in their oldest traditions and myths, whereas there is a curious silence about the pig and the chicken even in tribal memories. It is not difficult to account for this fact. It is known from genealogical studies that the New Zealand Maori arrived from the easterly area of Polynesia during the early part of the present millennium, and after a limited period of continued contact with the islands to the northeast, they isolated themselves completely from the rest of Polynesia and received no impulses from the outside world until Tasman arrived in 1642. Thus the crop plants and chickens and pigs which in this period of central Polynesian trade and maritime activity spread from Fiji never reached the isolated tribes on New Zealand. They remained in every sense the purest representatives of the original Polynesian stock. It is extremely significant to keep in mind that the inter-island diffusion which influenced and modified Polynesian culture in the last centuries prior to European arrival left the Maori unaffected. For this reason it is equally important to observe that even such a highly useful and important device as the outrigger never reached any Maori tribe nor their Moriori neighbors on the Chatham Islands, although it diffused with the other beneficial Fijian assets to nearly all the rest of the Polynesian islands.

With direct evidence to show that the Polynesians originally arrived without the Old World plants and animals, and even ignorant of both the double and single outrigger, we are not only deprived of the last arguments for the eastward-from-Indonesia theory, but we have to look for a completely different embarkation area whence the Maori-Polynesians could have reached the East Pacific still ignorant of the outrigger, the most desirable of the Asiatic navigational inventions. All through Indonesia, from Sumatra and the Philippines to the nearest tip of New Guinea, the Malays and Indonesians have since early times used the *double* outrigger to stabilize their craft, i.e., a buoyant boom fastened to crossbars on each side of the vessel. The Micronesians and the Melanesians used a *single* outrigger, that is on one side only, and for this reason the Micronesians built their canoes laterally asymmetrical. When the Polynesians adopted the single outrigger on their bilaterally *symmetrical* canoes they did not follow the Micronesian model but followed that of neighboring Fiji. In short, neither the Indonesian nor the Micronesian type of outrigger canoe reached the East Pacific.

An eastward-from-Indonesia migration reaching New Zealand and the other islands at a time compatible with the Polynesian settlement period is blocked by yet other stumbling stones. Among the many obstacles pointed out by observers is the fact that the Polynesians spread over their island area in the present millennium as pure Stone Age people, whereas not only bronze but even iron was in use in the Philippines by the second century B.C. and throughout Indonesia soon after.

F. W. Christian furthermore drew attention to the absence of the wheel throughout Polynesia, though it was known as early as iron in Indonesia.[7] Its absence in early America was once a main argument against contact with the Old World; why was the same argument never accepted in the case of Polynesia?

H. Petri, in his study of Pacific monetary systems, shows that stone and shell money belonged in Southeast Asia to the younger Stone Age and had an almost universal distribution throughout Indonesia, Micronesia, and Melanesia. He was accordingly surprised at the sudden and total absence of any monetary form throughout Polynesia; he found no other explanation but to speculate about possible "cultural retrogression."[8]

O. F. Cook took up the observation of his botanist colleague B. Seemann and claimed that the ignorance of alcohol in aboriginal Polynesia reveals that these islanders could not have come from any part of the Malay region "because colonists from Asia would certainly have brought the Asiatic art of bleeding the sap from the palms by cutting the young flower stalks, to make toddy and sugar from the juice. Such facts tend to show that the original inhabitants of the Pacific Islands did not derive their agricultural habits from Asiatic sources . . . since they have left the Polynesians in ignorance of the art of making toddy."[9]

Still more remarkable than the ignorance of alcohol in aboriginal Polynesia was the absence of the custom of betel nut chewing followed by millions of people in Southeast Asia. As G. Friederici points out, this custom was of great antiquity in the West Pacific, extending from India through Malaysia to the eastern limits of Melanesia, where it suddenly disappears. Throughout Polynesia the ceremonial drinking of *kava* appears instead, a salivary ferment made by women chewing certain plant fibers and spitting the pulp into warm water and later drunk after filtering. Friederici shows that the manufacturing method and associated drinking rites are so similar to those of ancient South America that it "makes a connection between the two highly probable."[10] Even early voyagers in the Pacific, like J. A. Moerenhout, said of the Polynesian *kava:* "The American Indians make exactly the same thing, but with other plants."[11] J. M. Brown quotes Brouwer's account from Chile in 1643, from which it appears that *cawau* was the aboriginal name there for a salivary ferment produced by women chewing a local root and spitting the pulp into a vessel of water precisely as with the *kava* of Polynesia.[12] Brown sums up the Polynesian use of *kava* instead of alcohol or betel as follows: "It is another mystery that the coco-nut should have been taken with them by the emigrants and its chief use abandoned for the far less intoxicating and seductive kava of the central Pacific, which has to go through the process of mastication and expectoration before it is ready to drink . . . This latter rather affiliates with chicha of the Pacific coast of South America, and goes no further west than to the southeast of New Guinea, where it meets the betel-chewing habit coming eastwards."[13]

In short the Polynesians abstained from the Old World habits of drinking alcohol and chewing betel nuts and maintained the *kava* drinking ceremonies instead, which closely follow the custom in the American high-culture areas, where the corresponding drink among the Inca was called *chicha,* although other local names were *aqha, acca* (Peru), *cawau* (Chile), *aha* (Colombia), and *kasava* (Brazil).

T. R. St. Johnston observed that the morticing of stones in Polynesia "implies an early separation from the mainland of Asia, before the use of mortar was in vogue."[14] The same conclusion is forced upon us from the pan-Polynesian ignorance of such early Asiatic elements as the arch in stone constructions, and rowlocks, rudders, and wooden nails in boatbuilding. The Polynesians follow the New World rather than the Old in their lack of all these ancient inventions. However, their universal ignorance, when Europeans arrived, of pottery making also, and of weaving, set them so clearly apart from their neighbors both to the east and to the west that no solution of the Polynesian problem is valid unless the background of all these remarkable and fundamental characteristics of Maori—Polynesian culture are fully explained.

Polynesian culture as encountered by the early Europeans was based on a few and rather simple culture elements following them about everywhere: the neolithic elbow adz, the dugout canoe, the specialized types of fishhooks, the bark beater, the *poi* pounder, the earth oven, and the *kava* drinking ceremonies. Since these traits are practically pan-Polynesian they must have been present already in the outside area from which the tribal ancestors spread all over the vast Polynesian triangle.

The pan-Polynesian elbow adz, with its variety of tanged and rectangular stone blades, is the cornerstone of Polynesian culture and yet the most controversial of the culture traits. H. O. Beyer was the first to note in 1948 that tanged and rectangular adz blades similar to those of Polynesia were known in very early archaeological periods in the northern Philippines, but nowhere else in Indonesia. He shows, however, that these tanged adz types were used in that area between 1750 and 1250 b.c.[15] The problem again arises as to how they could have reached Polynesia. R. Duff in various lectures has extended this distribution back to continental Southeast Asia, but this brings us no nearer to Polynesia. Tanged adzes are unknown throughout Melanesia, where the blade cross section is even uniformly cylindrical. Heine-Geldern, looking in vain for a local passage, admits that the tanged and rectangular adz could not have passed that way because of "the radical difference in Polynesian and Melanesian blade forms."[16] Buck, likewise looking in vain for a passage, concluded that the Polynesian adz forms could not have passed the Micronesian way for the simple reason that no stone existed on those atolls, thus the Micronesians were obliged to make their cutting tools from shell. He pointed out that the Polynesian adz forms could not have derived from Southeast Asia at all since the lack of raw material in the 4,000-mile-wise Micronesian area created a vast gap, forcing the Polynesians to invent their own adz forms independently upon reaching their volcanic islands in the East Pacific.[17]

We have seen in Chapter 2, however, that there is another and fully feasible sea route from Southeast Asia to Polynesia, the only one found possible by early European sailing ships. This route entirely avoids the Micronesian–Melanesian buffer territory and travels from the Philippine Sea with the Japan Current and westerly winds to the island-studded coast of Northwest America, where all the elements turn around and bear directly down upon Hawaii. Once we substitute this northern island area for Micronesia or Melanesia as roadside stations for Asiatic voyagers to the East Pacific, we immediately find steppingstones also for the tanged rectangular adz: it was the principal tool of the local Northwest Coast Indians right up to the arrival of Europeans. Captain Cook was the first to point out that the people of the Northwest American Coast used adzes similar to those of Tahiti and other Polynesian islands,[18] and Captain Dixon, after Cook, noted that the adz of these coastal Indians "was a toe made of *jasper,* the same as those used by the New Zealanders."[19] Captain A. Jacobsen stressed: "Also the adz-handle and the method of securing the blade to the wooden handle are exactly the same among the Polynesian people as among the Northwest Indians."[20]

Twentieth-century anthropologists have confirmed these early observations. W. H. Holmes emphasized that the tanged rectangular adzes of the Northwest Coast Indians resemble the adzes of the Pacific islands more closely than they do the corresponding tools of other American tribes,[21] and R. L. Olson wrote in his study of the Northwest Coast elbow-adz: "Its occurrence in Polynesia in a form almost identical with the elbow adz of America suggests a hoary age and extra-American origin."[22] It is accordingly possible that the tanged, rectangular adz, belonging only to a very early period in Asia and the northern Philippines, spread to Polynesia during a much later period, following the natural sea passage by way of Northwest America.

As stated earlier, the Pacific Ocean curves as a complete hemisphere; the equator is not a straight line, and what seems on a map to be a roundabout way up north is, in traveling time and effort, only a fraction of what would be needed to travel due east from Indonesia. As with the important tanged and rectangular adz, if we quite simply circumnavigate the problem areas of Micronesia and Melanesia and enter Polynesia by way of Hawaii rather than by way of Samoa, the whole series of familiar anthropological dilemmas will disappear, together with all the navigational problems. First of all, if the island area of the Northwest American Coast represents the steppingstones from Asia to Polynesia, the Polynesian physical type becomes a logical consequence rather than a continued problem. We found that the slender body build of the Indonesians places them among the smallest people in the world, whereas the Polynesians range among the very tallest. The Northwest Coast Indians on the mainland are slightly taller than the Malays, but the outlying Haida of the Queen Charlotte Islands and the Kwakiutl of northwestern Vancouver Island rank among the tallest people in the world. The figures given by F. Boas[23] for the Northwest Coast Indians and those given by H. L. Shapiro[24] for Polynesians coincide in showing tribes with an average stature of over 170 cms, and in both areas aborigines of six-foot stature were not infrequently seen.

The crania of the Indonesians and their neighbors are brachycephalic (short-headed) and so are those of most American Indians. But dolichocephalic (long-headed) skulls are well known from archaeological sites on the Northwest Coast and are frequently repeated in the mixed cranial forms of Polynesia. A. Hrdlička[25] gives the average cranial index of Northwest Coast Indians as 81.19 for males and 81.4 for females; this matches remarkably the 81.27 which, according to Shapiro, is the average cranial index of six main Polynesian groups, namely Hawaii, the Societies, Samoa, Tonga, Marquesas, and New Zealand.

The European-like features of most Polynesians have raised even more wild speculations than their tall stature, since their fair skin, their strong beard growth, often soft and wavy hair, sometimes tending to shades of brown, their thin lips, and commonly narrow aquiline noses set them far apart from the Indonesians and still further from the peoples of the intermittent territory. Whatever the cause, the aboriginal island tribes of Northwest America also had much fairer complexions than the other members of the Indo-American family, a fact emphasized by all the earliest European visitors like Cook, Dixon, and Vancouver. Their hair, too, showed the same non-Mongol peculiarities as among the Polynesians, since it was not uniformly coarse and black, but often soft in texture, and sometimes even of varying shades of brown. The early visitors were not less surprised a finding, among totally beardless people like the American Indians and Indonesians, Northwest coast aborigines who often had strong mustaches and, as described by Cook, "large and thick, but straight beards."[26] The narrow and very often aquiline nose of most Polynesians, contrasting with the broad and flat nose of the Indonesians, is as common among the Northwest Coast Indians as elsewhere in the New World, and so are their narrow lips and non-Mongoloid eye-form, all of which add to the European-like appearance that recurs in Polynesia. Captain Vancouver wrote of the maritime tribes in the central area of the Northwest Coast before their admixture with Europeans: "The prominence of their countenances, and the regularity of their features, resembled the northern Europeans."[27]

In view of this consistent concurrence in stature, cranial and facial characteristics, hair, and complexion, it is not surprising that local nineteenth-century investigators, so thoroughly familiar with the Northwest Coast Indians as Captain A. Jacobsen and Professor C. Hill-Tout, had difficulties in distinguishing Polynesian visitors from local Northwest Coast Indians. Jacobsen was struck by what he described as a remarkable similarity between the Haida, Kwatiutl, and Hawaiians, and added: "Thus I met once a Sandwich Islander on a small island near Vancouver, who was married there and had a family. I could not discover any noticeable difference between him, his children and his neighbors . . ."[28] And Hill-Tout adds: "I have seen members of the Squamish tribe whom I could with difficulty distinguish from some of the Samoans who returned from the Chicago fair this way, and camped at the Squamish village here."[29] Personally I spent the winter of 1939–40 among the Northwest Coast Indians of the Bella Coola Valley after I had spent a year among the Polynesians in the Marquesas group, and was struck by the person-to-person resemblance among some of the pure-blooded Salish Indians of Bella Coola to specific Polynesian friends in Tahiti and the Marquesas group.

In 1952, after I had visited both areas, I compiled for the first time all the then available data on blood groups A–B–O to show that the Polynesians, who differed profoundly from the Southeast Asiatics in blood gene frequencies, could well have come from northwestern North America. As a former biologist, I had been stimulated by G. A. Matson's discovery in 1946 that Blackfoot and Blood Indians of North America had A frequencies corresponding to those of the aboriginal Hawaiians.[30] The issue was immediately taken up by the Pacific serologist J. J. Graydon, who added the M–N and Rh blood groups to my earlier comparisons. He concluded that the blood evidence supported an American-Polynesian relationship, "making it probable that the islands of Polynesia have been settled largely by migrations from continental America."[31] In 1954 A. E. Mourant extended the analysis by compiling all blood group data available up to that time, and he, too, concluded, "a large part of the genetic constitution of the Polynesians can be accounted for on a basis of an American, and especially a northwest American origin . . ."[32] Challenged by these observations, R. T. Simmons, J. J. Graydon, N. M. Semple, and E. I. Fry came back with a complete study of the A_1–A_2–B–O, M–N–S, Rh, P, Le^a, Fy^a, and K groups concluding "that there is a close blood genetic relationship between American Indians and Polynesians, and that no similar relationship is evident when Polynesians are compared with Melanesians, Micronesians, and Indonesians, except mainly in adjacent areas of direct contact."[33] This important conclusion was finally confirmed in 1972 by an international work group composed of E. and Anne Thorsby, J. Colombani, J. Dausset, and J. Figueroa.[34]

Unfortunately the Northwest Coast Indians, although commonly considered descendants of some of the last immigrants to enter America from Asia, have changed their own speech so completely that it is impossible to know what it was originally. Though all the various Northwest Coast tribes are still intimately interrelated both physically and culturally, all tribes, even close neighbors, have developed seemingly unrelated languages, a process thought by some to be due partly to late intermixture with continental tribes and partly to the local practice of word taboo. Certainly the harsh, guttural Northwest Coast speech, particularly of the mainland tribes, seems to contrast with the soft vowel dialects of Polynesia. It might nevertheless prove to be interesting if some modern linguist took up the nineteenth-century challenge of the linguists J. Campbell and C. Hill-Tout. Campbell reached the conclusion that the Haida language of the central Northwest Coast ought to be included in the Oceanic group together with Polynesian.[35] Hill-Tout claimed to have found so many structural as well as lexical correspondences between the Northwest Coast Indian and Polynesian languages that he termed his findings "a chain of evidence of common origin and one wholly beyond the work of chance."[36]

The Northwest Coast Indians lived in a world of channels and islands covered by giant timber and shut off from inland America by precipices and wild mountains. As P. E. Goddard stated, "the Northwest-coast of America is exceedingly favourable for the development of a culture which depends almost entirely upon canoes for travel and transportation, and upon the sea for its supply of food."[37] The people who in some distant neolithic period came from Asia to settle this particular coast were blessed with a mild climate caused by the warm current from the Philippine Sea constantly washing the local shores and making it possible to live barefoot and dressed in bark cloaks the year around. The local level of culture when Europeans arrived matched in every sense that of the neolithic fishermen of Polynesia, their direct overseas neighbors to the southwest.

Second in importance to the specialized elbow adz common to both areas, and of particular interest in a study of Polynesian migrations into the East Pacific, is the seagoing canoe. A long acquaintance with the Northwest Coast people during the last century caused A. P. Niblack to pass the following flowery comment: "The canoe is to the Northwest coast what the camel is to the desert. It is to the Indian of this region what the horse is to the Arab. It is the apple of his eye and the object of his solicitous attention and affection. It reaches its highest development in the world among the Haida of Queen Charlotte Islands."[38]

In fact, some of the deep-seagoing craft have measured as much as 70 feet long, 6½ feet wide, 4½ feet deep, accommodating up to a hundred people.[39] With these large canoes the Haida, Kwakiutl, and Bella Coola Indians ventured into the exceptionally ferocious seas in the open ocean between Vancouver and the Queen Charlotte Islands, and in a modern experiment by Captain J. C. Voss one such Northwest Coast canoe was sailed from Vancouver Island directly to Tongareva in central Polynesia.[40]

We have seen that neither the proa nor the double outrigger canoe characteristic of Indonesia reached the East Pacific. The Polynesians arrived in large symmetrical single canoes or in pairs of canoes temporarily lashed together with crossbars to form the very sturdy and seaworthy vessel known as the double canoe. We have also seen that the outrigger, unknown to the Maori and Moriori, was a secondary acquisition only subsequently diffused into Polynesia from neighboring Fiji. Outside Polynesia the custom of sailing the unsheltered ocean in two equal canoes forming a temporary double canoe was known only among the Northwest Coast Indians, who according to the study of R.

L. Olson might have borrowed the custom from a similar practice with inferior boats among the Yukaghirs and Koryaks of northeastern Asia.[41] No other people navigating the Pacific by canoe would have such obvious access to Polynesia as the Northwest Coast mariners. J. M. Brown said of their canoes: "they are of all primitive craft the most fitted for meeting the conditions of oceanic voyaging, and have a great resemblance to the Maori war canoe . . ."[42]

Their strong conformity in size, structure, and decor to the largest Maori canoes comprises such details as the absence of keel, rudder, thwarts, rowlocks, and pegs in joining planks, whereas both people used sewing for adding elevated bow and stern pieces, and even side planks whenever needed, and both carved and painted elaborate figureheads, and decorated the final canoe with inlays of abalone shell. The correspondence is made still more evident by the common custom in both areas of temporarily lashing two such vessels side by side and covering them with a plank platform whenever a prolonged voyage was planned. The Maori and the Northwest Coast canoes had no fixed mast, and a clumsy mat was hoisted only to catch accompanying wind. On the Northwest Coast, as also on New Zealand, the peculiar custom was observed of turning the canoe around to hit the beach stern first on landing, as only supernaturals were supposed to land bow first.[43]

The paddles are also similar in both areas, and so is the maneuvering of the vessel. H. H. Bancroft wrote from the Northwest Coast: "When they embark, one Indian sits in the stern, and steers with a paddle, the others kneel in pairs in the bottom of the canoe, and sitting on their heels, paddle over the gunwale next to them. In this way they ride with perfect safety the highest waves, and venture without the least concern in seas where other boats and seamen could not live an instant."[44] And E. Best wrote about the Maori: "The crew on board war-canoes kneel two and two along the bottom, sit on their heels, and wield paddles from four to five feet long; the steersman, sitting in the stern, has a paddle nine feet long. Over tempestuous seas war-canoes ride like seafowl."[45]

Next in importance for the survival of the Polynesian mariners during their island discoveries were undoubtedly their three basic types of fishhook: the composite hook with stone or shell shank and bone barb; the incurved one-piece shell or bone hook; and the large composite wood and bone hook for shark or ruvettus. The distribution of these forms throughout Polynesia and partly also in Micronesia and adjacent parts of Melanesia makes an extra-Oceanic origin seem obvious. A most surprising fact is that fishhooks of any kind were unknown in Indonesia and all of Southeast Asia. The Malays and their neighbors had never learned to catch fish with line and hook. In the circum-Pacific area this practice was restricted to northern Asia and had spread from Alaska all the way down to Peru and Chile. The Ekholm–Heine–Geldern exhibit at The American Museum of Natural History in 1947 was the first to show that the incurved one-piece shell hook and the composite stone shank and bone barb hook of Polynesia concurred completely with archaeological fishhook types along the Pacific coasts of North and South America. Most remarkable was the concurrence of the highly specialized composite type where the cigar-shaped stone shank had a longitudinal notch near the base for the insertion of the bone barb, and transversal grooves encircling each pointed end for the attachment of the fishing line on top and a feather lure at the base. Common in Oregon, and particularly on the South American coast due east of Polynesia, this type has also recently turned up in archaeological middens among the Northwest Coast Indians, and specimens at the Provincial Museum in Victoria, British Columbia, closely match archaeological specimens from New Zealand. Whereas this type, as well as the one-piece shell or bone hook, could have spread into Oceania either from North or South America, the third Oceanic form, the large V-shaped wooden hook with incurved bone barb, is found nowhere else but among the Northwest Coast Indians who had developed it for fishing halibut. The correspondence is again so remarkable that E. W. Gudger included the Northwest Coast specimens in his special study of the Oceanic form due to "the remarkable resemblance in the fundamentals and construction."[46]

Another characteristic of pan-Polynesian culture was the grooved *tapa*—or bark beater—of either wood or whalebone used for manufacturing paper cloth. This primitive tool was a direct consequence of the surprising Polynesian lack of the loom and true weaving. The loom was known since very early times on both sides of the Pacific and particularly among nations sufficiently advanced to pursue maritime endeavors. The bark beater was also widespread on both sides, but only among backward tribes or isolated people with no nautical activities. The only marked exception was on the American Northwest Coast, where all the maritime tribes remained ignorant of the loom until Europeans arrived, and where they, just like the Polynesians, used grooved bark beaters of wood and whalebone to hammer the soaked inner bark of suitable local trees. Whalebone specimens have been found archaeologically in middens on the Northwest Coast, and the similarity to Polynesian whalebone specimens is striking. The inner bark of both the mulberry and breadfruit trees, which the Polynesians obtained from Fiji, produced fibrous paper cloth simply by crosswise beating, but the Maoris and the Moriois in the far south were ignorant of such trees and had to resort to "finger weaving" to unite the loose fibers they obtained by beating the inner bark of their own trees, precisely as the Northwest Coast people did. Captain Cook was again the first to point out this parallel when he visited the Northwest Coast: "In most of the houses were women at work, making dresses of the plant or bark mentioned, which they executed exactly in the same manner that the New Zealanders manufacture their cloth."[47] Captain Jacobsen said of the ready products: "Their articles of clothing look almost entirely like those of the New Zealand Maori, in form as well as in fabric and manufacturing method. The similarity is so great that some of the blankets from the two regions, when hung up beside each other, can hardly be distinguished."[48]

In his book on Samoa, E. S. Schurmann shows that bark blankets or mats were used as payment to local carpenters. "These mats," he says, ". . . are the Samoan symbol of wealth. The one who has many fine mats is rich, the one who has few is poor."[49] In fact, Petri, in his aforesaid work on Pacific monetary systems, showed that the Polynesians distinguished themselves markedly from all their neighbors to the west by their lack of stone or shell money, while mats in all essentials replaced currency in many parts of Polynesia. He says: "Many authors designate plaited mats as a sort of money typical for the Polynesians."[50] It is not difficult to detect from where this peculiar custom might have come. The Northwest Coast Indians also lacked any kind of *wampum* or other currency, but W. Dreyer wrote in the last century that they rewarded their carpenters with bark blankets. "The aforesaid blankets," he wrote, ". . . represent the standard of wealth, a kind of money. The wealth of a man, and the price of an article, is calculated to a certain number of blankets."[51]

Other than plaited mats on the earthen floor there was no furniture and there were very few utensils in the aboriginal house of Northwest America and Polynesia. However, any archaeologist working in Polynesia will be familiar with the conventional and beautifully shaped *poi* pounder of hard polished stone which was an indispensable chattel. Apart from the stone adzes and fishhooks no other pan-Polynesian artifact turns up in such quantities during excavations, and together with the large stone fishhooks of Easter Island this masterly executed tool has been considered the apogee of Pacific island stone-shaping art. Three highly specialized forms occur: the bell-shaped type with tall, slender handle terminating in a small disk or bulb, with the most perfect specimens from Rapaiti and the Marquesas group; the T-shaped variety with horizontal grip and upturned "ears," typical of the Society Islands; and the D-shaped variety occurring side by side with the bell-shaped in Hawaii. All these specialized forms appear as the principal food-preparing tools among the Northwest Coast Indians, and there, too, they represent the most common artifacts in archaeological excavations. The Northwest Coast forms differ from those in Polynesia only in having a flat base and were used as pestles, whereas the Polynesian counterparts have a slightly convex base and were used as pounders. J. F. G. Stokes, however, has shown that archaeological specimens in Hawaii reveal experimental and evolutionary stages from pestles used for dry food to pounders used for mashing taro and breadfruit into *poi*.[52] This is significant, since Hawaii is located as the natural steppingstone from the Northwest Coast archipelago to the tropical islands where taro and breadfruits were obtainable.

The pan-Polynesian use of the earth oven was in turn linked with their surprising ignorance of pottery. Wheeled pottery was known throughout Southeast Asia, including Indonesia, and coiled pottery in most of America and Melanesia since very early neolithic times. The first settlers of Polynesia must at one time have been familiar with the art of pottery making, for shards of coiled pottery have been found archaeologically both in the eastern and western extremities of Polynesian territory. However, the fact that historic and protohistoric tribes on every island in Polynesia were totally ignorant of ceramic art and for boiling in pots substituted baking in special stone-lined earth ovens is so remarkable that it requires explanation, since there is no lack of suitable clay that could have been used for pottery making. Again, in marked contrast to all other circum-Pacific peoples except the primitives of Tierra del Fuego, the maritime tribes of the Northwest Coast were all as ignorant of pottery as were the Polynesians. They, too, baked their food in the very same kind of stone-lined earth oven until

Europeans arrived. Among those who first saw the significance of this remarkable geographical distribution was the intrepid traveler J. Macmillan Brown, who wrote of the earth oven: "it is one of the most distinctive marks of the culture of the Polynesians and went with them wherever they went. It was probably bred in the frozen soil of the wintry north, and belonging to the natives of the northwest coast of America, as it does, it is one of the clues that seem to indicate affinity between them and the Polynesians."[53]

There are a few characteristic traits among all Maori tribes which are not pan-Polynesian although related vestiges appear elsewhere in Polynesia. Most striking are the conventionalized and beautifully fashioned short, one-hand fighting clubs of stone and whalebone. Both the Northwest Coast Indians and the Polynesians were familiar with the bow and arrow so popular among their neighbors, but they never used them in war, preferring to fight hand to hand with short clubs of conventional types that gave friend and foe the same chance. These beautifully shaped and polished clubs have been highly prized collectors' items since the days of the early voyagers, and Captain Jacobsen wrote: "We find among Maori weapons a war club which was formerly in common use. It was generally fashioned from whale-bone, or from nephrite and other stones. Exactly the same weapons were used by the inhabitants of the Vancouver and Queen Charlotte Islands. The resemblance in form and size is so remarkable that even the great discoverer Captain Cook was struck with it, when he first saw the weapons among the Maori and then in America."[54]

Challenged by the claim of Ratzel and other early founders of the science of ethnology, who pointed out that the fighting clubs of these two areas were just about identical, J. Imbelloni conducted a special investigation and reached the conclusion that it could hardly be a coincidence that the Maori and Northwest Coast warriors were alike in carving the same type of club from the same materials, namely the *patu onewa* from stone and the *patu paraoa* from whalebone. He showed that the drill hole to take the thong through the slim handle of the stone specimens requires such ingenuity and persistence that independent evolution is highly improbable. He drew attention, moreover, to the fact that the whalebone clubs in both areas also usually were alike in having a stylized bird's head carved in profile on the butt end, and he pointed out the presence on the Northwest Coast of such specialized Maori club forms as the *mere onewa,* the *mere pounamu,* and the *miti*. In conclusion he claimed that "it will be enough to remember the adzes, pestles, fishhooks, etc., of Polynesia and the northwestern coast of America in order to prove a transplantation of an integral patrimony."[55]

Imbelloni proposed, however, that the Northwest Coast clubs had been evolved by the Maori and brought to Northwest America from early New Zealand. It was an easy task for the Maori authority H. D. Skinner to rebut the claim by showing that there is no stratigraphic evidence for an evolution of these specialized clubs inside New Zealand, wherefore he proposed that the Maoris were themselves probably receivers from some unidentified common source somewhere in Asia.[56] Recent surveys have shown great antiquity with evolutionary forms and archaeological distribution inside Northwest America, but neither Imbelloni nor Skinner thought of reversing the direction of the distribution.

It is, in fact, puzzling that all those who have drawn attention to American-Oceanian parallels have always imagined the Polynesians as the donors. We do realize that the main problem of the Maori-Polynesians is the question of their own origins. We also know that the Northwest Coast people, just like the inhabitants of Indonesia, descend from ancestors in coastal East Asia, and that the current from their continental archipelago, quite contrary to that of Micronesia, bears directly down upon Polynesia with such a force that the islanders of Hawaii made their largest canoes of giant trees that had drifted from the Northwest American Coast. Further, the northeast tradewinds rise a couple of hundred miles off the Northwest American Coast and for the greater part of the year blow across Polynesia and all the way down toward New Zealand. Yet, we are so affected subconsciously by the one-time linguistic theory of a Polynesian descent from the Malays that when we find an area abounding in Polynesian parallels we reject them merely because we can prove that the Polynesians could not have been the *donors*.

In a paper on "Contacts with America Across the Southern Pacific," the prominent ethnologist R. B. Dixon stresses that the conformity between Northwest American and Maori-Polynesian cultures has been apparent ever since the days when the circum-Pacific coasts were first explored by Europeans: "Several of the earlier English explorers of the northwest coast of America, like Cook and Vancouver, who had previously been engaged in exploration in the South Seas, were much struck on coming in contact with the Indians in this region by the similarities between some features of their culture and those of the Maori of New Zealand. The solidly constructed plankhouses with their elaborately carved and painted decorations, the forts, the finely woven mantles, the short bone and stone clubs, recalled to their minds similar objects among the Maori and led them to speculate as to the possibility of some relationship between the two groups of people."[57]

For no apparent reason these speculations, which have continued through modern ethnographic studies, including Dixon's survey, have never attempted to see Oceania as the receiver, always as donor, which created new problems rather than solving existing ones. The Polynesians, themselves of unknown origin, could indeed have brought some artifacts and ideas to the ancient aborigines of coastal Northwest America, but they could not have made them ignorant of the loom and pottery, nor could they have influenced all Northwest Coast tribes so profoundly that physical appearance, blood groups, and all principal aspects of the local culture would follow the Maori-Polynesian pattern. In relation to the Northwest Coast tribes the Maori-Polynesians demonstrate the aspects of a daughter culture rather than a mother culture.

A trait-to-trait comparison between the Kwakiutl–Haida–Salish stocks of Northwest America and the Maori-Polynesians fails to disclose a single point of divergence greater than the island-to-island variation within either of these two adjacent areas. The list of concurrences goes far beyond that which will strike the eye, at first sight, although much has been casually or emphatically recorded by earlier observers.

Particularly striking is the Maori custom of erecting tall wooden posts or columns in the open, carved in the form of one figure standing on the head of another. Polack saw such Maori ancestor posts up to thirty feet tall,[58] and other early voyagers describe and illustrate them as common in Hawaii. In Tahiti several such figures were alternately standing on top of each other. The custom is a direct repetition of the characteristic Northwest Coast practice of raising so-called totem poles near their villages. M. Barbeau, in a special study of Northwest Coast totem poles, shows that the exuberant posts typical of this region in recent generations are a result of the introduction of European iron tools, for the pre-European specimens were more modest and generally confined to two superimposed figures, as so common in New Zealand. In fact, he found what he called a "compelling resemblance" to the corresponding posts in New Zealand, and stresses this point by introducing the illustration of a large Maori specimen among his North-west Coast samples.[59] In both areas these carved posts are sometimes set up as house decorations with a narrow opening carved between the straddling legs of the lower figure, through which the occupants gain entrance to the house.

The elaborate houses were the same in both areas, large and roomy with rectangular ground plan, and walls and roof of broad hand-split boards. The roof, resting on solid corner posts, was bluntly gabled to-ward long low side walls; there were no windows, and the short front wall had a small door and was often richly decorated either with carv-ing or painting. On the front gable, over the door, was commonly a lit-tle human figure carved in wood. The earthen floor was covered by plaited mats, and there was no furniture. In the Northwest Coast vil-lages such large plank houses could be up to 70 feet long, and Bach-mann describes a certain Maori plank house as 85 feet long, 30 feet broad, and 20 feet under the gable.[60] In such large buildings carved inner posts supporting the roof are described from both Maori and Northwest Coast areas. Surrounded by clusters of lofty ancestor poles, these villages, protected by wooden palisades, resembled nothing else in the Pacific area, since the hot climate of the rest of Polynesia caused the tropical Polynesians to prefer airy pole and thatch dwellings.

The social system was also the same in the two areas, as the North-west Coast people differ from all other Indians north of Mexico in di-viding the population into three social classes: a ruling aristocracy, commoners, and slaves. This system was closely followed by the Maori and a number of other Polynesian tribes. In Polynesia the clan system was patriarchal, in contrast with the matriarchal system prevalent among Indonesians and Melanesians; on the Northwest Coast both systems existed, according to tribe, but the patriarchal system was dom-inant among the Kwakiutl of the central area. Niblack compared the social systems of the two areas and found that "their political organi-zation of the tribe, their ownership of land, and their laws of blood re-venge are similar."[61]

Also common to both areas was the existence not only of medicine men but of *arioi* or *hametses* as well, a peculiar religious society like a group of medicine men who traveled about elaborately decorated, re-ceived with honors and veneration everywhere and splendidly treated, although they performed the most bestial cannibal ceremonies and ex-celled in unrestrained orgies. Next to them and to the tribal chiefs ranked the public orators in the local communities. Eloquence was greatly admired and speeches were given on all occasions, the public orators being well versed in local traditions and commonly distinguished by a ceremonial staff or other insignia when appearing before the people.

P. Drucker wrote in his survey of the aboriginal Northwest Coast culture: "Along with the system of graduated status in part based on ancestry was a marked interest in historical tradition. Genealogies were systematically remembered, to be recited on formal occasions. These family legends, which purport to cover the family's history from the time of its earliest ancestors, are far more than a recital of personal names and relationships—they tell also of war and conquest, and of movements of families from one place to another. The places referred to are actually long abandoned village sites. So matter of fact and internally consistent are these relations, and above all, so consistent are those of one family line with the traditions of their neighbors, that no ethnographer who has worked in the area has denied their historic value."[62]

This could equally well have been said of all Maori-Polynesian tribes.

In the last century G. M. Dawson lived among the Kwakiutl people of northern Vancouver Island and adjacent coasts and recorded their main tribal memories, which centered upon a migrant culture hero from whose younger brother the chiefly families reckoned their divine descent: "The name of this hero, like other words in the language, is somewhat changed in the various dialects. After hearing it pronounced by a number of individuals in the northern part of Vancouver Island and on the west coast, I adopted 'Kan-ē-a-ke-luh' as the most correct rendering. The 'Nawitti' people use a form more nearly rendered by 'Kan-e-a-kwe-a.'"

He also quotes a myth, however, where the same deity is referred to with yet another suffix, as Kānī-kē-lāq. The Kan-e legends end with the belief that he in the end married "a woman of the sea" and went away over the ocean, disappearing forever from mortal ken so that "the people suppose the sun to represent him. . . . The close connection of the culture-hero, Kan-ē-a-ke-luh, with the sun, has already appeared in the tales concerning him, together with the belief that the chiefs, or some of them, are related to Kan-ē-a-ke-luh by descent through his younger brother. Doubtless, also, in connection with this, we find that the sun, na-la, under the name Ki-a-kun-ā-e, or 'our chief,' was formerly worshiped and prayed to for good health and other blessings."[63]

Boas too, in his monograph on *Kwakiutl Tales,* shows that the hero he refers to as Qāneqelak or Kane-ke-lak was the principal god and divine ancestor of the local people, who finally departed, saying he wanted to go to more southerly latitudes.[64]

We need go no farther south than Hawaii, where like Fornander we find that tribal memories ascribe the discovery of their group to a mythical "wandering chief" who came from a vast island or mainland farther north which was never mentioned by its real name, but only alluded to as "the lost home of Kane." The sun, in Kwakiutl language *na-la* and Hawaiian language similarly *la* (*ra* in other Polynesian dialects) was also in Hawaii alluded to as "the resting place of Kane." Kane was venerated in Hawaii as the principal god and direct ancestor of ruling families, whereas the Kwakiutl people claimed descent from the younger brother of Kan-e. Collecting Kawaiian beliefs in the last century, A. Fornander stated: "This 'Kane' creed, such as it has been preserved in Hawaiian traditions, obscured by time and defaced by interpolations, is still a most valuable relic of the mental status, religious notions, and historical recollections of the earlier Polynesians. No other group in Polynesia has preserved it so fully, so far as my inquiries have been able to ascertain; yet I have met with parts of it on nearly all the groups, though more or less distorted, and in that case I hold that the universality of a legend among so widely scattered tribes proves its antiquity."[65]

One of Kane's full names in Hawaii was Kane Uakea, "Kane the Light,"[66] which corresponds closely to the Kwakiutl Kan-e-a-kwe-a recorded by Dawson.

There is no need to go into detail regarding the further creeds and customs in which various Maori-Polynesian tribes follow the pattern of their Northwest Coast neighbors, such as nose rubbing as a salute, topknots as masculine coiffure, feathers of big birds as hair decoration, head flattening, body tattooing, finger severance, fire walking, armor for combat, the tongue as a symbol of defiance, and weapons carved as stylized heads with an outstretched tongue as the blade, the ignorance of stringed musical instruments which had their main world center between India and Indonesia, and a Maori repetition of the Northwest Coast rattles, percussion instruments, and the wooden flute or flageolet carved as a grotesque human face with sound issuing through its wide-open mouth, the system of taboo, the dread of burial in the ground and preference in both areas of placing the dead on wooden platforms raised on poles, the dried-up remains or skeletons wrapped in bark blankets and deposited in a sitting position with knees below chin in caves, trees, or (also in both areas) in part of a canoe.[67]

It would seem as if the Northwest Coast archipelago alone, as a steppingstone from a much earlier abode at some as yet unidentified region of Southeast Asia, would satisfy any reasonable requirement for a geographically, anthropologically, and chronologically feasible source area of the peoples and cultures of the extreme East Pacific. This is not the case, however. We have seen that the Polynesian problem is complex and the Maori-Polynesians themselves claim that earlier people lived on all these islands when their ancestors arrived. As Buck shows, "Traditional narratives state that an early people were found in Hawaii, Cook Islands, and New Zealand by the later Polynesians . . . The later immigrants conquered their predecessors, who were not exterminated but absorbed."[68] Genealogical datings based on a period of about twenty-five years per Polynesian generation concur throughout Polynesia in showing that, according to locality, the various islands must have been settled by the present Maori-Polynesians during the first centuries of the present millennium. A. Fornander, a notable early Polynesian genealogist, after a lifelong study of Polynesian tribal history, claimed that about thirty generations reckoned from the end of last century brings us back to a period "when the aristocracy in almost all the groups took, so to say, a new departure." From then on, during a period of a few generations, all royal lines were interrupted and substituted by new ones: "a migratory wave swept the island world of the Pacific, embracing in its vortex all the principal groups, and probably all the smaller . . . Its traces were deep and indelible. It modified the ancient customs, creed and polity. It even affected the speech of the people." He shows that new tutelar gods succeeded earlier deities, new place names replaced old ones, and that the construction of pyramidal stone platforms also seemed to have ceased during this period.[69]

More than a century ago E. Shortland collected Maori tribal memories and wrote: "We learn from such authority that the ancestors of the present race came from a distant island named Hawaiki, lying in a northerly or northeasterly direction from New Zealand, or from a group of islands, one of which bore that name."[70] The same traditions survived in Tahiti, but there the island was named Hawai'i, and lay to the north of their own group. The legend of an ancestral arrival from Hawaiki or Hawai'i is widespread in central and southern Polynesia, but is conspicuously absent in the Hawaiian group. Apart from Hawaii in the Northeast Pacific only Savaii in the Samoa group has a name that would become Hawaiki in the Maori dialect. Savaii was long suspected of being the island referred to in the traditions, since its location would agree well with island hopping from the Malay domain. But as Maori traditions speak of long voyages undertaken by their ancestors between Hawaiki and the Samoan group, and since they expressly gave Rarotonga in central Polynesia as a way station *en route* from Hawaiki to New Zealand, Savaii was finally rejected and modern investigators all agree that the Maori did not come from Samoa but from somewhere in eastern Polynesia.

It is not difficult to identify the legendary Maori Hawaiki with Hawaii, the logical geographical steppingstone from Northwest America. Fornander made the following discovery in studying early Maori genealogies: "among other prominent names occurring in their ancestral tales, previous to their departure from Hawaiki, are four that appear also in the Hawaiian Ulu line between *Aikanaka* and *Paumakua*. In the New Zealand legends they appear as chiefs or *Ariki* of *Hawaiki,* following one another in the same succession as on the Hawaiian genealogy. Their names are—the Hawaiian pronunciation in brackets—*Hema* (Hema), *Tawhaki* (Kahai), *Whahieroa* (Whahieloa), *Raka* (Laka)." He admits, "It is hardly possible that there could have been two series of chiefs . . . with identical names and in the same succession; with one transposition alone, the same identity holds good in the names of three of their wives . . ." He also found that the Hawaiians themselves had a tradition about the life of an early local chief who eventually left Hawaii to seek a new settlement in distant lands, and he compares this Hawaiian tradition with a Maori memory of certain ancestral incidents in early Hawaiki, and finds the concurrence so marked "that it is easy to recognize that both legends are but different versions of one and the same event."[71]

Another well-known Polynesian genealogist, Percy Smith, discovered that among the notable Hawaiian chiefs who in about the years A.D. 1100 to 1200 left Hawaii to seek a new home in the southern islands was one named Olopana, whose wife was Lu'ukia. "Now Olopana's and his wife's names, if converted into Maori by known letter changes, would be Koropanga and Rukutia. As a matter of fact we do find in Maori history the names of Tu-te-Koropanga, whose wife was Rukutia, and that they lived in Hawaiki . . ."[72]

With the legendary island of Hawaiki and Hawai'i in Maori and central Polynesian tribal history identified as Hawaii, the northern corner of the large Polynesian triangle becomes the gateway of the present population of these islands. We have seen that Samoa, the western corner, subsequently became a principal contact point, acquiring important Melanesian assets from Fiji and sending downwind colonists into marginal regions of Micronesia and Melanesia. The third corner, Easter Island, is a lonely eastern outlier on the halfway mark to South America. We shall return to this island in later chapters of this book in search of a missing component in the mixed Polynesian culture, since we have seen that there is another and even stronger marine highway into the East Pacific which must be more suspect than any other in view of the constantly repeated argument that there is a substratum of some earlier people in Polynesia. There is ample physical and cultural evidence to justify some faith in the recurring claim, among the historically minded population from Easter Island to Hawaii and New Zealand, that others were already in possession of the islands when their own forefathers arrived by way of Hawaiki less than thirty generations ago. These former inhabitants and many of their beliefs and customs were absorbed more often than exterminated by the newcomers. They had not been carpenters splitting planks and excelling in wood-carving art like the historically known Maori-Polynesians and their northern neighbors along the forest-covered Northwest American Coast; rather, they had been expert masons, quarrying huge blocks from the solid mountainside, dressing and fitting stone for their temple structures and monuments like the inhabitants of the barren landscape of the Andes. These early settlers were responsible for the fitted megalithic structures and giant statues in human form raised and subsequently abandoned on the marginal islands nearest South America, for the introduction of the edible Maori-Polynesian dog, for the spread into Polynesia of the man-produced twenty-six-chromosome aboriginal American cotton together with the sweet potato and its South American name *kumara*, the bottle gourd and its various uses from container to rattle or fish-net float, and a whole series of other useful American plants to which we shall return in Chapter 9, among which is the important American fresh-water *totora* reed used by the Easter

Islanders for making their bundle boats identical with those of ancient Peru, and for thatching their circular and non-Polynesian stone houses which again were of South American type. Everywhere within the Polynesian area we find elements from this proto-Polynesian substratum, not always as archaeological vestiges, but more often as culture traits adopted and surviving right through the generations until historic times.

The tremendous thrust of the elements from Peru does not end in the Polynesian triangle but extends even into Melanesia, and there are several elements in Fiji and other marginal islands in this territory that can best be explained by downwind arrival from South America in the epoch when the as yet empty islands of Polynesia were first colonized. The difficult art and common practice of trepanation, unknown anywhere in Asia except in the Middle East, is one valid example; the ceremonial drinking of *kava,* already referred to, is another factor continuously distributed from Central and South America through Polynesia and ending abruptly where betel chewing comes in from Asia. The sling as a fighting weapon is unknown in Indonesia, and yet there are three specialized South Sea types, the band sling, the pocket sling, and the slit sling, all of which are direct repetitions of the three Peruvian types. Mummification was unknown in Indonesia, but in spite of the unfavorable climatic conditions which gave poor results, it was attempted in various parts of Polynesia by a process corresponding to that used in ancient Peru. Elaborate and colorful feather headdresses and feather cloaks for distinguished persons, characteristic of far-flung Polynesian culture, were unknown throughout the Far East including Indonesia, but were characteristic of ancient America and notably Mexico and Peru. The wooden tablets with boustrophedon* incriptions, and the complicated Polynesian *kipona,* or elaborate mnemonic system of knotted strings, have no equals anywhere in the West Pacific but have close counterparts in the New World. The veneration of the ancestor god Tiki, Kane's equal in most Polynesian groups, is found nowhere farther west but was the basis of pre-Inca worship in America. The list can be considerably extended, and this will be done in Chapter 13.

Evidence of a cultural substratum is also seen in the presence in Polynesia, already mentioned, of archaeological potsherds, small frag-

* Written alternately from left to right, and, inverted, from right to left.

ments having been excavated both in the Marquesas group and in the islands marginal to Fiji. In the same Marquesas group, also elsewhere in Polynesia as far as Fiji, a once cultivated and therefore long-linted cotton was growing wild when Europeans arrived, a clear indication of former planting by people versed in spinning and weaving. Pottery making and weaving, we have seen, could theoretically have reached these islands in pre-Maori-Polynesian times from the Old World as well as from the New. In Southeast Asia and Indonesia ceramic ware was made with the potter's wheel, whereas in the New World it was made by coiling continuous rings of clay on top of each other. The archaeological potsherds of Polynesia, and the vessels of the neighboring islands of Melanesia, where pottery was known, were made by coiling as in America, and in Fiji, where complete vessels were still in use when European collectors arrived, the highly specialized forms are so strikingly similar to early Peruvian effigy and cluster-shaped vessels that they would have been taken for a local variety if excavated from a pre-Inca burial ground on the North Peruvian coast.

The cotton plant which spread over the East Pacific from the Galápagos Islands to Fiji, but no farther, also speaks for itself. A modern chromosome study, as shown in Chapter 9, has disclosed that it has twenty-six chromosomes and thus belongs to a species artificially produced through hybridization by the ancient civilizations of Mexico and Peru, whereas all the cottons of the Old World, wild as well as cultivated, have only thirteen chromosomes, like the wild cottons of America. The potters who lacked the wheel and hence coiled their ceramic vessels, like the weavers who spun their yarn from twenty-six-chromosome American cotton, could well have come from Peru, but not from Indonesia.

To summarize: the Polynesian ocean area is vast, the land area insignificant, and the culture clearly composite, all confined to a triangle with one corner in Melanesia and the two others where ocean escalators come in respectively from Peru and Northwest America. An early cultural substratum from Peru, typified on Easter Island in the east, enriched by marginal contact with Fiji, centered upon Samoa in the west, and overcome by later Maori-Polynesian migrants entering by way of Hawaii in the north, will confirm the triple origins so often suspected for the composite culture within the East Pacific triangle. It may be said that, from the east came the American sweet potato, from the west the Melanesian breadfruit, but from the north the conquerors who reaped the harvest. These victors represented the Asiatic element in Polynesia, descendants from migrants who had come out of Southeast Asia without ever trespassing upon either Micronesian or Melanesian terrain.

Chapter 7

Incas Led the Europeans to Polynesia

THERE WAS not a single habitable island in the Pacific that had not been settled prior to the arrival of Europeans in this ocean. In spite of this we have named some European voyager as the discoverer of each of these inhabited islands. The Spaniard Alvaro de Mendaña is accredited with the discovery of the Marquesas Islands in 1595, the Dutch Admiral Roggeveen with the discovery of Easter Island in 1722, and the English Captain Cook of Hawaii in 1778, and so on. What is more, the first Europeans to learn that there were inhabited islands in the Pacific were even guided there by aboriginal Peruvians who volunteered their sailing directions.

Since the days of the Conquest it has been a peculiar habit of Europeans to disregard people with a different cultural background as almost non-human, at least until they have accepted the faith and learned the script we ourselves had received from Asia. Not until they have adopted our beliefs and customs do they become our equals and merit protection and credit for their own exploits. When it comes to our meetings with other branches of the human race in the New World and the still newer Oceania, the white man's feeling of superiority, backed by his gun, was strongly reinforced by the subordinate behavior of the vastly superior numbers of intelligent men and women who bid them welcome. We have seen in Chapter 4 that wherever the first European visitors advanced, from Mexico to Peru, they were received with awe and veneration as the returning envoys of white and bearded predecessors who had once before bestowed various blessings of civilization upon the local people. Precisely the same reception awaited the white man as he, guided by Inca informants, pushed on to the nearest oceanic islands.

S. Percy Smith, a noted authority on early Polynesian legends, wrote: "All through the race, everywhere we meet with it, we find a strain of light-coloured people who are not Albinos, but have quite light hair and fair complxion. With the Maoris this strain often runs in families for many generations; at other times it appears as a probable reversion to the original type from which the strain was derived. There are also traditions amongst the Maoris of a race of 'gods' called Pakepakeha, who are said always to live on the sea, and are white in complexion—hence the name Pakeha they gave to the white man on first becoming acquainted with us in the eighteenth century . . . We thus see that there is evidently a dim recollection of a white, or light-coloured, people retained in Polynesian traditions. When we come to inquire into the origin of this story, it is most natural to ascribe it to contact with a light-coloured race in very ancient times."[1]

In his study on *Polynesian Religion,* E. S. C. Handy wrote, after long residence in the Marquesas group, that the local islanders believed in two distinct ancestor gods, Tane, who "is said to have been 'white' and blond haired, and to have been the progenitor of the 'white' foreigners (*hao'e*), in contrast to Atea, the forefather of the native peoples, who was brown and darkhaired like them." He shows that on Mangaia it was another Polynesian god, Tangaroa (Tana-the-great), to whom blondness was attributed, his hair being of a red, sandy color, for which reason Captain Cook's party was received as the fair-haired sons of Tangaroa.[2] This confusion in early America and Polynesia between a venerated legendary people and the arriving Europeans brought fortune to the newcomers, although it cost Captain Cook his life. On his "discovery" of Hawaii he was mistaken for the white and fair-haired ancestor god Rono (Lono) and when the mistake was disclosed he was killed. His surviving companion, Captain King, afterward wrote: "they regarded us, generally, as a race of people superior to themselves; and used often to say, that great *Eatooa* [ancestor-gods] dwelled in our country."[3]

It is only against this historic background that we can understand why all these great people of ancient America and the adjacent ocean subjugated themselves so willingly to the European newcomers and permitted them to assume the role of supermen and discoverers.

The present chapter is a paper read for the 36th International Congress of Americanists convening in Barcelona in 1964 and subsequently published in the Congress Proceedings.

*   *   *

On 19 November 1567 two Spanish caravels left Callao harbor in Peru with an expedition of 150 men ordered by King Philip II of Spain to visit and convert to Christianity certain islanders in the Pacific Ocean not yet known to Europeans. The viceroy's nephew, Alvaro do Mendaña, was appointed commander of the two ships, and the party included the famous navigator and Inca chronicler, Sarmiento de Gamboa, on whose direct initiative the enterprise was organized. In 1559, after two years in Mexico and Guatemala, Sarmiento de Gamboa had come to Peru. Here he devoted his first seven years to a study of the aboriginal culture, which resulted in his important memorial to Philip II on the history of the Incas. Although it was Sarmiento who literally put an end to Inca history when he pursued and with his own hand captured the last Inca, Tupac Amaru, he was so interested in their oral literature that the Viceroy of Peru called him "the most able man on this subject that I have found in the country."[4] It was Sarmiento who first announced the repeated Inca claim that there were inhabited islands far out in the Pacific Ocean, and he was so insistent upon the truth of these Peruvian reports that he finally persuaded the Governor to dispatch an expedition to follow the old native sailing directions.

The favorable results of the two Mendaña expeditions are well known, but little attention has subsequently been paid to the Inca stimuli behind the Spanish enterprise. This is perhaps not so surprising. After all, the Solomon Islands encountered by the Spaniards were not in the area defined by the Inca informants. Furthermore, modern observers have assumed that aboriginal Inca craft were incapable of ocean voyaging. Nevertheless, in 1722, a century and a half after Sarmiento's attempt to follow the Inca sailing directions, the Dutch admiral Roggeveen accidentally stumbled across an inhabited island just where the earlier Spaniards had been told that it should be. However, when Roggeveen discovered Easter Island, the contemporary world had long since forgotten the Inca instructions which have survived for posterity only in the manuscript records of Sarmiento and his companions. This fact, combined with the present knowledge that balsa rafts equipped with *guara* in the Inca fashion are capable of return voyages to any part of the Pacific area, warrants a new background study of the Mendaña expeditions: that is, a re-examination of the original Inca reports and an analysis of Sarmiento's motives for believing the Peruvian accounts of extended voyages into the open Pacific.

The Spaniards had been associated with aboriginal Peruvians for forty years by the time Sarmiento convinced his government of the reality behind the Inca claims. In these early decades, before the great decline of the local culture, the conquistadors were unanimously impressed by the extent of aboriginal deep-sea navigation off Peru. The main attention of all the chroniclers was focused, naturally, on the important Inca headquarters in the interior highlands, where the tremendous wealth of the ruling classes was accumulated, yet history supports archaeology in describing a numerous and intrepid population of fishermen and merchants dwelling in large centers all along the unsheltered coast, basing their economy almost entirely on the riches of the offshore current.

Sarmiento and his contemporaries knew well that long-range Peruvian watercraft with Inca seafarers had been encountered by his countrymen nearly a year before they first reached the coast of Peru. Off northern Ecuador the first advancing forty-ton caravel, with ten Spaniards on board, encountered a northbound balsa raft of thirty tons' burden, with about twenty native men and women from Peru on board. The Spaniards were amazed at the fine rigging and the cotton sails used in the same manner as on their own caravel.[5] Five more merchant rafts navigating, like the first, with sails, were overtaken by Pizarro's advancing caravel before he reached Peru, and when finally approaching Tumbez, the Spaniards were met by a whole flotilla of balsa rafts standing out of the port and carrying Inca troops bound for Puna Island, forty miles beyond the horizon.

At the time of Sarmiento's own arrival in 1559, balsa rafts were still used for trade and transportation as far south as central and southern Peru, nearly two thousand miles from the actual balsa forests. The natives of the Chicama Valley communicated with Guayaquil, 500 miles to the north, with balsa rafts heavily laden with provisions and other cargo. Balsa rafts had also been employed by the Inca mariners for conveying guano from the Chincha Islands near Pisco and Paracas to the various provinces of the entire coast. Sarmiento's generation marveled at the aboriginal Peruvian seamanship and the buoyancy of their peculiar rafts. They spoke highly of the fine masts and yards, the native cotton canvas was praised as "excellent" and the native rope as "stronger than that of Spain."[6]

Until the time of Sarmiento the Spaniards had themselves made frequent use of the Inca mariners and their balsa rafts, which were able to enter surf and shallows where no European boat could venture. Oviedo describes, at the time of the Conquest, how Francisco Pizarro with all his people and horses were transported by sea to Puna Island on native sailing rafts navigated by local Indians.[7] Zárate also recorded how his contemporaries would embark with as many as fifty soldiers and three horses on individual balsa rafts, which they let the Indians navigate with their sails and paddles, "because the Indians are themselves great mariners."[8] Pedro Pizarro reported in 1571 how he personally, like Alonso de Mesa, Captain Soto, and many other prominent conquistadors, had been pushed off the rafts by the Peruvians in a heavy surf and were washed ashore half-drowned, while the skilled Inca mariners climbed back on to the rafts in the tumultuous sea and sailed away from the land.[9] Cieza de León and Zárate both wrote that the coastal Indians lived so much at sea that they had become like fishes, and recounted how they frequently detached logs from their rafts while at sea, so that their less seaminded enemies on board fell through and were drowned.[10] Inca Garcilasso reported that this treacherous trick was formerly repeatedly employed by the coastal dwellers when they were forced to transport highland Incas by sea. They cut the ropes and pushed their passengers into the ocean, saluting each other joyfully from balsa to balsa, "for those of the coast, being so used to the sea, had the same advantage over the inland Indians as marine animals have over those who live on the land."[11] These seaboard dwellers were daily on their large rafts and commonly spent weeks at sea with all their families and possessions. From the abundance of sea food harvested by them and the still more numerous owners of small reed boats in the treacherous current twenty to fifty miles off shore, even the inland Inca received fresh supplies of fish carried to the highlands by organized *caski* in two days.[12]

Inca Garcilasso shows that deep-sea fishing and long-range maritime trade and transport formed an integral part of the Inca economic system when Peru was conquered by the Spaniards.[13] References to this effect are made at least in passing by all contemporary chroniclers in spite of their reports being otherwise entirely focused on the riches and power of the highland rulers. In the judgment of Sarmiento and his contemporaries from Spain, Inca mariners with balsa rafts were able to venture as far into the unknown as any European vessel, and this explains why the conquistadors so readily believed in the Inca maritime information.

Turning next to some recorded examples of these rumors, traditions, and historical accounts that circulated throughout sixteenth-century Peru, we may well appreciate that they stirred the imagination of a navigator like Sarmiento and prompted him into action. As a leading Inca historian he became intrigued by the fact that the oral literature of the country contained repeated records of large-scale migration by balsa rafts, some departing, some arriving, and some representing lengthy two-way voyages with large numbers of rafts.

The region around the Ecuadorian harbor of Manta in the most northern extremity of the Inca Empire plays an important part in the seafaring accounts of the Inca. That was the area from which it was claimed that the supreme culture hero, Con-Tici-Viracocha, departed into the Pacific Ocean, and from which Inca Tupac Yupanqui, or Tupac Inca, subsequently left with his fleet in search of Pacific Islands. It is therefore noteworthy that Sarmiento and his companions did not select this northern area for their own departure, but started from the central Peruvian coast and headed for still more southern latitudes.

Tupac Inca was the grandfather of the Inca brothers the Spaniards met, and Sarmiento had forty-two of the leading Inca historians assembled at one time to get his history correct. He was therefore well aware of Tupac Inca's northern point of departure. About Tupac's conquest of the north coast, he wrote in 1572 that he was "fighting on land and sea in *balsas,* from Tumbez to Huanapi, Huamo, Manta, Turuca and Quisin. Marching and conquering on the coast of Manta, and the island of Puna, and Tumbez, there arrived at Tumbez, some merchants who had come by sea from the west, navigating in *balsas* with sails." Sarmiento goes on to record the story of how they gave information of some populated islands they had visited, accounts which tempted the highland Inca to seek his fortune at sea. "Yet he did not lightly believe the navigating merchants, for such men, being great talkers, ought not to be credited too readily."

However, Tupac's own necromancer gave him certain additional information through clairvoyance, and the Inca decided to visit the far islands. "He caused an immense number of *balsas* to be constructed, in which he embarked more than 20,000 chosen men; taking with him as captains Huaman Achachi, Cunti Yupanqui, Quihual Tupac (all Hanan-cuzcos), Yancan Mayta, Cachimapaca Macus Yupanqui, Llimpita Usca Mayta (Hurin-cuzcos); his brother Tilca Yupanqui being general of the whole fleet. Apu Yupanqui was left in command of the army which remained on land. Tupac Inca navigated and sailed on until he discovered the islands of Avachumbi and Ninachumbi, . . ."

The duration of this ocean voyage was recorded as nine months, whereas others among Sarmiento's informants said it took a year. When Tupac came back he had with him "black people" and other booty that was preserved in the Cuzco fortress until the Spaniards arrived. Sarmiento even interrogated the custodian who guarded these particular treasures.[14]

The Inca's northern starting point is also reported by Father Miguel Cabello de Balboa, who came to Peru a year before Sarmiento embarked in search of the Inca Islands. Of Tupac Inca, whom he referred to as King Topa, Balboa wrote: ". . . and having discussed his ideas and plans with his officers, he set out with his squadrons—now almost innumerable—and took lodgings in Manta, and in Charapoco, and in Piquara, because it would have been impossible in less space to lodge and sustain such a multitude of people as he had brought with him. It was in this place that King Topa Inga saw the ocean for the first time, upon which discovery he caused it to be profoundly worshiped, naming it Mamacocha, which means mother of the lakes. He got ready a large number of barges used by the natives, which were of hundreds of logs of notably light timber, fastened together one by one abreast, placing on top of the same a hundred floorings of reed-canes plaited together, making very secure and convenient vessels of the sort we have called Balsas. Then, having got together the abundance of these which would be needed for the number of troops who were to accompany him, and having chosen the most experienced pilots that could be found among the natives of these coasts, he went out on the ocean with the same courage and spirit that had governed his success since he was born. Of this voyage I say no more than can be readily believed, but those who have related the exploits of this valiant Inga, assure that on this voyage he remained at sea for the duration and extent of one year, some say more, and that he discovered certain islands which were named Hagua Chumbi and Nina Chumbi, and that these islands were situated in the South Seas, on the coast of which the Inga embarked."

Balboa reports also that "a great number of prisoners whose skin was black" were brought back to South America on board the Inca rafts.[15]

Before Sarmiento reached Peru, Betanzos, who arrived with the discoverers, had recorded the much older legend about the white Viracocha-people's departure from the same Manta coast, a tradition which filled the minds of the population throughout the Inca Empire far more than the recent voyage of Tupac Inca. It was firmly believed that the legendary culture hero Viracocha had walked with all his pre-Inca people northward from Tiahuanaco through Cuzco until they reached the Ecuadorian coast; assembling at Puerto Viejo near Manta, they then sailed away into the Pacific.[16] Sarmiento combined these universally believed Inca traditions with the historic fact stressed by him and known to all conquistadors, that when the Spaniards first appeared they were mistaken for white and bearded Viracocha people returning from the Pacific, a confusion which, as we have seen, permitted Pizarro and his little band of seafarers to conquer, without battle, the vast Inca Empire with its powerful armies and fortresses.[17]

That Inca Tupac chose to set sail from a northern port, which was selected also by his legendary predecessor, was probably no coincidence, for Manta is almost precisely where the equatorial line runs into the Pacific, and Tupac Inca, like Viracocha before him, worshiped the sun as his own ancestor and protector. Furthermore, Ecuador was the source of all balsa timber used for raft construction down the entire coast of the Inca Empire, and only by bringing his people to the local forests was it possible for the Inca to obtain the large quantity of balsa logs and bamboo required for building a whole fleet of seagoing rafts. It appears from Inca information which we will shortly consider, that the expedition subsequently steered toward the southern part of the ocean, a fact which led Sarmiento to search in a direction west-southwest from the harbor of Callao.

Seven hundred miles south of Manta, on the desert coast of northern Peru, the Spaniards heard equally vivid stories about Mochica migrations on balsa rafts. Father Miguel Cabello de Balboa wrote: "The people of Lambayeque say—and all the folk living with them—that in times so very ancient that they do not know how to express them, there came from the northerly part of this Piru, with a great fleet of

Balsas, a father of families, a man of much valor and quality named Naymlap; and with him he brought many concubines, but the chief wife is said to have been Ceterni. He brought in his company many people who followed him as their Captain and leader."[18]

The arrival of these balsa raft voyagers marked the establishment of the Chimu dynasty and culture, according to the natives of the north coast.

Corresponding stories with reference to the establishment of the Inca dynasty survived among the natives on the central coast of Peru until the last century.[19] According to the tribes around Lima, the first royal Incas came to power through fraud by deceiving the mountain people about their solar descent. This accusation was first recorded by the Jesuit Anello Oliva, who was one of the sixteenth-century settlers who came to live among the lowland population. He was told that the first royal Incas descended from mariners who sailed down from Ecuador: "Many made voyages along the coast and some were shipwrecked. At last one branch took up its abode on an island called Guayau, near the shores of Ecuador. On that island Manco Capac was born, and after the death of his father Atau he resolved to leave his native place for a more favorable clime. So he set out, in such craft as he had, with two hundred of his people, dividing them into three bands. Two of these were never heard of again, but he and his followers landed near Ica, on the Peruvian coast, and thence struggled up the mountains, reaching at last the shore of Lake Titicaca."[20]

Of course, Ica may never have seen the landing of the first Inca, but the rumors were there, and Ica could, since early pre-Inca times, compete with the coastal forest area in the north as a center of raft navigation. Father Joseph de Acosta recorded that the Indians at Ica, and also those of Arica 750 miles farther south, told the Spaniards that in ancient times they used to sail into the South Seas where they visited some islands very far away toward the west.[21] Acosta assumed that these pre-Spanish expeditions had taken place on rafts of inflated seal skin, but the numerous archaeological hardwood center boards and model log rafts excavated at Ica and Arica respectively show that precisely these two areas were very early pre-Inca centers of log-raft navigation.[22]

Arica and also Ilo, the two main ports on the coast directly below Tiahuanaco, were likewise specified as favorable starting points for the inhabited Pacific island described in Captain de Cadres' recorded interrogation of a wise old Indian named Chepo, said to be 115 or 120 years of age. Chepo said that the Indians used to embark at the ports of Arica and Ilo, and after two months' journey westward into the Pacific they would reach first a desert island called Coatu, in which there were three high mountains and many birds. On proceeding to the inhabited islands beyond they would keep this uninhabited bird island on the left, and would next reach an isolated island called Qüen, which was thickly populated and had a chief called Qüentique, and two others named Uquenique and Camanique. Ten days farther west was still another and larger populated island, Acabana. Threatened by death if he concealed the truth, old Chepo thereafter answered the eager captain with tales of great riches on these far islands. At last he volunteered of his own accord to add that rafts of wood were used for navigation. The contemporary Spaniards thought Chepo referred to the Solomon Islands, a name they used for all the rumored islands off Peru, but Amherst and Thompson, who published an English version of the old handwritten manuscript in 1901, thought he may have been relating a garbled version of an actual Indian voyage. They point out in a footnote that Easter Island, with barren Sala-y-Gómez in front of it, matches in a remarkable way the description recorded by Captain de Cadres.[23]

In fact, generations before Roggeveen came upon Easter Island by chance, old Chepo had given the Spaniards a precise sailing direction to that island from the most convenient ports on the south Peruvian coast. Today we know it to be a fact that, to reach the nearest inhabited island, a raft voyager from Ilo or Arica would first have to head for the barren bird island of Sala-y-Gómez, which for them is on a straight line to Easter Island. This raft voyage, aided by the trade winds and the southern curve of the outer Peru Current, would require roughly two months, exactly as stated by the old Indian. His description of Sala-y-Gómez is also to the point. The barren island is filled with birds that can be seen from great distances, and when first approached from the east it does actually look like three hills standing out against the sky. These three hills were recorded as the distinguishing feature by the first European discoverers and are so characteristic that modern maps frequently have Sala-y-Gómez marked erroneously as three separate islands. This impression is illusory, yet I have seen this islet almost awash in stormy weather, with only the three high points giving security to the numerous birds. Sala-y-Gómez must, quite correctly, be bypassed on the left side to keep the straight course from Ilo and Arica to Easter Island, the first of the inhabited islands. Mangareva is the next.

Chepo's reference to the supreme chief of Qüen as Qüentique is also interesting when considered with the fact that the Easter Island name for "chief" was recorded as *teque-teque*, probably *tiki-tiki*, by the first Spaniards who arrived in 1770.[24] Qüen-tique could therefore well be "chief" of the island Qüen.

Thus in south Peru the aborigines knew both the correct direction and the correct distance to Easter Island, and even pointed out the characteristics of the only landmark to be found *en route*. Exactly a thousand miles farther up the coast, at Callao, Sarmiento received equally precise sailing directions which show that the ancient Peruvians were able to pinpoint Easter Island's position through direct cross bearings. As is well known, internal trouble on the Mendaña expedition disrupted the original course set by Sarmiento on advice from the Indians, and it is here necessary to analyze briefly what happened.

In their excellent volumes on the expedition, Amherst and Thompson state that with the dawn of settled government in Peru the adventurers from Spain greedily absorbed the tales of undiscovered islands and a continent to the west which were current among the Indians and seafaring population of Callao. The babble of the taverns in time became debated questions at the Palace, and Pedro Sarmiento de Gamboa "professed to be able to fix the bearings of these islands; and the learned men in the colony were agreed that they were the outposts of a southern continent which stretched northward from Tierra del Fuego till it reached lat. 15 deg. S., about 600 leagues from Peru."

It is correct that there was general consent on the distance of about 600 leagues from Peru. In fact, as shown by the same authors, the provisions of the Mendaña expedition were calculated on the supposition that the land was 600 leagues distant from Callao harbor.[25] This is noteworthy, for, when Easter Island was first reached by Spaniards from Peru two centuries later, they gave the position as "about 600 leagues distant from Callao, and about the same from the mainland of Chile."[26] Actually, 600 leagues is slightly more than 2,000 nautical miles, and almost exactly the distance to Easter Island. Apart from the distance of 600 leagues there was one more point on which the members of the Mendaña expedition were in full agreement: the nearest island was supposed to be in a direction due west-southwest from Callao harbor. This is evident by comparing the narrative of the voyage written for Sarmiento with those written by his adversaries, the official expedition chronicler, Catoira, the expedition leader, Mendaña, the chief pilot, Gallego, and an anonymous manuscript by another educated member of the party. They must all have agreed that the reported island was due west-southwest from Callao, for all their logs show that for ten days (Gallego says twelve), they navigated tenaciously in that specific direction. This is the very precise bearing from Callao to Easter Island. At the end of November, still keeping this correct course, they had reached latitude 15° 45′ S, and here quarrels began. Sarmiento, although known as an uncongenial person, justly felt that he was the authority on the whereabouts of the islands. Writing in the third person he stresses that it was he, Pedro Sarmiento de Gamboa, who had given to the Governor of Peru "information concerning many islands and continents which he said existed in the Southern Ocean, and offered personally to discover them in the name of His Majesty, and with that intention he had collected proofs and made charts. . . . It was intended that they should follow the course west-southwest up to 23 degrees, which was the latitude that Pedro Sarmiento had fixed upon . . ."

Sarmiento's intention of searching in the ocean 600 leagues, i.e., about 2,000 miles west-southwest of Callao, would have brought him to the direct vicinity of Easter Island. His advance attempt at calculating the island's latitude was four degrees off, however, yet a fair error when we note that the chief pilot placed their own familiar port of Callao at 12° 30′ S, whereas it actually is 11° 56′. At 15° 45′ S it was this same chief pilot who suddenly disrupted the straight course for Easter Island, and began to sail due west. Sarmiento was furious at the interruption, and says in his report: "Pedro Sarmiento spoke to the General [Mendaña] about this change of course with much persistency, and told him publicly by word of mouth that he ought not to consent to it, and that he ought to have it altered, since he would miss the discovery and be lost . . ."

But young Mendaña supported the chief pilot, and the expedition now sailed west roughly along the 15th degree for twenty days. It was obvious to the entire expedition that the chief pilot broke the predetermined course far short of the 600 league mark stipulated by Sarmiento, but none objected. The reason was that Gallego, a long-time pilot along the coast of Peru and Chile, had personally received conflicting

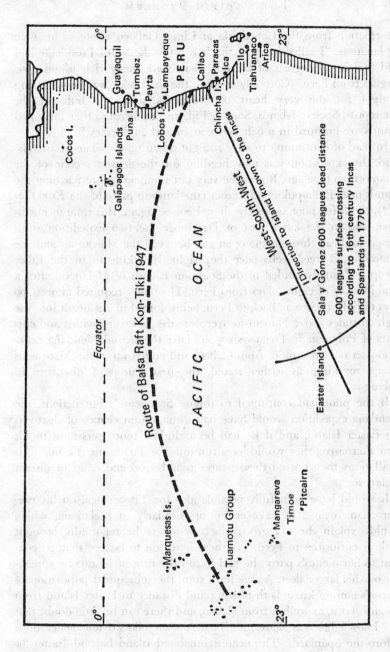

Sailing direction given by the Incas to the nearest inhabited island in the Pacific.

Within the image:

PERU

Guayaquil
Tumbez
Payta
Lambayeque
Callao
Ica
Paracas
Ilo
Tiahuanaco
Arica

Cocos I.
Puna I.
Lobos I.
Galápagos Islands
Chincha I.

0°
0°

23°

Equator

PACIFIC OCEAN

Route of Balsa Raft Kon-Tiki 1947

West-South-West known to the Incas

Direction to island to island distance

Sala y Gómez 600 leagues dead distance

600 leagues surface crossing according to 16th century Incas and Spaniards in 1770

Easter Island

Marquesas Is.

Mangareva
Timoe
Pitcairn

Tuamotu Group

23°
0°

information from the Cancillería at Lima. Gallego wrote as his own explanation: "I sailed in this latitude because the Señor Presidente had said that in 15 degrees of latitude there were many rich islands, 600 leagues from Peru." Correctly enough, the chief pilot was now steering straight for the very heart of Polynesia, since the bulk of the Tuamotus, Society Islands, Samoa, Fiji, and numerous other inhabited islands are grouped in a belt between 10 and 20 degrees S.

Instead of continuing to steer straight down upon isolated Easter Island, the expedition was now heading for the densest section of the Tuamotu archipelago. But at the very last moment before reaching the islands near Puka-puka and Raroia (the landing place of the *Kon-Tiki* raft), the fitful pilot suddenly altered course again, this time to northwest, and in the latter part of December the two expedition ships passed midway through the open gap between the Marquesas and the Tuamotus. Three weeks later they sighted Nukufetau in the Ellice group and finally landed in the Solomon Islands of Melanesia after a total journey of eighty days from Peru. They later required almost 400 days to fight their way back to Peru, being forced to sail north into the high latitudes above Hawaii to overcome the westward winds and currents of Polynesia.[27] Twenty-six years later the second Mendaña expedition set out once more from Callao, and ended up in the Marquesas group, marking, as earlier stated, the first European discovery in Polynesia.

If the pilot had continued to follow Sarmiento's instructions, the Mendaña expedition would have had a maximum chance of discovering Easter Island, and if he had been slightly more persistent in his own alternative, they would have run into the Tuamotus. Through his vacillations they missed these nearer islands and ended up in distant Melanesia.

It would have been fully possible also for Tupac Inca, on his pre-European voyage, to have ended up similarly in Melanesia, which would explain the numerous black prisoners he reportedly brought back as curiosities to Peru. Yet there is reason to believe that, in contrast to Sarmiento's party, he had found the nearest islands by spreading out his larger fleet. As we have seen, the subsequent population of Tupac's empire knew both bearing and distance to Easter Island from Ilo and Arica, as well as from Callao, and there can be little doubt that this knowledge was shared by Tupac's own pilots a few generations before the Spaniards. The nearest inhabited island beyond Easter Island is Mangareva at the southeastern extension of the Tuamotu archipelago. That this island was visited by Tupac and his fleet is corroborated by the local Polynesian population, whose main traditions are centered upon the visit of a foreign king named "Tupa." The local memory of this visitor was first published by F. W. Christian in 1924, who was unfamiliar with Inca history: "And the Mangarevans have a tradition of a chief named Tupa, a red man, who came from the east with a fleet of canoes of non-Polynesian model, more like rafts—surely a memory of some Peruvian *balsas,* or raftships."[28] Rivet in 1928, quoting Christian, was the first to suspect that the Mangarevans recalled a visit by Tupac Inca.[29] Buck next published additional details from the old Tiripone manuscript, written a few decades after the European arrival, by the son of a Mangarevan chief: "An important visitor to Mangareva was Tupa. The native history states that he came in the period of the brother kings Tavere and Taroi. . . . Tupa sailed to Mangareva through the southeast passage subsequently named Te-Ava-nui-o-Tupa (great-channel-of-Tupa)." Further: ". . . the voyager Tupa . . . sailed right down to Mangareva and lay afloat in the Great-pass-of-Tupa. He went ashore at the islet of Te Kava." The same native Polynesian manuscript states that before Tupa returned to his own country "he told the Mangarevans about a vast land . . . which contained a large population ruled by powerful kings."[30]

The Kava islet on the east reef where, according to Mangareva traditions, Tupa disembarked, and the Great Ava of Tupa, which was the mooring place of his fleet of rafts, directly recall the Inca reference to Ava-island, or Ava-chumbi, one of the two islands visited by Tupac's fleet. The other island was referred to as Nina-chumbi, or Fire-island, a perfect name for Easter Island as it would appear to an arriving voyager. All the early visitors, from Roggeveen and Gonzalez to Beechey, describe how the natives lit numerous fires and sent up columns of smoke around the coast, possibly to signal to the newcomers when they approached. Several observers have suggested that Fire-island may refer to the Galápagos group, with its normally extinct volcanoes, but, as we shall see in Chapter 10, the Galápagos group was well known to the Incas and had no permanent inhabitants.[31] The "black" people could well have been selected from among the aboriginals of Mangareva, where Beechey, the European discoverer, found some individuals in the extremely mixed population who were as dark as Melanesians.[32] Black captives would be the only curiosity for the powerful Inca to bring home from the poor Stone Age people of the Pacific islands. He must have returned to Peru just as disappointed as the gold-greedy Mendaña expedition, and possibly along a similar northern route, touching Mexico or Central America, where the dark-skinned prisoners could be supplemented by the metal throne and other souvenirs seen by the Spaniards at the time of Tupac's grand-children.

The lack of gold and other treasures on the islands discovered, combined with the extremely difficult return voyage to Peru, will explain why all the Mendaña discoveries were lost again for about two centuries, until rediscovered by other Europeans in the latter half of the eighteenth century. Even in this indifference toward the possibility of taking possession of the poor islands they had discovered, the Spanish rulers of Peru followed the pattern set by their Inca predecessors.

Chapter 8

Balsa Raft Navigation

THE GENERAL impression among visitors to modern Polynesia is that dugout canoes with a single outrigger are the only type of watercraft familiar to the aboriginal settlers of these islands. We have seen in Chapter 6, however, that the Polynesians reached the East Pacific ignorant of any kind of outrigger. The double outrigger typical of Indonesia never reached any Polynesian tribe, but whereas the Maori of New Zealand remained forever without any outrigger on their canoes, the tribes on the tropical islands obtained the Melanesian single outrigger secondarily upon marginal contact with neighboring Fiji.

But what about rafts? Surely they would not be appropriate to a maritime people like the Polynesians? This is another erroneous conception common to those who take a superficial attitude to the problem. When the *Kon-Tiki* raft landed on Raroia of the Tuamotu group, the first exclamation by the islanders who found us was that our vessel was a *paepae,* the widespread Polynesian term for a raft. Indeed, those who feel that rafts are out of place in Polynesia might equally have asked, when some years later I had Polynesians re-erect a stone statue on Easter Island: Why work with stone colossi in Polynesia, for everybody knows that the Polynesian tribes are exclusively carpenters and wood carvers who never quarry stone? This is in fact true. However, the fact that the present-day Polynesians carve only wood and that they fish from outrigger canoes does not necessarily exclude stone sculptors and raft voyagers from having formed an early substratum within this same area. We must not forget that the

Polynesian culture is a composite one; more than one people entered the island area of the East Pacific.

In their exhaustive three-volume study, *Canoes of Oceania,* A. C. Haddon and J. Hornell refer to reports about balsa-like rafts formerly seen in use in the Society Islands, and add: "This information brings the Society Islands into line with the Marquesas Islands and with Mangareva, Samoa, Tonga, Fiji, and New Zealand, whose people were all well acquainted with the navigational use of rafts. It supports the view that rafts were utilized freely in some at least of the movements from island to island of the first migrants into Oceania."

Speaking subsequently of the wash-through type of raft-ship which was the only watercraft of the Chatham islanders, they say that its presence in this Polynesian group "lends weight to the hypothesis that much of the earliest movement in the Pacific was effected by men who employed some form of sailing raft in their voyaging from island to island."[1]

In a special study of South American balsa rafts, Hornell diverges into the adjacent island area with the following comment: "Everywhere throughout Oceania we come across evidence of the present or past use of rafts. In Mangareva . . . virtually the easternmost island of any importance in Polynesia with the exception of Easter Island, sailing rafts are or were until recently in use approximating closely in form to that of the sailing balsa of Ecuador."[2]

Indeed, on Mangareva, the very island where the memory of the visit of the foreign king Tupa is preserved, no other vessels were in use when Captain Beechey arrived by way of South America and came upon the island in 1825. He found no canoes at all in the Gambier group, but published drawing of thirteen Mangarevans sailing a log raft, and stated that these rafts were from forty to fifty feet long and would carry upward of twenty persons.[3]

Side by side with the log raft, the second type of Peruvian watercraft, the reed boat, also had a scattered distribution in former Polynesia, recorded from all three corners of the Polynesian triangle. In her paper on *Traces of Reed Boats in the Pacific,* R. Knudsen shows that Hawaiian folklore includes several references to canoes made of reeds. Important legendary ancestors like Kana and the blond god Lono for which Cook was mistaken are associated with navigation in boats made of reeds and wickerwork.[4]

On Easter Island reed boats like those of Peru were still in use dur-

Old drawing of balsa raft from Guayaquil, from Juan and Ulloa, 1748: (a) bow; (b) stern; (c) thatched hut; (d) poles serving as masts; (e) kind of bowsprit; (f) centerboards; (g) centerboard serving as rudder; (h) cooking place; (i) water bottles; (k) mainstays; (l) flooring or deck.

Early drawing of Easter Island statues still standing on stepped *ahu*

platforms, with topknots on head (from La Pérouse, 1786).

A long-ear of Easter Island as drawn by Captain Cook's artist, Hodges, in 1777.

ing religious competitions when Europeans first arrived, and as seen in the following chapter the reed used was the same as the *totora* of the Peruvian reed boats. According to a test made with a totora reed boat brought from Lake Titicaca to the Pacific coast by W. Castro in 1956, after fourteen months of continuous immersion in salt water it showed no signs of waterlogging, rot, or damage by marine fauna. This papyrus-like and very buoyant reed is, however, a strictly American fresh-water plant that had reached no further than the crater lakes of Easter Island. In spite of the lack of suitable local reeds, however, the tradition of reed boat construction survived as far west as New Zealand when the Europeans arrived there. J. S. Polack, an early trader residing among the Maoris from 1831 to 1837, wrote: "Among the early occupants of New Zealand canoes were made entirely of the bulrush. We have seen, between Kaipara and Hokianga, one of these vessels of olden time, nearly sixty feet in length, capable of holding as many persons, but they are wholly in disuse. They were remarkably thick, formed entirely of rushes, except the thwarts, and resembled the model of a canoe in every particular. They were remarkably light . . . though many bundles of rushes were consumed in forming them, and were paddled with much velocity, until saturated, when they settled down in the water. These vessels are no longer formed, and specimens are extremely rare."[5]

In his study of *The Maori Canoe,* E. Best reproduces an old sketch of such a Maori reed boat, termed *mokihi,* together with a drawing of a South American reed boat from Lake Titicaca, to show the striking resemblance.[6] Hornell, too, is aware of this conformity with Peruvian boatbuilding, and adds with reference to a second type of Maori reed craft: "A still more primitive form of the *mokihi,* as these rafts were called, was analogous to the *caballito* of Peru astride which the fisherman sits, propelling himself by paddling." He adds: "A detail which may have considerable bearing upon the elucidation of the problem under consideration is the fact that in the binding together of the reed bundles of the Titicaca *balsas,* plaited reed braid is used instead of cord laid in the manner of rope. The Polynesians similarly employed plaited braid for all kinds of lashings, but in their case it was made of coconut fiber, the most suitable material available to them. The 'sennit,' as it is called, is made by exactly the same technique as the reed braid of Peru."[7]

Since canoes were thus by no means the only vessels known inside

Polynesia, and since Polynesia lies well within the reach of South American watercraft as so far shown by thirteen manned rafts in recent decades, it is relevant to include an examination of aboriginal Peruvian maritime activities in the study of Polynesian origins.

The present chapter is based on a combination of my article "The Balsa Raft in Aboriginal Navigation off Peru and Ecuador" published in the *Southwestern Journal of Anthropology* (Vol. 11, no. 3) by the University of New Mexico in 1955, and a lecture on "Guara Sailing Technique Indigenous to South America" delivered before the 33rd International Congress of Americanists in Costa Rica in 1958 and subsequently published in the *Acts of the Congress.*

*   *   *

The Seaworthiness of Balsa-wood Sailing Rafts in Early South America

Aboriginal navigation in Peru and adjoining sections of northwestern South America is a subject that has been little known and still less understood by modern boatbuilders and anthropologists. The apparent reason is that the local boatbuilding was based on principles entirely different from those of our own ancestry. As earlier commented upon, to the European mind the only seaworthy vessel is one made buoyant by a watertight, air-filled hull, so big and high that it cannot be filled by the waves. To the ancient Peruvians the size was of less importance; the only seaworthy craft was one which could never be filled by water because its open construction formed no receptacle to retain the invading seas, which washed through. Their object was thus achieved by building exceedingly buoyant, raft-like vessels of balsa timber or other very light wood, or of bundles of reeds or canes lashed together in boat fashion, or by making pontoons of inflated seal skins carrying a sort of deck.

Such craft tend to appear primitive, incommodious, and unsafe to anyone who is unfamiliar with their qualities at sea, and this can be the only reason for the widespread and erroneous assumption that the peoples of ancient Peru were without seagoing craft or capable sailors in spite of their 2,000 mile coastline and their outstanding cultural level in nearly all other respects.

When I first attempted, in 1941,[8] to call attention to the possibilities of early Peruvian navigation, the balsa raft was accorded little interest among the few anthropologists who were familiar with its existence as a pre-European culture element, and many had even overlooked the fact that it went under sail in pre-European time. Regular sails were not recorded from other parts of aboriginal America. The general impression appeared to concur with the judgment of Hutchinson in his *Anthropology of Prehistoric Peru* of 1875, where the balsa raft was merely described as "a floating bundle of corkwood."[9] Three modern writers, Lothrop,[10] Means,[11] and Hornell,[12] had presented interesting papers on aboriginal Peruvian craft and navigation, with excellent descriptions of the building principles of the balsa raft, but, on purely theoretical grounds, as we shall see later, they all judged the balsa raft to be water absorbent and useless for navigation in the open sea.

It was against a background of such prejudice that I was stimulated to a further study and reappraisal of Peruvian navigation, since I was led by other observations to suspect that Peruvian balsa rafts had traveled as far as to the islands at Polynesia, 4,000 miles away.

The first record of a Peruvian balsa raft antedates the actual discovery of the Inca Empire. When Francisco Pizarro left the Panama Isthmus in 1526 on his second and more progressive voyage of discovery down the Pacific coast of South America, his expedition encountered Peruvian merchant sailors at sea long before he discovered their country. His pilot, Bartolomeo Ruiz, was sailing ahead to explore the coast southward near the equator, when off northern Ecuador his ship suddenly met another sailing vessel of almost equal size, coming in the opposite direction. The northbound vessel proved to be a large raft, and its crew were the first Peruvians ever seen by Europeans. Immediately afterward a report was sent to Charles V by Juan de Sáamanos, and the episode was recorded even before Peru itself had been visited.[13] The event was also narrated in 1534 by Pizarro's own secretary, Francisco de Xeres.[14] From both sources we learn that the large balsa raft was captured by the Spaniards, who found a crew of twenty Indian men and women aboard. Eleven were thrown overboard, four were left with the raft, and two men and three women were retained aboard the caravel to be trained as interpreters for the later voyages.

The balsa raft was a merchant vessel heavily laden with cargo. The Spaniards estimated its capacity at thirty toneles, or about thirty-six tons, as compared with the forty tons of their own caravel, which carried only half as many persons as did the balsa raft. The cargo was carefully listed by the Spaniards, and included some items which could only have come from Peru proper.[15]

The craft was described by Sáamanos as a flat raft, composed of an underbody of logs covered by a deck of slender canes raised so that crew and cargo remained dry while the main logs were awash. The logs as well as the canes were lashed securely together with henequen rope. Sáamanos says of the sail and rigging of the raft: "It carried masts and yards of very fine wood, and cotton sails in the same shape and manner as on our own ships. It had very good rigging of the said henequen, which is like hemp, and some mooring stones for anchors formed like grindstones."[16]

Ruiz now returned to Pizarro with his prisoners and booty, and a few months later a new expedition, led by Pizarro, pushed southward to the northern coasts of the Inca Empire. On the way to Santa Clara Island in the open Gulf of Guayaquil, Pizarro overhauled five sailing balsas in two days, and opened favorable negotiations with their crews. Then he crossed the Gulf to the Peruvian port of Tumbez, the home of some of his raft captives. When approaching the coast the Spaniards saw a whole flotilla of balsa rafts standing toward them, carrying armed Inca troops. Running alongside the fleet Pizarro invited some of the Inca captains aboard his vessel, and by establishing friendly relations through his interpreters—those captured from the first raft encountered—he learned that the whole flotilla was bound for Puna Island, which was then under Peruvian rule.

Other balsa rafts came out of the bay with friendship gifts and provisions for the Spaniards, and we learn from Francisco Pizarro's cousin, Pedro, that a little farther down the Peruvian coast the Spaniards overtook some balsa rafts, aboard which they found precious metals and some of the clothes of the country, all of which they kept, so that they might take them to Spain to show the king.[17]

But even before Ruiz captured the first merchant balsa off Ecuador, the Spaniards had already heard rumors about Peruvian navigation from the natives of Panama. The chronicler Las Casas, son of Columbus' companion, stated that the aborigines in Peru possessed balsa rafts in which they navigated with sails and paddles, and that this fact was also known in pre-Conquest times to the eldest son of Comogre, a great chief in Panama, who spoke to Father Cabello de Balboa of a rich coastal empire to the south where people navigated the Pacific Ocean with ships a little smaller than those of the Spaniards, propelled by sails and paddles.[18]

Several of Pizarro's contemporaries recorded details of the craft navigated by the coastal natives of Ecuador and northern Peru, notably Oviedo, Andagoya and Zárate.[19] Their similar accounts describe rafts made of "long and light logs," an odd number—five, seven, nine, or eleven—tied together with cross beams covered by a deck; the navigation with sails and paddles; the ability of the large ones to carry up to fifty men and three horses; and the construction of a special cooking place on board. Oviedo describes, as we have seen, how Francisco Pizarro and all his people and horses were transported by sea to Puna Island on native sailing rafts navigated by local Indians. Andagoya, who took part in the earliest expeditions of discovery northward and southward along the Pacific coast, was particularly impressed by the quality of the native henequen rope, stronger than that of Spain, and the excellent cotton canvas. In describing the ability of the local natives to navigate with regular sails, Zárate stated that the raftsmen of Peru were great mariners (*grandes marineros*). As we have seen in the previous chapter, they played fatal tricks on many of the Spaniards who had voyaged as passengers on their balsa rafts.

The Italian traveler Girolamo Benzoni, who came to Peru about 1540, published a very primitive drawing of a small-sized Peruvian balsa raft of seven logs, carrying eight Indians navigating offshore with a small sail hoisted on a straddling double mast. In his text he states that there were rafts for navigating which were much greater, made up of nine or eleven logs, carrying sails which varied according to the size of the raft.[20]

Inca Garcilasso de la Vega, who was of Inca descent and left Peru for Spain in 1560, devotes most of his attention to the wash-through fishing craft of reeds or rushes which were numerous and by far the dominant vessel along the Peruvian coast; he says they usually went from four to six leagues off the coast (fifteen to twenty-four English miles), and more if necessary. He adds that when the natives wanted to convey large cargoes they used the rafts of wood on which they hoisted sails when they navigated the open sea.[21]

Father Reginaldo de Lizarraga, who came to Peru in the same year that Inca Garcilasso left, says of the natives of the Chicama Valley: "These Indians are great mariners; they have large rafts of light timber with which they navigate the ocean, and while fishing they remain many leagues out at sea." He also told how the native merchants of the Chicama Valley communicated with Guayaquil, five hundred miles to the north, by means of their balsa rafts heavily laden with sea food and other cargo.[22]

As we have seen, Father Cabello de Balboa, who came to Peru in 1566, learned from the Inca historians that some two or three generations before the arrival of Pizarro, Inca Tupac Yupanqui had descended to the coast, and, selecting some of the best local pilots, had embarked with a whole army upon a vast number of rafts and sailed away from the coast. He was absent for about a year before he returned with his flotilla to his own empire.[23] Also, the chronicler Sarmiento de Gamboa in 1572 recorded these Inca accounts of voyages by balsa rafts to distant Pacific islands, and, as shown, this famous navigator admits that it was the rumors of Peruvian merchant sailors with balsa rafts and the account of Inca Tupac Yupanqui's voyage of discovery which prompted him to urge the Peruvian viceroy to organize the Mendaña expedition.[24]

The prominent early historian of Peru, Bernabe Cobo, went into considerable detail in describing the remarkable qualities of the balsa timber used for the ocean-going rafts, and also the native ability to navigate and swim. He added: "The largest rafts used by the Peruvian Indians living near the forests, like those of the harbors of Payta, Manta, and Guayaquil, are composed of seven, nine, or more logs of balsa timber, in the following manner: The logs are lashed one to the other lengthwise by means of lianas or ropes tied over other logs which lie as cross beams; the log in the middle is longer than the others at the bow, and one by one they are shorter the closer they are placed to the sides, in such a way that, at the bow, they get the same form and proportions as seen on the fingers of an extended hand, although the stern is even. On the top of this they place a platform so that the people and the clothing on board shall not get wet from the water which comes up in the cracks between the large timbers. These rafts navigate on the ocean by means of sail and paddles, and some are so large that they are easily able to carry fifty men."[25]

The next crude illustration of a balsa raft under sail was drawn by Admiral Joris van Spilbergen on his voyage around the world in 1614 to 1617. Spilbergen states that when this balsa raft entered Paita harbor, 120 miles south of the Peruvian port of Tumbez, its crew of five natives had been away fishing for two months, and came back with enough provisions on their raft to distribute to the whole Dutch fleet anchored in the bay.[26] The interesting feature in Spilbergen's otherwise crude drawing of the event is that it shows the crew in action on board the raft, two of them attending to the sail, while the other three are navigating the raft without paddles or steering oar, simply by raising and lowering centerboards inserted in cracks between the logs. The use of centerboards was an art which was completely unknown to boatbuilders in Europe until about 1870, more than 250 years later.

The first unsuccessful attempt to introduce centerboard navigation to Europe was in 1748, by the Spanish naval officers G. Juan and A. de Ulloa. Twelve years earlier they had made an interesting survey of the ingenious art of aboriginal balsa raft navigation in Guayaquil Bay. They published an excellent drawing of a balsa raft at sea, showing such details as the arrangement of the bipod mast with its sail and rigging, the thatched hut amidship, the cooking place with open fire and the storage of water jars astern, and the position of the centerboards inserted near the bow and stern. They claim emphatically that a native crew with sufficient skill in manipulating the centerboards could sail a balsa raft in any wind as well as a regular ship.[27]

Later M. Lescallier published another drawing of a large nine-log balsa raft with a spacious dwelling amidship and a crew navigating at sea simply by means of centerboards and a huge square sail on a bipod mast. Lescallier's work, published in 1791 under order of the King of France to serve as instruction for the naval cadets, included a good description of the aboriginal balsa raft and its remarkable steering principles still employed only among the natives on the northwest coast of South America. With Juan and Ulloa as his main source, Lescallier emphasized that if the principles of this native centerboard navigation had been known in Europe, many shipwrecked men would have saved their lives by sailing their rafts to the nearest port.[28]

In 1801 J. Charnock, in his great history of marine architecture, made another fruitless effort to introduce the ingenious art of centerboard navigation to the outside world, stating that this method of steering was an art peculiar to the coastal Indians of Peru and Ecuador and hitherto unknown in Europe.[29]

Alexander Humboldt in 1810 presented a beautiful illustration in water color of a large sail-carrying balsa raft with centerboard and fireplace astern;[30] and in 1825 W. B. Stevenson gave an excellent description of the larger balsa rafts that still covered the coast of the former

Chimu habitat as far down as to Huanchaco, south of Chicama. Some of these larger rafts had thatched bamboo huts with four or five rooms, and they were "beating up against the wind and current a distance of four degrees of latitude, having onboard five or six quintals (25 or 30 tons) of goods as a cargo, besides a crew of Indians and their provisions." Stevenson, too, describes the centerboards and says: "By raising or lowering these boards in different parts of the balsa, the natives can perform on their raft all the maneuvers of a regularly built and well-rigged vessel . . ."[31]

In an unpublished manuscript of 1840, written by George Blaxland and preserved in the Mitchell Library of Sydney, the author reproduces a drawing of a nine-log balsa raft, with sail and centerboards as the only means of navigation. The manuscript also contains a report from an officer of one of Her Majesty's ships, who had encountered a native Peruvian family on a balsa raft at the island of Lobos de Afuera about sixty miles off the Peruvian coast. The natives were just preparing a raft voyage to the invisible mainland against a contrary wind: ". . . they had been absent from their Native Village three weeks, and were about to return with a Cargo of Dried Fish, the family consisted of Nine persons, with a Number of Dogs, and all their goods and chattels. . . . The Vessel I was in, a schooner of 40 tons, sailed for the same place in company, and it was surprising to see the manner the raft held the Wind, going at the rate of four or five knots an hour; we kept together for some time and arrived the next day within a few hours of each other; . . . The whole of the lading of vessels on some parts of the Coast is made entirely by these balsas and at Lambeyeque in consequence of the heavy surf rolling on the shore, a landing cannot be effected but by them; they also carry salt from one port to another two or three hundred miles apart, another proof they are trustworthy."[32]

In 1841 we get a detailed technical draft by F. E. Paris in his essay on naval construction among non-European peoples. Paris was in South America in time to see the aboriginal Peruvian balsa rafts before they were displaced by European boat types at the turn of the century, but he studied them only while they were moored in the bay. Although he carefully drew and described the centerboards, or *guara,* as they were termed by the natives, he did not fully understand their technique or function, stating merely that: "These are driven in to a greater or lesser degree, fore or aft, in order to luff or go about. The rafts have no other methods for steering on the ocean . . ."[33]

It is quite obvious that a *guara,* or centerboard, as opposed to a paddle or steering oar, could only be used in connection with a sail. Without a sail a centerboard had no function and no effect. This has already been pointed out by S. K. Lothrop[34] and others, and is an important fact in view of the many centerboards which are found archaeologically in the desert graves on the north and south coast of Peru. The beautifully ornamented hardwood centerboards from the numerous graves of Paracas and Ica in southern Peru show that sail-carrying rafts were important culture elements even in these southern latitudes, and at periods which not only antedate written history, but even take us right back into pre-Inca time. W. C. Bennett, for instance, illustrates one of these beautifully carved and painted centerboards from a pre-Inca tomb on the south coast of Peru.[35]

Archaeology also furnishes with some minor but rather important details which remained unrecorded by the early chroniclers and historic observers, namely, how the lashings were secured to the slippery logs, and how the individual logs were shaped in the bow and stern to diminish the water resistance. Such information may be gained from the tiny model rafts—more properly intended as spirit rafts—which have been found in great numbers in the Arica desert graves on the Pacific coast below Lake Titicaca. These prehistoric rafts were left there more than a thousand years before the arrival of Pizarro and the first Europeans, and show that the lashings, of hemp rope or strips of seal hide, were fastened in grooves cut around the logs. They also show that to decrease the water resistance each log was pointed boat-fashion fore and aft.[36] One small raft excavated by M. Uhle and published in 1922 was fitted with a square sail of reeds similar to that used until the present day by the neighboring mountain Indians of Lake Titicaca.[37] It was this discovery in a grave from the primitive fisher population at Arica, dated to the first centuries A.D., which made E. Nordenskiöld conclude that "The sail was probably known on the Peruvian coast earlier than pottery and weaving . . ."[38]

As earlier quoted from Inca Garcilasso, the most numerous craft along the desert coast of aboriginal Peru was the reed raft of the individual fishermen; the wooden rafts with sail were used only for transporting heavy cargo and for regular ocean voyaging. The principal Peruvian ports for wooden rafts in Inca time were Paita and Tum-

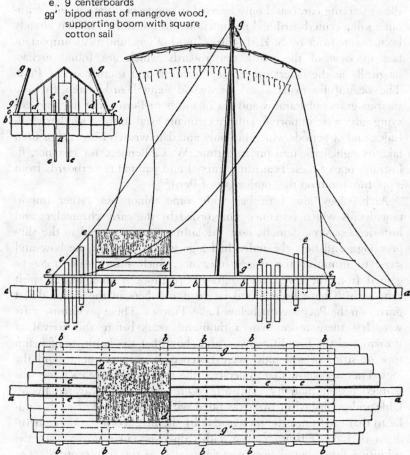

a . 9 main balsa logs
b . 7 cross beams of balsa
c . elevated deck platform
d . hut of canes with thatched roof
e . 9 centerboards
gg' bipod mast of mangrove wood,
    supporting boom with square
    cotton sail

Length of raft up to 80.90 ft.
Width of raft up to 25.30 ft.
Carrying capacity 20.25 tons.

The building principles of the aboriginal balsa raft of northwestern South America. Plan made in Guayaquil by F. E. Paris (1841–43).

bez and other villages on the northern coast near the great balsa forests of Ecuador, but until about 1900 important balsa raft ports were recorded as far down as Sechura, Lambayeque, Pacasmayo, and Huanchaca, 500 miles south of Guayaquil. In Inca time the balsa rafts were employed still another 500 miles to the south, conveying guano for fertilizer from the Chincha Islands near Pisco to the various provinces of Peru. The Incas even transported balsa logs overland for the construction of buoyant rafts in remote corners of their empire. Thus, when the first Spaniards under Hernando Pizarro advanced down the highlands of the Andes from Cuzco, they found in what today is Bolivia great quantities of large balsa timber transported there on the backs of native laborers to build wooden balsa rafts on Lake Titicaca for the pleasure of Inca Huayna Capac.[39]

By combining historical and archaeological information, we thus possess a considerable knowledge of the construction principles and local importance of the peculiar raft which permitted aboriginal navigation in Peru and adjacent Pacific waters. Accordingly, when the noted Americanist S. K. Lothrop in 1932 compiled material for his interesting paper on "Aboriginal Navigation off the West Coast of South America" he was able to give a good picture of the local balsa raft. However in judging its seagoing ability, he stated that it "absorbs water rapidly and loses its buoyancy completely after a few weeks. Owing to this characteristic it was necessary to take the *Jangada* (balsa raft) apart at intervals, haul the logs ashore, and there allow them to dry out completely." Lothrop therefore concluded that the balsa raft was unfit for oversea voyages, and that it could not travel as far as to the Polynesian islands, not even to the Galápagos group a few hundred miles offshore.[40]

Lothrop quoted G. Byam as his source for this information. Byam, however, a nineteenth-century British traveler, was personally unacquainted with balsa rafts. In his book of 1850 we find indeed that his sailing ship met a seafaring balsa raft off Cabo Blanco in north Peru. But the raft is described as merely sighted in the distance while tacking southward against a fresh breeze, and whatever additional information Byam gave concerning its buoyancy was merely quoted as the theoretical opinion of the captain of his ship.[41] Inadvertently Lothrop thus came to introduce a heresy of wide consequences into anthropological literature.

Lothrop's study was otherwise a valuable contribution, and few anthropologists have afterward cared to penetrate further into the question. Some additional material was brought up by the noted Inca authority P. A. Means in 1942. In his interesting paper on "Pre-Spanish Navigation Off the Andean Coast," referring to Lothrop, Means accepts the same negative view in his theoretical judgment of the balsa raft, saying: ". . . it was obviously a type of boat that would awake nothing but scorn in the breasts of shipbuilders of almost any other maritime people in the world." He concludes: "Altogether, we are justified in concluding that in Peruvian native navigation prior to the Spanish conquest, the balsa-log raft, with sails, deckhouse, and cargo space, was the least contemptible and the least inefficient of craft known. This, admittedly, is faint praise; but, in view of the facts, it is the best that can be given to the boatbuilding art of those singularly unmarine-minded people, the ancient Andeans."[42]

The noted authority on aboriginal craft and navigation J. Hornell was led to bring up the same subject in 1945, first in his paper, "Was There a Pre-Columbian Contact Between the Peoples of Oceania and S. America?" and next in 1946 in his paper "How Did the Sweet Potato Reach Oceania?" Hornell was confident that the early Peruvians had influenced the Polynesian island agriculture, and was therefore careful in his judgment of the balsa raft, yet he concludes: "Certainly no ordinary, untreated balsa raft could make a prolonged oversea voyage unless the Incas' seamen knew of an effective method of treating its absorbent logs with some kind of waterproofing composition . . ."[43]

The confident negative attitude among the few Americanists who had actually surveyed the main principles of Peruvian boatbuilding had a double effect on modern anthropology. By labeling the balsa raft as "not seaworthy," they deprived the aboriginal Peruvians of their principal means of navigation and generally deemed them a notably unmaritime and landlocked people. This one-sided picture of the early high cultures in Pacific South America penetrated the technical as well as the general literature, and it soon biased the study of important problems in Polynesian anthropology as well.

In 1932 the prominent Pacific scholar R. B. Dixon succeeded in proving that the sweet potato had been carried by man from Peru to Polynesia in pre-Spanish time, accompanied by its Quechua-Peruvian name *kumara,* and pointing to the balsa rafts, he suggested that Peruvian or other American Indians had been responsible for the transfer.[44] In the same year Lothrop published his aforesaid survey of Peruvian navigation, and two years later Dixon came back with a new publication, now staring: "Since we have no evidence that at any time the Indians of the Pacific Coast of South America where the sweet potato was grown had either the craft or the skill for making long sea journeys, we are forced to conclude that the transference of the plant was carried out by Polynesians."[45]

Correspondingly, the Polynesian archaeologist K. P. Emory had originally written in 1933, with regard to the ancient great-stone masonry of Easter Island, the Society Islands, the Marquesas, Hawaii, Tubuai, and the Tonga group: "It is quite within reason to entertain an American origin for a cultural element so specialized as this stone facing. It is a conspicuous element localized in the part of America nearest to Polynesia, a part where currents strike out and flow in the direction of Easter Island and the Tuamotus. . . . May not one of the seagoing rafts of the early Incas have been swept into this current carrying survivors as far as Easter Island 2,000 miles to the west?"

In a subsequent publication of 1942 he too was led to abandon his view, since, as he states, Dixon had in the meantime pointed out to him that the balsa raft of Pacific South America quickly became waterlogged.[46] In a publication by A. E. Morgan of 1946 the author in turn quotes Emory, who wrote to him on request that "balsa rafts become waterlogged in a few days if not taken out of the water to dry."[47]

At this time the verdict on the balsa raft had virtually grown into an axiom, and when Buck in 1945 published his *Introduction to Polynesian Anthropology,* he eliminated one half of the Pacific borderlands by simply stating: "Since the South American Indians had neither the vessels nor the navigating ability to cross the ocean space between their shores and the nearest Polynesians islands, they may be disregarded as the agents of supply."[48]

With the same confidence J. E. Weckler wrote in 1943 in his monograph on *Polynesian Explorers of the Pacific* that "no American Indians had seagoing ships that were capable of such passages as the voyage to Polynesia."[49]

This belief had such a firm grip on the minds of both Americanists and Pacific anthropologists that, when I attempted to oppose it in a publication of 1941,[50] I naturally met with no response. There appeared to be in the end only one way to settle the dispute, namely to construct a replica of the craft under discussion and to derive a satisfactory answer through a practical test. Therefore, in 1947, I organized and led what became the *Kon-Tiki* expedition.

The raft, named *Kon-Tiki* after the departed culture hero of Peru and the pan-Polynesian ancestor god Tiki, was composed of nine two-foot-thick balsa logs, ranging in length from thirty to forty-five feet, the longest in the middle, and lashed to cross-beams supporting a bamboo deck and an open hut. A bipod mast, carrying a square sail, five *guara* (centerboards), and a steering-oar completed the construction. The raft was launched off the Callao harbor in Peru on April 28, 1947, with a crew of six men; ninety-three days later the first inhabited Polynesian island was sighted and passed. After a total journey of 4,300 miles in 101 days, the *Kon-Tiki* grounded on the reef of Raroia atoll in the Tuamotu Islands, with crew and nearly all the cargo safe.

The object of the expedition had been to test and study the true qualities and abilities of the balsa raft, and what was more, to get an answer to the old and disputed question of whether the Polynesian islands were within feasible reach of the raftsmen of ancient Peru.

It proved to be an exceedingly seaworthy craft, perfectly adapted for carrying heavy cargoes in the open and unsheltered ocean. Of all the valuable qualities none surprised and impressed us more than its outstanding safety and seaworthiness in all weather conditions. Next to its unique ability to ride the waves came perhaps its carrying capacity, which however, was no surprise, since balsa rafts capable of carrying up to thirty tons or more were described by the early Spaniards.

The theoretical judgments of the balsa raft had deemed it not seaworthy because of the water-absorbent nature of the balsa wood, which would make it sink if not regularly dismantled and dried; also because it was thought that the rope lashings which kept the logs and the whole craft together would be worn through by friction when the great logs began to move at sea. The light and porous wood was also considered to be too fragile should high ocean seas lift the bow and stern up while crew and cargo were weighing upon the central part. Finally, it was considered that a one and a half foot freeboard on the flat and open raft would leave crew and cargo entirely exposed to the fury of the ocean.

Our experience provided the answers to these problems, and showed that the ancient culture peoples of Peru and Ecuador had their good reasons forevolving—and abiding by—this very type of deep-seagoing craft.

Dry balsa wood, as commercially distributed and generally known today, is exceedingly water-absorbent and unsuitable for raft construction, but green balsa wood, put into the sea when freshly cut and still filled with sap, is very water-resistant, and although the water gradually penetrates the sun-dried outer section, the sap inside prevents further absorption. *Kon-Tiki* was still capable of holding tons of cargo when it was finally pulled ashore for preservation in its Oslo museum more than a year after the expedition.

The balsa logs did not chafe off the rope lashings. The reason was that the wet surface of the logs became soft and spongy, and the ropes were left unharmed in their grooves as if pressed between cork. The two-foot-thick balsa logs proved to be tough enough to resist the assault of two storms with towering seas, and even an emergency landfall on an unsheltered reef in Polynesia.

The secret of the safety and seaworthiness of the unprotected balsa raft, in spite of its negligible freeboard, was primarily its unique ability to rise with any threatening sea, thus riding over the dangerous water masses which would have broken aboard most other small craft. Secondly, it was the ingenious wash-through construction which allowed all entering water to disappear as through a sieve. Neither towering sloping swells nor breaking windwaves had any chance of getting a grip on the vessel, and the result was a feeling of complete security which no other open or small craft known to us until then could have offered. Moreover the shallow construction of the raft, and the flexibility allowed by all the independent lashings, made it possible even to land directly on an exposed reef on the windward side of the dangerous Tuamotu archipelago. As mentioned in Chapter 2, since the voyage of *Kon-Tiki* many other balsa rafts have sailed from the South American coast to Polynesia, Melanesia, and even Australia.

During the voyage of *Kon-Tiki* a few experiments were carried out with what the natives call *guara,* the aforesaid centerboard. It was found that five *guara,* six feet deep and two feet wide, when securely attached, were enough to permit the raft to sail almost at right angles to the wind. It was also ascertained that by raising or lowering a *guara* fore or aft, the raft could be steered before the wind without using the steering oar.

However, an attempt to tack into the wind failed completely, and the raft's crew therefore yielded temporarily to the generally held claim that the Peruvian balsa raft, like any other flat-bottomed vessel, could only be sailed in the general direction of following winds. But subsequent to the expedition I was gradually led to suspect that this failure in our attempt to tack was probably due to the inexperience of the raft's crew rather than to limitations in the early Peruvian marine architecture. This suspicion incited me to organize a second balsa raft experiment to which we shall return in the following section.

Guara Sailing Technique

To gain information on the indigenous steering method used in the aboriginal navigation off the west coast of South America we are largely dependent on the records of the early chroniclers, and to some extent on archaeology, not least the iconographic art of the pre-Conquest population on the coast. Sometimes details not seen, or at least not recorded in writing by the early Spaniards, were illustrated in realistically molded effigy jars, or painted with line drawings on ceramic pots, even woven into textiles, by pre-European artists in Peru. Many, in fact most, of such maritime motifs go back to pre-Inca time. The majority of truly impressive reed ships and log rafts were illustrated in the art of the Early Chimu, or Mochica, i.e., the very early pyramid builders who were among the founders of South American civilization. Large reed ships with many passengers and cargo, often with a double deck and forked stern, are not uncommon in Mochica ceramic art. Effigy jars illustrating voyagers on rafts of straight logs lashed together also occur, but specimens are rare.

The earliest written records reporting the use of sails on aboriginal Peruvian watercraft are presented by Sáamanos, Xeres, Andagoya, Oviedo, Zárate, Las Casas, Balboa, Gamboa, Garcilasso, Benzoni, and Cobo, all of whom concur in stating that the art of sailing was indigenous to the Inca Empire and employed on the balsa rafts at sea. In the highlands, sails were in use even on the Lake Titicaca reed boats, but Inca Garcilasso says of the coastal population: "They do not put up sails on their boats of rushes, . . . but they hoist sails on their wooden rafts when they navigate the sea."[51]

We have seen that the first Peruvian sailing raft met by Europeans was beating up against the wind and the strong Niño Current with more than thirty tons of cargo when captured by Pizarro's pilot. This truly difficult marine maneuver was not accomplished by paddling, a feat which for practical reasons alone would be impossible for a broad log raft carrying twenty men and women and thirty tons of cargo. We learn from Sáamanos's pre-Conquest report to Carlos V in 1526 that this colossal cargo raft was properly equipped for regular navigation. It carried masts and yards of very fine wood, with an excellent rigging of henequen hemp, and "cotton sails in the same shape and manner as on our own ships."

Subsequent chroniclers also infer that Inca fishermen and merchant sailors were capable of premeditated raft voyages with successful return into the wind, a feat which has been deemed impossible by modern experts on rafts and navigation. Wartime experiments with rubber dinghies and life rafts of wood or aluminium convinced naval and civil authorities of the inaptitude of sailing rafts as means of reaching given destinations, for the flat-bottomed rafts would yield to all winds and move sideways or backwards as helpless prey to the elements. In spite of a raft's superior safety in rough seas, it was said, no appliance of rudder or steering oar could make it navigable as was the case with a lifeboat with hull and keel. It is the more remarkable therefore, to learn from early eyewitnesses that the Inca seamen could set sail and bat their way toward Panama, Puna Island, the Lobos and Chincha Islands, etc., or go far into the treacherous rapids of the Humboldt and Niño currents to return after weeks of absence with heavy burdens of dried fish.

It is no secret that the Inca sailors achieved their marine exploits by means of the aforesaid *guara,* the kind of hardwood centerboards we tested with limited success on the *Kon-Tiki.* The balsa raft *guara* vary considerably in dimensions according to the size and type of the craft, and according to the dimensions of the hardwood material available. They are usually from four to seven feet long and from five to ten inches wide, although off the jungle areas of Ecuador they could be as much as three or four yards long and half a yard wide. The *guara* are rectangular boards without shaft but with a knob or handle on the upper end. We may be dependent on the early chroniclers and on more or less conventionalized native art for information on the early Peruvian watercraft, but we are still able to inspect and study the actual hardwood *guara* employed by the ancient local mariners. Such *guara,* usually carved from the hard and enduring algarrobo tree, are among the most commonly occurring wooden artifacts in the pre-

Conquest graves of coastal Peru. Thanks to the splendid art and work-manship embodied in some of them, they are very familiar objects in Peruvian museum exhibits all over the world. Most of the *guara,* how-ever, were crudely manufactured without ornamentation of any kind, and as these strictly utilitarian pieces failed to make an impression on treasure-seeking collectors, many have been lost in the hands of igno-rant *huaqueros.* It may perhaps be fair to say that the ratio between trained archaeological work and mere treasure hunting in Peruvian coastal sites is as clearly reflected in the ratio between the plain and the exuberantly ornamented *guara* as it is in the ratio between Peruvian plainware and beautifully decorated effigy jars saved for museum collections.

The most elaborately ornamented specimens of *guara* come from the Pisco, Paracas, and Ica region on the south-central coast. Yet, here too, plane and crude algarrobo *guara* are found by excavation. Whereas the ornamental *guara* from the Chimu area on the north coast usually have no more than a bird or an animal figure carved in the round on top of the grip, as on the local paddles, the finest Paracas specimens often have the grips with carved and painted birds, fishes, men, or ornamental symbols superimposed in two or three rows. The upper row is sometimes composed of six or eight men standing side by side and holding hands in such a manner that they form a wave mo-tive.

It has been suggested that some of the most artistic specimens are purely ceremonial emblems of rank, and this is probably true. Yet I have failed to find a single specimen which could not serve its purpose if put to use, because of the hardness of the wood employed and the carefully selected placement of the carvings which never impede the proper movement of the *guara.* The carving is always restricted to the upper grip and if, on rare specimens, it extends somewhat further down, it always follows the lateral edge of the board in such a way that it does not at all interfere with the free sliding of the hard board through the crack or slot between the soft balsa logs. It is indeed noteworthy that the carvings are consistently limited to that part of the *guara* which, when in use, is standing free and visible above deck, whereas the section which is left submerged below the raft, and thus is invisible to crew and passengers, is left plain and unornamented along its full length like a ceremonial ax handle or a staff, and not be left rude and plain for the major part of its length. In view of the function

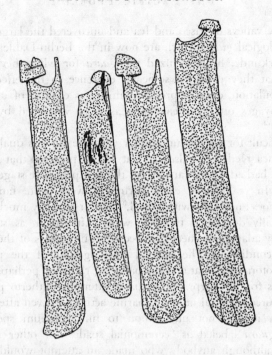

Unornamented, utilitarian *guara* archaeologically found in coastal tombs of southern Peru (from Heyerdahl 1952, plate LXXIV).

of the *guara,* which implies that the handle and upper section is standing visible and exposed to no strain or wear whatsoever except for a very slight occasional touch by a hand, we may safely assume that the great bulk even of the best ornamented specimens were actually in use too, although probably by men of rank in the coastal community.

When the first elaborately carved Pisco specimens were excavated and spread to museums and private collections in the latter part of the last century, they were treated merely as fine samples of pre-Inca wood-carving art, and although they were identified by W. Gretzer as marine *guara* in 1914, very little attention has since been paid to their actual function.

After a lifetime in coastal Peru, Gretzer had adequate opportunity of observing the last lingering balsa rafts which, maneuvering with *guara,* still carried tons of dried fish northward to Ecuador, and lumber and other cargo southward to Peru. When he started his excavations in the valleys of Pisco and Ica and uncovered the large collection of archaeological *guara* which are now in the Berlin-Dahlem Museum für Völkerkunde, he recognized the *guara* for what they were. He stressed that they provided sufficient evidence to the effect that the coastal population, even in pre-Inca time, was capable of undertaking regular voyages on the ocean such as were witnessed by the early Spaniards.[52]

It is difficult for anyone unfamiliar with the curious qualities of the buoyant Inca reed and balsa rafts at sea to perceive that the coastal population had advanced far beyond the first primitive stage in marine evolution. In reality, the early Peruvians were quite familiar with dugout canoes and boats with a hull,[53] but at sea they much preferred their specially developed types of watercraft which, as stated, were marvelously adapted to meet the special requirements of the local geographical conditions. The general misjudgment of the presumably primitive totora reed boat and the balsa log raft may perhaps be one of the reasons for the surprisingly sparse attention hitherto paid to the existing source material on local marine activities. Even after Gretzer's publication it was not uncommon to find museum specimens of Peruvian *guara* labeled as "ceremonial spades" or other similar descriptions, although anybody who made an attempt would soon find out that the *guara* was most unsuited for any kind of agricultural work. When specimens were excavated *in situ* and not merely obtained as stray artifacts in the hands of collectors, it became gradually evident that they were some sort of marine accessory, since they were generally interred with fishermen's equipment or other artifacts implying marine activity rather than agriculture. It was also rather striking that the special ornamentation on the grip precisely matched that of the local paddle handles, and the *guara* have therefore in recent years commonly been exhibited as "a special kind of paddle" or even as "a rudder."

A study of the grip alone will suffice, however, to show that this curious artifact could have served as neither. The principal quality of a paddle is a perfect balance: the grip must be set symmetrically on top of the central axis to prevent the blade from twisting during the stroke. The grip of the broad *guara,* however, is set entirely out of balance, far over to one of its corners, in such a way that paddling or rowing with it would be quite hopeless. Nor does the *guara* have a shaft allowing a balanced grip for the lower, second hand. Most of the south coast *guara* have the handle carved as a mere slot for the insertion of the fingers, like the carrying handle of a bag. It is obvious that the specialized *guara* handle is intended merely for a vertical one-hand raising and lowering of the wide board, and not to gain momentum through a balanced two-hand stroke. Nor does the grip of the *guara* in any way tally with—or function as—the tiller of a rudder, and we are left with the apparent fact that the practical functions of the *guara* differ from those of boat accessories occurring on common European watercraft.

More recently, in 1963, D. Eisleb completed a systematic study of the large archaeological collection of plain and ornamented Peruvian *guara* preserved in the storerooms of the Berlin-Dahlem Museum für Völkerkunde. He discovered that one of the characteristics common to all these boards was that they were shaped like knives, with one edge narrower and sharper than the other, so as to enable this navigation instrument to cut the water with minimum resistance.[54] This shape excludes all other functions but that of a centerboard.

When Lothrop published the first systematic study of aboriginal Peruvian navigation in 1932, he happened to be as familiar with sailing techniques and marine matters as with the local field of archaeology, and like Gretzer, Lothrop realized that the strange marine accessories were *guara,* the special kind of centerboard which was still in use on the north coast until the turn of the century. He also emphasized that the presence of *guara* in early pre-Conquest graves on the Peruvian coast provides archaeological evidence of the pre-Columbian use of sail in this area. He says: "it is obvious that a centerboard is useless unless a vessel has sails."[55] As distinct from a rudder or steering oar the movable *guara* is purely a sailing tool, superfluous and unusable on any craft propelled by oars or paddles.

The first Spaniards, arriving in caravels, showed no interest in the *guara* as such, praising only the remarkable skill of the local mariners in the handling of their rafts. But in his early drawing of a balsa raft at Paita, Peru, published in 1619, the Dutch admiral Spilbergen illustrates two cloaked Indians standing by the sails issuing orders to three others who squat on the raft's deck, each holding the upper section of his own *guara,* which is thrust down vertically through the cracks between the logs. The raft has no steering oar or rudder In the text Spilbergen makes no comment whatever on the *guara,* he merely states, like the Spaniards before him, that this was a very wonderful craft, adding that the sailing raft had been at sea fishing for two months, and had returned to Paita habor with sufficient fish to supply all the ships of Spilbergen's fleet.[56]

It is here important to bear in mind that the *guara* meant nothing to the artist who provided Spilbergen's interesting drawing, for the use of even regular centerboards was not yet known to contemporary Europe. So Spilbergen, although leaving for posterity the very first illustration of the principles of centerboard navigation, refrained from any comment beyond the fact that the raft and sails "were very wonderfully made."

A hundred and thirty years more had to pass before the two Spanish naval officers Juan and Ulloa became sufficiently intrigued by the navigation technique employed by the local Indians to look further into the mystery of the indigenous *guara*. After an excellent description of the various sizes and types of balsa raft they saw in Guayaquil, they wrote in 1748: "Hitherto we have only mentioned the construction and the uses they are applied to, but the greatest singularity of the floating vehicle is that it sails, tacks, and works as well in contrary winds as ships with a keel, and makes very little leeway. This advantage it derives from another method of steering than by a rudder, namely, by some boards three or four yards in length, and half a yard in breadth, called *guaras,* which are placed vertically, both at the head and stern between the main beams, and by thrusting some of these deep in the water, and raising others, they bear away, luff up, tack, lay to, and perform all the other motions of a regular ship. An invention hitherto unknown to the most intelligent nations of Europe . . . a *guara* being let down in the fore part of a vessel must make her luff up and by taking it out, she will bear away or fall off. Likeways on a *guara*'s being let down at the stern, she will bear away, and by taking it out of the water, the balsa will luff, or keep nearer to the wind. Such is the method used by the Indians in steering the balsas, and sometimes they use five or six *guaras,* to prevent the balsa from making leeway, it being evident that the more they are under water, the greater resistance the side of the vessel meets with, the *guaras* performing the office of leeboards used in small vessels. The method of steering by these *guaras* is so easy and simple that when once the balsa is put in her proper course, one only is made use of, raising and lowering it as occasions require, and thus the balsa is always kept in her intended direction."[57]

They were so impressed by this Peruvian sailing technique that they strongly recommended an introduction of the same system in Europe. Yet, when Lescallier and Charnock published their comprehensive world histories of navigation in 1791 and 1801 respectively, they could still only quote Juan and Ulloa's observations in Ecuador, and stress that the centerboard steering method was entirely peculiar to the coastal Indians of that area and not yet known in Europe. As stated, in his instructions for French naval cadets, Lescallier actually made an effort at recommending *guara* navigation for European life rafts, but with no result.

Further reports on Peruvian *guara* navigation were published by Humboldt in 1810 and by Stevenson in 1825. The latter had seen balsa rafts in Peru which, merely by means of *guara,* were "beating up against the wind and current" for hundreds of miles, with twenty-five or thirty tons of cargo.[58]

In 1832, B. Morell reported that balsa rafts could still be seen fifty miles from land and able to "beat to windward like a pilot boat . . ."[59]

Before Paris in 1841–43 published his voluminous essay on non-European watercraft, he went to northwestern South America to study the balsa rafts. He wrote: "In Peru they have preserved the use of rafts as constructed by the ancient inhabitants, which are sufficiently well suited to local conditions to be still preferred to all other craft." He published the drawing of a balsa with *guara* inserted, here reproduced on page 212, but he had no opportunity to observe rafts tacking at sea. He was in fact rather skeptical about Juan and Ulloa's eyewitness report on the unlimited possibilities of *guara* navigation, and wrote: "We have not been able to observe these ingenious rafts sufficiently to be sure that they really do carry out all these maneuvers . . ." Yet he admitted: "The rafts have no other means of steering in the ocean."[60]

A few years later, in 1852, C. Skogman observed balsa rafts with *guara* far into the ocean off northern Peru, and he reported that they made voyages to the Galápagos Islands, some 600 miles off the mainland.[61]

Another twenty years were to pass before the first centerboards were used on European boats, and little or no credit was then given to the ancient people who had employed the system for many centuries. According to Lothrop, some experiments of fitting centerboards to certain small boat models were made in England in 1790, but the actual use of centerboards in England and in the United States began about 1870.

Until then only leeboards had been used by European sailors, their sole function being to serve as a keel for reducing leeway.

About the turn of the century, true *guara* navigation of rafts disappeared with the last lingering traits of aboriginal culture along the coasts of Peru and Ecuador. With the twentieth century the secret of raft navigation was lost before it had spread to European life rafts.

When the *Kon-Tiki* raft was equipped with *guara* for its voyage in 1947 opinion among ethnologists and marine authorities was unanimous that they would be useless for controlled maneuvering, and although the expedition members verified that it was possible with five *guara* to fall off and bear almost at right angles to the wind, yet we failed in all our efforts to turn about and tack the raft against the wind. We returned from the expedition sharing the impression of Paris and subsequent scholars that the raft could only be navigated before the wind.

However, in 1953, with the kind assistance of the late Emilio Estrada of Guayaquil, it was possible to resume practical tests with a regular-sized balsa raft off the bay of Playas in Ecuador, where tiny three-log rafts of the Brazilian *jangada* type were still employed by local fishermen. Some of them helped us build a balsa raft slightly smaller than the *Kon-Tiki* but similarly constructed from nine logs lashed together and covered with a bamboo deck. Together with Estrada and me on board were the two archaeologists E. K. Reed and A. Skjölsvold. Once more a square sail was hoisted on a bipod mast in native fashion, and six *guara* were again inserted between the logs, two in the extreme bow and two in the stern. Two more were set at random, for they were to remain in a fixed position and serve only as leeboards. No paddles, rudder, or steering oar were carried on the raft as we hoisted sail and left the coast with the lessons obtained by Estrada from the local fishermen. It was found that a correct interplay between the handling of the sail and the lifting and sinking of the *guara* fore and aft enabled us, after some experiment, to tack against contrary wind, and finally to sail back to the exact spot on the beach where we had set off. Once known, the *guara* method of steering was astonishing through its simplicity and effectiveness. We had already discovered on the *Kon-Tiki* that if we lifted the steering oar out of the water while we were under sail the raft would set its own steady course at some angle off the course of the wind, an angle that would alter if we changed the ratio of the *guara* fore and aft. Actually, a

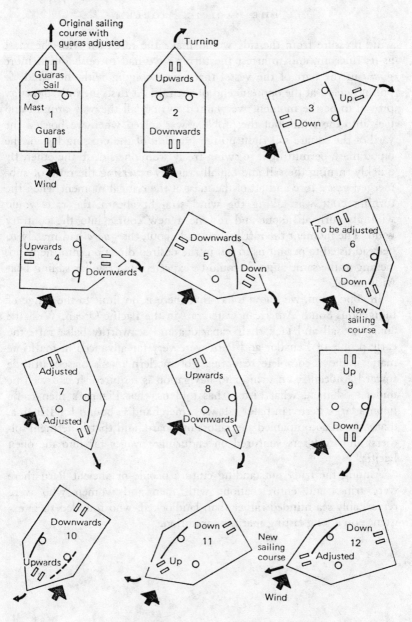

The principles of *guara* navigation.

wind pressure from the side would make the raft turn with the mast as its fulcrum, and to arrest the turning we had to push down more *guara* in the part of the vessel that was swinging with the wind, or pull up *guara* at the opposite end of the raft. At first, the only difficulty proved to be the moment we wanted to turn all the way around and tack into the wind, but the problem was solved when we hoisted the yard of the square sail right up the junction of the crossing legs of the bipod mast, permitting it to swing freely from one side to the other. By quickly turning the sail and equally rapidly reversing the ratio of submerged *guara* fore and aft of the mast at the critical moment when the turning craft was taking the wind straight abeam, the raft would willingly turn all about and resume a new course into the contrary wind. The moment the raft had turned about, the *guara* had merely to be readjusted to permit us to sail in the desired direction into the wind, tacking at the same angle as could be expected in a regular sailing boat with a keel.[62]

In conclusion, we know today that there is no limit to the range of indigenous South American watercraft in the Pacific Ocean. With the ability to sail and tack their capacious and seaworthy balsa rafts the early people of Ecuador and Peru were very far advanced in maritime matters, and a complete reappraisal of modern man's biased attitude toward Andean seamanship and navigation is required. It can well be understood then, what history has told us, that Pizarro's men came upon a large Peruvian balsa raft with merchandise bound for Panama, that women accompanied the sailors on board, and that fishermen, soldiers, and explorers ventured on enduring voyages far into the open Pacific.

Among the truly outstanding culture people of ancient Peru there were tribes and entire nations with men and women who were remarkably sea minded rather than landlocked, who founded their existence on a long-lasting maritime tradition.

Chapter 9

Culture Plants and
Early Navigators

THE AMERICAN anthropologist and plant geographer G. F. Carter once said with reference to independent evolution: "Any fool can make an arrow-point, but only God can make a sweet potato." The argument was launched in an attempt to alert the attention of scientists in other fields to the extreme importance of genetics in tracing the lost wakes of early travelers in the Pacific. A corresponding point was raised by another friend and colleague, E. N. Ferdon, who upon conducting archaeological excavations in East Polynesia initiated a thorough library research to check observations made by the first European visitors to these islands. He wrote that one of the most interesting things he came across was in Bryon's journal of his voyage from 1764 to 1766, in which he records of the Takaroa atoll, just where the Peru Current comes in from South America at its greatest speed: "The Birds we saw ashore were Parrots & Parekets, and a beautiful kind of Dove, which were so tame, that they came close to us, and often went into the Savage's Hutts."[1] Parrots do not belong to Polynesia. On the Pacific coast of South America they were man's companion even at sea, to judge from Humboldt's water color of a huge balsa raft loaded with fruits and other cargo and with a green parrot sitting in the stay. A parrot also happened to be given to us in Peru as a pet aboard the *Kon-Tiki* raft which landed in the same group as Takaroa. They were extremely popular in ancient Peru, where stuffed parrots and parrot feathers are common in pre-European tombs. Any artist can draw a parrot, but only navigators can carry live specimens of a short-range jungle bird thousands of miles across an ocean.

The dog in Polynesia is another genetic indicator of human movements. The Polynesian dog, *Canis Maori,* is a different breed from the wild dingo of Australia, the paria-dog of Southeast Asia, or the husky of the Arctic, and what little is known from skeletal remains found in the Marquesas, skins collected in New Zealand, and descriptions from the early voyagers indicates close genetic relationship to the aboriginal breeds of Mexico and Peru previously mentioned. Whereas we have seen that pigs and chickens spread to Polynesia from Fiji after the isolation of the Maori began, dogs could not have reached Polynesia from Melanesia where they seem to have been absent until the Europeans arrived. Cook's companion, G. Forster, wrote from nuclear Melanesia: "Hogs and common poultry are their domestic animals; to which we have added dogs, by selling them a pair of puppies brought from the Society Islands. They received them with strong signs of extreme satisfaction; but as they called them hogs (*puaha*), we were convinced that they were entirely new to them."[2]

The Maori believe that the dog accompanied the *kumara,* or sweet potato, on its original voyage from the ancestral fatherland. J. White in *The Ancient History of the Maori, His Mythology and Traditions* shows that the memory of the dog and the sweet potato goes back to the days before the progenitors of the Maori set out for their final Polynesian home. The legend says that the early ancestors in the fatherland cut down "light-timbered trees, which they dragged together to the source of the River Tohinga. They bound the timber together with vines of the *Pirita* and ropes, and made a very wide raft (*Moki*)." They also "built a house on the raft, and put much food into it, fernroot, *Kumara,* and dogs."[3]

In his opening of the ethno-botanical symposium at the Tenth Pacific Science Congress in Honolulu in 1961, the chairman, botanist J. Barrau, recommended that the entire evidence pertaining to relationship and spread of Pacific island plants ought to be re-examined in the light of the new evidence that aboriginal raft voyagers could have crossed the ocean gap between South America and Polynesia before the arrival of Europeans.

The account given in the present chapter is an extended version of a paper first published under the title "Plant Evidence for Contact with America before Columbus" in *Antiquity* (Vol. 38) in 1964.

*   *   *

No other field of science has been as profoundly affected as botany by preconceived opinions among anthropologists concerning possible ranges of primitive navigators. Botanists commonly do not consider themselves authorities on aboriginal navigation and primitive craft, and in marine matters have turned to the anthropologists for expert advice. Anthropologists have willingly volunteered such advice, and next used the response from the botanists to bolster their own isolationist view on American prehistory.

A prominent botanist A. de Candolle published in 1884 a pioneering work, *Origin of Cultivated Plants,* and in a sense became the father of the science of ethno-botany. De Candolle accumulated the botanical evidence available at that time, and drew the conclusion that, "In the history of cultivated plants, I have noticed no trace of communication between the peoples of the old and new worlds before the discovery of America by Columbus."[4] This was a genetic argument of paramount importance in the discussion that went on among contemporary ethnologists and prehistorians. Although De Candolle had been careful in drawing conclusions, his failure to find proof of any pre-Columbian exchange of crop plants across the Atlantic and Pacific oceans was in line with a growing tendency of isolationism in the interpretation of cultural evolution. From then on an increasing number of anthropologists began to ask, if there had been contact between pre-Columbian America and the Old World, why had none of the Old World cereals been introduced to early Mexico or Peru, or American corn to the rest of the world?

At the beginning of the twentieth century another prominent botanist E. D. Merrill sided unconditionally with the isolationists, trusting the validity of their claim that no vessel prior to the evolution of the European caravel could have reached America by sea. As a close follower of De Candolle, on whose teachings he based his view, Merrill adopted and developed the modern thesis that there had been no contact between the Old World and the New prior to the arrival of the Vikings and Columbus. By the strength of his opinions and the vigor of his arguments, Merrill became one of the foremost propounders of the now growing hypothesis that the great oceans surrounding the tropic and temperate zones of the New World had provided a complete and successful barrier to any form of prehistoric navigation. Merrill, however, went further than De Candolle. Whereas De Candolle had only concluded that plant evidence available to him failed to indicate Old World contacts with aboriginal America, Merrill insisted that the negative plant evidence did prove that there could have been no such contact.

Among the first botanists to argue that plant evidence actually proved aboriginal contact had taken place between America and Polynesia were two of Merrill's American colleagues, O. F. and R. C. Cook. During the first two decades of the present century they produced various plant evidence to show the spread of aboriginal American agriculture to Polynesia.[5] Merrill opposed their botanical reasoning with an anthropological argument: "The generally accepted theory among ethnologists supports an *eastward* culture movement across the Pacific rather than a *westward* one." If there had been any American–Polynesian contact at all, he argued, "it would be much more reasonable to view it as coming from the Pacific to America rather than as evincing a migration from America into the Pacific."[6]

As late as 1937 Merrill wrote: "As agriculture in America was autochthonous [of local origin], we may assume that so were the cultures based upon it." This rather categorical and constantly reappearing statement from a leading botanist—one of the few to enter early into the field of ethno-botany—could not fail to impress contemporary anthropologists.

However, Merrill's conclusions were gradually challenged by other prominent botanists and plant geographers holding a conflicting view. Among the most notable were O. F. and R. C. Cook, who gradually got support from C. O. Sauer, G. F. Carter, J. B. Hutchinson, R. A. Silow, S. G. Stephens, C. R. Stoner, and E. Anderson, all of whom produced historical or genetic evidence arguing that cultivated plants *had* been carried by aboriginal man across the tropic oceans surrounding the New World. The progress of modern archaeology yielded important botanical information not available at the time of De Candolle, and it became increasingly difficult for Merrill to sustain the categorical view which he had defended with such tenacity in the 1920s and 1930s.

The validity and strength of Merrill's negative reasoning depended on the absolute and unconditional absence of cultivated plants of common origin in the two hemispheres. Such negative evidence, although not conclusive, weighed heavily as an argument against transoceanic voyages. However, a single plant making an exception to his rule would invalidate his argument. Merrill had, so to speak, to keep his barrel watertight. The loss of a single stave would render it unserviceable and turn his negative reasoning against him with the multiple force of positive testimony.

A culture plant that had long puzzled anthropologists by its presence throughout Polynesia when Europeans arrived was the sweet potato, *Ipomoea batatas*. Although it was a strictly American plant prior to the arrival of the Spaniards in the New World, it had long since found its way to the islands in Polynesia, where it was the principal crop plant from Easter Island to New Zealand prior to European arrival. No other plant is so important in Maori–Polynesian legends about the early ancestral voyagers and the original fatherland, and throughout Polynesia, from Easter Island to Hawaii and New Zealand, the sweet potato was referred to as *kumara,* with slight dialectic variations. *Kumara* was also the aboriginal name for this same American species in ancient Peru, and from Peru northward to Panama the sweet potato was known as *ckumara, cumar, umar, kumal, umala* and *kuala*.[7]

Frequent attempts had been made by anthropologists to eliminate the sweet potato as argument for pre-European contact between Polynesia and America. It had even been seriously proposed by scholars that a sweet potato had perhaps been caught between the roots of a fallen tree on the coast of Peru and drifted without human aid to Polynesia. The theory failed to explain how the name drifted across together with the plant and it never gained much support. An alternative proposal of wide appeal was that the sweet potato with its native Peruvian name had spread to Polynesia when the first Spanish caravels sailed from Peru on their discoveries of the East Pacific in the late sixteenth and early seventeenth centuries. In 1932, however, the noted anthropologist R. B. Dixon published his survey "The Problem of the Sweet Potato in Polynesia," in which he succeeded in demonstrating that the sweet potato was already firmly established throughout the Polynesian triangle long before the arrival of the Spaniards in the sixteenth century.[8]

Merrill was forced to accept Dixon's historic evidence, and, realizing that a vulnerable sweet potato tuber can only spread across an ocean by human agency, so far as this specific American culture plant, unknown anywhere as a wild species, is concerned, he gave way. In 1946 he tore the first stave from his barrel and admitted that aboriginal navigators had crossed the ocean from the New World at least as far as the islands of Polynesia. He wrote: "they did introduce into Polynesia one important food plant of American origin, the sweet potato, and spread it from Hawaii to New Zealand . . . well before the advent of the Europeans in the Pacific." Soon he went even further and in 1954 pointed out the great care needed for such a successful transmission, stating that the aboriginal navigators must have carried their *kumara* from America as a living plant, in soil, otherwise no sweet potato tuber could possibly retain its viability in a humid atmosphere, at sea level, for longer than a month or at the most six weeks. He pointed to the fact that the *Kon-Tiki* raft, under sail, took over three months to make the passage. He even added: "It would be foolish to assert that there were no communications across the Pacific in pre-Magellan times . . ." and held that the pan-Polynesian cultivation of the American sweet potato offers positive evidence of pre-European contact.[9]

In the meantime the pre-European distribution of the coconut too had taken on a new aspect. This highly useful palm had first been encountered by Europeans as they pushed on into Southeast Asia and Indonesia, and was then considered an Asiatic species. Later, when the Europeans also reached the West Indies and tropical America, they found the same palm there, and it even grew wild in the tropical forests of the northern Andes and in cultivated groves all the way from Ecuador to Guatemala. As early as 1832, in his natural history of the palms, C. F. P. de Martius had come to the conclusion that coconuts from the Guayaquil area of Ecuador and the islands near Panama had drifted across the tropical Pacific all the way to Asia.[10]

De Candolle first accepted the obvious botanical evidence for an American origin of the coconut palm, *Cocos nucifera*. The numerous species of the sub-family (*Cocoinae*) to which the coconut belongs, are all characteristic of tropical America and none occurs in Asia. It was only the cultivated and highly useful species with its edible nuts that was found by the Europeans in aboriginal settlements from Meso-America all the way across the Pacific to coastal Asia. Its occurrence in a wild state in South America, and firm traditional and historic records of a recent introduction in coastal Asia, resulted in a flurry of contradictory theories among the botanists, in which De Candolle took a leading part: "The inhabitants of the islands of Asia were far bolder navigators than the American Indians. It is very possible that canoes from the Asiatic Islands, containing a provision of coconuts, were thrown by tempests or false maneuvers on to the islands or the west coast of America. The converse is highly improbable."[11]

A return to Martius' original view was stimulated in 1906 by the English botanist H. B. Guppy after four years of personal research in the Pacific. He realized that geographical conditions would not have permitted coconuts to spread with drift voyagers from Indonesia to South America, and concluded: "It is . . . to be inferred that it came originally from the home of the genus in America, perhaps as a gift brought by the Equatorial Current from the New World to Asia."[12]

At the turn of the century a natural trans-Pacific dispersal of the coconut was therefore considered as an adequate solution among many botanists. However, even this hypothesis was challenged. By 1941 experiments with floating coconuts had been conducted in Hawaii. The results disproved the old belief that a coconut could float across almost any ocean gap and germinate when washed ashore at the other end. It was discovered that the eyes of a floating coconut would be attacked by fouling organisms and lose their viability on an extensive drift like the one between the New World and Polynesia.[13]

Merrill was then gradually forced to yield his second stave and wrote: ". . . to add another statement which may seem shocking, it is most certain that the Polynesians introduced the coconut on the west coast of America between Panama and Ecuador, not too long before the Spaniards arrived." Fighting to the last against an American origin of the coconut palm, he argued: "The last word has not yet been said as to where the species originated . . . One thing is certain: the coconut palm was thoroughly established along the wet Pacific coast of Panama and adjacent Colombia before the arrival of the Spaniards."[14]

Merrill had no sooner stated that he needed to change his earlier published views concerning the human transportation of the sweet potato and the coconut between pre-Columbian America and Polynesia than yet another important culture plant fell out of the same barrel— the gourd, *Lagenaria siceraria*. The gourd was recognized as one of the principal culture plants with pan-Polynesian distribution in pre-European time.

Contrary to Linnaeus, De Candolle and, with him Merrill, had established that the gourd was entirely unknown to the aboriginal population of America prior to the arrival of Columbus. Then archaeologists began to find seeds and artifacts made from the gourd in early pre-European graves of Peru and Chile. This plant now became an ethno-botanical dilemma. In 1931 E. Nordenskiöld pointed to the great similarity of artifacts made from dried gourds in pre-Spanish South America and Oceania, and referred to the plants as "the principal proof of pre-Columbian communication between Oceania and America."[15]

In 1938 Buck began to see the gourd as evidence that Polynesian voyagers must necessarily have reached South America during their long canoe trips in the early part of the present millennium. Repeating his claim in 1945, two years before the *Kon-Tiki* crossing, he argued that: "Since the South American Indians had neither the vessels nor the navigating ability to cross the ocean space between their shores and the nearest Polynesian islands, they may be disregarded as the agents of supply."[16]

The opinion of this much quoted anthropologist once more influenced contemporary botanists, and A. J. Eames and H. St. John wrote in 1943: "It is now believed that before the thirteenth century Polynesian voyagers starting from Mangareva or the Marquesas sailed eastward, reaching Peru, and then returned. Such a voyage would provide a possible explanation of the introduction of the sweet potato . . . to Polynesia, and the gourd . . . to South America."[17]

In 1950 even Merrill admitted that the gourd no longer supported his earlier views, "for it is clear that this cultivated plant did occur in both hemispheres before Magellan's time." He added: "It may owe its presence in pre-Columbian America to the Polynesian voyagers . . ."[18]

Even this supposition did not hold up in the light of the now gradually accumulating evidence. Contemporary with the *Kon-Tiki* expedition, which showed the feasibility of a raft voyage from Peru, Junius Bird excavated a deep refuse midden on the coast of Peru and revealed that the gourd was cultivated and used for the production of various artifacts by a fishing culture in South America more than 3,000 years ago, at a period long before any Polynesians had settled in Oceania.[19] Chronological evidence accordingly demonstrated that the gourd was older in Peru than in Polynesia, and thus must have been carried from the former area to the latter rather than vice versa. In 1954 Merrill gave up the idea that the Polynesians had brought the gourd to America. He now suggested Africa as the original homeland of the gourd while proposing that it reached aboriginal America across the Atlantic. He claimed that man was obviously responsible for its distribution within America and Polynesia too.

It was now pointless to argue for isolation merely by holding back other loose staves in what was left of the barrel. Merrill therefore abandoned his opposition to the growing evidence that the Old World banana was cultivated in pre-Columbian Peru and Brazil, and not introduced by the Portuguese as he had formerly theorized. He changed his former opinion and wrote in 1954: "We may reasonably admit that one, or a few of the numerous Polynesian plantain varieties may have been carried by the Polynesians themselves to South America, for the 'eyes' (buds) can very easily be transported, over long distances, with a minimum of care and still retain their viability. It might be that a form introduced on the coast of Peru was transported over the Andes, thus reaching the upper waters of the Amazon."[20]

It was at this point that yet another Polynesian plant, overlooked by everyone, entered the discussion. A linted cotton grew wild in the Marquesas group, the Society Islands, Hawaii, and Polynesian-affected Fiji when the first Europeans arrived. The plant was for many years not an ethno-botanical suspect since the historical Polynesians were ignorant of weaving and produced their clothing, like some Indonesians and all American Northwest Coast tribes, by the simpler bark-beating method. The possibility that the loom, and even pottery, might have been known to a culturally distinct substratum had not yet been suspected. When Europeans arrived they found the Society and Marquesas island cotton to be spinnable, but the contemporary islanders were uninterested in European attempts to encourage organized cultivation of this inedible plant and its eventual laborious spinning and weaving. For years therefore the only noteworthy peculiarity about the linted Polynesian cotton was its geographical distribution: both wild and cultivated cotton of any sort were absent from the rest of the Pacific, including Australia and Indonesia, whereas it grew in the uninhabited Galápagos Islands, bridging the gap to the wild and cultivated cottons of the New World.

In 1947 Hutchinson, Silow, and Stephens published their earlier cited genetic analysis of wild and cultivated cottons throughout the world. They found, much to everyone's surprise, that the Polynesian

cottons were of the twenty-six-chromosomed American species produced through interbreeding and cultivation by the aboriginal cotton
domesticators of Mexico and Peru. All wild cottons in America have
thirteen chromosomes, and so do all the cultivated and all the wild species in the Old World. But the early cotton domesticators of America
had, as stated, managed to hybridize species which combined thirteen
large and thirteen small chromosomes, and had thus artificially produced linted cottons which were tetraploids, i.e., twenty-six-
chromosomed. Including the Polynesian species and varieties, they are
the only tetraploids in the entire cotton genus. On purely botanical
grounds the three botanists were therefore forced to suggest that the
linted cotton had necessarily reached Polynesia "since the establishment of civilization in tropic America."[21]

C. O. Sauer showed in 1950 that this late and yet pre-European
spread of cultivated cotton from America to Polynesia could not be assigned to sea birds, which do not eat *Gossypium* seeds, or to ocean currents, cotton being most unsuited to such long-range dispersal by floating. He showed that, although the *wild* thirteen-chromosomed cotton
might have reached America by natural means in remote geological
periods when world geography as a whole was different from today,
this explanation could not apply to "the much later time when the tet-
raploid group originated. Nor does such a hypothesis help to explain
the occurrence of cottons with strong American parentage, ranging
from the Galápagos to Fiji. Perforce then we must consider human
agencies in the geographic distribution of the *Gossypium* genus. The
problem relates entirely to the lint-bearing forms useful to man."[22]

G. F. Carter asked in 1950: "Was cotton originally carried as a
source of oil seeds, as suggested by Hutchinson, Silow, and Stephens?
Or was weaving later given up in the Pacific area to bark cloth?"[23]

The spinnable Polynesian cotton had entered into the field of ethno-
botany with the same genetic force as the sweet potato, the coconut,
and the gourd. Even Merrill, in 1954, speaking of the identification of
the Polynesian cotton as an American hybrid, says: "This hybrid may
well have reached Tahiti, through the agency of man, before the voyages of the Polynesians had ceased."

Confronted with the steadily increasing evidence of direct American–Polynesian contacts in pre-Columbian times, Merrill now loosens
all the staves of his isolationist barrel: "That there were occasional and
accidental associations between the peoples of Polynesia and America,

and even occasional ones between the American Indians and the eastern Polynesian islands, actually must be accepted . . ." He no longer
considers the Polynesians to be the only Pacific navigators, but even
adds: "We must admit . . . that natives of South America may have
reached some of the Pacific islands on balsa rafts."[24]

By making these concessions in his last publication before his death,
Merrill had turned a page and marked a milepost in American and
Polynesian ethno-botany. No one had fought for the doctrine of complete American isolation in pre-Columbian times with more passionate
conviction than he. To Merrill and his followers any ocean, regardless
of its currents, was seen as a barrier to human movements rather than
a mobile sponsor of voyages and drifts. Their critical attitude has undoubtedly served as a most valuable obstacle to the surge of diffusionist
theories that would otherwise have marred American anthropology
today. It should be duly stressed that the concessions regarding oversea
contacts, in line with the gradually accumulating evidence, are
confined to aboriginal voyages across the comparatively short open
stretch of water between South America and Polynesia. Botanical evidence for direct contact with Asia or Indonesia is lacking. No Old
World crop plants of Asiatic origin have been found in Polynesia except as earlier stated those obtained from Melanesia through marginal
contact with Fiji.

One more botanical species of pan-Polynesian importance has been
subject to ardent discussion among ethno-botanists. Only those who
have sojourned among the aboriginal Polynesians and participated in
their daily struggle for survival will understand how a rather inconspicuous plant like *Hibiscus tiliaceus* was of profound importance to
the island communities. The hibiscus, as distinct from the plants mentioned hitherto, has seeds adapted for natural dissemination by sea, and
therefore might well have preceded any human voyage to Polynesia.
Yet the plant has entered into ethno-botanical discussion because of its
deliberate cultivation in Polynesia, combined with associated linguistic
observations. The botanist F. B. H. Brown justly refers to the hibiscus
as, "One of the most useful of all types cultivated by the early
Polynesians."[25] O. F. and R. C. Cook first brought the hibiscus, or
maho, into the ethno-botanical discussion by arguing in 1918 that
"Though many botanists have written of the *maho* as a cosmopolitan
seashore plant, its wide dissemination may be due largely to human
agency, as with the coconut palm." They show that the tree in a wild

state is an abundant or even dominant species in many localities of Middle America, down to the banks of the Guayaquil River on the Pacific coast of South America, where it was used by the aboriginal population for bark cloth manufacture, for the production of water-resistant cordage and string, and for kindling fire. They demonstrated that both the special uses and the names of this plant were much the same among the Polynesians. Thus in tropical America the tree was known as *maho* or *mahagua,* or some variant of this name, and in Polynesian dialects it was known as *mao, mau, vau, fau, hau,* and *au.* The two authors concluded: "The *maho, mahagua,* or linden hibiscus is one of the economic plants to be taken into account in studying the problem of contacts between the inhabitants of tropical America and the Pacific islands, in prehistoric times. Though considered a native of America, the *maho* appears to have been distributed over the islands and shores of the Pacific and Indian oceans before the arrival of Europeans. Readiness of propagation and of transportation by cutting renders this plant well adapted for cultivation and dissemination by primitive peoples. Although human assistance in transportation does not appear to be so definitely required with the *maho* as with the sweet potato and other plants that are grown from only cuttings, the names of the *maho* afford almost as definite indications of human contacts as in the case of *kumara,* a name for sweet potato already known to have been shared with the Indians of Peru. The name *maho* or *mahagua,* with numerous local variants, is widely distributed in tropical America and is closely approximated in many of the Pacific islands in relation either to the plant itself or to its principal uses for fiber, bark cloth, and fire making. . . . That the primitive Polynesians were in possession of the *maho* before they became acquainted with the similar Asiatic plants may be inferred in view of the indications that Polynesian names of other important cultivated plants—the paper-mulberry (*Papyrius* or *Broussonetia*), the rose of China (*Hibiscus rosa sinensis*), and the screwpine (*Pandanus*)—were derived from names of the *maho*. The making of fire by friction of wood, and of cloth by beating the bark of trees with grooved mallets, are specialized arts which may have been carried with the *maho* from America, across the tropical regions of the Old World."[26]

Merrill at that time (1920) opposed this view, arguing that the species was never *cultivated* outside Polynesia. The reason for its cultivation in Polynesia, he says, was undoubtedly that it was the best, or one

of the best, of the few fiber plants available to the primitive Polynesians. He maintained that the *Hibiscus tiliaceus* is a species of natural
pantropic distribution and that it had been disseminated by ocean currents. Still quoting at that time the current anthropological doctrine of
an aboriginal American ineptitude in marine matters, he insisted that
if man was responsible for the transfer it would be much more reasonable to suspect a voyage from the islands to America rather than vice
versa.[27]

The conflicting theories of the two botanists were subsequently reviewed by Carter in 1950: "These arguments seem to me to be excellent specimens of the result of fixed ideas. Cook was so intent on proving the American origin of agriculture that he was incautious, if not
unwise, in using a halophytic plant with a seed well adapted to water
transportation as *proof* of man's carrying plants across the ocean. Merrill on the other hand was either so incensed by Cook's special plead-
ing or so allergic to trans-Pacific contacts (or both) that the violence of
his reaction blinded him to the virtues of Cook's arguments. . . .
Winds and currents suggest that if the plant was carried across the
Pacific by natural means it must have been from America to Polynesia.
But natural carriage would leave the problem of usage and name to be
solved. . . . The identity of names and uses in Polynesia and
America, when coupled with the positive evidence from the sweet potato, makes it certain that whether or not the plant crossed the sea by
natural means, man carried the name for the plant and quite possibly
the usages across the same seas. It even seems probable that he carried
the plant also."

Carter also wrote in the same paper: "Clearer proof for contact between peoples from the Pacific with the peoples of Middle America
could hardly be asked than that supplied by the sweet potato and by
the hibiscus known as maho."[28]

As we have already seen in Chapter 6, although looking for a
human passage from Indonesia, Buck admitted that none of the
Polynesian plants could have come from that area, as the dry and
sandy coral atolls of Micronesia represented a buffer territory. He
showed that the Old World food plants grown in Polynesia (breadfruit, wet-land taro, sugar cane, etc.) had all been obtained by the
Polynesians in recent centuries of lively interisland contacts, when visitors to Fiji from Samoa and Tonga had spread them to most, but not
all, Polynesian islands. Together with the Fijian type of outrigger, as

well as the chicken and the pig, these Melanesian plants had gradually diffused from one island to the next after the Maori had separated themselves from all their kindred in Polynesia proper. Rice, the staple diet of Indonesia and Southeast Asia since the earliest times, was unknown in Fiji and the rest of Melanesia and therefore never diffused to any Polynesian tribe.

Although the vicinity of Fiji greatly affected Polynesian economy in the centuries prior to European arrival, Fiji alone cannot account for all the useful plants growing in various parts of Polynesia when the first Europeans arrived. It is well known that the indigenous flora of Polynesia must have been exceedingly poor in useful plants prior to the arrival of the first human settlers, yet this was by no means the case by the time the first European visitors arrived. We have seen how the pan-Polynesian cultivation of sweet potato, gourd, coconut, and the local presence of cotton and hibiscus provoked lively discussion among scholars accustomed to consider these islands outside the range of aboriginal South American craft. And yet there are many more plants of the same non-Melanesian category to be added to the list, although their presence inside Polynesia has a more restricted distribution.

The three island territories forming the Polynesian front toward America are, from south to north, Easter Island, the Marquesas group, and Hawaii. They have all provided remarkable botanical evidence for contact with America which has puzzled botanists and called for an unbiased explanation.

Easter Island is the nearest Polynesian territory to South America. Like Hawaii and New Zealand, Easter Island economy was entirely based on the cultivation of the American sweet potato when Europeans first arrived. Several varieties were grown and locally known by their Peruvian name, *kumara*. The Dutch discoverers were presented with great quantities of sweet potatoes,[29] Captain Cook's party observed this plant in extensive plantations,[30] and the first missionary to settle ashore wrote: "They cook the eternal sweet potatoes. It is the everyday dish, the invariable staple food of the natives, big and small . . . the uniformity is perfect: always sweet potatoes, everywhere sweet potatoes . . ."[31]

The early visitors also found gourds growing in fields,[32] and when W. J. Thomson arrived to carry out his important survey for the United States National Museum, he recorded: "A wild gourd is common, and constitutes the only water jar and domestic utensil known to the natives." And: "These calabashes grow in profusion on the island, but are worthy of note on account of the prominent place they occupy in the traditions, and because the seed was introduced by the original settlers."[33]

It is noteworthy that when the Spaniards arrived from Peru they were received by Easter Islanders who presented them with "plantains, chili peppers, sweet potatoes and fowls."[34] These plants were all known in pre-European Peru and are present in early pre-Inca burials on the mainland coast. The American chili pepper (*Capsicum*) also seems to be an early introduction in the Marquesas group, where it often grows wild near abandoned village sites, but nowhere is the historic record so unambiguous as in the case of Easter Island. All species of *Capsicum* are of American origin and none is indigenous to the Old World.

An immediate problem to botanists was the fact that a small tomato and a little scrubby variety of semi-wild pineapple were conspicuous in the otherwise extremely poor flora. Thomson wrote last century that "Tomato plants were also found growing wild, and on several occasions proved a valuable addition to our limited fare."[35] By the turn of the present century, however, W. Knoche, speaking of the local presence of the chili pepper, says: "From the same family derives a small tomato (*Solanum zycopersicum*) which has disappeared from Easter Island." He also states that the small semi-wild and scrubby pineapple was by now almost lost due to lack of cultivation.[36]

The tomato and the pineapple are strictly American plants which could not have come from Fiji. They were recorded growing wild in pre-missionary settlement areas on the east coast, an area abandoned by the Easter Islanders who all moved to Hangaroa on the west coast when the first Europeans settled ashore in that place. Problem plants also growing in the same abandoned areas were manioc, arrowroot, and tobacco, all American species and nevertheless claimed by native tradition to be of ancestral import as opposed to the various vegetables they recognize as of foreign introduction. In the first decades of European colonization, Thomson wrote: "We saw tobacco plants growing in secluded spots, but were unable to determine by whom or when they were introduced. The natives maintained that the seed was included among that which was brought to the island by the first settlers."[37] The local name for the plant was *ava-ava*, indicating that the leaves had been chewed, like *ava* or *kava*, whereas European smoking tobacco is *odmo-odmo,* to suck, or *puhi-puhi,* to blow. In the Andean area prior to the European introduction of the North American smoking habit, tobacco was cultivated for chewing.

It is important to note that the first foreign plants successfully introduced to Easter Island were those carried by the first missionaries to settle there, who arrived two decades before Thomson. Otherwise the first recorded attempt to introduce foreign plants was that of La Pérouse in 1786; his gardener planted cabbages, carrots, beets, maize, pumpkins, peaches, plums, cherries, oranges, lemons, and cotton,[38] all of which were eaten or destroyed by the local natives before they had a chance to take root.

When the Spaniards arrived on their first voyage from Peru they recognized another important American plant. They recorded that the Easter Islanders had plantations and made their houses of the same *totora* reeds as those grown and used by the natives of Peru.[39] Today this American plant, *Scirpus riparius,* still of paramount importance in the economy of Easter Island, only grows wild in the large bogs of the partly overgrown crater lakes on the island. On European arrival no other plant was as important to the Easter Islanders as building material for their houses and boats; their only furniture were mats made of *totora* reed; hats and baskets were plaited from it; fish nets, cords, and large braided cables were made from the same extremely tough fibers; and the dead were buried in *totora* wrappings. This Easter Island reed was the only representative of this otherwise strictly American species to be found growing outside of the New World. Carbon datings of funeral wrappings, pollen borings, and historic records all combine to show the pre-European introduction of the plant to Easter Island.[40] As a fresh-water species grown only in irrigated fields on the coast of Peru, the *totora* tubers cannot spread with ocean currents, nor are the seeds eaten by sea birds, nor are they carried in their feathers on a two-thousand-mile flight. Its use on aboriginal Easter Island in the manufacture of reed boats of the very type built by the ancient fishermen all along the Pacific coast of South America creates a problem where the botanists have again left the solution to the anthropologists. The plant had originally been named *Scirpus riparius* var. *paschalis,* but in 1956 the noted authority on Easter Island flora, C. Skottsberg, re-examined the plant and found that it did not deserve to be distinguished as a variety, as it was identical with the *Scirpus riparius* of Peru. He admitted that an aboriginal introduction by man was the only feasible explanation: "A direct transport of seeds across the ocean without man's assistance is difficult to imagine, and it is futile to speculate in land connections."[41]

Easter Island tradition insists that one of their early ancestors, Ure, had brought with him the first *totora* root stocks and planted them in the Rano Kao crater lake. It is noteworthy that Uru is the name of the once very important tribe of the Lake Titicaca area, which more than any other people bases its economy on *totora* reeds. Most of the Uru people today are noted for living on floating *totora* islands, building their boats and houses of the same material.

The only plant growing together with the *totora* in the Easter Island crater lakes, apart from a peat-forming moss, is *Polygonum acuminatum,* another strictly American fresh-water plant of aboriginal introduction. Its oversea spread creates the same problem as the fresh-water *totora*. It was used by the early Easter Islanders, as among the natives of the Titicaca basin, as a medical plant.

The wild, or presumably wild, flora of lonely Easter Island was otherwise remarkably poor. It was examined in 1934 by Skottsberg, who found that it comprised only thirty-one flowering plants, of which eleven were pantropical or widespread while twenty species had a distribution restricted either to the east or to the west of the island. Only seven of these were of direct importance to the economy of Easter Islanders: two had come from Polynesia and five from South America.[42] The presence of the two useful Polynesian species could readily be explained through the recognized arrival from Polynesia of the ancestors of the present-day Easter Islanders, but the five useful South American species greatly puzzled the scholars. Skottsberg first wrote in 1934: "From a botanical point of view the plants, with the exception of the American species, offer no great difficulties, provided that we can rely upon the actuality of the transoceanic migration . . . but the presence of an American element is in any case surprising." When the *Kon-Tiki* experiment had shown that South American balsa rafts had a range at least twice as far as that needed to bring seeds and rootstocks to Easter Island, Skottsberg reviewed on new premises the enigmatic origin of the Easter Island flora, and asserted that aboriginal human introduction at least of the two fresh-water species was not only likely but would greatly ease the difficult botanical problem of transplantation in pre-European time.[43]

With Easter Island found to be well stocked with genetic evidence

of aboriginal plant import from the American continent, we may next
turn to the Marquesas group, which is twice as far from South
America though in the main sweep of the Peru Current. The flora of
the Marquesas group was thoroughly studied by F. B. H. Brown and
published in a three-volume report by the Bernice P. Bishop Museum
in 1931–35. Brown recognized that the important breadfruit tree and
wet-land taro, staples of the Marquesas, unknown on Easter Island,
were evidence of aboriginal import from Fiji, yet he was led on purely
botanical grounds to challenge current thought in anthropology by arguing that other plants in the Marquesan flora with equal certainty
revealed human voyages from South America in pre-European time.

We shall see in Chapter 11 that the Marquesas Islanders had
definite tribal traditions of a distant land to the east, in the direction of
South America, from where their ancestors had brought the first coconuts to their islands. Furthermore, the gourd was the only water container here as elsewhere in Polynesia. The sweet potato—kumara—
was grown here as on the other islands, although of less importance
than on Easter Island and Hawaii, due to the preference of the more
easily harvested breadfruit. The domesticated lint-bearing cotton was
growing wild. Brown extended the New World list with the pineapple, Ananas sativus, a strictly American plant with a small fruited
form growing spontaneously from Brazil to the Andean highlands. He
argued that its pre-Columbian growth in the Marquesas group implies
an early crossing of the East Pacific by native craft: ". . . A native of
tropical America, it is evidently of ancient aboriginal introduction in
the Marquesas, where it is to be found in all inhabited valleys. A few
plants occur here and there at low altitudes, but it seems to have been
planted more commonly in the arid uplands . . . One of the largest
pineapple plantations in the Marquesas is in eastern Fatuhiva, on the
dry, rocky, exposed slopes of Mouna Natahu, at an altitude of 900
metres."[44]

In 1937 I lived for some months in the completely isolated Ouia valley at the foot of this mountain, and could witness that these plants
grew wild in an almost inaccessible part of the island hardly seen by
any other Europeans than the intrepid botanist Brown.[45] The mountain-girt valleys on the east coast of Fatu Hiva have never seen any European settlement and were depopulated and abandoned even by their
early Polynesian occupants shortly after first contact with the missionaries. The smallish aboriginal pineapple was abandoned in the

deserted areas of the Marquesas Islands when the larger and better quality was introduced by the Europeans, and the islanders made a clear distinction between the two types, the modern pineapple invariably growing near the historic settlements. It is on record that this better quality was first introduced to the Marquesas in the valley of Taiohae on Nukuhiva at the beginning of the nineteenth century.[46] Brown presents other evidence for its presence in pre-European clearings: "The native names are *haa hoka* (northern dialect) and *faa hoka* (southern dialect) in the Marquesas, *hara* in the Cook Islands . . . The fruit, which is small in comparison with that of commercial varieties, is extremely fragrant and superior in flavor. The following six names and cultivated varieties, all of which were an integral part of the ancient material culture, were evidently originated by the Marquesans from the single Brazilian species. This fact seems fairly positive evidence that the early Polynesians, through contact with America, obtained their original stock long before the discovery of the Marquesas by Europeans."[47]

The papaya, *Carica papaya,* is another fruit incapable of propagation by sea. It belongs to the genus *Carica,* native of tropical America, with a smaller, less tasty variety from Colombia to Peru, where it was often modeled by the pre-Inca pottery makers on the coast. Brown writes: "Carica Papaya . . . At least two varieties are present in the Marquesas: *vi inana* (*vi inata*), recognized by the Marquesans as one of their ancient food plants, is doubtless of aboriginal introduction. Its fruit is smaller and less palatable than the *vi Oahu* which is claimed by the natives to have been introduced from Hawaii by the early missionaries. Both kinds yield abundantly. The native name of the species is *vi inana, vi inata,* or *vi Oahu* in the Marquesas; *ita* in Tahiti; *ninita* in Rarotonga; *eita* in Rimatara; and *hei* in Hawaii. The sap of the papaya, preferably that from a male tree (mamee), is used as a poultice. A native of tropical America; of aboriginal introduction in Polynesia."[48]

Brown was as struck by the presence of a strong South American element in the Marquesan flora as was Skottsberg with regard to Easter Island, and although admitting that several species could have arrived with the natural drifts from the New World, he pointed out that others had as certainly been intentionally or unintentionally introduced by aboriginal voyagers. Since his genetic findings were not in line with current anthropological theories, Brown concluded: "Although it appears that the main stream of Polynesian immigration came from the west, just the opposite direction from which the indigenous flora came, undoubtedly some intercourse may have occurred between the natives of the American continent and those of the Marquesas."[49]

Turning next to Hawaii, this group is far north of the doldrums and therefore outside the range of any natural feeder from South America. W. Hillebrand, in his *Flora of the Hawaiian Islands,* pointed out that these islands lie entirely within the domain of the continuation of the Japan Current deflected from the Northwest American coast, yet he was led to purely hypothetical speculations of a subsidiary feeder coming up from South America: "This accessory stream may or may not account for the important American element of the Andean regions which is apparent in the Hawaiian flora."[50]

This Andean element in Hawaii included the pineapple, already discussed in relation to Easter Island and the Marquesas group. In his 1919 essay on the genus *Ananas,* M. S. Bertoni was among the first to point out that this crop plant seems to have spread into the Pacific island area from South America in pre-Columbian time.[51] In 1930 O. Degener shows in his study of Hawaiian plants that written records testify that the first pineapples imported by Europeans were planted on Hawaii in 1813, i.e., a generation after Cook's discovery of the group, yet he adds that "the Hawaiians had been growing the plant in a semi-wild state long before."[52] In his study of the history of the pineapple J. L. Collins also calls attention to its early presence in Hawaii, showing that it was known as *hala Kahiki* among the local aborigines.[53] The term Kahiki is the Polynesian name for the legendary ancestral fatherland, and *hala* is the same root as *ha'a* and *hara* which, as we have seen, were the aboriginal names for the same plant in the Marquesas group and the Cook Islands respectively.

Hawaii is still another of the Polynesian islands where linted cotton was found growing wild on the arrival of the Europeans. This cotton, *Gossypium tomentosum,* was once thought to be endemic in Hawaii, but in 1947 the aforesaid analysis by Hutchinson, Silow, and Stephens proved it to be a direct derivation of the artificially produced twenty-six-chromosomed cotton brought into existence by the aboriginal culture people of Mexico and Peru. They state that "in view of its close relationship to the New World cottons, *G. tomentosum* can only have reached Hawaii since the establishment of civilization in tropical America."[54]

One other remarkable species in the series of American crop plants in aboriginal Hawaii is the husk tomato, *Physalis peruviana*. Hillebrand says that it is naturalized and records the native name as *poha*. It was used in early Hawaii for its edible berries which keep for several months.[55] The husk tomato is an American crop plant, native of the region from Mexico to Peru. Two types were cultivated in the New World, but the Hawaiian form, *Physalis peruviana,* was principally grown by the aborigines of Peru. Carter extracts nine species of American-Hawaiian plants from Hillebrand's early flora, and states that the entire list deserves to be studied from an ethno-botanical point of view. He says about the husk tomato: "Like cotton, sweet potato, and *Hibiscus, Physalis* points again toward Peru." And: "Even these few notes from an old botany suggest a clue to the origin of the American element in the flora of Hawaii. It would be strange indeed if it should prove that only the 'cosmopolitan weeds' used by man in America were transported by nature to Hawaii and that the same uses found in America traveled with them as in the case for *Argemone.*"[56]

The growth in Hawaii of the strictly American *Argemone* (*A. alba* var. *glauca*) had already been noted by Captain Cook on his discovery of the group, and as a result has caused considerable scholarly headache. In his account of the genus *Argemone,* D. Prain states that its presence in aboriginal Polynesia "is difficult to explain."[57] and his colleague F. Fedde, in a later parallel study merely repeated that it "is really difficult to explain."[58]

The white-flowered Hawaiian *Argemone* was found closest related to a species grown on the Pacific coast of South America. *Argemone* was grown in aboriginal Peru for its narcotic and anesthetic properties,[59] and was used for the same purposes in Hawaii. Naturally then, this plant soon attracted the attention of ethnologists. J. F. G. Stokes of the Bernice P. Bishop Museum in Hawaii was among those who were intrigued by the importance of the American sweet potato in ancient Hawaii, and wrote: "Were there early contact between Hawaii and Central America, it might not be so surprising that the Mexican poppy (*Argemone mexicana*) was found in Hawaii by Cook's people. It might have been ship-borne instead of wind-borne as generally stated."[60]

At last Carter took the full step and suggested: "We are dealing with no weed, but a plant with culturally determined usages. That the plant and its specific usages traveled together suggests purposeful rather than accidental transport. . . . It has the same arbitrary medical uses as in America: not only the use of the seed oil, but also the application of the milky sap to chronic skin diseases. The plant was present when Cook discovered the islands. Fedde long ago noted that this plant grew in open spaces, a characteristic of the introduced plants of the islands as Engler had even earlier noted. Fedde considered it not an ancient introduction. Such evidence certainly suggests that man carried it to Hawaii." Also: "*Argemone* suggests that the exchange of knowledge went beyond food plants into medicine and its associated magic and ritual."[61]

As already stated, it is a mistake to visualize Polynesia as an island paradise prior to the arrival of the first human settlers. Wherever tradition is preserved we learn that the islands had scarcely any useful vegetation in pre-human times. The tradition about the now verdant Mangareva group states that, "When Miru and Moa arrived there, this place had no people. Also there were no tall trees from the beach to the foot of the mountain. Bare stood the land."[62]

Although certain American plants, like the totora reed and the papaya, apparently spread no farther than to the Pacific islands marginal to the American continent from which they originated, others, like the linted cotton, spread through the Society Islands as far as Fiji. Still others, like the sweet potato, spread deeper into Melanesia wherever Polynesian outliers were founded, but no farther. But the coconut seems to have found its way right across the Pacific into Indonesia and the territories beyond, a few centuries prior to European arrival. The reason may be very obvious: the coconut palm was a plant well adapted to survive diffusion by way of the arid intermediate coral atolls of Micronesia, and once successfully introduced it would be a sure companion of long-range voyagers because of its durable contents of flesh and milk.

We have seen in Chapter 2 that the first European discoverers, and even several of the twentieth-century balsa raft voyagers, happened to bypass the tiny islands of Polynesia and sail straight into the negroid domain of Melanesia before touching land. The same might indeed have happened in pre-European time. Even if some Polynesian islands had just been found by pre-Maori-Polynesian explorers from Peru, these would at the time have had little or nothing to offer man other than fish and seabirds, and the voyagers would be apt to push on beyond these uninhabited and uncultivated islands until they reached the large jungle-covered lands of Melanesia, where a very old semi-continental population could offer tropical crops from their own settlements.

An early intrusion in Melanesia from aboriginal America is suggested, not only by the archaeological and historic presence of coiled pottery of American type in this area, combined with an array of other cultural concurrences, but by the presence of spinnable cotton which, unlike the sweet potato and the gourd, would not have been planted by tapa-producing Maori-Polynesian voyagers. Furthermore, an additional number of useful New World plants had found their way as far west as the Samoa-Tonga-Fiji triangle. B. Seemann in the last century had found a large part of the Fijian plants to be of American origin,[63] and Merrill had admitted: ". . . yet even as the Polynesians themselves may possibly have introduced the sweet potato from America into Polynesia, at the same time they may also have introduced a few American weeds."[64] Again, however, the proportion of *useful* plants was conspicuously high. Among them was *Heliconia bihai,* a strictly American fiber plant reappearing unexpectedly in the Polynesian–Melanesian border territory. J. G. Baker discovered that this Pacific Island *Heliconia* appeared to be only a cultivated form, closely related to the species grown by the aboriginal population in Mexico and Peru.[65] Cook again was the first to see the likelihood of human transportation, since the leaves were used by the aboriginal cultivators for making hats, mats, baskets and roof thatch, and the starchy rootstocks were eaten. He said: "Though no longer cultivated by the Polynesians, it has become established in the mountains of Samoa and in many of the more western archipelagoes. In New Caledonia the tough leaves are still woven into hats, but the Pandanus, native in the Malay region, affords a better material for general purposes and has displaced Heliconia in cultivation among the Polynesians."[66]

The taro is always regarded by ethnologists as introduced to Polynesia from Melanesia and this is undoubtedly correct for the true taro, *Colocasia antiquorum,* which will only grow in swampy land and irrigated fields. However, it is not true for the dry land taro, *Xanthosoma atrovirens,* known in Tahiti and the Marquesas as *tarua,* the only kind of taro which in Easter Island grows locally in the dry soil between scattered lava blocks.[67] The dry-land taro can only have come from America, where all species of this genus are at home. Like Cook, Sauer shows that, as in the case of taro, the cultivation of

Xanthosoma in America is usually in moist lowlands. On the Peruvian jungas the roots are dried and stored.

The American yam bean, *Pachyrrhizus,* belongs to the same Polynesian–Melanesian border area. Since it is closely associated with the growing of yam, *Dioscorea,* it may be appropriate to discuss the yam first, since it has had a more problematic history. The yam is generally considered a Melanesian plant brought with the breadfruit into Polynesia. This is by no means certain. The genus had a trans-Pacific distribution in pre-Columbian time, being found by the advancing Europeans from Atlantic Central America to Indonesia. The plant geographer C. O. Sauer shows, in his survey of the cultivated plants of South and Central America, that the New World tropics hold a number of wild species of *Dioscorea,* some with edible tubers.[68] Carter shows that the yam, with its native name *ajes* (pronounced ahes), has been described in detail ever since the first Spaniards landed in the Caribbean, the first mention being in Navarette's account of Columbus' voyage: "Here then is another plant which, like the sweet potato, is propagated vegetatively and hence most unlikely to cross the seas by wind, drift, birds, or other non-human agencies, but which crossed the ocean in pre-Columbian times."[69]

Brown was also fully aware of the fact that the aboriginal yam could have reached the Marquesas from the New World rather than from Melanesia. Learning from the natives that their name for this tuber was *puahi,* he recorded: "The material is not sufficient for accurate determination, but it appears to be near to, if not identical with, *Dioscorea cayennesis* Lamarck, a native of Africa, widely cultivated at an early date in tropical America. . . . The subterranean tubers are highly esteemed by the natives for food. . . . Very rare in the Marquesas. Only a single specimen was found in Fatuhiva, the southernmost island of the archipelago. Doubtless of early aboriginal introduction, and, if *D. cayenensis,* which it closely resembles, it would further indicate contact with America."[70]

The yam was also listed by M. W. Jakeman together with the sweet potato, cotton, hibiscus, the coconut palm, and *Argemone* as an ethnobotanically related group of culture plants grown in the Pacific island area prior to any contact with Europeans: "These, however, probably originated in America and were carried from there to the Islands, since the tradition of agriculture is apparently much older than in the New World, and because the main currents of the Pacific run westward from America to the Islands. That most of these plants were not merely carried to the Islands accidentally by the currents but were transported purposely by one or more migrating groups of ancient Americans is proved by the fact that few of them, i.e., those which can live in salt water, could have crossed the ocean without man's aid . . ."[71]

An argument in favor of the yam having reached the islands from America rather than from Indonesia is seen in the aforesaid association with the yam bean, *Pachyrrhizus*. The yam bean, known by the Quechua Indians of Peru as *ajipa* (pronounced ahipa) is found archaeologically in the pre-Inca graves of the red-haired centerboard navigators at Paracas on the coast of Peru,[72] and is known to be a native of the Andean area, cultivated by the local tribes with yam because of its insecticidal properties.[73] In spite of the important medical qualities its main use is as food, since the watery tubers are delicious and sweet. Guppy was struck by observing the yam bean in Oceania: ". . . the home of the *Pachyrrhizus* is in America. One may indeed wonder how a plant with such a history ever reached the Western Pacific. . . . Though I searched diligently, it never presented me with its seed. In Tonga, according to Graeffe the plant is much employed in preparing the land for yam cultivation . . ."[74]

Again Cook was apparently the first botanist to realize that "in time and labor of travel the Pacific islands were closer to the coastal dwellers of aboriginal Peru than were many of the inland regions conquered by the pre-European rulers of that empire." This, he suggests, will explain how the edible tuber of such a leguminous vine as the yam bean could have spread from Peru to Tonga and Fiji. He says: "The natives of the Tonga Islands no longer cultivate *Pachyrrhizus* for food, but they nevertheless encourage its growth in their fallow clearings in the belief that it renders them the sooner capable of yielding larger crops of yams. . . . the plant sometimes figures in an unexplained manner in their religious ceremonies, an indication of greater importance in ancient times."[75]

Against this mass of genetic evidence of important elements in early Pacific island agriculture having been carried by man from South America, only a single counterargument has been launched: maize, the classic American staple of great antiquity in the New World, was never cultivated in Oceania prior to European introduction. Since this was an undeniable fact in line with current thought on New World isolation from any oversea territories except Siberia, no other botanical observation has so profoundly biased ethnological students. It would therefore be useful to point out that when the Mendaña expedition in 1595 discovered the first Polynesian islands—the Marquesas group—it came from Peru and it brought maize. The expedition explicitly recorded that the crew "sowed maize in presence of the natives."[76] Nevertheless, no maize grew in the Marquesas group when Captain Cook later rediscovered these islands in 1774, nor is maize grown in this group today. Correspondingly, we have seen that La Pérouse in 1786 sowed maize on his visit to Easter Island, yet no maize was found when the missionaries arrived and sowed maize for a second time nearly a century later. Nobody would dispute the historic arrivals of Mendaña in the Marquesas and La Pérouse on Easter Island because the maize they sowed did not catch on. It is, of course, the great number of American crop plants that can be shown as pre-European in Polynesian settlements that tell the story of oversea voyages and not one species that can be shown to be missing. If a missing plant can be used to argue the lack of contact, the absence of the Indonesian staple, rice, should have been given the same attention.

In conclusion, any scholar who has followed with interest the growing body of hard ethno-botanical evidence of the present century can only agree wholeheartedly with the statement of J. Barrau in his opening remarks as chairman of the "Symposium on Plants and the Migrations of Pacific Peoples" at the Pacific Science Congress in Honolulu in 1961. Admitting that Pacific botany had too long been guided by almost universally accepted dogma concerning one-way human traffic in the Pacific, he found it necessary to re-examine the entire botanical evidence in light of the fact that it had now been demonstrated that balsa raft voyagers from South America could well have contributed to the Andean element in the pre-European flora of Oceania.[77]

STEPPINGSTONES FROM SOUTH AMERICA

PART IV

STEPPINGSTONES
FROM
SOUTH AMERICA

Chapter 10

The Pre-Spanish Use of the Galápagos

THE ARRIVAL of the *Kon-Tiki* balsa raft in Polynesia with its crew alive so surprised the scientific world that one noted Americanist publicly announced that he refused to believe the voyage had taken place, a conviction he held until confronted with the documentary film of the expedition. It was now recognized that a balsa raft, contrary to previous opinion, was a seaworthy craft, and that Polynesia lay within the possible reach of aboriginal raft voyagers from South America. The argument next brought up by the isolationists was that, although the balsa raft was shown to be capable of crossing the ocean, the early Peruvians still could have used it only for inshore voyages. Why else, was the common argument, were the islands nearest America, i.e., Juan Fernandez, the Galápagos group, and Cocos Island, not inhabited like distant Polynesia when the Europeans came to the Inca Empire? Why would anyone bypass these islands a few hundred miles off the coast and settle islands thousands of miles farther out?

A map with printed names on an ocean leaves an impression different from seeing the local geography. Did these islands have the same to offer human settlers as the islands farther out? Apparently not. Why else did neither Juan Fernandez, the Galápagos group, or Cocos Island appeal to either Indians or Spaniards once they were officially discovered by Europeans? History shows that the Galápagos group, so favored by iguanas, giant tortoises, seals, and birds, was shunned by human settlers for the lack of a permanent water supply. Only recently a small group of settlers, mainly from Ecuador and Norway, have managed to wrench a living from the cactus-covered land-scape by storing water from the rainy season in modern tanks. Juan Fernandez was not anyone's choice, although Alexander Selkirk, the original model for Defoe's *Robinson Crusoe,* lived there from 1704 to 1709. Cocos Island, although regularly ravaged by fortune hunters looking for a rumored Inca treasure, even today remains uninhabited by man.

The mere existence of an island does not, accordingly, mean that it occasions human settlement any more than do vast regions on the mainland which have failed to attract inhabitants. Polynesia is one of the regions that have always appealed to man. Yet even here islands for various reasons have been left uninhabited until the present time, although this is not evident from looking at a map. On each side of Easter Island, for instance, Sala-y-Gómez, Ducie, and Oeno Islands are all uninhabited but were well known to the people of Easter Island and Mangareva. Uninhabited Henderson Island is important in the economy of the Pitcairn islanders, who go there by longboat to collect timber for wood carving. Pitcairn itself, for unknown reasons, was found uninhabited when Fletcher Christian and the mutineers of the *Bounty* arrived there in 1790 and established the present colony. Yet Pitcairn had been known to aboriginal voyagers, as proven by the mutineers finding small stone statues and other vestiges of former occupation, including non-Polynesian arrowheads of quartz and basalt now in the Pitt Rivers Museum in Oxford.[1]

Could it be that such a large group as the Galápagos, comparatively close to the coast of Ecuador and in the main sweep of the Peru Current, had been known to the South American mariners without tempting them to permanent settlement? Apart from the extreme poverty of the cactus-covered terrain with all the available water in the rainy season immediately filtering away into the porous lava ground, active volcanoes were known to have caused havoc on these islands even in historic times.

A search in the available literature on this group showed a unanimous claim among the authors that there were no archaeological remains in the Galápagos Islands; no one had set foot ashore prior to the arrival of Europeans. This statement, however, never derived from the personal observations of any archaeologist, but was invariably the opinion of zoologists, botanists, geologists, or authors of travel books who, it appeared, merely quoted each other and repeated what had become an axiom. It gradually became apparent that no archaeologist had ever attempted to investigate the Galápagos Islands because it was assumed that the 600-mile distance from the mainland was too far for any aboriginal South American craft.

Rather curious circumstances brought the Galápagos group to the attention of archaeologists. A photograph of a peculiar stone head found by a botanical expedition to the island of Floreana had circulated among archaeologists at The American Museum of Natural History.[2] Partly overgrown by lichen and partly shaded by foliage the head looked so authentic that the Easter Island ethnologist A. Métraux was convinced that long-range Polynesian voyagers must have been responsible for this carving so far away from land. It was the general consensus that the surrounding terrain had to be investigated. I invited two noted archaeologists, E. K. Reed, head of the Archaeological Department of the U. S. National Park Services, and A. Skjölsvold, chief curator of the Archaeological Department of Oslo University, to initiate the first systematic search for pre-European habitation sites in the Galápagos group.

The photograph from Floreana proved to be highly deceptive; a confrontation with the real stone head proved it to be freshly carved by a kindly German settler who had merely retouched a natural lava outcropping to entertain his children and had not the heart to say so when he saw the joy he had given the visiting botanists. No less humorous, however, was the fact that this same settler, Mr. Wittmer, upon learning of our mission, conducted us to his chicken yard, where the poultry had long surprised him by kicking up old potsherds. Recently more of the same material had come to light in the sides of a small ravine as the result of an unusually heavy cloudburst. It happened that chickens, not scientists, uncovered the first bits of archaeology in the Galápagos group.

Our local survey was restricted to the islands of Floreana, Santa Cruz, and Santiago. Our method in selecting promising sites for archaeological test digs was very simple: we went around the islands in a small boat and went ashore wherever anybody before us could possibly have been tempted to make a landing. Such landing areas proved to be extremely limited in the Galápagos group. Eroded cliffs and rugged lava flows with sharp outcroppings left few places for landing, and in the areas where landing was at all possible it was rare to locate a feasible camping ground, since sharp rocks and lava boulders hardly left enough level ground to lie upon. There were, however, a few exceptions on all three islands visited, and these were precisely the places where the archaeologists' trowels were able to verify that aboriginal campers had been ashore before us.

The following chapter is based on a paper entitled "Archaeology in the Galápagos Islands" delivered before the Tenth Pacific Science Congress in Honolulu in 1961. A full and illustrated report on the findings of the Galápagos expedition is published jointly with A. Skjölsvold as *Archaeological Evidence of Pre-Spanish Visits to the Galápagos Islands*, a Memoir of the Society for American Archaeology, Number 12, 1956.

*   *   *

Archaeological investigations of the Galápagos group have until recently been neglected on the assumption that these islands lay outside the range of primitive craft from either South America or Polynesia. It is noteworthy, however, that observers from the sixteenth to the nineteenth centuries, who were familiar with *guara*-operated balsa rafts, considered the Galápagos group well within the range of aboriginal vessels from South America. The conviction that these islands could only be reached by European ships arose when balsa rafts were no longer seen at sea.

We have mentioned that both Miguel Cabello de Balboa and Pedro Sarmiento de Gamboa had known and personally described balsa sailing rafts before they recorded the memories of Inca Tupac's prolonged ocean voyage. The Galápagos group was then already known to the Spaniards, but not yet Polynesia, and Balboa suggested that it might have been the Galápagos group the Inca fleet had visited. Sarmiento de Gamboa, however, had collected so much information that he possessed very exact sailing directions, and he talked the viceroy into dispatching the Mendaña expedition in search of an island 2,400 miles (600 leagues) south-southwest of Callao harbor, remote from the Galápagos Islands.

A brief synopsis of early post-Spanish activities in the Galápagos will here be needed since the prehistory of these islands may be better understood as a background for historic events.

The group was visited for the first time by Europeans in 1535, when a ship carrying the Bishop of Panama, Tomás de Berlanga, was helplessly caught by the offshore current while sailing southward along the mainland coast bound for Peru. In the area where the Niño and the Humboldt currents join forces Berlanga's sailing vessel was caught in a six-day lull and immediately started a rapid drift away from the coast. After drifting helplessly in the doldrums for ten days the vessel came in sight of an island on the tenth day of March. In a subsequent report from Tomás de Berlanga to the emperor of Spain, dated April 26, 1535, the bishop speaks of the futile search for water on this newly discovered island where the ship's crew encountered strange iguanas resembling serpents, and tortoises so large that each one could carry a man on its back. Not a drop of water was found on the island, which was about four to five leagues round. The water supply on board the ship gave out, and the Spaniards, as well as their horses, began to suffer great hardship. The following day one more island was sighted, this one still larger and with high mountains. Because of the currents and the calms it took three days to cross to this island, which proved to be about ten or twelve leagues round. When the ship was anchored everybody went ashore; some were sent inland to search for water and others were put to dig a well, out of which came water "as salty as from the sea." Not a drop of fresh water was found on the island for two days, but the Spaniards survived by eating and squeezing the juice from the leaves of a local cactus. Seals, turtles, tortoises, and iguanas were found on this island as on the first, besides various birds so tame that many were caught in the hand.

The bishop doubted that a place could be found on the island where one might sow a bushel of corn, the surface being like worthless dross with cactus instead of grass and covered by rocks to such an extent that "it seems as though God had sometime showered stones." Because of the shortage of water the Spaniards lost two of their men and ten horses. Finally sufficient water was discovered in a ravine among the rocks to gather eight hogsheads in the boat's barrels and jugs.

From this island two others were seen, one of medium size but the other much larger than the rest, and estimated to be at least fifteen or twenty leagues round. Their altitude was found to be between $\frac{1}{2}°$ and $1\frac{1}{2}°$ south. The Spaniards did not investigate these two latter islands, but thinking that the newly discovered group, which they had reached so very easily, was only some twenty or thirty leagues from the coast of Peru they set sail for the mainland with the meager water supply already mentioned. They soon discovered the strength of the westbound current, however, and they sailed eleven days without sighting land. Then, by finding the latitude to be 3° south, Berlanga realized that the direction they were taking had gradually led them into a still stronger section of the westbound ocean drift. He made the crew sail on the other tack and after ten more days the ship reached the bay of Caráques in Ecuador, no nearer to its destination in Peru than prior to the accidental discovery of the Galápagos.

A second visit to the group, even more hasty and superficial than the first, took place in 1546. During the civil war between Pizarro and the viceroy of Peru, Captain Diego de Rivadeneira stole a ship at Arica, on the north coast of present Chile, and, prevented from an intended landing at Quilca, set sail hoping to escape to New Spain. After twenty-five days at sea without instruments and charts, his vessel came within sight of a very high island which was circumnavigated in three days. A heavy sea prevented the party from landing, and the vessel struggled about in the rapid local currents until twelve more islands had been sighted, all smaller than the first. Only on one of the smaller islands did some of Rivadeneira's twenty-two men finally manage to get ashore, but they did not take time to make more than a cursory search for water for fear that their comrades on board would sail away and leave them in that desolate spot. They hastily returned to the beach, bringing only a few birds back to the ship, which set sail and left the arid group without water supply. Rivadeneira and his men suffered great hardships until a rainstorm quenched their thirst. They finally reached the coast of Guatemala, where Rivadeneira reported his discovery and described the giant Galápagos tortoises, iguanas, sea lions, and birds they had observed.

Some other Spanish caravels sailed into the Galápagos Sea in the latter part of the sixteenth century, but they made no use of the islands, which they found to be desert and without fruit. The local currents and eddies constantly threw their vessels off course and made it seem as if the strange islands were floating about on the surface of the ocean. The group was therefore referred to as *Las Islas Encantadas,* and as Enchanted Islands they remained of no use to man until the English buccaneers landed on the group toward the end of the seventeenth century. From then on the local enchantment was gone, and the buccaneers chose to refer to the group by its more realistic name *Galápagos,* a name actually used for the first time by the Flemish cartographer

Abraham Ortelius in 1570 in honor of the giant local tortoises that had so much impressed the first discoverers.

The first buccaneer expedition that tried to stop in the Galápagos was one commanded by Captain Bartholomew Sharp in 1680. His southbound sailing vessel first followed the coast toward Peru, but turned into the ocean off Punta Parina to avoid being detected by the Spaniards. Out there, where the impact of the Humboldt Current strikes out toward the Galápagos, and in the midst of what the buccaneers describe as a very stiff offshore gale, they encountered a merchant balsa raft under sail. Their own pilot advised them not to meddle with its native crew, "for it was very doubtful whether we should be able to come up with them or not . . ." We learn from the same early buccaneer record that these aboriginal balsa rafts sail "excellently well," and that some are so big as to carry two hundred and fifty packs of meal from the valleys of Peru to Panama without wetting any of it.[3]

In 1684 the pirate ship *Bachelor's Delight* entered the Pacific, where she joined the *Nicholas* and captured three Spanish merchant vessels near the Lobos Islands off the coast of Peru. One of the participating British buccaneers, William Ambrose Cowley, describes the historic event in a manuscript which is preserved in the British Museum. Cowley says ". . . wee sailed away to the Westwards to see if wee could find those Islands called the Galipoloes, which made the Spaniards Laugh at us telling us that they were inchanted Islands and that there was never any but Capitaino Porialto that had ever seen them but could not come near them to Anchor at them, and they were but Shadowes and no reall Islands."[4]

The original entry as quoted here was partly omitted and partly mutilated when the manuscript was published in 1699 by Hacke in his *Collection of Original Voyages* as "Capt. Cowley's Voyage round the Globe."

After three weeks' sailing Cowley and his buccaneer companions did find the Galápagos, where they anchored for twelve days and divided the treasure among themselves while their sick commander, Captain John Cook, was attended to ashore. Several of the islands were visited and Cowley, claiming to be the first to come to anchor there, gave all of them individual names. He also took time to make the first chart of the group. Cowley and his companions, including William Dampier, Edward Davis, Lionel Wafer, Basil Ringrose, and John Cook, found no fresh water on any of the islands they visited, except at

James Bay on James or Santiago Island (referred to by Cowley as Albany Bay on the Duke of York's Island). Here they found "excellent good, sweet Water," and they put ashore a few thousand bags and packs of flour and eight tons of quince marmalade which was part of their strange pirate booty from the Spanish merchant ships. Subsequent visitors have frequently referred to the great quantity of broken "Spanish jars," all large and of one type, found at this place, and they undoubtedly date back to the marmalade booty of the *Bachelor's Delight*.

After depositing their cargo ashore, the buccaneers sailed northward again to try a second time to find fresh water among the other islands, but they came into a current so strong that they did not even manage to get back to James Island to replenish their dwindling water supply. They were forced to steer north-northeast and finally reached the coast of New Spain.

During the next months of 1684–85 the *Bachelor's Delight* joined other privateers that had entered the Pacific and played havoc with Spanish ships off the northwest coast of South America. The viceroy of Peru learned of the provisions and live goats the British pirates had stored in the Galápagos, and sent a party out to destroy the supplies and to put dogs ashore to kill off the goats. In 1685 the *Bachelor's Delight* returned to the enchanted islands to recover only 500 sacks of flour that had been cached, and these had been partly spoiled by birds. During this visit the buccaneers had better luck in finding water, probably due to an unusually heavy rainfall, and they discovered some of the small areas with good soil.

In the next few years the Galápagos group became an important base for the buccaneers harassing the South American coast. Here they were so far from the routes followed by Spanish shipping that they had no need to fear a sudden assault; thus the location was ideal for a secluded retreat between cruises and battles. Animals were let ashore to run wild and supplement the diet of tortoise, turtle, iguana, bird, and fish, and the pirates gradually came to know the very few spots where fresh water could usually be obtained even in the dry season.

Following the British buccaneers, a French expedition of two ships arrived in the Galápagos in 1700. This expedition, led by M. de Beauchesne-Gouin, had traded on the South American coast northward to Callao, but had encountered much trouble because it was constantly mistaken for the buccaneers who were still fresh in the memory of all. The French finally decided to leave the coast to explore the Galápagos group, known by this time to some of the crew who were actually former buccaneers. The expedition visited four of the islands and spent one month in the group, but they found very poor firewood and hardly any water at all, and left the group in contempt, describing it as "the most horrible place in the world" (Beauchesne's hand-written journal in the Dépôt de la Marine).

In 1709 the Galápagos group was twice visited by the *Duke* and the *Duchess* which were sponsored by Bristol merchants for privateering. Like Beauchesne, the commander, Captain Woodes Rogers, was much less enthusiastic about the Galápagos than the buccaneers who had given rather favorable descriptions of the group twenty years earlier.

After these British and French visitors, the turn of the Spaniards came again. Charles III organized expeditions to explore the Pacific waters of America, and in 1789 Alonso de Torres sailed to the Galápagos group, where he renamed all the islands and made a new map, inferior to that of Cowley a century earlier. As far as records show, Don Alonso's visit to the Enchanted Islands was the first of any consequence by a Spaniard since Berlanga's discovery in 1535, a fact of considerable importance in our interpretation of the local ceramic refuse material later to be discussed.

The following year, in 1790, Alessandro Malaspina led the first brief scientific expedition to the Galápagos, with two ships, *Descubierta* and *Atrevida*. On his return Malaspina was unfortunately involved in politics and subsequently imprisoned, for which reason his manuscript papers were never published.

In 1793 another expedition reached the Galápagos and opened an important phase in the local history. Captain James Colnett of the Royal Navy was sent to the Pacific with the ship *Rattler* to explore the whaling grounds and investigate islands and harbors where the whaling boats could put in for repair and refitting. Colnett found the Galápagos to be conveniently located for whalers; here they could also beach their boats and secure fresh provisions, including vast quantities of tasty and readily caught tortoise. He drew the first modern map of the Galápagos group and renamed such islands as he could not identify. He found the watering place of the buccaneers on James Island entirely dried up, but suspected that other water holes might exist further inland. A considerable number of the Spanish jars left by the buccaneers were still scattered about and some of them were found to be undamaged. Old daggers, nails, and other implements similarly recognized by Colnett's party as remains from the buccaneers were also found in the same place.

With the publication in 1798 of Colnett's extensive report on his mission the whaling era of the Galápagos group began. The buccaneer era of the islands had long ended. Only in 1816 did the group again have a very brief visit from such adventurers, when the corsairs Buchard and Brown sailed to the group to divide their loot. Whereas the buccaneers in their day had favored James Bay on Santiago, the whalers made use of the good anchorage with fresh water at Tagus Cove on the west coast of Isabela, and thenceforward Post Office Bay on Floreana became a regular port of call where mail was left in a barrel by outward-bound vessels and unofficially collected by others that were homeward-bound.

War came to the Galápagos in 1812 when Captain David Porter in the United States frigate *Essex* arrived with the intention of clearing the Pacific of British whalers. He was guided by an American whaler from the South American coastal waters to the barrel in Post Office Bay. There he found important intelligence in the mail waiting to be picked up by homeward-bound British whalers, and was thus able to capture a great number of enemy ships.

At that time the Galápagos group had also just received its first resident in historic times. An Irish sailor named Patrick Watkins had quarreled with the captain of his ship, and was set ashore near Post Office Bay on Floreana at his own request. About a mile inland he built a hut where he found a spot with sufficient soil and moisture to raise about two acres of potatoes and pumpkins, which he brought to the coast and sold to the regularly passing whalers. Captain Porter, in the journal of his own cruise, published in London in 1823, gives a vivid description of the hermit who resorted to rum in his solitude, and finally through trickery and violence managed to get four sailors from other vessels ashore where he kept them entirely as his slaves. Describing how Patrick and his weird companions finally escaped in a stolen boat, Captain Porter prophesied that the Galápagos group would remain unpopulated for many generations to come. A little more than a decade later, however, the first organized attempt to colonize the islands was planned by José Villamil.

The Galápagos group had so far remained unclaimed territory, but as Ecuador had just received its independence, Villamil, an Ecuadorian general, conceived the idea of organizing a colonization company and in 1832 he took official possession of the islands in the name of the government of Ecuador. He renamed the group Archipélago de Colón. Villamil obtained pardon for eighty soldiers who had been condemned to death after a rebellion, and he sent them with a number of their women to Floreana Island to form the first historic settlement of the group a few miles inland from Black Beach. Here, in the garua zone, at an altitude of 1,000 feet, the island has a very small but good spring in the rocks and sufficient soil to permit modest agriculture and support a few domestic animals. But trouble came to the settlers when the government had the place converted to a penal colony and increased the local population with a couple of hundred convicts. After a few years Villamil was discouraged and resigned as governor of the group; trouble and uprisings resulted, and most of the convicts escaped. In 1845 the colony, now reduced to a fraction of its former size, was transferred to Wreck Bay on San Cristobal, where fresh water was discovered on the high land in the interior. Only a few of the colonists remained on Floreana, all of them criminals in exile.

About this time the Swedish captain C. Skogman, on his world cruise in 1851–53, sailed through local waters and reported meeting balsa rafts navigating with sails hoisted on bipod masts and with long *guara* sunk between the logs fore and aft. It is important to note that these rafts apparently kept up a long tradition, since Skogman expressly recorded that they even visited the distant Galápagos group.[5]

A second attempt to colonize Floreana was made in 1870 by Valdizian, but the government again interfered by converting the colony to a penal settlement. Valdizian was murdered by the convicts in combat and the remaining colonists left the island altogether. Deserted orchards and wild cattle remained and tempted Antonio Gil in 1802 to make a third attempt to colonize the same island, but after four years he and his party also gave up and left for Isabela, where they founded a settlement on the southeast coast. While depending on some brackish water found between the rocks near the coast, they made a living by shipping sulphur from the local crater to Guayaquil in Ecuador. The local port on Isabela was named in honor of Villamil, and a small garrison was established there in 1902.

At this time San Cristobal was the convict center, and a certain Manuel Cobos had acted as a local dictator, brutally treating the convicts on the sugar plantation he had started in the interior garua plateau in 1880. Subsequently the convicts were transferred to Villamil on Isabela, while Wreck Bay on San Cristobal has today become the main port and center of the island government, with a small Ecuadorian garrison. A local water line was built by American engineers during the Second World War, bringing to the bay garua water which was formerly lost into the sea through a waterfall on the uninhabitable side of the island.

In the twenties and thirties of the present century a few Norwegian, Ecuadorian, and German emigrants reached the islands, occasionally in organized groups. Nearly all of them have left because of the local water shortage. A few, however, settled in Academy Bay on Santa Cruz, some among the ash and cactus near the bay, where brackish water was found by clearing a well between some rocks, and some at the end of a trail leading a few miles up the hills on a garua area that had soil and where rain could be gathered in tanks during the wet season. A few Ecuadorians have since then joined the European settlements in Academy Bay, which represents the only inhabited area on the island of Santa Cruz, and a very small Ecuadorian garrison is now located on Seymour, an arid little isle at the north end of Santa Cruz where the United States Air Force built a landing strip during the Second World War. It is dependent on imported water. Wreck Bay has remained the only settlement area on San Cristobal, and Villamil the only one on Isabela. Recently a dozen Ecuadorians resettled Black Beach on Floreana, and a German settler has successfully found a living for his small family higher up in the hills at the little spring first chosen by Villamil and his pioneers. For the rest, the Galápagos group has remained entirely uninhabited and unexploited other than for its almost inexhaustible fish supply. A modern attempt to establish a fishing settlement in Post Office Bay failed entirely, as did an attempt to export salt from a crater lake in James Bay on Santiago. A limited quantity of salt was removed from the crater in the thirties of the last century, the local deposits having been first recorded by the buccaneers. In recent years a few individuals have attempted to settle in this same bay and in one or two other localities on the islands, mainly in Floreana, but their visits have been of short duration and few traces are to be seen of their camps and huts.

With the twentieth century began the first scholarly discussions of possible pre-Spanish visits to the Galápagos. Experts in Inca history from C. R. Markham in 1907 to P. A. Means in 1942 have been so impressed by the obviously historic aspect of Inca Tupac's ocean voyage that they believed his raft armada to have visited the Galápagos, since these were the nearest oceanic islands. T. J. Hutchinson in 1875 had already termed the balsa raft a "floating bundle of corkwood,"[6] and Means, although believing the Incas had reached the Galápagos, underestimated the raft which had taken them there, stating it was "obviously a type of boat that would awake nothing but scorn in the breasts of shipbuilders of almost any other maritime people of the world."[7]

As we have seen, S. K. Lothrop made a more comprehensive study in 1932 of the practical aspects of such a voyage, but was misled by an erroneous nineteenth-century source into believing that the Galápagos could never have been reached by balsa rafts, because in a few weeks at sea, it was believed, they lost their buoyancy and needed to be taken ashore to dry. From this Lothrop concluded that a balsa raft could not have remained afloat at sea long enough even to complete a voyage to the Galápagos, and he suggested that Tupac may instead have transported an army to the mainland north of Guayaquil, and plundered it.[8]

J. Hornell in 1946 quoted Lothrop, but suggested that perhaps the early Peruvians used some preparation of gum, resin, or wax in some solvent with which they treated the logs, and that this had helped the Inca rafts to remain afloat as far as the Galápagos.[9]

However, the erroneous assumption concerning the balsa rafts deprived archaeologists of any motive for investigating the uninhabited Galápagos. General visitors to the group, instead of being alerted to the possibility of finding pre-Inca vestiges, denied that such could exist. For example, V. W. von Hagen in 1949 was led to assert: "Whatever islands the Inca sailed to, he did not sail to the Galápagos." He supported this assertion by citing presumably authoritative statements to the effect that the Andean seaboard dwellers were "majestically inept" in marine matters, and concluded that an Inca landing on the Galápagos "was a mainfest impossibility."[10]

Subsequent experiments have shown that these modern assessments of the balsa rafts were mistaken since, as we have seen, balsa rafts subsequent to 1947 have landed in the Galápagos from both Peru and Ecuador and many others have gone on to Polynesia, Melanesia, and even Australia. Thus the Galápagos are well within the feasible range of aboriginal South American vessels, such as actually witnessed by Skogman in the middle of the last century.

It was with full confidence in the balsa raft, after sailing it to Polynesia in 1947, that I left for the Galápagos accompanied by the archaeologists E. K. Reed and A. Skjösvold in 1953. No attempt was made to accomplish an exhaustive survey of the group or any single island, and areas for investigation were selected with consideration of the apparent geographical possibilities of aboriginal occupation, together with landing facilities for primitive vessels.

Four pre-Spanish occupation areas were located on three different islands. The largest site was on the plateau above James Bay on Santiago Island, where eight different aboriginal camp sites were located. A mountain ridge separated these from another site at Buccaneer Bay on the same island. The two other sites were encountered respectively at Whale Bay on Santa Cruz and at Black Beach on Floreana. Subsequent to our departure, a further prehistoric site was located at Cabo Colorado on Santa Cruz by J. C. Couffer and C. Hall.

The material excavated from the sparse soil and located in lava cracks was aboriginal ceramic shards, a bird-shaped Mochica terra-cotta flute, molded Chimu frog appliqués, a chalk stone spinning whorl, and

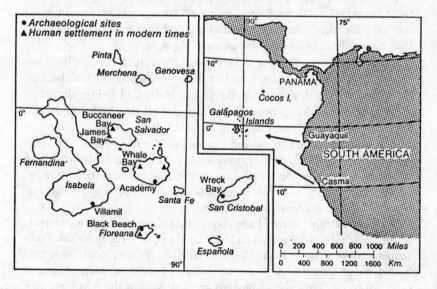

Archaeological sites in the Galápagos Islands.

several flint and obsidian scrapers. The combined sites yielded in all 1,961 aboriginal ceramic shards, representing at least 131 different pots, probably more. Of these, forty-four pots were identifiable with known ceramic wares from the coasts of Ecuador and northern Peru, and thirteen additional pots are probably identifiable with ware from the same area. The remaining seventy-four pots represent aboriginal ware of which sixty-seven are unidentified merely because of insufficient characteristics in the limited material preserved, whereas seven aboriginal coiled pots are unidentifiable in spite of striking characteristics. Some sites produced only Peruvian shards, while others yielded both Peruvian and Ecuadorian material. The ceramic types from the north coast of Peru were studied and identified by the leading contemporary authorities on prehistoric ware from that area, C. Evans and B. J. Meggers of the Smithsonian Institution, U. S. National Museum. The Galápagos material was identified as follows:

La Plata Molded ware is represented by three pots from two different localities in James Bay. San Juan Molded is represented by one pot from another locality in James Bay. Queneto Polished Plain is represented by two pots from two different localities in James Bay. Tiahuanacoid ware is represented by three pots from two different localities in James Bay. San Nicolas Molded is represented by one pot from James Bay. Tomaval Plain is represented by at least fifteen pots from James Bay, Buccaneer Bay, Whale Bay, and Black Beach. Another five pots from three sites were probably Tomaval plain. Castillo Plain is represented by at least ten pots from James Bay, Whale Bay, and Black Beach. The latter site also produced a Mochica-type clay whistle. Another six pots were probably Castillo Plain. The other identifiable pots were characteristic plainware from the Guayas area in Ecuador.

With the exception of three pots of hitherto unknown non-European type, represented by 377 rim, handle, and body shards of a very thin ware with thick, glossy, red slip, and complex form, no distinctly new types of ceramic ware were encountered. In other words, the material collected is in itself of scant scientific value. Its only importance is embodied in the fact that it has been left behind in the Galápagos Islands with distances varying from 600 to 1,000 miles from its identifiable mainland points of origin.

Naturally the question arises: to what extent may some of these

remains have found their way to these oceanic islands in post-Columbian times?

As we have seen, the group was accidentally discovered by Europeans in 1535, when Bishop Tomás de Berlanga was caught by the
strong offshore set of the current while sailing from Panama, bound
for Peru. A day was spent on one island and two on another in a futile
search for water, whereupon the Spaniards barely managed to tack
back to Ecuador. Coming from Panama, however, the bishop and his
party could scarcely have brought aboriginal Peruvian or Ecuadorian
ceramics to the Galápagos.

A second visit to the group was the one in 1546, when Captain
Diego de Rivadeneira stole a ship at Arica in Chile and set sail for
Guatemala. He rediscovered the Galápagos, and a brief and futile
search for water was made on one of the smaller islands, whereupon
the ship immediately left the group without anybody setting foot on
any of the other islands.

We know that a few other Spanish caravels sailed into the Galápagos Sea in the latter part of the sixteenth century, but it is also
known that they made no use of the islands, which they found to be
desert, without fruit or water. It is possible that some of these caravels
carried Indians aboard, and that some of these went ashore with ceramic pots, a few of which were broken there, but it is hardly likely
that they carried a minimum of 131 aboriginal pots ashore and broke
them all at different sites. Nor would they even have brought along
such a variety of ware, representing widely separated geographical regions and cultural epochs in aboriginal Peru and Ecuador, some of
which existed only archaeologically in historic time.

We have seen that to the Spaniards this remote group in the treacherous Peru Current remained *Las Islas Encantadas* until British buccaneers found it a convenient hide-out toward the end of the seventeenth
century.

There is, accordingly, no foundation for any hypothesis of post-
European introduction of the aboriginal refuse in various sites in the
Galápagos group. The identification by Evans and Meggers of the
Peruvian ware shows that the local deposits consist of pre-Inca material
dating back through Estero, La Plata, and Tomaval periods on the
mainland, which means that refuse from at least two of the Galápagos
sites are datable to coastal Tiahuanaco times.

The discovery of shards from a minimum of 131 aboriginal pots, broken and left behind in the Galápagos, implies a considerable human activity in pre-colonial times. It is quite obvious that our cursory survey failed to reveal all sites and uncovered only part of the material still available. Owing to the general scarcity of soil on the coastal cliffs, much of the refuse must also have been washed into the sea. It is clear, moreover, that we are dealing with repeated visits rather than permanent habitation, as the latter would have left thicker deposits and a more homogeneous ware. Local development would scarcely have succeeded in achieving an independent evolution in pottery that closely followed the mainland pattern from Castillo and Tomaval Plain ware through Polychrome Tiahuanacoid, San Nicolas Molded, and finally the three characteristic types of Chimu blackware as represented by Queneto Polished Plain and San Juan and La Plata Molded. Geographically, the refuse deposited represents ceramic types from the Guayas area of Ecuador down to the Casma Valley near the transition to the central coast of Peru, 1,000 miles away.

To summarize: the use of the arid, cinder-covered Galápagos Islands, probably as a fishing outpost, is not of European origin, but the continuation of an aboriginal pattern that appears to date at least as far back as the Coastal Tiahuanaco period in the Peruvian archaeological sequence.

Chapter 11

The Coconuts of Cocos Island

THE THREE ISLANDS of Juan Fernandez are located in the north-bound sweep of the Antarctic current so far south of the Inca empire and so remote from the area formerly frequented by balsa rafts that they can hardly have been of much importance to aboriginal South American navigators. This was not so with the Galápagos group and Cocos Island. The Galápagos group lies exactly on the equatorial line and thus in the precise latitude of Manta, where, according to Inca legends, Con-Tici-Viracocha embarked with his white and bearded men and where Inca history also locates the point of departure for Inca Tupac's long balsa raft expedition.

We have learned from archaeology that the Galápagos group has been visited from the mainland since Tiahuanaco times and history records that balsa rafts still sailed to these desert islands in the first half of the last century. It is not difficult to understand that the Galápagos, although deprived of permanent water supply, still had a great attraction to aboriginal food gatherers and merchants. The islands were stocked with enormous quantities of large edible iguanas and giant tortoises, both species easily caught by hand, the later particularly suitable for long-range transport as oil and food supply. Attempts at cultivating cotton on these dry islands are also indicated by the fact that botanists have now reduced the endemic wild cotton of the Galápagos, *Gossypium darwinnii,* to a mere variety of the twenty-six-chromosomed *Gossypium barbadense* which was the South American species artificially produced by the pre-European civilizations in Peru. This secondarily wild Galápagos cotton still has spinnable, even though not particularly attractive lint, and will explain why an aboriginal type of chalkstone spinning whorl was among the artifacts excavated by our expedition in the Galápagos. The main attraction of the group, however, lies in the enormous wealth of fish which still attracts fishing vessels from all parts of the Pacific. Since, as we have seen, this group is located right on the equator, it is surrounded by a chaos of currents and upwellings stimulating marine life. Cold westbound waters of the Humboldt or Peru Current wash the southern islands of the group while the warm Niño Current from Panama and equatorial upwellings surround the northern part of the group. These currents, as we have seen, were so strong that they dragged the early sailing ships westward with such a speed that early mariners, and some even in the present century, considered the islands to be drifting about, hence they became *Las Islas Encantadas,* The Enchanted Islands.

The discovery that the Galápagos Islands, although possibly never properly settled, had been more important to the pre-European mariners of Ecuador and Peru than to the Spaniards who arrived later, warrants a re-examination of the puzzling prehistory of lonely Cocos Island. Cocos Island, unlike the cinder-covered Galápagos group, has plenty of water and rich soil. Although in modern times a convenient port of call for cruising ships from Panama, the island has never tempted post-Columbian settlers. Was it correspondingly unimportant in pre-European times? There is no reason to suspect the contrary.

This chapter is based on "Notes on the Pre-European Coconut Groves on Cocos Island" which appeared as Part 17 of the second volume of *The Norwegian Archaeological Expedition to Easter Island and the East Pacific,* published in 1965.

*   *   *

Cocos Island is located 5°35′ N, about 500 miles west of Panama, and thus lies in the doldrum belt of confused currents interjacent between the two vast and westward-moving North and South Equatorial currents. This is too far north to have had any bearing on possible sailing routes from South America to Polynesia. Cocos Island lies only 300 miles southwest of Costa Rica, however, on a direct line between Guatemala and Ecuador. Since modern archaeologists have found accumulating evidence of direct pre-European trade contact between Guatemala and the coast cultures of Ecuador and North Peru, it has been pointed out by M. D. Coe[1] and others that Cocos Island would be ideally located as an intermediate port of call for aboriginal voyagers between these two areas. Here they could provision their vessels with any desirable quantity of green coconuts filled with refreshing and preservable liquid.

Other observers have been struck by the strong resemblance between the stone statues discovered in Colombia and Ecuador and those on the nearest islands in Polynesia, i.e., in the two easternmost islands of Hivaoa and Nukuhiva in the Marquesas group. Returning to Panama with our expedition ship, after completing the excavation of these two statuary sites in the coconut groves of the Marquesas, Cocos Island lay right on our route and we decided in July 1956 to make a call to get acquainted with the local geography.

Cocos Island is defended all round by vertical cliffs, about 300 to 600 feet high, which fall abruptly from the coastal highland into the pounding ocean. The island covers an area of about eighteen square miles (about forty-five square kilometers), and the interior hills rise to an altitude of about 3,000 feet (911 meters). Only at the north end of the island are the coastal cliffs broken by two permanent streams, the mouths of which have built up small mud flats to form Wafer Bay and Chatham Bay. These two bays extend some way inland as closed, mountain-girt valleys. Neither reach the interior highlands, as both are closed on the landward sides by steep walls.

Rainfall is very heavy, creating innumerable waterfalls that leap directly from hanging valleys or from the tops of the cliffs into basins hollowed out of the shore shelf. Because of the great humidity, the steep valley walls as well as the inland plateaus and ridges are covered by dense and impenetrable tropical jungles, and dense moss and foliage cover most of the vertical cliffs around the coast. It is impossible to penetrate into the interior, other than part way up the two main river beds, except by clearing a passage through the undergrowth.

The general vegetation has greatly changed since the island was first named and described by Europeans. Coconut palms are now so few that the name Cocos Island seems truly exaggerated in relation to other islands closer to the Isthmus or farther out in the Pacific. That the island formerly merited its descriptive name, however, is apparent from the verbal accounts given to Captain Dampier by the contemporary Spanish discoverers. Dampier writes: "The Island Cocos is so named by the Spaniards, because there are abundances of Coco-nut Trees growing on it. They are not only in one or two places, but grow in great Groves . . . This is the account that the *Spaniards* give of it, and I had the same also from Captain Eaton, who was there afterwards."[2]

Among the very first visitors was Captain Wafer, who called at the island in 1685 and whose name was given to the landing place: "Our men being tolerably well recover'd, we stood away to the Southward, and came to the Island *Cocos,* in 5 Deg. 15 Min. N. Lat. 'Tis so called from its Coco-Nuts, wherewith 'tis plentifully stor'd. 'Tis but a small Island, yet a pleasant one: For the Middle of the Island is a steep Hill, surrounded all about with a Plain, declining to the Sea. This Plain, and particularly the Valley where you go ashore, is thick set with Coco-nut Trees, which flourish here very finely, it being rich and fruitful Soil. They grow also on the Skirts of the Hilly Ground in the Middle of the Isle, and scattering in Spots upon the Sides of it, very pleasantly. But that which contributes most to the Pleasure of the Place is, that a great many Springs of clear and sweet Water rising to the Top of the Hill, are there gathered in a deep large Bason or Pond, the top subsiding inwards quite round; and the Water having by this Means no Channel whereby to flow along, as in a Brook or River, it overflows the Verge of its Bason in several Places, and runs trickling down in many pretty Streams. In some Places of its overflowing, the rock Sides of the Hill being more than perpendicular, and hanging over the Plain beneath, the Water pours down in a Cataract, as out of a Bucket, so as to leave a space dry under the Spout, and form a kind of arch of water; which together with the Advantage of the Prospect, the near adjoining Coco-nut Trees, and the Freshness which the Falling Water gives the Air in this hot Climate, makes it a very charming Place, and deleightful to several of the senses at once.

"Our Men were very much pleas'd with the Entertainment this Island afforded them: And they also fil'd here all their Water-Casks; for here is excellent fresh Water in the Rivulet, which those little Cataracts form below in the Plain, and the Ship lay just at its Outlet into the Sea, where there was very good Riding: So that 'tis as commodious a Watering-place as any I have met with.

"Nor did we spare the Coco-nuts, eating what we would, and drinking the Milk, and carrying several Hundreds of them on board. Some or other of our Men went ashore every Day: And one Day among the rest, being minded to make themselves very merry, they went ashore and cut down a great many Coco-trees; from which they gathered the

Fruit, and drew about 20 Gallons of the Milk. Then they all sat down and drank Healths to the King, and Queen, & c. They drank an excessive Quantity; yet it did not end in Drunkenness: but however, that Sort of Liquor had so chilled and benumb'd their Nerves, that they could neither go nor stand: Nor could they return on board the Ship, without the Help of those who had not been Partakers in the Frolick: Nor did they recover it under 4 or 5 Days Time."[3]

The presence at one time on Cocos Island of these extensive pre-European coconut groves must be explained either by local activity of planters arriving from America or from Polynesia, or else by natural dispersal of the nuts with the ocean current. All three hypotheses have been expounded. As is often the case with Pacific botany, the conclusions of botanists, of great importance to anthropological reconstructions, have to a great extent been founded on current ideas of human movements. The question of the origin of *Coco nucifera* has been touched upon in Chapter 9.

The coconut palm was first known to Europeans by its existence in India and Indonesia only because they came to that area long before they discovered America. Apollonius of Tyana saw the coconut palm in Hindustan at the beginning of the Christian era, when it was regarded as an Indian curiosity. Its arrival in continental Asia from the Malay archipelago was probably not much before that time. The earliest Chinese descriptions are from the ninth century of our own era, and its arrival in Ceylon is ascribed to an almost historic epoch.[4]

When Columbus discovered Cuba on his first voyage to America, his Journal recorded that he found a beach with many very tall palms and "a large nut of the kind belonging to India." When the Spaniards reached the Isthmus of Panama, Oviedo recorded in 1526 that "there is both in the firm land and the ilandes a certain tree called Cocus . . . ," whereupon he proceeds to give a most detailed description of the coconut and its uses.[5]

Botanists of the seventeenth century often continued thereafter to regard the coconut palm as an Asiatic species, but in the nineteenth century Martius (1823–50) and Grisebach (1872) arrived at the conclusion that the plant, for botanical reasons, must be of New World origin. De Candolle originally shared their view, since eleven related species of the genus *Cocos* were American, while none was Asiatic. However, as we have seen in Chapter 9, De Candolle, himself the founder of ethno-botanical teaching, was gradually so influenced by the ethnologists that he began to waver. Although still admitting that strictly botanical evidence argued an American origin, the navigational problems, combined with a variety of names and uses in Indonesia, led him by 1884 to conclude that the origin of the coconut was obscure. He proposed that canoes from Indonesia, loaded with coconuts, might have been "thrown by tempests or false maneuvers on to the islands or the west coast of America," and that "the converse is highly improbable." De Candolle therefore assumed that even the coconut palms of Cocos Island might have been brought there by Polynesian voyagers rather than by the coastal dwellers of nearby South America.[6]

We have seen that a number of scholars have followed De Candolle in his theory on the spread of the coconut, resting heavily on ethnographic arguments, whereas others have equally consistently followed Martius and Grisebach in pointing to the absence of related species in Indonesia and continental Asia. The most active protagonist for an American home for this species was, as earlier shown, O. F. Cook, who also deserves credit for having brought Cocos Island into the heart of the discussion. He wrote: "If the coconut could be submitted as a new natural object to a specialist familiar with all known palms, he would without hesitation recognize it as a product of America, since all the score of related genera, including about three hundred species, are American. With equal confidence the specialist would assign the coconut to South America, because all other species of the genus Cocos are confined to that continent, and he would further locate it in the northwestern portion of South America, because the wild species of Cocos of that region are much more similar to the coconut than are those of the Amazon Valley and eastern Brazil. Thus, from a purely biological standpoint, it is reasonable to suppose that the vigorous and productive coconut palms reported by Humboldt in the interior districts of Venezuela and Colombia may have been growing near the ancestral home of the species." And: "The uses of the coconut have been most highly developed in the Pacific islands because lack of other plants has compelled the inhabitants to depend on it more and more. Necessity has given rise to the multiplicity of uses, but the palm itself had to be brought from the only part of the world where such palms grew—South America.

"The presence of large numbers of coconuts on Cocos Island in the time of Wafer (1685) and their subsequent disappearance should be considered as evidence that the island was formerly inhabited, or at least regularly visited, by the maritime natives of the adjacent mainland . . . Even without a permanent population the coconuts may have been planted and cared for by natives of the mainland for use during fishing expeditions, a plan followed in some localities in the Malay region. The serious disturbances that followed the arrival of the Spaniards in the Panama region would naturally tend to interrupt such visits. Ethnologists may find in this hitherto unsuspected primitive occupation of Cocos Island additional evidence of the maritime skill of the Indians of the Pacific coast of tropical America, and thus be more willing to consider the possibility of prehistoric communication between the shores of the American continent and the Pacific islands."[7]

Today the majority of botanical opinion inclines to the view that America must have been the original homeland and first center of domestication of *Cocos nucifera*. Cocos Island lies no further away from the pre-European coconut groves in Costa Rica, Panama, and Colombia than a coconut could reasonably be expected to float without losing its buoyancy. Self-propagation across such extensive spans of ocean as that which separates Cocos Island from Polynesia would be more than improbable, however, since the viability of a coconut is lost long before its buoyancy.

We have also seen in Chapter 9, from experiments conducted by Edmondson with floating coconuts in Hawaii, and by us with coconuts submerged under the deck of the *Kon-Tiki,* that sea water gradually penetrates the soft area of the coconut eyes, causing micro-organisms to destroy the nut's ability to germinate after a couple of months at sea. Upon an extensive drift, like the one between Cocos Island and Polynesia, a coconut would no longer sprout even if granted ideal conditions by being carried to a cleared area and properly planted in sand mixed with soil. If the coconut palm reached Cocos Island from any part of Polynesia, this must have happened through the agency of man.

The nearest possible area within Polynesia whence the coconuts could have been carried to Cocos Island is the Marquesas group. It is noteworthy that the Marquesas islanders were well aware of the existence of an island far to the east of their own group, a fact that much puzzled the early Europeans. Even on the remarkably correct sailing chart made for Captain Cook by his native informant, Tupia of Ulitea, an unidentified island named Utu by the Polynesians (and spelled Ootoo by the Englishmen) was marked in the ocean to the east of the Marquesas group. Later Captain Porter was told independently by the natives of the Marquesas that there was an island to windward, i.e. to the east, of their own group, known to them as Utupu (Ootoopoo). Over a century and a half ago he wrote: "None of our navigators have yet discovered an island of that name, so situated; but in examining the chart of Tupia . . . we find nearly in the place assigned by the natives of *Nooaheevah* [Nukuhiva] to Ootoopoo an island called Ootoo . . . this chart, although not drawn with the accuracy which could be expected from our hydrographers, was, nevertheless, constructed by Sir Joseph Banks, under the direction of Tupia, and was of great assistance to Cook and other navigators in discovering the islands . . . Of the existence of Ootoo or Ootoopoo there cannot be a doubt; Tupia received such information from the accounts of other navigators as enabled him to give it a position on his chart nearly fifty years ago, and the position now ascribed to it by Gattenewa [of Nukuhiva], differs little from that of Tupia."

Of particular interest for the present study is that the easterly island of Utupu was remembered in Polynesian traditions specifically because it was where the ancestors had obtained the extremely important coconut palm. Porter laid emphasis on this significant piece of Marquesan tradition: "The coco-nut tree, as I before remarked, was said to have been brought from Ootoopoo, an island which is supposed by the natives to be situated somewhere to the windward of La Magdalena [Fatu-Hiva]."[8]

The folk memory that the coconut was introduced from an island lying to the east of the Marquesas, where the Europeans also actually discovered a lonely Pacific island so full of coconut palms that it became the one Pacific island named after a plant, speaks strongly for Cocos Island being identical with the island of Utupu in Polynesian traditions. There is no other island to the windward of the Marquesas but Cocos and the cinder-covered Galápagos, where no coconut palms grew.

Botanical evidence to indicate that the coconut palm spread from an original home in northwestern South America and westward across the Pacific is therefore strongly supported by ethnographic records which even pinpoint the route from Cocos Island to the nearest group in eastern Polynesia. The remaining question is how the coconut palm first reached oceanic Cocos Island from one of the aboriginal centers of coconut domestication in Colombia, Panama, or Costa Rica. The object of our brief visit was to investigate the possibility of a natural spread by acquainting ourselves with such details in the local topography and vegetation as could not be gained from the sparse literature and rather sketchy maps of the island.

An inshore cruise around the precipitous coast sufficed to show beyond question that the high cliffs and hanging walls of Cocos Island would not give the least foothold for a seaborne coconut anywhere except at the two narrow river mouths of Chatham Bay and Wafer Bay on the north coast. The expedition ship anchored off Chatham Bay, and landings were effected both there and at Wafer Bay.

The change of vegetation since Wafer's visit in 1685 was so pronounced that it would have been tempting to suspect that he had visited another island, had he not given an exact position which precludes confusion. Whereas Wafer's party had no difficulties in visiting the highland plains and hills in the middle of the island, our party had considerable difficulty in penetrating merely the overgrown valley where Wafer landed.

During the single day we had at our disposal on the island, none of the expedition reached beyond the steeply rising walls at the bottom of Wafer Valley or the ridges near the landing. Further, we had noted that according to L. J. Chubb, during his geological survey, he was unable to explore the interior sufficiently to investigate the existence of a possible crater lake such as was suggested by Wafer's description.[9] Undoubtedly, a determined effort to cut a trail uphill and inland is fully possible, but it does not appear that this was necessary during the Englishmen's visit, when the inland plain and the valley where his party had gone ashore were "thick set with Coco-nut Trees, which flourished here very finely . . ."

Unquestionably, during more than two and a half centuries the jungle had encroached upon the existing coconut groves, and recaptured the former clearings. Our reconnaissance, with a view inland, revealed that in the elevated interior forest area, and at widely separated points on top of the densely jungle-covered ridges, there were single isolated coconut palms, kilometers apart. Some very few isolated palms also emerged from the compact roof of the jungle in the interior of the two valleys. Only a very small piece of level land close to the beach in

Wafer Bay preserved a cluster of coconut palms large enough to be considered a very small grove. This area near the beach showed evidence of recent clearing, and some of the palms have been chopped down, possibly during the brief local establishment of a Costa Rican penal colony.

But for Wafer's original description of extensive former inland groves, it might have been tempting to suspect that on Cocos Island *Cocos nucifera* was not a littoral plant but a truly wild palm that grew spontaneously as an integral part of the rain forest. This, then, would have been the only locality where *Cocos nucifera* could be found growing in a truly wild state, and the question of origin would have been conclusively answered.

The cluster of palms near the beach in Wafer Bay could theoretically have been the result of drifts from continental America prior to Wafer's visit. From this beach the coconut palms might have spread inland along the bottom of the ravine by natural propagation, provided the present jungle was not there to arrest and suppress the progress of the extremely sun-craving young palms. A professional copra planter, A. Kinander, who accompanied the expedition group from the Society Islands, was fully convinced that a sprouting coconut would be completely choked by the dense canopy before it could penetrate the local jungle roof. In fact, nowhere in the underbrush did we observe a sprouting nut or young palm, except in the clearing near the beach. The few coconut palms observed were all old and had their lofty crests above the close grasp of the jungle. The dense jungle of the inland plateaus and the ridges is separated from the two deep ravines by steep mountain sides. These walls, which enclose the abruptly ending lowland valleys, are so high that a falling coconut could not without human aid reach the lofty interior parts of the island, where Wafer had seen extensive groves and we could still see individual palm crests far apart.

Unless we ignore Wafer's report, and assume that *Cocos nucifera* is a wild plant native to Cocos Island, it seems evident enough that man must once have cleared considerable areas in the bottom of the ravines and on the interior plateaus and ridges, utilizing the clearings for coconut plantations of quite considerable extent and distribution prior to the arrival of Europeans.

Apart from the coconut palms we saw at a distance, no other evidence immediately suggesting aboriginal activity was seen during our brief visit, with the possible exception of Chatham Bay. Excavations were not attempted. A more detailed inquiry near the mouths of the two rivers and in the overgrown interior highland may be worth while for future archaeological investigators.

At Chatham Bay two very small beaches were separated by a high and dominating promontory, with its steep sides and artificially leveled crest all covered by an extremely dense grass taller than a man and interwoven with creepers. This vegetation formed a marked contrast with the surrounding jungle, and the evidence of former human activity at this point was clear, although it might have been of post-European origin. The tall grass could be penetrated only with the aid of machetes, and several small terraces formed by cut and fill were encountered *en route*. Their function remains obscure, unless they were constructed to support small dwellings. The leveled and equally overgrown summit plateau, which measured about sixty meters wide and about twice as long, could not have been formed without considerable labor. A vertical cut about four meters deep through the rock and soil on the inland side formed the western limit of the leveled area, and the masses removed along the originally narrow crest had been used as fill to widen the artificial plateau. On the north side a deep and wide ravine came up the slope and cut into the plateau like a natural moat. In a few obviously quite recent clearings old sheets of corrugated iron and other remains of camp sites revealed the activities of modern visitors, possibly treasure hunters.

We knew that a Costa Rican penal settlement had been on the island for a short period, and it seemed possible that the terraced promontory was the site of it, the only plausible alternative, it seemed, to aboriginal activity. It has later been ascertained, however, that the penal colony, on the island from 1878 to 1881, was not located in Chatham Bay at all, but in Wafer Bay. There is no known record of agricultural or constructional activity in the area of Chatham Bay, so if the penitentiary was located in Wafer Bay it is difficult to ascribe the leveling and terracing on the Chatham Bay promontory to the historic period, because, apart from the prisoners and some brief and casual visits by treasure hunters, Cocos Island has been uninhabited throughout historic time.

Test pits, made by early and recent treasure-hunting parties, were found everywhere near the beaches of Chatham and Wafer Bays and in clearings near the outlets of the two rivers. The treasure hunters, who paid a fee to the Costa Rican government, were authorized to dig and were the only regular visitors to the island, which, because of its impenetrable jungle and precipitous coastline, has held no other commercial or tourist attraction. All accessible terrain in the limited area of the landing places, had been dug and redug, some of it even blown up by dynamite, and wild pigs have continuously aided in the havoc by turning over loose stones and moldy soil, destroying all original features.

At Wafer Bay, about fifty meters from the sandy beach and parallel to the foot of the hill, the remains of two short rows of boulders, deeply set in the soil, had escaped destruction, but the surrounding soil was too disturbed to permit identification of original function, which was difficult to associate with any practical purposes. The penal colony, however, had been near this locality.

To ascertain the antiquity of the artificial features in Chatham and Wafer bays would require more time than our brief call would permit, and sufficient evidence to suggest prehistoric human occupation of the island was deduced only from the many vestiges of former clearing for coconut plantations.

In conclusion, prehistoric planters must have found the location of Cocos Island worthy of the vast amount of labor spent in clearing the natural jungle for planting coconuts. It is difficult to see why Polynesians, unless involved in considerable trade with the Panama region, of which there is no evidence, should go to such labor on an island at least four thousand miles from their own settlements. It is equally difficult to see why American Indians should go to the same trouble in clearing large jungle areas on a remotely offshore island, when the coconut was of secondary importance in their own diet and there was ample space for clearing in their own jungle territory on the mainland coast.

It is my opinion that the extensive Cocos Island groves would be of little use to anyone unless it is assumed that the island was either densely inhabited at one time or was favorably located for voyagers who frequented the area and were in need of convenient supplies. From personal experience I know that there is no more suitable natural product for open boat voyages than newly picked, scarcely mature coconuts, which will withstand almost any amount of spray and rough storage, and yet yield fresh liquid and substantial food for weeks of navigation. According to the observations of the archaeologist Ferdon, large quantities of husked green coconuts were still being used as the primary water supply for ocean-going *Imbabura* dugouts sailing from northern Esmeraldas, Ecuador, to Tumaco and Buenaventura, Colombia, in 1943, and green coconuts were also immediately brought as the only water supply by the Ecuadorian raftsmen who, in 1947, floated my party downstream to Guayaquil with the balsa logs for the *Kon-Tiki*.

The clearing of the indigenous jungle from the coastal valleys and interior highlands of Cocos Island was such a major task for anyone that the original planters who filled the island with coconut groves in pre-European times must have had special reasons for doing so. The only apparent reason would become clear once we have seen the geographical location of this island in relation to the rapidly accumulating evidence of oversea contact between Guatemala and northwestern South America in pre-Columbian times. As pointed out by Coe, the dearth of concurring archaeology in the deep coastal bend of the Isthmus area separating Guatemala from Ecuador, combined with former local expertise in *guara* navigation, testified by our Galápagos findings, as well as the geography of Cocos Island, make it an ideal port of call for aboriginal merchants trafficking the open sea off Panama.

As demonstrated by O. F. Cook, the Spanish conquest of the mainland, and the serious disturbances that followed, would suffice to interrupt all visits to Cocos Island and leave the tropical jungle the chance to recover the land once so laboriously cleared by early human hands.

Chapter 12

Easter Island Statues

IT HAS OFTEN been fruitful in the academic world to switch from one branch of science to another somewhat related field of study. With the same training in scientific thought and procedure, but unbiased by the tendency any disciple has to accept the doctrines of his tutor, the trespasser from one discipline to another will often take a new and un-traditional approach to accepted dogma. When I left the University of Oslo as a biologist to live for a year as a native among the Polynesians in the Marquesas group, the purpose of my field work was to investigate how living species of the animal world had come to inhabit these remote oceanic islands. My academic background was zoological and geographical, but after three years with access to the world's largest private library on Polynesia, the Kroepelien collection in Oslo, I was better prepared in all matters pertaining to the Polynesian people than by following a formal course in anthropology.

Returning from the Marquesas Islands in 1938 with a considerable archaeological collection, it seemed natural for me to take one step up the biological ladder. From a former study of how oceanic islands had received their first fauna I began to devote all my time to the problem of how they had first been reached by primitive man. A year on the isolated island of Fatuhiva with outrigger canoes and an open lifeboat as the only means of transportation in an ocean where waves and clouds move from east to west all the year around made me critical of current theories which brought the Stone Age discoverers of these is-lands ten thousand miles against the westward rotating elements. Hav-ing more than once fought for my life in the ocean to get back to land,

I had learned from practical experience that Fatuhiva was in the midst of a marine conveyor belt.[1]

The decisions to drift from South America to Polynesia on a balsa raft, and to look for archaeological remains in the Galápagos group, were the contest of an undoctrinated mind against scientifically unproven dogmas. The next speck of land in the ocean beyond the Galápagos was Easter Island. Located midway between South America and the nearest neighbors in Polynesia, Easter Island was at the time of European discovery the loneliest inhabited land in the world. With its more than 600 giant stone statues and impressive megalithic walls of unknown origin it offered laymen and scholars alike one of the most baffling riddles of archaeology. This island, too, was wrapped up in uncontested dogma. It was the farthest from Asia and accordingly, it was said, it had to be the one last reached and with the shortest period of human settlement.

The logic of this generally accepted conclusion rested on the theory that man had actually hit upon this island as a result of a headwind migration from Asia rather than upon a downwind ride from America. So convinced were contemporary scholars of a very recent settlement of Easter Island that no one had attempted stratigraphic excavations in search of sub-surface vestiges, in spite of the fact that this island had attained more fame than any other Pacific island for the vast amount of its surface remains. After brief calls by nineteenth-century ethnologists, the first thorough surface survey of visible Easter Island statues and ruins was conducted by the British party led by Mrs. Katherine Scoresby Routledge in 1919. A complete inventory of all important surface remains was subsequently compiled by the resident missionary, Father Sebastian Englert. The only professional archaeologist to visit the island prior to the arrival of our team was the Belgian professor H. Lavachery, who, in company with the French ethnologist Alfred Métraux, continued surface work on the island in 1934, concentrating his attention on the hitherto unrecorded petroglyphs.

The great many authors who had written on the local archaeological material without setting foot ashore accepted the views of the few scholars who had seen this totally unforested island. The barren island was so remote and out of the way for men arriving from Asia that there could have been no time for man-made products to be covered by slowly accumulating soil; therefore, excavations seemed superfluous.

The *Kon-Tiki* raft had sailed twice as far as from Peru to Easter Island, and the Galápagos shards were witness to pre-Inca sailings since Tiahuanaco times; therefore there was nothing to my knowledge that could have prevented voyagers from South America from reaching Easter Island long before migrants from distant Asia, no matter what route the Asiatics might have taken. To voyagers from Peru, Easter Island would be the nearest habitable land in the ocean, and they alone would have come from an area where it was customary to erect colossal statues in human form on stone platforms in the open.

To come upon lonely Easter Island from any direction would require either considerable luck or the custom of sailing a fleet spread over a broad front, or extensive traffic back and forth in the local area. Whatever might have been the actual case, voyagers from South America would have had all the advantages. If aboriginal voyagers, like the Europeans subsequently, had entered Oceania from Peru, they too might well have by-passed Easter Island initially and come upon larger, more closely packed islands in central Polynesia or even Melanesia. Whatever the succession of discoveries in Polynesia might have been, Easter Island would at any rate be the one island, out of hundreds, lying as a stage halfway between the continental mother country and the newborn island world; this fact alone would account for Easter Island's Polynesian name, *Te-Pito-o-te-Henua,* "The Navel-of-the-World." There would have been little to make Easter Island a virtual temple ground littered with sacred *ahu*-altars and giant statues, but for its unique geographical location in relation to America. Its poor soil and naked landscape, its lack of both running water and a protected harbor, and its modest size of seven by fourteen miles, hardly made it a competitor to Tahiti, Hawaii, New Zealand, or the big and verdant islands clustered on the edge of Melanesia.

Until the local airport was opened in recent years, archaeological work on Easter Island was impeded by difficulty of access. A brief annual visit by a Chilean naval vessel provided the only established contact with the outside world. To carry provisions and equipment for a year's archaeological work in this extreme eastern corner of Polynesia, I found it necessary to charter and convert for our purposes a 150-foot Greenland trawler, which we anchored off our main camp in Anakena Bay. The ship's officers and crew, as well as large groups of islanders, assisted in the excavations which were organized by four senior archaeologists: E. N. Ferdon, Jr., then staff archaeologist of the Museum of New Mexico; W. Mulloy, professor and head of the department of anthropology at the University of Wyoming; C. S. Smith, professor and head of the department of archaeology at the University of Kansas; and A. Skjölsvold, then director of the department of archaeology at the Stavanger Museum in Norway.

The combined results of our excavations on Easter Island in 1955–56 are published in the two volumes of *The Reports of the Norwegian Archaeological Expedition to Easter Island and the East Pacific* (Vol. I: *Archaeology of Easter Island,* and Vol. II: *Miscellaneous Papers,* 1965). The ethnographic observations and collections are incorporated in *The Art of Easter Island* published in 1976. This chapter is based on a lecture given before the Swedish Society for Anthropology and Geography and printed under the title "Statuene på Påskeöen: problem og resultat" in the ethnographic journal *Ymer* in 1962.

*   *   *

Both geographically and archaeologically Easter Island stands out conspicuously among the thousands of islands in the Pacific hemisphere. No other island has held a population that lived so far away from other land in any direction, and so remote from Asia. Nevertheless, no other island has such impressive and extraordinary remains of a former high culture as this tiny and barren outpost facing America. There are tens of thousands of islands and atolls in the Pacific Ocean, but Easter Island alone possesses the remains of an aboriginal writing system; spectacular temple platforms of gigantic blocks of various sizes shouldered, polished, and fitted together with absolute precision; and a vast variety of heterogeneous art; as well as several hundred anthropomorphic stone colossi, with red stone wigs, set up around the coast. Ever since this island was first stumbled upon by three Dutch ships coming westward from South America two and a half centuries ago, the non-Polynesian aspects of the local remains have been a puzzle to the scientific world.

When lay brother Eugène Eyraud was landed on Easter Island in 1864 as the first European to settle ashore, he and his missionary colleagues soon managed to put an end to Easter Island's aboriginal history. With him the curtain dropped on the final tragic act of one of the strangest dramas ever to take place on a lonely oceanic isle, thousands of miles from any eye witness.

We depend on archaeology and other means of prehistoric research reconstruct the main features of Easter Island's period of greatness. Today we may state with certainty that nothing but the last phases of a dying culture was witnessed on Easter Island by the arriving Europeans. The first of all foreign visitors was the Dutch admiral Jacob Roggeveen, who approached the island in the evening twilight of Easter Sunday, 1722.[2] As the sun rose above the sea next morning the Dutchmen brought their ships close inshore and observed a mixed crowd of fair-skinned and dark-skinned people who had lit fires before some enormous statues standing in a row. The people ashore were squatting in front of the statues, with their heads bent while they alternately raised and lowered their arms. When the sun rose they prostrated themselves on the ground facing the sunrise, their fires still flickering before the stone colossi. The statues were even then so old and eroded that Roggeveen could with his bare fingers break pieces away from the decomposed surface, wherefore he concluded that the giant figures were simply molded from clay and soil mixed with pebbles. The Dutchmen left the island after a single day's visit.

Nearly fifty years passed before the Spaniard Felipe Gonzalez and his companions rediscovered the same island, sailing from Peru in 1770. The Spaniards were not satisfied merely to look at the eroded surface of the statues; they struck them so violently with pickaxes that sparks flew and thus discovered that the statues had been carved from a very hard and heavy stone. They recorded that the thirty-foot-tall monolithic statues carried large cylinders of a different stone atop their heads. On top of these cylinders lay human bones, wherefore they concluded that the monuments served the double function of being gods as well as receptacles for burials.

The Dutch and Spanish visitors concurred in pointing out that Easter Island lacked timber and ropes large and strong enough for erecting such colossal monuments. As stated, Roggeveen believed he had the solution to this riddle, arguing that the statues were made from clay, but the Spaniards disproved this assertion and brought to a wondering world the first reports of the huge monoliths in human form which stood erect in great numbers among a mixed population of primitive aborigines on a barren island thousands of miles from any other land. During the two centuries that followed the mystery of

Easter Island strengthened its grip on human imagination throughout the world.

Four years after the Spaniards, Captain James Cook reached the same island, and after him the French arrived under La Pérouse. All these early visitors emphasized very strongly that the Easter Island monuments represented relics of extremely great antiquity, and that the poor and primitive contemporary island population had had no hand in their production. Cook was the first to note that many of the statues lay intentionally overturned on the ground beside their destroyed altar-like masonry foundations, and he pointed out that the islanders did not even keep up the maintenance of the old structures.

Cook brought with him a Polynesian interpreter who had the greatest difficulty in understanding the local language, but he understood enough to learn that the numerous statues represented dead kings and chiefs. There was no further evidence that the stone images were worshiped, as was witnessed by the Dutch, indeed many had been overthrown. But the English and French concurred with the Spaniards in finding skeletal remains strewn about the statues, and therefore described them as funerary monuments.

Regardless of what the statues might have signified to the contemporary islanders, they continued to overthrow them from their foundation platforms. The Russian Lisjanskij was in 1804 the next to visit Easter Island. He reported that four statues still stood erect on their masonry platforms in Cook's Bay, and seven more in Vinapu. Twelve years later, in 1816, another Russian expedition under Kotzebue called. He found all the statues in Cook's Bay overturned, and out of the seven in Vinapu only two remained standing.

The last report on statues still erect on their masonry platforms derived from Du Petit-Thouars, who observed nine standing statues north of Cook's Bay in 1838. During the years that followed they too were overthrown, and when Eugène Eyraud arrived in 1864 to settle ashore as the first European, there was not a single statue left erect on the numerous image platforms; all had been overturned from their former foundations, many were broken during the fall, and the large stone cylinders they had supported on their heads had often run like heavy steam rollers down the nearby slopes. The only standing statues that none had managed to capsize were the unfinished ones that Captain Cook's advanced party had first discovered partly buried in the descending silt at the foot of the overgrown and long-abandoned image quarries on the slopes of the Rano Raraku crater.

Eyraud was driven from the island after nine months, but he returned in 1866 with other missionaries. He and his colleagues were the first to learn to converse with the aborigines on Easter Island. They attempted by direct questions to find the answers to the riddles of Easter Island. The contemporary natives could give no better explanation than that once upon a time all the statues had walked by themselves to the various *ahu* platforms on orders from the creator god, Makemake.

Seven years later the missionaries were once more driven from the island. Shortly afterwards the Tahitian sheep ranger Tati Salmon arrived, and subsequently a Chilean meteorologist, Martinez. Both of them were to live in intimate contact with the local aborigines, and through them some highly interesting and not yet distorted pre-European traditions have survived.[3]

According to the earliest recorded traditional memories, the ancestors of the still surviving population were distinguished as "Short-ears"; they had reached Easter Island with a chief named Tuu-ko-ihu, who came from another island far toward the west, i.e., in the direction of Polynesia proper. On their arrival they had discovered that this island was already inhabited by a different people, the "Long-ears." This earlier population had reached the island under the leadership of the true discoverer, King Hotu Matua, who had come from the opposite direction, from the east, reaching Easter Island after a sixty-day oversea voyage from a huge country in the direction of the sunrise, where it was so hot that the vegetation in certain seasons was scorched and shriveled by the burning sun. The Long-ears, arriving first, had been raising *moai,* or statues, ever since they landed with Hotu Matua. The Short-ears, arriving subsequently, assisted the Long-ears for two hundred years (*karau-karau*) in building *ahu* walls and long-eared statues, until the peaceful coexistence ended in a disastrous civil war; the Short-ears massacred all but one of the Long-eared men in a pyre lit in an extensive defensive trench across the Poike peninsula. The one Long-ear was saved to continue the propagation of his kin. During the period that followed these massacres, tribal feuds took place among the surviving Short-ears on Easter Island, and all the statues were gradually overthrown by undermining and pulling them down with ropes, according to the same traditions.

In 1914 the archaeology of Easter Island was begun when the

aforesaid Mrs. Katherine Scoresby Routledge arrived on her English yacht. No professional archaeologist participated in the expedition, but Mrs. Routledge's popular book on the visit contains most important scientific observations and has so far been the principal source of general information on Easter Island archaeology.[4] Her extensive unpublished ethnographic notes, undoubtedly of considerable value when analyzed, were lost in spite of all efforts to locate them, until recently encountered in the archives of the Royal Geographical Society.

Twenty years later, in 1934, the island was visited by a Franco-Belgian scientific team, but unfortunately the French archaeologist died en route and his Belgian colleague Henri Lavachery was therefore left to study prehistoric remains alone, while the French ethnologist Alfred Métraux made an important study of the ethnology.

Mrs. Routledge suspected that an unknown and later exterminated people, possibly of Melanesian origin, had inhabited Easter Island prior to the present Polynesians, but Métraux and Lavachery rejected this idea and asserted categorically that no other people had visited this isolated island before the Polynesians arrived about the twelfth or thirteenth century A.D. They advanced the subsequently popular theory that the inhabitants of Easter Island had started erecting giant statues because, on this naked and barren island, they found no material with which they could continue wood carving such as was practiced in the other, forest-covered islands of Polynesia proper. This theory seemed sufficiently plausible to discourage further archaeologists from visiting the island, and stratigraphic excavations were never attempted.

Had Easter Island been as barren as assumed by the anthropologists when the first aboriginal voyagers settled ashore? This was one of the most important questions we hoped to answer by bringing modern equipment for pollen borings to the island. The pollen analytic borings which we undertook around the crater lakes in the extinct volcanoes Rano Raraku and Rano Kao on Easter Island produced a rich paleobotanical material which was analyzed by Professor O. H. Selling at the National Museum of Natural History in Stockholm.

The pollen deposits reveal that the natural environment found by the first people who settled Easter Island was different from the one we know today, different from the one that has been characteristic of Easter Island ever since its discovery on Easter Sunday 1722. This island, which is now poor in vegetation, had formerly a richer flora, including even trees of families which later became extinct. Between the trees were bushes of various species. It was a vegetation which in certain ways must have resembled the original lowland vegetation on, for instance, the lee side of Hawaii or the Marquesas islands, although many species differed. Before the stone sculptors started their work in the crater walls of the now completely barren volcano Rano Raraku, the slopes of this volcano must have been covered by palms of a species unknown on the island today, the pollen of which filled every cubic millimeter of the bottom strata of the crater lake. One of the most surprising discoveries was the pollen of a shrub related to the coniferae (*Ephedra*), which was so far unknown throughout the Pacific, but which is closely related to, if not directly identical with, a South American species. Dr. Selling has found pollen of the same species in the Marquesas Islands.

It was possible to follow the gradual disappearance of this primeval vegetation of Easter Island in our series of borings eight meters (c. twenty-six feet) deep, containing stratified pollen. While trees still surrounded what was then open crater lakes, an American fresh-water species, *Polygonum amphibium,* suddenly appeared for the first time, probably brought as a medicinal plant from the coast of South America by the first settlers to arrive. Then soot particles began to appear in certain pollen strata simultaneously with a rapid impoverishment of the original flora. The soot particles can only have derived from vegetation fires sending a rain of ashes across the crater lakes. These fires were evidently caused by the aboriginal immigrants as the population increased and needed land for settlement and cultivation; subsequently the fires were perhaps caused deliberately during warfare. The destruction was eventually so effective that in the upper strata hardly anything survived of the original vegetation, whereas grass and ferns gradually intruded upon the burned-out landscape.

This local scene shifting on Easter Island represents a discovery that has more than botanical interest. It shows that we have had wrong conceptions concerning life on Easter Island during the first local period of cultural development. The stone masons who went ashore and began to cut and join enormous blocks of basalt had not reached a barren and grass-covered island where they could drag their enormous monoliths about the plains at will; rather, they first had to cut down trees and clear land to get access to quarries, and to allow freedom of movement for themselves and their monuments. This discovery immediately invalidates the long-accepted argument that the people of

Easter Island began to carve the mountainside because they had landed on an island where they could not carve in wood as in the other islands in Polynesia. The environment in which the first Easter Islanders settled was essentially the same as on the other islands, and it is accordingly the more striking to note the peculiar cultural characteristics which, as shown below, they brought along when they first arrived.

Another and entirely different contention, also generally accepted, that had unnecessarily complicated the problems pertaining to the Easter Island statues proved to be based on a series of misinterpretations of one of the observations by the Routledge expedition. Mrs. Routledge had sand and gravel removed from the lower portion of some of the statues partly buried in silt at the foot of the Rano Raraku quarries. She wrote in her narrative of the expedition that a particular one among these statues proved to have a pointed base, and she assumed that it was carved in this way because it was intended to be set in the earth and not to balance on top of an *ahu*-platform like all the other statues, scattered about the island.[5] Métraux and Lavachery interpreted this discovery to mean that every one of the sixty statues which stood partly buried in the silt at the foot of the quarries had a similarly pointed base. Without further examination Métraux wrote in his monograph on the ethnology of Easter Island that there are two fundamentally different classes of statues on the island, one with a peg-shaped base, to be set in the ground, the other with a wide flat base, carved to stand free on top of the *ahu* walls of the island.[6]

Sir Peter Buck, the leading authority on Polynesian culture, who never visited the island, increased the confusion by believing that Métraux meant that even the 170 unfinished statues which lay exposed in the open shelves of the quarry proper had pointed bases and accordingly had been designed to be set in the earth. One single statue, which actually proved to be merely defective, had thus become 230 statues in the published literature, and in *Vikings of the Sunrise,* his most widely distributed publication, Buck draws the following far-reaching conclusion: "The images with pegged bases were never intended to be placed on the stone platforms of the temples, but were to be erected in the ground as secular objects to ornament the landscape and mark the boundaries of districts and highways. Because the images remaining in the quarry all had pegged bases, it would appear that the orders for the platforms had been filled and that the people had embarked on a scheme of highway decoration . . ."[7]

It was a simple matter for our expedition to ascertain that not a single one among all the statues that remained in the quarries had a pointed base, in spite of the fact that Arne Skjölsvold, who led the investigations in Rano Raraku, discovered about fifty statues in addition to those that had been known so far.[8] When we initiated the excavation of the partly buried giants standing at the foot of the quarries, we discovered that each of these, too, except one defective specimen, had a full body with long arms and slender fingers placed at the lower end next to a wide and flat base, which was in no way pointed so as to be sunk in the ground, but on the contrary was so designed that the statue would stand fully exposed on a platform.

Our investigations disclosed that all the 600 or so statues so far known on Easter Island represented one basically homogeneous type, including unfinished specimens representing different stages of work on that same type. The statues could be recognized and divided into four main stages of production. In the first stage the statue had its back still attached to the crater wall, whereas the front and the sides were partly or completely finished, sometimes to the very last detail including a perfect surface polish. Only the concavities of the eyes were lacking. In the second stage even the back was detached, and the statue was temporarily erected in the refuse silt at the foot of the quarries to make it possible for the crude back to be carved into shape and receive its final polish, including in some instances symbols in low relief. On the steep slopes of the volcano the statue was readily tipped upright with its wide flat base standing on an excavated terrace crudely paved with unworked lava boulders. At the third stage, when the statue was finished except for the deep concavities of the eyes, it was laid prone once more and transported from the volcano along the paved roads; only at the fourth stage, when it was lifted on to its specific *ahu,* did the statue receive its excavated eye sockets. In addition, a large red stone cylinder was placed on top of its head, referred to by the local natives as *pukao,* or "topknot."

With this discovery the entire problem was simplified; none of the statues represented landscape or highway decoration. The stone carvers had been engaged in one enterprise: to produce homogeneous monuments with red topknots, erected side by side on *ahu* platforms around the entire coast.

But other problems of Easter Island still remained to be solved. While Skjölsvold directed the excavations at Rano Raraku, Mulloy and Smith began the first systematic investigations and excavations of the *ahu* ruins on which the statues had formerly been standing. They discovered that the masonry covered earlier structures, which had subsequently been partly rebuilt and partly extended and strengthened. The original constructions had not been designed to carry heavy monuments, and in addition they represented a different architecture and a different technique of stone work.[9]

As excavations advanced it was clearly seen in the various rebuilt structures that the prehistory of Easter Island could be divided into three distinctly separate strata, which the archaeologists denominated as Early, Middle, and Late periods. In the Early Period there was no production of true *ahu* images, although statues were carved. The temples were altar-like elevations of very large, mutually dissimilar, and most precisely cut and joined stones. They had their façade toward the ocean and a sunken court on the inland side. Astronomically oriented, they were constructed by highly specialized stone masons who studied the annual movements of the sun and incorporated their observations in the religious architecture. During the Early Period different types of sculptures were erected on the ground inside the temple court.

Not until the next cultural period, the Middle one, were the giant statues of the well-known type carved and placed on terraced stone platforms. By this time the original temple constructions had been partly destroyed or altered, and upon them was superimposed a different masonry to form the later well-known *ahu*. These *ahu* were built without astronomical orientation, and were designed for the first time to support rows of giant monuments, which had their backs to the ocean while facing the old inland court.

Whereas the architects and image sculptors in the Middle Period concentrated all their energy and interest in erecting their enormous monuments of Rano Raraku tuff, the previous population on Easter Island, in the Early Period, were far better experts in the art of shaping and fitting together vast polished blocks of hard basalt, forming their altar-like religious structures.

The third and final period, the Late one, was initiated by the sudden end of all work in the Rano Raraku quarries, and the simultaneous interruption of the transport of statues along the roads. During this period the statues were one by one overthrown from the *ahu*. A new burial custom was introduced. The non-Polynesian custom of cremation had been practiced earlier, with burned bones and burned artifacts deposited in stone-lined cremation cists next to the *ahu*. From now on wood carvers, lacking skill in megalithic sculpture or masonry, buried the dead beneath piles of unworked boulders thrown together in formless heaps on top of the destroyed *ahu,* or in large multi-burial chambers roughly constructed underneath the bellies or faces of the overturned giants. The Late Period was everywhere marked by decadence, warfare, and destruction. Thousands of spear points of obsidian characterize all strata of this final period, whereas weapons did not occur, or were extremely rare, in each of the two earlier periods.

This discovery not only disclosed a stratification on Easter Island, but caused the previously hypothesized local evolution to be reversed. Mrs. Routledge had actually suspected that the Easter Island *ahu* had been rebuilt, and that their original appearance was different, but Métraux and Lavachery had rejected this and claimed that the Easter Island culture was homogeneous and without any sign of stratification.[10]

All observers had concurred in pointing out the striking similarity between the largest and best preserved *ahu* façades on Easter Island and corresponding structures in the Andean area. They had assumed, however, that the best walls on Easter Island were of late date and represented the result of local evolution. Polynesians were assumed to have reached Easter Island ignorant of this specialized type of stone masonry, and only as time passed on this treeless island did they gradually become expert stone masons and the equals of the foremost experts in South America in carving and joining megalithic blocks. This picture, however, had now to be reversed. It was the first settlers on Easter Island who had started to build the best walls of the same type as found in Peru and the adjoining sections of the Andean area, after first clearing trees away from quarries and temple sites. The people in the Middle Period did not master this specialized masonry technique at all, and merely erected their giant statues. Furthermore, the final period showed no signs of evolution in any type of stonework and was typified by decadence, mass destruction, and deterioration of everything created earlier. Hence the situation was reversed, and an arrival from the stone-carving cultures of South America could no longer be excluded, since there was no other region in the entire Pacific from where immigrants might have brought a ready developed skill in specialized stone masonry.

The complex nature of Easter Island culture proved to extend beyond religious structure and burial customs, and to include the secular dwellings of the aboriginal population. After the initial surveys of the local surface archaeology, Ferdon began to suspect that there were vestiges of entirely different types of houses in various sections of the island. Ethnologists and archaeologists had so far agreed that, apart from underground caves, there existed only one house type on Easter Island: i.e., long, lenticular reed houses resembling a boat turned upside down. A frame of arched poles supporting a thatch of reed and grass was set into narrow drill holes in a boat-shaped foundation wall of dressed stone. The expedition's archaeologists first excavated a number of these house foundations, all of which proved to originate from the time immediately before or after European contact, i.e., within the span of the Late Period. Subsequently Ferdon and Skjölsvold turned their attention to certain circular masonry walls remaining in large quantities in various sections of the island.[11] Earlier ethnologists and archaeologists had accepted the present population's claim that these structures represented the garden plots of their ancestors, and that the circular walls were built to protect the *mahute* plantations against the wind on the barren island. The Swedish botanist Carl Skottsberg, who visited Easter Island in 1917, confirmed that the circular walls were used as garden plots, and he illustrated them as such in a publication on the flora of Easter Island, later adopted and reproduced in Métraux's work on the ethnology of the island.[12] Our excavations revealed that this function of the circular walls was entirely secondary, and began in the Late Period of the island. Actually these structures represented the thick masonry walls of circular houses which had been covered by reed roofs, and by excavation we found the floor filled with refuse and tools from a long-lasting occupation. A cooking place was located either in the center of the floor or immediately outside the wall, and in one instance Skjölsvold found an oven filled with charred remains of baked sweet potatoes and sugar cane that had been abandoned in a hurry. Radiocarbon datings disclosed that this utterly non-Polynesian house type had been in use on Easter Island during the Middle Period, when the large statues were erected, and in some cases continued into the Late Period together with the entirely unrelated boat-shaped pole-and-thatch dwellings. Ferdon, who was fully familiar with South American archaeology, recognized these circular stone houses—unknown throughout Polynesia—as concurring with a type characteristic of the adjacent slopes of the Andean region directly facing Easter Island.[13]

Our excavations on the plains of Vinapu disclosed a third, and also entirely divergent house type, with a solid slab roof covered with earth. It was secondarily used for the burial of a decapitated person. An entire village of similar stone houses remains on the summit of the highest volcano on Easter Island, and has been known ever since the arrival of the missionaries as the most important ceremonial center. In this village, named Orongo, the whole population of the island gathered each year at the period around the spring equinox. They then sat as spectators and judges during an annual competition in which the participants swam with small *totora* reed boats to the bird islets off the coast in search of the first egg of the sooty tern, to gain the title of the sacred bird-man of the year.

Routledge and Métraux had both paid considerable attention to this peculiar annual ceremony at Orongo which had continued well into historic times, but no one had regarded the stone houses at Orongo as more than a purely ceremonial village unique to Easter Island, since this form of crypt-like masonry dwelling was unknown throughout the rest of the Pacific. While directing extensive excavations at Orongo, Ferdon encountered the same cultural stratification at this site, and discovered that these peculiar houses, which had survived as ceremonial structures at the top of the volcano, actually represented the continuation of a building form which had previously served for dwellings in the Early Period on Easter Island. This corbeled house type, too, unknown elsewhere in Polynesia, could be traced to ancient Peru and adjacent sections in the Andean area.

Projecting barren rocks in Orongo village were entirely covered by bird-men carved in relief. They represented the locally well-known crouching figures with human bodies and limbs, but with bird heads and long hooked beaks. One bird-man was embracing a realistic incision of the sun. While excavating some of the low ceremonial houses, which frequently had caved in, Ferdon discovered several hitherto unknown fresco paintings on smooth slabs of the walls and ceilings. The dominating motifs were sickle-shaped reed boats, double-bladed paddles, and the "weeping eye," all non-Polynesian traits characteristic of American high cultures.[14]

Ferdon's stratigraphic excavations disclosed that, with short interruptions, this site at the top of the highest of Easter Island's volcanoes had represented a ceremonial center throughout the three cultural periods of the island. In the bottom layer he exposed an Early Period solar observatory which registered the sun's position at sunrise both at the December and the June solstice and at the equinox. There was no evidence of a ceremonial village at this site during the Early Period, but sun symbols which included petroglyphs as well as a small, hitherto unknown statue of entirely aberrant type, were exposed in direct association with the solar observatory. The sun-measuring structure represents the first of its kind ever known inside Polynesia. Once more it was necessary to turn to the Andean area for comparable features.

In the Middle Period the beautifully faced and fitted masonry of the solar observatory was superimposed by a crude *ahu*-like temple structure. The stone-house village was now constructed in the intimate vicinity, and the bird-man cult was suddenly introduced in a ready developed form and mixed with the earlier sun worship, gradually to displace the latter almost entirely. A comparatively small, beautifully executed Early Period stone statue of dark basalt, now in the British Museum, was moved at the beginning of the Middle Period from its original site in the solar observatory and incorporated as inventory inside the largest and most important stone house in the cult center of Orongo village. Primitive bird-men and double-bladed paddles were secondarily cut across the original Early Period sun symbols on its back, an observation that had first been made by Routledge, although she had not attempted an explanation. This important Orongo statue differed from all the Middle Period *ahu* statues of Easter Island in having a convex rather than flat base, and in not being carved from the usual yellowish-gray tuff, but rather from hard black basalt, wherefore it could not have come from the stone quarries in Rano Raraku. As will be shown later, this Early Period statue may possibly represent the prototype for all the *ahu* images subsequently erected during the Middle Period on the island.

As excavations advanced on the lowland below, statues of hitherto unknown types were encountered there as well. Some of these earliest statues were found deliberately broken, and their fragments had been used as masonry blocks in the walls of the circular stone houses of the Middle Period. Others were dishonored by being set face into the wall as mere construction blocks in the crude *ahu* platforms supporting the large statues of the Middle Period. Some of these early, demolished and dishonored statues were carved from dark basalt like the statue at Orongo, others were of various types of red scoria, and still others of the yellowish-gray tuff from Rano Raraku. However, all could be distinguished from the standard type of Easter Island statue so far known, and respectlessly incorporated as crude building material in the walls of Middle Period structures, they almost certainly represented vestiges from the Early Period image carvers.

The statues we discovered from Easter Island's earliest period could be divided into four basically different types, out of which three were not previously known on the island nor in any other part of Oceania. Monument Type I is represented by squared, sometimes flattish, stone heads without body or limbs and with a rounded rectangular outline. The plane face carved in low relief has invariably enormous eyes and prominent eyebrows that run in a Y-shape into the flat nose. Other details like ears and mouth are insignificant or missing. Several specimens were found, generally made unrecognizable merely by having been turned face down near an *ahu* or in a stony field.

Monument Type II is represented by a rigid, pillar-shaped, and highly unrealistic figure, also with a rounded rectangular cross section, but with a complete body and stunted legs. The thin arms carved in relief are flexed at right angles and the fingers of the hands almost meet on the stomach. One finished, but broken, and two unfinished quarry specimens were found, all of red scoria.

Monument Type III is represented by a remarkably realistic figure of a naked giant kneeling in such a way that the soles of his feet are turned up behind as support for his bulging buttocks. The knees project forward at right angles to the body, and the hands are resting on each thigh near the knees. The face gazes slightly upward, the oval eyes are not hollow but vaguely convex, and the cheeks project. The small mouth has pursed lips, and the chin has a small goatee beard. Only one example was encountered, buried under silt from the oldest part of the Rano Raraku quarries.

Whereas these three newly discovered types were formerly entirely unknown in Oceania, Monument Type IV, also from the Early Period, was more familiar, as it approaches closely the only Easter Island statue type so far known, i.e., the Middle Period *ahu* image of which many were still standing at the time of the first European visits. The Early Period Type IV is, in fact, clearly a prototype of the subsequent stone giants that were to give Easter Island its fame. This type is a stiff, conventional bust without legs, truncated just below the genitals, with nipples and navel and with long slender arms down the sides, the hands flexed at right angles along the base in such a manner that the tips of the extremely long, thin fingers reach the sides of the genitals. Nose and ears are prominent, the mouth is pursed, and the forehead projects above the eye region. The eyes differ markedly from those outlined in relief on the other statue types of the Early Period, and merit special attention: Type IV has deep cavities in the place of the eyes, a peculiar characteristic later repeated in all Middle Period specimens of this same type.

It is a general misconception that the large monuments of Easter Island are blind stone heads. This misapprehension derives from the fact that the only statues that have remained in an upright position until modern times are the unfinished ones at the foot of the quarries. Standing with their bodies buried in fallen quarry rubble, they were blind simply because the eye sockets were not to be carved until the images were erected at their destination on an *ahu* platform. As we have seen, all the finished and formerly standing giants had been overthrown during the Late Period of civil war, and they had almost without exception been capsized in such a manner that they rested face down. We initiated the re-erection of fallen *ahu* images in 1955 and others have continued the process, so that several statues are now back in their original position, all with deep, hollow eye sockets. These deep cavities in the place of eyes on the Type IV images have caused some to propose they were meant to represent hollow-eyed crania, a theory that must be rejected since the fleshy parts of ears, lips, and nose are realistically shown. Continued research has of recent years convinced me that the Type IV statues of Easter Island's Early and Middle Period originally had inlaid eyes. Some of the colossal stone statues in human form left by the Hittites, and some of the life-sized stone men of pre-European Mexico, have precisely the same deep, oval depressions in the place of eyes, but in those cases we know that the inlays have in fact fallen out, since other specimens in both areas have the eye concavities filled with white marine shell enclosing a central disk of black obsidian. In fact, on Easter Island too, all the well-preserved wooden statuettes collected prior to missionary influence had precisely the same type of eyes: deep, oval concavities filled with white bone or shell surrounding a black obsidian pupil. W. J. Thomson collected a detached Easter Island stone statue head with such an inlay in 1886.[15] Even the giant *tapa* images (*paina*) of Easter Island's Late Period had applied eyes, made from white disks cut from human skull bone, surrounding a pupil of black sea shell.[16]

The most noticeable difference between the Type IV statues of Easter Island's Middle Period and their generally smaller Early Period prototype is that the Middle Period specimens had the top of the head flattened to support a superimposed red stone topknot (*pukao*), and their bases were flattened so as to balance securely on a stone *ahu*. The Early Period specimens had both base and top rounded, for they had no topknot and were set in the earth of the temple plaza.

Tradition has it that the first immigrants to arrive from the east started to carve stone statues. If we look for inspiration outside the area we find none of the four types represented elsewhere in Oceania or in Southeast Asia. Only the Marquesas group, Raivavae and formerly Pitcairn—all in the extreme eastern part of Polynesia—had large stone statues, but these all represent disproportionately stout men with bulging stomachs, short slightly flexed legs, and big round heads with diabolic features in low relief. They conform well with the variety of large-headed and short-legged stone men erected on elevated stone platforms or set in the ground all the way from the Valley of Mexico by way of San Agustin in Colombia to Lake Titicaca in Peru-Bolivia. Although all these statues invariably have extremely short legs, busts with no legs at all are common only at archaeological sites in the Huaraz region of Central Peru, and appear sporadically around Lake Titicaca. The statues of the bearded Con-Ticci-Viracocha at Tiahuanaco and at the neighboring site of Mocachi have no legs, and one bulky stone giant at the Tiahuanaco site of Taraco on the north shore of the same lake is truncated below the abdomen and, as I have illustrated elsewhere, closely approaches the Monument Type IV of Easter Island as it appeared in its original Early Period phase.[17] Nevertheless, legless busts must be considered an exceptional form in the Andes, and undoubtedly developed into a dominant statue type only as a result of local selectivity during the transition from the Early to the Middle Period on Easter Island.

However, the other three newly discovered Early Period types, equally unknown elsewhere in Oceania, are most familiar in the Andes. They happen to concur closely with the three types of stone statues which the Andean archaeologist W. C. Bennett listed as characteristic for the pre-Inca monuments of Tiahuanaco. The three Easter

Island forms follow the three Tiahuanaco forms in every peculiar detail, the rectanguloid bodiless head with large eyes and Y-shaped nose as well as the squared pillar-statue with arms flexed and hands on the abdomen, and the realistic kneeling statue with hands on thighs and each of the other characteristics listed above.[18] Skjölsvold, who excavated the large kneeling giant from the refuse silt below the oldest part of the quarries, compares all its very peculiar details to the corresponding Tiahuanaco specimens which Bennett dates to the earliest pre-Classic period of this site. Skjölsvold states that "the similarity between this Tiahuananco statue from South American and our specimen is so great that it can scarcely be put down to chance, but must be ascribed to a close relationship, which implies that there is a connection between these two examples of ancient stone sculptures in the Andes and on Easter Island."[19]

Against the background of the newly discovered Early Period types it is possible to visualize an evolution behind the Easter Island *ahu* monuments. So far only the homogeneous giants from the Middle Period had been known, and they had no similarity to statues either on the islands to the west or to those on the continent to the east. This was one of the reasons why their isolated occurrence on Easter Island had created such an enigmatic problem. The new discoveries show that, during a still earlier period hitherto not recognized, the earliest population had experimented with various qualities of rock on Easter Island, and with four different types of anthropomorphic monuments, out of which three proved to be characteristic early forms in Tiahuanaco on the nearest mainland to the east. In addition, the fourth type was also present among Tiahuanaco stone statues although it developed into a more specialized form on Easter Island by the end of the Early Period. Later the latter type was unanimously accepted as a norm for the several hundreds of giant monuments erected on the rebuilt *ahu* during Easter Island's second period.

Why was this? To obtain an explanation for the evolution and the peculiar subsequent local stagnation demonstrated by the archeologists, we have to resort to assistance from ethnology. There is no reason to doubt the verbal information from the surviving aborigines of the Late Period, as obtained by Cook, La Pérouse, and other early visitors while several of the statues still stood erect on their *ahu:* the statues represented no idols in the true sense of the word; they were monuments of kings, chiefs, and other important persons, set up on or near their burial sites. Each single statue was erected in honor of a certain deceased person, and even subsequent to the tribal feuds which involved the overturning of the statues, during the Late Period, several old natives could remember the names of specific *ariki* or chiefs represented by certain statues. Our excavations revealed that prepared tombs and other burials were restricted to the *ahu* during the very last part of the Middle and the entire Late Period, while we found no evidence of burial in the astronomically oriented altar-like structures without statues in the Early Period. As stated, crematoria with multi-burials were excavated in front of the façade of the finely dressed and fitted and astronomically oriented temple walls. This, too, was a surprising discovery, since it was not previously known that cremation had ever been part of Easter Island burial tradition.

Another question naturally emerges. Why did all these powerful chiefs in the Middle Period want their mortuary monuments to be stereotype copies of the Early Period IV statues? The question is the more pertinent since they had destroyed or mutilated all Early Period statues, even those of Type IV, with one single exception: the beautiful basalt statue from the solar observatory on top of the volcano Rano Kao had been saved and brought into one of their own ceremonial stone houses at Orongo. This was in fact the only freestanding Easter Island statue not overthrown even in the Late Period, but venerated almost until the time when it was removed and taken to the British Museum.

Was this Orongo statue of some particular significance? We may undoubtedly answer affirmatively. With its convex base it was not merely the only statue on the island to be erected on the earthen floor inside a building, and the only one to survive all the three cultural periods, but it was the only statue on Easter Island which was known to have been the object of worship and religious attention from the entire island population irrespective of family or tribe. All the other statues, together with the *ahu* on which they stood, belonged to separate families and for this reason were overthrown and demolished as an act of revenge in the savage tribal feuds of the Late Period. Even some of the unfinished statues standing at the foot of the Rano Raraku quarries had deep scars from attempts at decapitation by aborigines who had been unable to overturn them because most of the trunks were deeply buried in silt. But that single statue in the Orongo stone house was left untouched and was still the object of fertility worship in important rituals for all the intercombatant tribes on the island when the missionaries arrived in the latter half of the last century. Our excavations revealed that large quantities of charcoal from ceremonial fires were accumulated in front of the entrance to the large central stone house which had enshrined this important little basalt figure.

In all probability this statue had originally been associated with the local sun rituals during the Early Period. It had the symbol of the sun and the rainbow carved in relief on its back until it was moved into a newly constructed stone house during the Middle Period; then the bird-man symbols of this new period were crudely added to the earlier motifs on its back. Yet it resumed its central position in the cult of the island as a sort of creator or fertility god, worshiped at ceremonies during the annual spring equinox. Whereas the other statues, which the people of the Middle Period now began to erect on family *ahu,* represented deceased human individuals, the Orongo statue continued to be a common deity venerated by all families on the island. This may explain the monoform funerary art as expressed in the *ahu* images. The fact that the kings of Easter Island, as elsewhere in Polynesia and in Peru, counted their descent from the supreme deity makes it understandable that they wished their portrait to resemble to the greatest possible extent this divine ancestor, known to them all through the image in their common ceremonial center at Orongo. While maintaining a physical resemblance to this omnipotent progenitor, the only divergence they allowed themselves in their own sculpture was, to an ever increasing extent, to make their mortuary monuments as large and towering as possible to show off their own power and importance.

Once we had found a sub-stratum of statues that antedated the stone giants which had brought Easter Island its fame, it became apparent that the theoretical datings of Easter Island's first settlement were no longer tenable. The Easter Islanders had themselves given early visitors two royal genealogical lines, the earliest counting fifty-seven generations back to Hotu Matua, the first immigrant king. Since it was assumed that the immigration came from distant Asia this long line was arbitrarily discarded in favor of a shorter royal line which variously comprised between twenty and thirty names. It was important during our excavations to search for organic remains suitable for radiocarbon dating, for all previous attempts to date the Easter Island settlement had been based on legendary genealogies.

Routledge believed that two unrelated immigrations had reached

Easter Island; of these the Polynesians arrived about A.D. 1400.[20] Knoche similarily suspected that two different people had reached the island, the first between the eleventh and the thirteenth centuries A.D.[21] Lavachery and Métraux both held the opinion that Easter Island culture was young and homogeneous, and that the island remained undiscovered until between the twelfth and the thirteenth centuries A.D.[22] Englert shared the view that there was apparent evidence of a local conglomeration of two cultures, but he believed that neither of them had reached lonely Easter Island until about A.D. 1575.[23]

Our excavations indicated that Easter Island was inhabited by a considerable population already occupied in constructing extensive defensive works as early as about A.D. 380 plus or minus 100 years. This was more than a millennium earlier than anybody had hitherto suspected, and represented the earliest date up to that time reported for any island in Polynesia. It was possible through the discovery of stratigraphically placed charcoal and bone material to produce seventeen different carbon-14 datings from Easter Island. Two of the most interesting derived from the legendary ditch which divided the Poike peninsula from the rest of the island. According to claims consistently repeated by the island population from the time of the earliest historic records, this was a man-made ditch where the final decisive battle between their own ancestors and the "Long-ears" had taken place, and in which the latter were cremated alive in a defensive pyre at the bottom of the nearly two-mile-long trench.

However, geologists had so far concurred with anthropologists in suspecting that the Poike ditch was but a natural geological depression,[24] and both Métraux and Lavachery had concluded that the natives invented the tradition to explain a natural geological phenomenon.[25] In consequence the associated tradition about the "Long-ears" and the "Short-ears" was also commonly discarded as a mere fable. As soon as we sank test pits into the Poike ditch, however, it was found to contain large quantities of charcoal from a huge and intensive fire, and the carbon-14 tests dated this fire to about A.D. 1676 plus or minus 100 years.[26] This was in remarkable agreement with A.D. 1680, the date estimated in advance by Father Sebastian Englert on the basis of aboriginal tradition, which insisted that the battle along the Poike pyre took place twelve generations ago.[27]

Smith's excavations showed that this defensive ditch was built long before the feuds resulting in the pyre of about 1680: when this pyre was lit the ditch was already an old structure partly blown full of aeolian dust and drifting sand. Smith found obsidian flakes at the very bottom of the ditch. The Poike trench proved to be a natural depression which had once been artificially transformed and extended to a depth of twelve to fifteen feet and a width of thirty-five to forty feet, while being nearly two miles long and severing the peninsula from the rest of the island. Gravel and debris dug up from the bottom of the ditch had been used to build a defensive embankment along its uphill side, and during this procedure charcoal from a fire had become embedded beneath the displaced debris, disclosing that preparations for defense of the precipitous peninsula were in progress as early as about A.D. 380.[28] This would seem to indicate local feuds at that early period, or perhaps, rather, a fear of pursuit by enemies from the original homeland, since references to such a pursuit actually form an important element in all the earliest legends of the island. In fact, the legendary first king, Hotu Matua, was claimed to have fled from his original fatherland toward the east to escape capture and death after being defeated in three great battles.

At the foot of the Rano Raraku quarries lay a row of grass-covered hillocks and sloping ridges, which had hitherto been considered natural formations. On top of one of the highest of these was the foundation wall of what until missionary times had been the sacred dwelling of the annually elected bird-man, a structure which Routledge and Métraux associated with the earliest rituals of Easter Island. Skjölsvold's excavations revealed that all these hillocks were entirely artificial. They constituted enormous rubble mounds of debris, broken basalt picks, and ashes transported from the quarries located in the mountain side above. Remains from early fires embedded in this refuse made possible the dating of activities in the Middle Period when work still went on in the Rano Raraku quarries. The discovery of the artificial origin of these hillocks disclosed that the superimposed house of the bird-man did not represent the earliest rituals of Easter Island at all, but was a purely secondary contrivance, built during the Late Period on top of refuse from the Middle Period, after the abandonment of work in the image quarries.[29]

As a result of the various radiocarbon dates the expedition archaeologists established the following three cultural periods for Easter Island: the Early Period from some time at least prior to A.D. 380 to about 1100, the Middle Period from about 1100 to about 1680, and the

Late Period from about 1680 to the full introduction of Christianity in 1868.[30]

To obtain a basis for chronological and typological comparisons, our expedition, upon leaving Easter Island, visited Pitcairn and Raivavae, as well as Hivoa and Nukuhiva in the Marquesas group, the only four islands in the whole Pacific, other than Easter Island, where monumental stone statues occurred.

Pitcairn and Raivavae formerly possessed a limited number of smaller statues evidently of comparatively recent origin, and no attempts have ever been made to suggest that these had inspired the ancient sculptors of Easter Island.[31] On the other hand, Buck[32] and others thought they saw the primitive forerunners of the sophisticated Easter Island monuments in the roughly man-sized, but plump and diabolic, stone images on two temples sites in the Marquesas,[33] the latter group being located as far from Easter Island northwestward as is Peru eastward. Skjölsvold succeeded in finding charcoal at two different levels beneath the masonry platform supporting the Hivaoa statues, and Mulloy and Ferdon excavated charcoal below the foundations of the Nukuhiva statues, revealing that the Marquesan monuments were erected as recently as about A.D. 1316 and A.D. 1516 respectively: i.e., far into the Middle Period of Easter Island.[34] The possibility that they might have inspired the first artists of Easter Island may therefore be disregarded, since, as we have seen, statuary art was an important element during Easter Island's Early Period too, which antedated the Marquesan images by a thousand years. Stylistically or chronologically these fourteenth- to sixteenth-century Marquesan products could not have influenced the mass producers of *ahu* images even during Easter Island's Middle Period, which began about A.D. 1100. On the other hand, the possibility of an influence spreading in the opposite direction, i.e., from Easter Island to the Marquesas, cannot be excluded on chronological grounds.

As has been described elsewhere, the modern descendants of Ororoina, the sole survivor of the "Long-ears" during the massacres in the Poike ditch, showed our expedition through practical demonstration how the large statues were carved from the hard crater walls of Rano Raraku until twelve generations ago by means of roughly pointed hand picks of hard andesite; furthermore, how a few hundred men could transport the giant monuments across the terrain; and how twelve islanders with no other expedients than two logs, cord, and a

pile of crude boulders could erect a twenty-ton giant on the upper platform of an *ahu* in a matter of eighteen days.[35]

Although much archaeological work remains to be done on Easter
Island, as also at Tiahuanaco in the Andes, it is now at least possible to
attempt a reconstruction of some of the major pre-European events on
this, the loneliest of all human habitats.

At some unidentified date at least prior to A.D. 380, that is more
than fifteen centuries ago, the first settlers landed on Easter Island. All
local volcanoes were long since extinct and there were open lakes inside three craters. The people who landed found a verdant island covered by various species of trees and shrubs, including palms. They
therefore had to make clearings for their own stone-house settlements,
for their religious masonry structures, and for their various image
quarries. Although there was thus no shortage of wood on the island,
they did not build their dwellings in the Polynesian manner from pole
and thatch, but they opened quarries and selected stone to construct
circular masonry houses and boat-shaped dwellings of corbeled slabs.
Some of these dwellings were slab-roofed, others thatched with *totora*
reed. This plant was necessarily transported as root stock from an irrigated field on the desert coast of South America and planted by the
settlers in the fresh-water crater lakes together with the equally American medicinal plant *Polygonum amphibium*. In spite of the local presence of wood they also built peculiar watercraft from the same *totora*
reeds, following again the characteristic construction principles of the
inland Tiahuanaco waterways and the Pacific desert coast of ancient
Peru. They cleared, and finally exterminated with fire, the indigenous
palms covering the verdant slopes of the extinct Rano Raraku volcano,
to get access to the solid tuff below the soil. This selected rock, as well
as scoria and basalt in other quarries, they attacked with remarkable
expertness and experience, using flaked and pointed, non-Polynesian
hand picks of American type of shape colossal blocks which they
dressed and fitted in a variety of forms, designed nevertheless to match
each other so precisely that not a knife's edge could be inserted between them.

Their highly specialized masonry technique was unknown elsewhere in Polynesia, but was of the type characteristic of ancient Peru
from the Cuzco Valley to Tiahuanaco. The religion brought by these
early immigrants must have been a form of solar cult, since their impressive religious structures were altar-like megalithic platforms pre-

cisely oriented to the movement of the sun. They also chose the summit of the highest volcano for constructing a solar observatory and a cult site for the sun. Rather than carving wood in the usual Polynesian fashion they sculptured statues from very hard basalt and from various kinds of tuff and scoria, and these statues were erected in the earthen temple courts. The statues included specialized types, all unknown throughout the Pacific island area but characteristic of the dynamic culture center of Tiahuanaco. A defensive structure was built across the Poike peninsula, perhaps for fear of enemy pursuit from the original homeland to this isolated refuge.

What finally happened to the founders of this Early Period culture is not known. Archaeological evidence at Vinapu and Orongo seems to indicate a temporary abandonment of the local temple structures, and the entire island might perhaps have been abandoned for a period interjacent between the Early and Middle Period. But from the sparse carbon datings so far available nothing can yet be said with absolute certainty concerning the transition from the Early to the Middle Period.

What seems evident, however, is that the people subsequently occupying the island were hostile to their predecessors, tore their temples apart and rearranged the building blocks with no regard for the original fitting of their exquisitely shaped and dressed surfaces, and without interest in the annual movements of the sun. The old stone images were also broken and dishonored, their remains serving as crude building material in the walls of a new architectural manifestation: the image *ahu*.

In spite of hostility and marked difference in religious concepts, the new culture was sufficiently related to the old one to make it reasonable to suspect arrivals from the same general geographical region. It is thus possible that the whereabouts of Easter Island was not unknown to the immigrants marking the commencement of the Middle Period. On their arrival about A.D. 1100 the bird-man cult was suddenly introduced to dominate religious activities. Intimately associated with the bird-man cult the newcomers venerated their deceased ancestors. Large ancestor statues became the central feature in their architectural development and dominated all creative efforts, and the many different burial sites became the private cult centers of the respective families. During a period of less than six hundred years, more than six hundred giant ancestor statues were sculptured from the now naked crater walls of Rano Raraku, where man had long since cleared the verdant slopes until the Rano Raraku palm forest had been transformed to wind-blown ashes. As time passed, the acquisition of a mortuary statue be-came a matter of prestige, and successive generations, protected through isolation from disturbing external wars, became increasingly ambitious in exceeding each other in the dimension of their individual family images. At the end of the Middle Period the treeless island had thus become entirely surrounded by *ahu*-platforms supporting mortu-ary stone giants, all facing the inland temple court with their backs to the ocean. At the end of this period, too, cremation burials in front of the *ahu* seem to have been replaced by multiple burials in or on top of the *ahu,* a custom that became almost universal throughout the Late Period.

When image production reached its peak—immediately prior to the disruption of the Middle Period—the island engineers were able to erect statues up to forty-six feet (14.02 meters) tall, that is, one-piece sculptures as high as a four-story building. The largest statue lifted on to an *ahu* platform five miles from the quarries weighed more than eighty tons, and although it was thirty-two feet tall it balanced a red stone cylinder weighing twelve tons, i.e., the weight of two grown ele-phants, on top of its head. It is difficult to visualize how this evolution would have ended. A monolithic statue seventy feet (21.33 meters) tall, i.e., as tall as a seven-story building, was left almost completed by the sculptors in the quarries when the catastrophe occurred about A.D. 1680. The work in the quarries, along the roads, and on the *ahu* was suddenly arrested and was never again resumed. In this final period of manslaughter and barbarism, families hid themselves and all their property in secret underground caves which abound in the lava fields and coastal cliffs. Thousands of obsidian spear points were now manu-factured for the first time, and they dominate all refuse levels through-out the following era. The *ahu* images were overthrown, the reed houses burned until the foundation stones cracked, and the masonry walls were torn down.

The victor, who remained alive, was Polynesian. He was not a stone mason or a carver of stone monuments; he built pole and thatch houses and gathered driftwood along the coast to make wooden fig-ures and tiny canoes like those elsewhere in Polynesia. On Easter Is-land his most important traditional wood carving, still today produced by the hundreds for commercial purposes, is of a peculiar emaciated person termed *moai kavakava,* with goatee beard, strongly aquiline nose, and long ear lobes pendant to the shoulders. This, the Easter Islanders claim, was the appearance of the foreign people found by their ancestors on the island and exterminated in the Poike pyre.

The Polynesians who came to Easter Island did not bring with them the *poi* pounder or the *tapa* beater, the two most important household implements characteristic of the pan-Polynesian culture. There is indeed little or no material evidence to mark the time of their arrival. It is as if they had come in a very modest manner and quietly adopted the local non-Polynesian beliefs and customs. From which island they had departed cannot yet be stated with any certainty. Their own tradition, as collected in the last century, insisted that they arrived *karau-karau*—i.e., 200 years—prior to their own uprising, which led to the battle of Poike. This would agree well with the estimates of Routledge and others, based on the shortest of the two distinct Easter Island genealogies, which included twenty-two generations, whereas Hotu Matua was said to have come from the east fifty-seven generations ago.

There are many indications that they did not come to isolated Easter Island on their own initiative to assist the long-eared stone sculptors in their fanatical megalithic enterprises. The possibility is present that they might have been fetched by Middle Period Easter Islanders who could very well have visited the Marquesas group about the fourteenth century A.D.

At any rate, history found them as the dominant population group living among war-ridden ruins and toppled statues on a naked, treeless island. Among them on the scene when Roggeveen raised the curtain for European spectators were some white-skinned and red-haired individuals, but the main show had long since ended and the leading actors had left the stage.

Chapter 13

The World's Loneliest
Meeting Place

THERE IS hardly a habitable place on earth which does not prove to
be a meeting place, if not a melting pot, of different peoples and cultures. On the continents and continental islands every nation has
changed ownership or received foreign immigrants at least once, the
high culture areas of the Mediterranean world several times. The
Phoenicians were early explorers but never the first in any place; even
on the Canary Islands they were preceded by the Guanches. The Vikings found their own northern land the home of Laplanders; they met
Welsh monks when they settled Iceland, and Eskimos when they
reached Greenland.

Was Polynesia an exception? There is little reason to believe so.
Polynesian culture has been lost and the population so mixed with
modern Asiatic and European settlers and visitors that nothing approaching a true picture of original conditions can any longer be observed. But the early European voyagers were all very emphatic in
insisting that three clearly distinct people had intermixed within the island area we have called Polynesia. The dominant type had fair to
light copper-colored skin, black hair, prominent and almost European
features, the ability to grow mustaches; yet they had a slight Mongoloid stamp and an imposing stature of nearly six feet. This basic type
appears throughout Polynesia, concurs with the common norm of
New Zealand Maori, and concurs again with the physical type we
have found to be characteristic of the island tribes of the Northwest

American coast. These were the islanders who considered themselves normal human beings, the *tangata*.

The second type showed Melanesian affinities, for they were reported to be remarkably dark-skinned, with very flat, broad noses, thick lips, more frizzy hair, and shorter stature. Such people were regarded by the islanders from Hawaii to New Zealand as descendants of the legendary *Menehune* or *Manahune*. The third type, however, had a quite unusually fair skin, reddish or brown hair, and very prominent nose, and were often described as having "Jewish" or "Arabic-Semitic" features.[1] They were found in purest form among the pre-Maori New Zealand refugees who had settled the Chatham Islands. This type is known in Polynesia as *Keu, Uru-keu,* and *Ehu,* or *Haole* and *Hao'e,* and in New Zealand even as *Pakeha, Turehu,* or *Patupaiarehe.*[2] Buck states that where a fairer skin and reddish hair exist in full-blooded Maori, they are believed to descend from a Patupaiarehe ancestor. He adds that certain Maori tribes are said to have had more than their share of red hair, and in these tribes it is said to occur in certain families.[3]

The early European observations and firm Polynesian beliefs were brought into science by Sullivan's aforesaid pioneering study of available skeletal remains. He concluded that "The now rapidly accumulating data on the inhabitants of Polynesia are beginning to indicate clearly that the 'Polynesians' are in no sense to be considered a uniform racial type. The 'Polynesian type' is an abstract concept into the composition of which have entered the characteristics of several physical types." Observing that these same physical types appear unevenly distributed on different Polynesian islands he assumed that the racial mixture had not taken place *before* the dispersal into Polynesia: ". . . it is clear that they must have entered the Pacific at different times, and possibly by different routes. Certainly they must have had different languages and cultures."[4]

R. Linton concurred in Sullivan's views and wrote that "Recent studies of physical type have proved conclusively that the Polynesians are not a pure race but are made up of at least three racial elements."[5] E. S. C. Handy next summed up the consensus among Polynesianists: "Sullivan, Dixon, and Shapiro have all indicated the composite nature of the racial type in Polynesia and the varying distribution of its distinctive elements. Dixon, Linton, and the present writer have analyzed one or another phase of the culture and have demonstrated the presence of several distinct strata or groups of culture elements. And Churchill nearly twenty years ago segregated Polynesian linguistic elements into two distinct groups."[6]

Nothing has subsequently been brought forward to invalidate these conclusions, and since Easter Island forms the eastern outlier of the Polynesian triangle it should offer an interesting possibility for tracing the source of this complexity through an analysis of the anomalous local culture.

The text of this chapter is based on a lecture entitled *"How Far is Easter Island Culture Polynesian?"* given before the Seventh International Congress for Anthropology and Ethnology in Moscow in 1964, and some additional data are extracted from the more recent monograph, *The Art of Easter Island,* of 1976.

*   *   *

The idea that lonely Easter Island represents a melting pot of cultures was not born of recent excavations. The Dutch discoverers in 1722 describe different racial types living together on the island. Among the first to come on board was an islander of apparent rank who had greatly extended ear lobes and who "was an entirely white man." The complexion of most of the Easter Islanders was otherwise described by the Dutch to be about as brown as the hue of a Spaniard, "yet one finds some among them of a darker shade and others quite white, and no less also a few of a reddish tint as if somewhat severely tanned by the sun."[7] The Spanish rediscoverers in 1770 described some of the men as "thickly bearded, tall, well set up, white, and ruddy." They divided the skin color of the local people into "white, swarthy, and reddish," and found the hair to be "chestnut colored and limp, some have it black, and others tending to red or a cinnamon tint."[8]

The Late Period, with its continuous overthrow of ancestral statues and civil war, must have taken another toll of the population by the time Cook arrived in 1774, for he found a decimated, starving and war-ridden population of recognized Polynesian affiliations, whom he firmly dissociated from the monolithic sculptures on the island, which he identified as vestiges from an earlier island era, not even maintained by the contemporary islanders.[9]

When the first Europeans actually settled ashore and learned to communicate with the Easter Islanders, they were told, as we have seen, that two different people with different languages had formerly lived together on the island as the result of two distinct arrivals, the first from the east and the second from the west. The idea of erecting statues came with the first settlers, the "Long-ears," but the bulk of the present islanders descended from the second group of immigrants, the "Short-ears," who, after a long period of peaceful coexistence, finally rebelled and exterminated the male "Long-ears" in the Poike ditch. A careful interrogation of all the elderly natives conducted in 1886 by W. J. Thomson, with the Tahitian settler A. P. Salmon as his interpreter, convinced him of the truth in the local claim that there had been more than one immigration to this easterly island.[10]

W. Knoche shared this opinion after observing diversity in the local culture. He concluded that a non-Polynesian sub-stratum had preceded the now dominant population, yet he rejected the proposal of the Inca historian Sir Clements Markham, who in 1870 had suggested a possible inspiration from Tiahuanaco. Knoche's counterargument was the accepted dogma that South American balsa rafts were incapable of any voyage in the open ocean, and he postulated instead that Easter Island had received a pre-Polynesian sub-stratum from Melanesia.[11]

H. Balfour next concluded categorically that Easter Island culture was composite, with at least one pre-Polynesian arrival, probably from Melanesia.[12] Balfour's view was developed further by Haddon, who proposed that three separate migrations had reached this lonely island, respectively from Australia, Melanesia, and Polynesia. He based this view on the craniological studies of Volz, Hamy, Joyce, Pycraft, and Keith, all of whom had pointed to non-Polynesian features in the Easter Islanders.[13]

Next Routledge went to the island in 1919 to carry out the first systematic archaeological surface survey. She wrote: "Roggewein's description of the people as being of all shades of color is still accurate. They themselves are very conscious of the variations, and when we were collecting genealogies, they were quite ready to give the color of even remote relations. (Described as either 'black' or 'white.') . . . It is obvious that we are dealing with a mixed race. . . ."[14]

H. L. Shapiro, approaching once more the problem within the field of physical anthropology, failed to find any unanimity of opinion, but his personal conclusion was that, "the association of Easter Island with Melanesian or Australian stocks . . . does violence to the known facts."[15] This dismissal of a Melanesian element was considered conclusive by Métraux, and in his monograph on the ethnology of Easter Island he claims that an examination of the archaeological remains had convinced him "that Easter Island culture is one."[16] However, Métraux's archaeologist companion, Lavachery, stressed that their work had been restricted to surface investigations, and he cautiously concluded: "The Polynesians probably found Easter Island devoid of monuments and uninhabited; but this statement lacks proof."[17]

Prior to my own visit to the island I doubted the validity of Métraux's conclusion, and revived in 1941 the arguments for cultural complexity. Instead of resorting to a Melanesian sub-stratum I suggested, like Markham, one from the Andean culture area. Although I had so far had no experience of balsa raft navigation, I did not believe in the assumed South American ineptitude in marine matters, and believed the Easter Island was well within the range of pre-Inca navigators from Peru.[18] Shortly after that, Father Englert, who has resumed locally the archaeological surface surveys, also challenged the conclusions of Métraux and Lavachery. He reverted to the original view of Routledge and others who had proposed a racial and cultural sub-stratum beneath the Polynesian, but modified the old hypothesis of a voyage from Melanesia by pointing as well to some of the existing parallels in ancient Peru.[19]

This brief survey of opinions shows that, prior to our introduction of stratified archaeology on Easter Island, various fields of science had lent themselves to arguments for cultural complexity.

Linguistically there was less reason to suspect an alien sub-stratum. Englert, however, who made the most thorough study of modern Easter Island language, refers to the traditional claim that an earlier and alien people on the island had a different way of speaking, and he says that some synonymous words which still exist may have their origin in this difference of languages. He also speaks of traditional texts pronounced by old people when making certain string figures, but found the words so utterly incomprehensible that he failed to attempt to record them.[20]

The first vocabulary of ninety-four Easter Island terms was collected in 1770 by Agüera of the Spanish expedition. The list contained many characteristic Polynesian words, and some which were equally obviously non-Polynesian. Among the foreign words were the numerals, recorded from one to ten. They were, with the present Polynesian numerals of the island in parentheses:

Coyana	(etahi)
Corena	(erua)
Cogojui	(etoru)
Quiroqui	(eha)
Majana	(erima)
Feuto	(eono)
Fegea	(ehitu)
Moroqui	(evaru)
Vijoviri	(eiva)
Queromata	(angahuru).[21]

To account for the seemingly uncalled-for foreign words, which do not conform with their theories of a monoform origin of the local people, A. S. C. Ross, and with him Métraux, suggests that they probably have a meaning entirely different from that assumed by the recorder.[22] If this were so, these words are equally foreign, however, because they have no other meaning in Polynesian!

As shown by Englert, the disastrous Hotu-iti war must have raged over Easter Island about 1772–74, immediately prior to the arrival of Cook.[23] The plantations had been destroyed and some disorganized groups of war-ridden Polynesians living in extreme poverty were all there was left to greet the disappointed Englishmen, who could not even obtain provisions. Cook and his companions were well aware of the marked difference between the few hundred surviving Easter Islanders seen by their expedition and the flourishing population of mixed types described by the earlier visitors. Both he and Forster recognized the Polynesian element, but describe the survivors as small, lean, timid, and miserable, and believe a catastrophe to have hit the island, leaving only harassed monuments as witnesses of the past.[24] Modern observers have usually overlooked this drastic transfiguration in the local overall picture between the two European visits of 1770 and 1774. Nevertheless, as we have seen, tradition about the Poike ditch, supported by archaeology, indicates another similar annihilation

of a major population group as early as about 1680, prior even to Roggeveen's visit.

To what extent non-Polynesian terms survived at the time of Cook's
visit we do not know, since Cook and Forster for the sake of comparison collected only a small list of such very specific words as were recognized by them and their Tahitian interpreter as having equivalents
in Tahiti, whereas terms they did not recognize were not recorded at
all.[25] That Cook's selected list of twenty-eight Tahitian-kindred words
was not representative of the contemporary Easter Island language was
admitted by the author himself, as he says of the first Easter Islander
who boarded the ship, while the Tahitian interpreter Otiti was present: ". . . his language was, in a manner, wholly unintelligible to all
of us."[26]

In 1864, before the local language had been recorded, Eyraud settled
ashore as missionary with a group of Mangarevans and the only survivors from the disastrous Peruvian slave raids, who were repatriated by
way of Tahiti. Tahitian language was now introduced to the decimated Easter Island population both in speech and writing. Some
years later Roussel (1908) compiled a Rapanui vocabulary, published
post-mortem,[27] but during Roussel's local sojourn Palmer recorded
that "Their language has so much altered that it is impossible to say
what it was originally."[28]

The adjustment to Tahitian speech was augmented further in 1871,
when most Easter Islanders moved to Mangareva and Tahiti, while
Polynesian-speaking sheep rangers from Tahiti and a Tahiti-schooled
catechist from the Tuamotu Islands came to settle among the remaining Easter Islanders, whose total number in 1877 had sunk to 111.[29]
Most Easter Island vocabularies have been obtained from their descendants, whose schooling continued to be in Tahitian. No wonder
that Churchill wrote in 1912, when comparing his own much quoted
vocabulary with the Rapanui text recorded by Thomson on Easter Island a generation earlier: "Of the text we need but say that it is not
such language of Rapanui as is recorded in the pages of this vocabulary, nor is it consistently the known speech of any Polynesian people,
but a jumble of several."[30]

Englert also wrote: "Today it is not possible to reconstruct completely the grammar and the vocabulary of the original language . . .
the natives were civilized as Christians in the Tahitian language which
belongs to the same linguistic group as Polynesian . . . because of this

and other reasons the ancient pure Rapanui language is already partly lost."[31]

Regardless of the otherwise split opinion on the validity of glottochronology, calculations based on existing Easter Island vocabularies, such as attempted by K. P. Emory and others, cannot result in meaningful information.[32]

The intrepid Tahitian-speaking groups that imposed their own language on the small and susceptible Easter Island stock were all converted Christians, however, and did not bring the vocabulary of the Polynesian mythology to the island. As a result the gods and goddesses of Easter Island were never confused with or affected by those of Tahiti and the rest of Polynesia. For this reason it is most significant to observe that the supreme pan-Polynesian deities, Tu, Tane, Tangaroa, Tiki, and Maui, played no part in the religion of the Easter Islanders. Hiro, Rongo, Tangaroa, and Tiki existed only as traditional names but were not worshiped or venerated. With due reason Métraux stresses: "The most striking feature of Easter Island religion is the unimportance of the great gods and heroes of other Polynesian religions." Métraux suggests that: "The importance given in the Easter Island mythology to gods whose names are unknown in the rest of Polynesia shows that the emigrants who settled on the island substituted for some of the principal Polynesian deities lesser gods who took their rank and attributes."[33]

However, there are no lesser gods in Polynesia with the names that were worshiped on Easter Island. The supreme god of the Easter Islanders was Makemake, and with him Haua was the only deity to receive offerings and prayers.[34] Neither Makemake nor Haua were known, not even by name, in any other part of Polynesia. It would seem more likely that these non-Polynesian gods were adopted from another cultural tradition on the same island, than that the Polynesian emigrants upon arrival on an empty island discarded all the prominent pan-Polynesian gods to sacrifice to some self-conceived novelty unknown to their own ancestors. Such an act would be utterly un-Polynesian. Makemake was indeed no deified man, but the supreme god of Easter Island, who created earth and ocean, sun, moon, stars, man, and all living creatures. He rewarded the good and devoured the spirit of the evil after death, while he made his anger known by thunder. Ferdon has demonstrated that the Makemake symbols were

closely associated with the sun-measuring device and other vestiges of
solar worship on top of the highest volcano at the Orongo village.[35]
This ceremonial village with its stone houses was the nucleus of the
Makemake worship and of all pan-Easter Island religious activity; and
yet the entire structure as well as the local ceremonies were as clearly
non-Polynesian as was Makemake himself. The prepared solar observatory, designed to measure the sun's position at the time of the
equinox and summer and winter solstices, has no known parallel in
Polynesia or adjacent island territories. Such prepared devices were
common in Peru on the mainland next to Easter Island, however,
where they, as on Easter Island, were associated with sun ceremonies
and special fires.[36]

We have stated that even in architecture the paramount ceremonial
village of Orongo is not Polynesian. Nowhere in Polynesia is this concept of joining different houses into a compact unit repeated. This is a
common feature in ancient Peruvian architecture both in the highlands
and on the coast. As unique in Polynesia is the specialized building
technique of each individual Orongo house, with its masonry walls,
corbel-vaulted roof, and slab cribwork at the corners. Although nothing parallel is known in Polynesia, stone houses with the technique of
corbeling, or false arch construction, and slab cribwork are architectural features of nearby Peru and adjacent regions of western South
America.[37]

Archaeology reveals that the Makemake worship associated with the
sun was later supplemented by, or assimilated with, the subsequently
all-important bird-man cult, where the non-Polynesian deity Haua
played a principal part. From the Middle Period of Easter Island history all rocks around Orongo were covered by the human figures with
a hook-beaked bird's head. The bird-man rites involved the annual
swimming on tusk-shaped *totora* reed floats to an off-shore islet in
search of the first bird's egg, the winner becoming the sacred bird-man
of the year with almost unlimited social privileges. Métraux writes:
"The importance of the bird cult cannot be denied in the face of the
Orongo ruins and the numerous images of bird-men carved on the
rocks. Traditions, testimonies of early missionaries, and records of travelers confirm the exceptional importance of the cult ritual as well as
the social order built on this annual competition. . . . The complex of
the bird cult . . . has no parallel in the rest of Polynesia . . . nowhere

else was there open competition resulting in the election of a sacred man."[38]

Ferdon sees no reason to exclude the continent nearest Easter Island from consideration, and writes: "although the artistic representations of Easter Island bird-men at present appear to be unique, the evidence of a bird-man cult at Tiahuanaco, Bolivia, and another in the Chimu culture of northern coastal Peru, suggests an American origin for the Easter Island cult."[39]

The tusk-shaped reed floats used in the bird-man competition embody another non-Polynesian feature. Reed-bundle vessels were formerly used in New Zealand, but they were made from local *Phormium tenax,* which quickly became waterlogged. Tusk-shaped reed boats of the size and type used in Easter Island, and of the very same reed, were the most common watercraft of ancient Peru. On Lake Titicaca, and especially along the Pacific coast, reed boats occasionally took on prodigious dimensions, and, as shown in Chapter 3, it is noteworthy that bird-men with long hooked beaks, as on Easter Island, are frequently depicted in Early Chimu art, navigating reed vessels. We have also seen in Chapter 9 that the leading authority on the flora of Easter Island, Professor Skottsberg, has now shown that the aboriginal Easter Island reed is the non-Polynesian *Scirpus riparius,* an American aquatic plant dependent on human aid for its transfer from irrigated areas in coastal Peru to the fresh-water lakes on Easter Island. Again Ferdon asserts that the occurrence on Easter Island of the South American-type craft and the very plant from which it was made "is strong evidence of American contact and suggests the means by which American-derived traits could have reached Easter Island."[40]

Large and small reed boats play an important part in the mural paintings on the slabs of the Orongo houses. Among them are also the conventionalized mask of the double-bladed paddle so important in Easter Island ceremonies and symbolic art. Double-bladed paddles did not exist elsewhere in Oceania, not even for religious dances such as on Easter Island, but were widespread in America. They were observed on reed boats off California until the last century, and they were used until the arrival of the Spaniards and are also found archaeologically on the coast of Peru and Chile. The carved and painted paddles, buried together with pre-Inca raft models from the early pre-ceramic fisher population on the Pacific coast below Tiahuanaco, are double-bladed like the ceremonial paddles of Easter Island. Thomson's com-

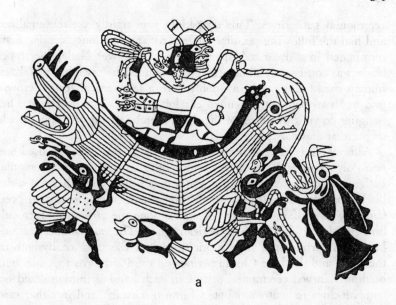

a

b

Reed boats with bird-men from pre-Inca Peru. Painted decorations on Mochica ceramic jars. (a) from Joyce 1912; (b) from Leicht 1944.

ment on the fine Easter Island specimens he brought to Washington in the last century is that they were used in ancient times "in a similar manner to that practiced by the Indians of America."[41] More remarkable still, however, is that these large double-bladed paddles, termed *ao* on Easter Island, were also carried about as emblems of rank during ceremonial gatherings. This *ao* paddle was rigidly conventionalized and had the following peculiar characteristics: The long, slender shaft terminated in a decorated upper and a plain lower blade; the upper blade was consistently either carved or painted to resemble a stylized human mask; this mask invariably bore a tall vertical feather-crown, and had two pendant, extended ear lobes carved like lateral pouches hanging down to the level of the shaft, thereby giving the upper blade its peculiar angular form.

Although it is in itself remarkable that the Easter Islanders used this non-Polynesian and typical American boat accessory as a ceremonial badge ashore, it was not until recently that I discovered that a double-bladed paddle with all the specific characteristics of the *ao* had been similarly carried as an emblem of rank among the earliest pre-Inca culture people on the South American coast. The *ao* paddle was unknown in Peru in Inca and historic times, but was used locally both in the Early and the Late Chimu periods on the Pacific coast. A hierarch holding a carved ceremonial paddle in each hand is immortalized on both Mochica redware and Late Chimu blackware, and in either case the right-hand paddle has every one of the very unusual characteristics of the Easter Island *ao* as specified above.[42] This concurrence is far beyond the range of chance, and the reappearance of the proper *ao* in the religious art on the mainland coast windward of Easter Island is a fingerprint that can be interpreted only as a Peruvian inspiration behind a basic ceremonial art manifestation on Easter Island. The Late Chimu period is generally reckoned to have begun about A.D. 1200, simultaneously with the estimated first century of the Middle Period on Easter Island, but the Mochica (the Early Chimu) Period falls into the first half millennium A.D., concurring in time with the Early Period on Easter Island. The fact that the *ao* was illustrated in Peruvian ceramic art from both these early periods, but was unknown in Inca times, identifies the overseas introduction to Easter Island to the Early or Middle but not the Late Period.

Still another South American element appears as an important detail on the masks which are painted, together with reed ships, *ao* paddles, and bird-men, in the ceremonial stone houses of Orongo: the "weeping-eye" motif.[43] This conventionalized symbol, so extremely important in early Easter Island art, is unknown elsewhere throughout Polynesia. Again, as pointed out by Ferdon, it is a diagnostic feature of early cultures in Peru and in wide areas of adjacent America, typical for instance of the sun god and the bird-men at the Gateway of the Sun in Tiahuanaco. In fact, P. A. Means shows the extreme importance of the "weeping-eye" motif in Tiahuanaco art, where it is symbolic of the supreme pre-Inca deity Viracocha, i.e., the white and bearded leader of the Long-ears from Tiahuanaco who departed into the Pacific. He accords with T. A. Joyce in identifying the tears as drops of rain falling from the eyes of the heavenly sun god to cause life to prosper on earth.[44] Means also shows that the Weeping God's head in Tiahuanaco wears a feather headdress representing the rays of the sun, a peculiar detail which is invariably repeated on the weeping-eye masks on Easter Island.

The supreme god Makemake was also carved at Orongo as a feline figure. Thomson thus said of some Orongo rock carvings which he estimated to antedate all others: "the most common figure is a mythical animal, half human in form, with bowed back and long claw-like legs and arms. According to the natives this symbol was intended to represent the god 'Meke-Meke'. . ." He claimed it bore a "striking resemblance" to a form he had seen in Peruvian art.[45] A feline figure with arched back, drawn-up abdomen, tall legs, and a round head with gaping mouth is commonly found incised with bird-men on the Easter Island tablets. Bishop T. Jaussen's much quoted theory that this animal is a "rat" is as farfetched as at all possible and solely dictated by the fact that rats were the only mammals on Easter Island and, what is more, feline animals do not exist on any Pacific island.[46] Yet felines were present in America and dominated the religious and symbolic art all the way from Mexico to Peru since Tiahuanaco times, and, as in Mesopotamia and Egypt, consistently as a symbol of the creator god.

In addition to the important intertribal cult center at Orongo, each extended family had its individual image platform, which served for ancestor commemoration. In its historic phase this image *ahu* at the end of an open temple court has much in common with religious structures elsewhere in southeastern Polynesia, which all in turn are related to similar elevated stone platforms with temple courts typical of adjacent South America, including Tiahuanaco. We have shown, in the previous chapter, that the *ahu* is built over an earlier structure with different plan and purposes. This earlier structure was astronomically oriented and had no counterpart in Oceania. It had its front where the image *ahu* has its back, and consisted of core filling covered up and elegantly faced with exquisitely shaped and fitted blocks. All the numerous statues of the image *ahu* were consistently turned to face *inland,* and the inland plaza was the center of ceremonial attention. In the previous period, however, the ceremonial attention had been in front of the high *seaward* wall, which was carefully oriented to the yearly movements of the sun. Here irregularities in the huge rectangular and multiangular blocks were patched with scrupulously matched angular and vaulted stones, and surfaces were ground smooth and slightly convex. This highly specialized masonry technique has no known counterpart in Polynesia. Walls of fitted blocks do occasionally occur on some islands, but the finishing is not the same, and they are not oriented to the sun. Core-filled walls, oriented to the sun and fitted and finished with the specialized Early Period Easter Island technique, occur over wide areas in pre-Incaic Peru from the Cuzco Valley, with Rumi-Kolke, to Ollantay-Tambo and Tiahuanaco.

Buck suggested that the Easter Island statues must have received their inspiration from the few life-sized stone figures in the Marquesas.[47] As shown in the previous chapter, this hypothesis is no longer valid in view of recent excavations and carbon datings. The Marquesan image structures in question are so late in time that they even postdate the commencement of the Middle Period statue making on Easter Island. When the Early Period statues were carved on Easter Island there were no stone giants on any other Pacific island, whereas colossal stone men raised in the open were characteristic of the contemporary cult sites in northwestern South America. We have already shown how the non-Polynesian types of Early Period statues on Easter Island have close counterparts in Tiahuanaco.

The complexity of burial customs on tiny Easter Island is particularly noteworthy, and was augmented by Mulloy's excavation of contiguous cists with numerous cremation burials, first found in front of the sun-oriented wall at Vinapu, and subsequently in front of other Easter Island *ahu.*[48] Cremation is reported from New Zealand, is unknown elsewhere in Polynesia, but has a sporadic occurrence both in Melanesia and in some western regions of South America.[49] Equally unknown throughout Polynesia is the thick-walled, core-filled, and boat-shaped masonry tomb with a long central tube for secondary burials, so common on Easter Island;[50] and un-Polynesian is also the cylindrical and corbeled masonry tower known on the island as *tupa,* which in all its details is a duplicate of the South American burial tower, known there as *chulpa,* and abounding in the regions around Tiahuanaco.

Proceeding to secular dwellings, we find the same non-Polynesian picture. Ferdon, in his special study of Easter Island house types, writes: "One of several features that make the Easter Island material culture complex stand out as markedly different from those of other Polynesian islands is its variety of dwelling structures . . . the fact that every one of these buildings, in their total construction, appears to be unique in Polynesia, presents a further problem that is not immediately answerable in terms of independent invention."[51]

One of the principal types of early dwelling on Easter Island, the remains of which are found in vast quantities, especially on the eastern side, are circular stone houses with thick, low, core-filled masonry walls, built-in storage cists, and entrance through a presumably conical thatched roof. Such circular stone houses are sometimes clustered together in contiguously walled units, forming regular village patterns.[52] They do not have any relationship to Polynesian architecture, but reappear, even to the detail of the entrance through the roof, in the circular and thick-walled contiguous-room houses of the Pacific slopes below Tiahuanaco.[53] As important as the core-filled circular houses were the long, boat-shaped slab houses built with masonry cribwork at the pointed ends, corbel-vaulted roof, and tunnel-shaped side entrance. The ceremonial village at Orongo is the best preserved sample of this remarkably non-Polynesian architecture, although single buildings and ruins of an extensive village of this type existed elsewhere on the island.[54] The Easter Island reed house, rather than being rectangular or oval like the pole and thatch houses of Polynesia, follows the lenticular plan of the ancient cribwork stone houses, where the pointed ends were dictated by constructional needs. Thus, in its peculiar ground plan, and also in being built from the South American totora reed, with its poles resting in drill holes in elaborately cut and fitted curbstones, even the historic Easter Island house differs from dwellings elsewhere in Polynesia.[55] The ever-present basaltic curbstones, *paenga,* are among the most characteristic archaeological remains on Easter Island, and have no counterparts in Polynesia. Stones of the same shape and form, with closely corresponding drill holes similarly placed on the narrow side, are found secondarily incorporated in the rebuilt walls of temple platforms in Tiahuanaco, precisely as is the case on Easter Island.[56]

The peculiar Easter Island masonry cooking place, found archaeologically throughout the island and, quite unlike the pan-Polynesian earth oven, is built from narrow rectangular blocks set on edge half above the ground in square or pentagonal shape, is a repetition of a characteristic oven known from excavations of habitation sites in ancient Peru.[57]

It has been customary to ascribe the unexpected presence of stone houses, fitted megalithic walls, and giant statues to a special evolution on Easter Island encouraged by the local lack of wood for carving and construction. This theory is no longer tenable, as explained earlier. Pollen borings reveal that the island was formerly covered by now extinct species of trees and shrubs, even palms, and that the original settlers immediately started to clear the woods with fire to create openings for stone quarries and masonry structures.

A distinguishing mark that was evidently considered of paramount importance to the entire population of Easter Island was the fact that one ancestral group practiced the custom of artificial ear extension whereas all others maintained their normal ear lobes. The custom is reflected in every one of the Middle Period stone statues, and even today the local population distinguish between the minority among them who claim descent from Long-ear lines and those who descend from the victorious Short-ears. Ear extension was in fact practiced right into historic time, probably surviving through maternal lines, since the most consistent of all tribal memories on the island refers to all but one of the Long-ear men as massacred during the Poike battle whereas certainly the women, and probably even the children, were left to intermix with the victorious Short-ears.

In Uapou of the Marquesas group the supreme Polynesian god Tiki was worshiped under the name "Tiki with large ears,"[58] and the Hervey islanders at the time of Captain Cook had a god called "Big-ears," yet artificial ear extension cannot be said to be a Polynesian custom. It was, nevertheless, one of the most striking characteristics of Easter Island. Behrens, who came with Roggeveen when the island was first visited by Europeans, saw amid the people ashore "a few of a reddish tint as if somewhat severely tanned by the sun. Their ears were so long that they hung down as far as to the shoulders."[59] Beechey later saw some with ear lobes so long that, to keep them out of the way, they would sometimes "fasten one lobe to the other, at the back of the head."[60]

Turning again to Peru, the custom of artificial ear extension was of great antiquity and extreme social importance. Markham shows that the right to enlarge the ear lobes was a privilege reserved for the Incas of royal blood and obtained for them the name meaning "the great-eared people," which the Spaniards turned into *Orejones*.[61] Pedro Pizarro, who arrived in Peru with his cousin Francesco during the Conquest, wrote: "There were some orejones who had ears so large that they came down to the shoulders. He who had the largest ears was held to be the finest gentleman among them."[62] Inca traditions maintained that the legendary god-men who built Tiahuanaco also extended their ears and called themselves "Big-ears."[63]

Pizarro's companion, Juan de Betanzos, who married an Inca woman, recorded that the white and bearded Tiahuanaco hierarch Ticci, leader of the departing *Viracochas,* had stopped over in Cuzco on the way from Lake Titicaca to appoint a local successor before he descended to the Pacific coast at Manta. The last act he performed was "leaving orders as to how they should produce the orejones when he was gone"; then "he assembled with his own people and went out on the ocean never again to be seen."[64]

Ticci the legendary god of the "Big-ears," who left the coast of Peru, and Tiki-with-large-ears who, according to Marquesan myths, led humanity to Polynesia, is very likely the same legendary personage, yet it was solely on Easter Island that ear extension assumed a social importance equal to that of ancient Peru, and where realistic traditions maintain that "Long-ears" came with King Hotu Matua's party of aboriginal discoverers from a great land in the direction of the sunrise.

Apart from the Middle Period statues, no other vestiges of a formerly high cultural standing on this island, with its unique geographical location, have been given so much public attention as the incised written tablets, termed *kohau rongo-rongo*. They were found suspended from the roof in every hut on the arrival of the first missionary, but on his order the majority were burned, others hidden in secret family caves where they perished, and very few were saved for posterity. It was clearly documented by all the early missionaries that not even the most intelligent and best informed of the local islanders could provide the meaning of a single sign among those engraved on the tablets, nor could they give the ideogram for the simplest word. They knew each tablet to represent a specific text, but disagreed about which text belonged to which tablet. If one tablet was substituted for another in the middle of their recital, they continued the original text uninterruptedly. The text was recited with a singing rather than speaking voice. They piously copied the original old tablets on new boards, and regarded them as magic objects of the greatest value.[65]

When two of the same natives were later transferred as laborers to Tahiti, they pretended to be learned *rongo-rongo* scribes. One was caught in a fraud by T. Croft as he recited three different texts to the same tablets three Sundays in succession;[66] the other, Metoro, invited as a guest of Bishop Jaussen, continued for fifteen days on end to read an incoherent and meaningless text from the few ideograms on five small tablets put before him. The credulous bishop filled more than two hundred pages with concocted recitals, but the ingenious Metoro escaped the trap by stating that the bulk of the words were not written and were thus invisible. Thus the bishop attempted to compile a *rongo-rongo* dictionary, in which, for instance, appear five different signs all meaning "porcelain," a word the Easter Islander had never even heard before he came to Tahiti. The resourceful Metoro even translated one single *rongo-rongo* sign to signify "he opens a porcelain tureen," another as "the three wise kings," and one sign as "canoe which rolls well with man and feathers."[67] When such signs were put together the resultant text, of course, became entirely meaningless.

Bishop Jaussen's pages of *rongo-rongo* dictionary somehow found their way back to Easter Island, where they were welcomed by the local natives, and with the aid of the Tuamotuan catechist were copied as sacred gospel and finally hidden with pagan relics in secret family caves. Their existence as treasured heirlooms was not disclosed to anyone until our expedition members in 1955–56 were given access for the first time to a few of these family caches. We thus obtained the first of these post-missionary paper manuscripts to which pages of genuine tribal memories had been added. Subsequently others have continued to emerge from the caves.

In the meantime T. Barthel made his sensational claim of having deciphered the *rongo-rongo* script. He had studied the bishop's original manuscript of Metoro's simulations preserved with the rest of his collection at the Congrégation des Sacrés-Coeurs in Rome, and obtained world-wide attention by claiming that these notes helped him read the *rongo-rongo* tablets. According to Barthel, when deciphered, the tablets recorded that the first Easter Islanders had come from the island of Raiatea in about the fourteenth century A.D.[68] Previous to

Barthel, Dr. A. Carroll had similarly claimed to be able to read the tablets, but he had simply "read" the old tradition recorded by Thomson: that the first settlers had come from the direction of South America as they steered toward the setting sun.[69] When challenged by the Easter Island archaeologists Mulloy, Skjölsvold, and Smith[70] to present a word-by-word translation of just any one of the several preserved tablets, Barthel, like Carroll before him, evaded the issue. The *rongo-rongo* boards thus remain undeciphered, although other unsubstantiated claims of reading them, with completely different results, have not been wanting.[71]

Script is another utterly non-Polynesian element on Easter Island. Why such a sign of true civilization, characteristic of great nations, should have evolved independently (and been subsequently forgotten) on lonely Easter Island has caused more scholarly disagreement than any other problem. On the other Polynesian islands the only mnemonic device was a system of knots on strings, which especially in the Marquesas group attained a striking similarity to the complex *quipu* typical of the Inca period in Peru. Theories have been proposed that the Easter Island script had been brought by voyagers from Mohenjo-Daro in the Indus Valley on the exactly opposite side of the earth; that trans-Pacific migrants from China to Mexico had stopped over on Easter Island and left the concept of writing; that the *rongo-rongo* was not script at all but merely native doodles; or that the natives had seen the early Europeans writing and thus invented their own script. These theories have all been duly disproven. The *rongo-rongo* is today known to be a script with a certain number of signs repeated at irregular intervals in lines arranged in boustrophedon, i.e., in a continuous serpentine band where every seond line is turned upside down. Europeans, Chinese, and the Indus Valley people never wrote in boustrophedon, nor was the *rongo-rongo* invented subsequent to European arrival, but already forgotten by then. A theoretical sailing from China to Mexico would be forced north along the sub-Arctic caravel route and would by-pass Easter Island by thousands of miles. The Indus script was not convincingly similar to the *rongo-rongo;* it went into disuse millennia before man reached Easter Island, and it was geographically so remote that a theoretical circum-global voyage from that region would be infinitely easier if passing by way of the Atlantic and America.

Métraux, who for some time doubted that the *rongo-rongo* was real script, was one of the most ardent opponents of the once popular Indus Valley theory. He wrote: "I could compare the Indus script with the pictographs of the American Indians and find as much resemblance. . . . If scientists insist upon connecting Easter Island with the Indus Valley, I claim the same privilege for the neglected Cuna Indians of the modern Republic of Panama."[72]

Actually, the Cuna Indians, who wrote on wooden tablets, live 900 miles closer to Easter Island than do the Polynesians on Tonga. Even the ancient American centers of writing in Mexico and Nicaragua are nearer to Easter Island than are many islands in Polynesia. The first seriously to suspect a contact between the Cuna and the Easter Island script was E. von Hornbostel, although he proposed that the spread of script had gone from Easter Island to the Cuna of Panama, and thence to the early civilizations of Mexico.[73] R. von Heine-Geldern took up this idea and wrote: "The Cunas today generally write on paper. But besides this, written wooden tablets also exist, and the Cunas say that these were the original writing material. The tablets seen by Nordenskiöld were intended to be hung up in the houses during celebrations. The ideograms are painted on with colors. However, according to information by D. L. Gasso . . . the ideograms were formerly carved on wooden tablets. This recalls the written tablets of Easter Island. Also the writing in boustrophedon, and with the succession of lines running upwards from the bottom, recall the Easter Island script." Further: "All the correspondences here presented, when put together, may well justify the presumption that a relationship of some kind actually exists between the Easter Island writing and the writing of the Cuna."[74]

The Cuna signs, however, although continued in boustrophedon, are not directed with the heads downward in every second line, and they are also individually dissimilar enough from the *rongo-rongo* signs to indicate that, although we may be on the right track, these Panama Indians halfway between Mexico and Peru were not the voyagers who brought the tablets to Easter Island. The Easter Islanders are very specific in their claim that the first immigrant King, Hotu Matua, brought sixty-seven written tablets with him when he came from his barren, simi-desert home in the Far East, and that a certain Hinelilu, who accompanied him in a boat with Long-ears, "was a man of intelligence, and wrote *rongo-rongo* on paper he brought with him."[75]

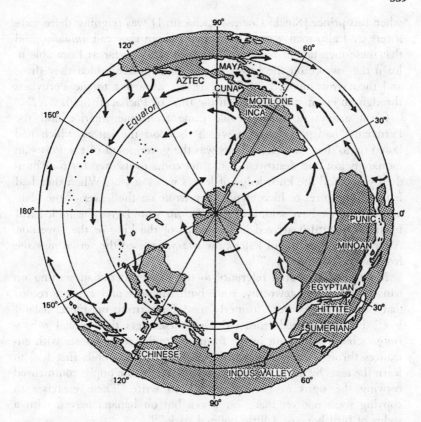

The globe seen from the Antarctic.
A hypothetical migration from the Indus Valley or Mesopotamia to Easter
Island is longer by way of the Pacific than by way of the Atlantic Ocean.

The Russian *rongo-rongo* expert, J. V. Knorozov, has pointed out
that the only place in the world outside Easter Island where a system
of writing has been found with every second line upside down, i.e., in
"reversed boustrophedon" is in ancient Peru.[76] On the arrival of Europeans, however, only the Indians of the Lake Titicaca area still continued a primitive form of picture writing. The *quipu* system, with knots
on strings, was otherwise used universally in the Inca Empire. Father
Montesinos was the only chronicler who recorded local information referring to *pre-Inca* times: "The *amautas,* who know the events of those
times by very ancient traditions passed from hand to hand, say that

when this prince [Sinchi Cozque Pachacuti I] was reigning there were letters, and also men very wise in them whom they call *amautas,* and that these men taught reading and writing . . . as far as I am able to learn they wrote on the leaves of the plantain-tree which they dried and then wrote upon, . . . These letters were lost to the Peruvians through an event which befell in the time of Pachacuti Sixth . . ."

Great armies of fierce people came from the interior and the Peruvians "had great wars in which they lost the letters, which had lasted up to that time. . . . Thus was the government of the Peruvian monarchy lost and destroyed. It did not come to its own for four hundred years, and the knowledge of letters was lost . . . When they had letters and figures or hieroglyphs they wrote on the leaves of the plantain-tree, as we have said, and one *chasqui* would give the folded leaf to the next until it arrived in the hands of the king or the governor. After they lost the use of letters, the *chasqui* passed the verbal message from one to another . . ."[77]

Montesinos' repeated reference to the former Peruvian writing on banana leaves is noteworthy, since both Métraux and Englert record that banana leaves were formerly used for writing on Easter Island too.[78] Englert learned from old Easter Islanders that special *rongorongo* schools were built in the form of circular stone houses with entrances through conical thatched roofs, where the pupils first had to learn the texts by heart. "After learning to recite, the pupils commenced copying the signs to get accustomed to write. These exercises in copying were not yet made on wood, but on banana leaves, with a stylus of bird bone or a little pointed stick."[79]

That writing was also formerly practiced on wooden tablets in Peru appears from the records of Father Christóval de Molina, a priest in the hospital for the conquered Incas at Cuzco: "And first with regard to their idolatries, it is so that those people had no knowledge of writing. But in a house of the sun called Poquen-Cancha, which is near Cuzco, they had the life of each of the Yncas, with the land they conquered, painted with figures on certain boards, and also their origin."[80]

Sarmiento de Gamboa, upon consulting an assembly of forty-two learned Inca *amautas,* or historians, recorded: "They heard their fathers and ancestors say that Pachacuti Inga Yupanqui, ninth Inga, issued a general call to all the old historians of all the provinces he subjected, and even of many others more from all those kingdoms, and he kept them in the city of Cuzco for a long time, examining them concerning the antiquities, origin and notable facts of their ancestors of those kingdoms. And after he had well ascertained the most notable of their ancient histories he had it all painted after its order on large boards, and he placed them in a big hall in the house of the sun, where the said boards, which were garnished with gold, would be like our libraries, and he appointed learned men who could understand and explain them. And nobody could enter where those boards were, except the Inga, or the historians, without express license from the Inga."[81]

Although we are not able today to pinpoint any exact locality outside Easter Island where the tablets can have had their origin, it is still very clear that all the basic elements of this aboriginal writing system, from the use of banana leaves and wooden boards to the very system of writing in reversed boustrophedon, recur in the ancient high-culture area of America. Nothing remotely similar is found in the hemisphere west of Easter Island.

A closer examination of the various ideograms in the Easter Island script shows that many are completely non-figurative, whereas others are simply ornamented at their extremities with animal and human features. The basic and constantly reappearing motifs used as complete ideograms or lending their heads and limbs as embellishment to non-figurative signs, are indeed very few: human figures always shown *en face* with a triangular or quadrangular head, large ears, and three fingers on each hand whenever the hand is shown; birds or bird-headed men always shown in profile with long or short, sharply hooked beaks; a round-headed mammal always shown in profile with gaping mouth, long flexed legs, and arched back; straightforward fish; peculiar double-headed versions of these same four creatures; and the same figures holding one or two staffs. All other representations are clearly of secondary importance, whereas these constantly reappearing motifs or parts of them added to non-figurative symbols dominate the *rongo-rongo* script.

None of these symbols are Polynesian, whereas they are all characteristic of Andean symbolic art. In the relief ornamenting the monolithic Gateway of the Sun, the most celebrated pre-Inca monument at Tiahuanaco, the centrally placed sun god is shown *en face* with quadrangular head and three-finger hands; in each hand he holds a staff ornamented with double heads of hook-beaked birds; from his elbow hang two long-eared human trophy heads, and their very long and pendant ear lobes terminate again in hook-beaked bird heads. Surrounding the sun god are three rows of hook-beaked bird-men, all shown in profile, also with three-fingered hands carrying staffs, some terminating in double-headed birds and some in double-headed fish. A curved fish is also shown in Easter Island fashion as a moon-shaped pectoral on the chest of the central deity, and heads and tails of fish are added at random to embellish the terminal points of the feather crowns and plumed wings of the bird-men. The only mammal represented is feline, and six of the plumes radiating from the central deity's feather crown terminate in feline heads; other feline heads are carved in pairs on his arms and at each end of his girdle. The sun god himself is illustrated standing on the upper platform of a stepped, *ahu*-like structure flanked by two puma heads and ornamented with a non-figurative ideogram which in Easter Island manner terminates in heads of hook-beaked birds and felines. Heads of one or more of these three animals—the feline, the hook-beaked bird, and the fish—are added elsewhere in a symbolic-ornamental way to the decorative ideograms which complete the lintel area of this extraordinary sample of pre-Inca religious sculpture. In short, all the artistic concepts on this South American monument coincide with those on the Easter Island tablets; there are none in addition and none missing.

If we turn to the small-scale free sculpture in stone and wood on Easter Island, we find an individualistic freedom and weird imagination which sets this island clearly apart from any other region of Polynesia. Lavachery, art historian as well as archaeologist, was the first to point out a remarkably non-Polynesian individualism in art revealed through his own survey of Easter Island petroglyphs.[82] After my own recently completed survey of all known Easter Island art objects contained in sixty-four public and private collections throughout the world, I can confirm that this individualism goes beyond the petroglyphic motifs.[83] The large number of small sculptures in stone and wood removed from Easter Island prior to missionary arrival and the subsequent introduction of commercial art, shows that it is utterly erroneous to believe, as has been the case so far, that Easter Island art is repetitive and monotonous and slavishly follows a few given norms, a misconception which has survived solely because the few published sculptures from Easter Island are constant repetitions of those which were in fact intentionally standardized for specific reasons. The great *ahu* monuments were carved alike to resemble the divine progenitor of all important genealogies, whose image was universally venerated at Orongo, and as mortuary monuments they reflect no less artistic imagination than does the Christian repetition of crucifixes in religious art. Also the ribbed, wooden *moai-kavakava* had to be carved in a rigidly unchanging fashion because, as tradition had it, this was a portrait of the last survivor of the "Long-ears." The extremely flat, female *moai papa* or *pa'a-pa'a* had to maintain its traditional form because it represented one important deity, the earth mother, and it is in fact equally flat in all its versions from the early Mediterranean to Mexico and Peru. The beautiful male *moai tangata*, literally "mankind figure," and the winged and hook-beaked *tangata-manu*, "man-bird," also represented fixed ancestral deities which could not be altered by the artist. Finally, the double-bladed *ao* paddle, the twin-headed *ua* staff, the sickle-shaped *rei-miro* pectoral, and the egg-shaped *tahonga* ball were all standardized emblems of rank recognized because of their never-changing shape and characteristics. All these well-known Easter Island carvings were either erected outdoors as fixed monuments or else carried openly during religious dances and other ceremonies.

There was another class of sculpture, however, called *moai maea,* of which Geiseler wrote on his visit in 1882: "These images always remain in the huts, and are a kind of a family image, of which each family possesses at least one, whereas the wooden images were brought along to the feasts."[84] Thomson wrote as a result of his visit four years later: "The small wooden and stone images known as 'household gods' were made to represent certain spirits and belong to a different order from the gods, though accredited with many of the same attributes. They occupied a prominent place in every dwelling and were regarded as the medium through which communications might be made with the spirits, but were never worshiped."[85]

On the introduction of Christianity a large number of these heterogeneous *moai maea* left the island with early visitors and found their places in museum showcases or storage rooms, and an even larger number disappeared into the many secret family caves from which nearly a thousand specimens were disclosed to our expedition in 1956. Some of the most eroded of these sculptures were duplicated one or more times by subsequent generations of artists, but otherwise museum and cave specimens alike revealed an infinite variety in motifs and a vivid individualistic imagination which, as subsequently shown by Lavachery, could only be matched in ancient Peru. He wrote:

"Easter Island is unique in Polynesia in the way its artists have adapted their styles and products to the material used. The imagination of the proper Polynesian is poor compared to that of the Easter Islanders. Even on the islands where art is most abundant, as in the Marquesas group or in New Zealand, this poverty is only overcome by a repetition of great numbers of motifs of a similar character. Thus, in the Marquesas the motifs are continuously tied to the conventional mask with large, round eyes and to the traditional arabesque decoration, whether it is applied to free sculptures in stone and wood, to low relief on shell, bone, or wood, to petroglyphs, or tattooing. On the other islands in Eastern Polynesia the art motifs show even more limitation in inventiveness. Does, then, the capricious and varied art of Easter Island present us with another mystery? Undoubtedly, as with so many of the problems of this island, we ought to direct our attention towards South America . . ."[86]

Turning next to the tools and implements of Easter Island, we find no close affinity to Polynesian norms. Undoubtedly the most common local artifact is the principal Easter Island weapon, the *mataa*, or broad, tanged obsidian spearhead of utterly non-Polynesian characteristics. It has long been a puzzle that only two such obsidian *mataa* have been found outside Easter Island, both found in an aboriginal South American burial site at Llolleo near the Chilean coast. Recently, however, further obsidian *mataa*, equally indistinguishable from the Easter Island specimens, have been uncovered at two additional archaeological sites on and near the coast of Chile, i.e., at Zapallar and on Mocha Island.[87]

The neolithic cutting tools of stone from Easter Island contain both Polynesian and non-Polynesian types. Double-beveled axes, or celts, are not considered a Polynesian feature, yet they have been found in datable Middle Period contexts. Double-pointed or single-pointed hand picks, *coups de poing,* are far more common than any other local cutting tools, yet they are never reported as a Polynesian tool, whereas, like the celt, they are common in South America.

We have seen in Chapter 6 that any kind of fishhook was unknown in Southeast Asia, including Indonesia, and that their universal presence in Oceania closely followed aboriginal Arctic and American forms. The simple and composite bone fishhooks of Easter Island concur with those found archaeologically from South America to New Zealand, but the most remarkable Easter Island type is an incurved one-piece

fishhook of polished stone, which in its perfection of design and balance has been considered the apogee of Oceanic stone work. With the
exception of three similar pieces from the Chatham Islands, the only
specimens found outside this easterly island come from archaeological
middens on the islands and mainland coast of Southern California.
The correspondence with the Easter Island specimens amounts to near
identity, and caused Heine-Geldern and Ekholm to exhibit specimens
from both areas side by side at the American Museum of Natural History in 1949, to bolster their theory of transpacific migrations. Whatever may be the connection between these distribution areas, the
Easter Island specimens remain non-Polynesian.

The only household furniture in the Easter Island dwellings described above were sleeping mats and stone pillows. The mats were
made of South American totora reed. The surprising non-Polynesian
use of stone pillows was tentatively accounted for by Métraux as due to
the formerly assumed local shortage of wood,[88] which seems unlikely,
since there was always enough driftwood and *toromiro* to carve the variety of figurines and badges already mentioned.

Our surface survey of former Easter Island sites revealed a considerable number of quite non-Polynesian grinding stones indistinguishable from the typical American *metate*. Their use on the island remains
inexplicable, and so does the function of a considerable number of
beautifully carved and polished hemispheric basalt bowls found complete and as shards in various parts of the island. Similar stone bowls
and *metate* are unknown elsewhere in Polynesia, but common in ancient Peru, where several specimens of both categories have been found
on the Pacific coast below Tiahuanaco.

Once we have analyzed all principal aspects of pre-European beliefs,
customs, and artifacts on this easternmost outlier of Polynesia, it seems
appropriate to ask: Where are the Polynesian elements? With the exception of part of the vocabulary and some of the primitive wood-cutting tools, we have found no recognizable, purely Polynesian culture
traits on Easter Island. If, on the other hand, we asked, what in fact
can be termed typical Polynesian culture elements, we have seen the
answer in Chapter 6: apart from adz types and fishhook types, which
are as American as they are Polynesian, and the earth oven, which on
Easter Island was found side by side with a South American type of
fireplace, the traits generally considered to be pan-Polynesian are the
poi pounder, the *tapa* beater, and the *kava* drinking ceremonies. Sur-

prisingly as it may seem, none of these were present in the culture of Easter Island.

It is indisputable that the beautifully carved and polished stone *poi* pounder is a principal artifact in all Polynesian cultures, and most notably in the Marquesas, from where the Polynesian component in the Easter Island population is supposed to have come. Yet it is conspicuous by its complete absence from Easter Island, although *taro* is grown, and *poi,* the pan-Polynesian and indispensable Marquesan staple, is locally an unknown dish.

The grooved wooden or whalebone *tapa* beater, which, together with the *poi* pounder, is the most important woman's tool throughout Polynesia, was unknown on Easter Island until introduced in missionary times. The Easter Islanders used rounded and polished beach stones for beating their *mahute* bast into strips which were fastened together in a completely non-Polynesian manner, with bone needle and thread. Métraux writes: "Easter Island is the only place in Polynesia where strips were fastened together by sewing. Elsewhere in eastern Polynesia the strips were felted together; in western Polynesia they were pasted."[89] The bone needles used on Easter Island reappear in an identical form in ancient Peru.[90]

Kava, the ceremonial beverage considered diagnostic of Polynesian culture and related to the South American *chicha* or *cawau,* was unknown on Easter Island.

It is difficult to escape the conclusion already reached in the previous chapter, that the important Polynesian contingent which came to Easter Island preserved little of their own mother culture but their basic wood-carving tools, the earth oven, and part of their own vocabulary. In a sense then, it could be said that pre-Polynesian culture survived on Easter Island into historic times, although in a highly reduced and degenerate form, and sustained by another population group than the one which originated it. The fact that on reaching Easter Island the Polynesians, as their traditions admit, abandoned their own culture and adopted the customs of their predecessors on the island, leaves us without a clear archaeological break to date their arrival. The only hint is the traditional memory that the two people lived peacefully together for two hundred years before the descendants of the newcomers from the west got tired of toiling for their predecessors from the east, and made the Poike revolt which both archaeology and tradition date to about A.D. 1680. If this is a valid indicator, the Polynesians would have arrived on Easter Island in the late fourteen-hundreds, which tallies fairly well with Routledge's calculations of about A.D. 1400, based upon a most careful study of local genealogies. We have seen that the few stone giants in the Marquesas group were erected roughly about 1316 and 1516, and it might be interesting to speculate as to whether this had anything to do with possible local visits from Easter Island monument makers at that time. Apart from the spectacular size of these specific Marquesan monuments there is a marked stylistic difference between them and their Easter Island counterparts, as the Marquesan stone giants, like all other Marquesan art, slavishly follow the pattern of the stereotyped Tiki images.

If we assume with Routledge, and in accord with local traditions and genealogies, that the Polynesians reached Easter Island between 1400 and 1480, they were too late to be responsible for the local switch from the Early Period sun worship to the Middle Period bird-man cult. There was no bird-man cult in the Marquesas group or elsewhere in Polynesia anyhow. The carbon datings of our expedition indicated a stratigraphic change in the architecture of the *ahu* examined, which appears to have taken place at some time around 1100. More excavations are needed to know whether all *ahu* were rebuilt at that period, or, what seems more likely, whether rebuildings continued over a longer period, according to the needs of the newcomers. Although the Early and Middle Period cultures have so much in common that they must have been basically of the same stock and must have come from the same general region, yet they clearly did not descend from the same ancestry, since the Middle Period architects were ancestor worshipers and would never have destroyed the architecture and monuments of their own progenitors. In fact, we find exactly the same on Easter Island as in all the adjacent high-culture area of South America: an archaeological stratification of different and yet basically related cultures. This is as conspicuous of Tiahuanaco, with its superimposed cultural epochs marked by the destruction and rebuilding of the local stepped temple terraces accompanied by changes in statue styles, as it is on the Pacific coast, where the Early and Late Chimu replace each other in the north and the Early and Late Nazca in the south. Superimposed on all these early Peruvian civilizations comes at last the Inca culture. If the carbon dating of around 1100 is correct for the beginning of the Middle Period on Easter Island, this date coincides with the rise of the Inca Empire in Peru. Since not only the Early but also the Middle Period characteristics point to Peru rather than to Polynesia, it is important to note that the beginning of the Middle Period culture on Easter Island corresponds with the coming to power of the first Inca with all the belligerence that this involved throughout the Andean area. The Easter Island traditions of Hotu Matua, their first king, makes him no hero; in fact they are very specific in stating that in his days there were great wars in the large and sun-scorched eastern kingdom where he resided, and it was because he was defeated in battle that he fled with his followers and their families into the open Pacific in the direction of the setting sun.

Chapter 14

Review and Discussion

THE EVOLUTION of navigation is like the course of a river: tributaries from inconspicuous inland sources join together and gain in magnitude until they enter the open sea. Once primitive man had tried to cross calm water by straddling a floating tree, it did not require much ingenuity to sense that to stop it rolling over, another trunk had to be joined to the side of the first one. This was the inevitable step toward a crude log raft.

It is fair to assume that the carrying capacity of a solid log was apparent to early man before he thought of the combined buoyancy of many reeds, and that log rafts therefore preceded bundle boats in primitive navigation. The respective availability of timber or reeds, however, would be a decisive factor in the trend of local evolution.

Shapeless makeshift rafts were undoubtedly first made to cross a deep river or to reach a tempting island. When primitive man discovered the advantage of watercraft even for extensive inland and coastwise travel, for heavy transport and for lake fishing, he diminished the raft's water resistance by pointing its bow and thus increased its velocity. More sophisticated forms of log rafts and bundle craft were thereby gradually developed. The most elaborate representatives of these two basic categories in use until recent times were the balsa log rafts and the totora reed vessels of the coasts of the former Inca Empire.

A great step ahead, but following a different idea, was to scoop out the inside of one big trunk and retain buoyancy through the uplift of water displaced by air rather than by the weight of the removed wood. This sidetrack from raft to dugout canoe also reduced water resistance to the minimum of a single pointed log, and at the same time increased the freedom of movement on narrow waterways.

Undoubtedly the canoe was the first watercraft kept afloat through the principle of the hull. Yet we shall probably never know if the watertight canoe or the wash-through bundle craft was the first vessel to be built with the shape of a true boat. We do know, however, that the invention of the canoe as such was a blind alley, whether built from a scooped-out tree trunk or made from a framework covered by hide or bark. The principle of the hull was to enter into regular shipbuilding through quite different channels. Indeed, the largest and most elaborate examples of canoes ever known were those of the American Northwest Coast Indians and their Oceanic neighbors from Hawaii to New Zealand. Enormous canoes were also built in pre-European times for use in the Caribbean Sea and off the west coast of Africa. In Polynesia especially, side planks were commonly sewn to the dugout bottoms whenever giant logs were not available, but nowhere in the world has any dugout canoe been found with an interior frame added to increase its dimensions and shape to those of a true ship with a ribbed hull. There is no foundation for the popular belief that the ships of the first civilizations developed out of dugout canoes.

The first ships known were built from bundles of reeds and not from timber or split planks. They were built according to the simple principle of wash-through self-buoyancy and not according to that of water displacement by a watertight hull. We know these earliest ships from prehistoric art in northern Africa and western Asia. Their shape and size can be judged from pre-dynastic petroglyphs in Egypt, rock paintings in the Sahara, and incisions on the earliest Mesopotamian seals. The first use of mast and sail goes back to this initial reed ship period. A ceramic boat model in the Iraq Museum, with a cylindrical footing for its mast, shows that the art of sailing in that area goes back at least to 4000 B.C. A large pre-dynastic pot in the British Museum is decorated with what is said to be the earliest Egyptian representation of a ship under sail; it carries a cabin on its deck and is dated to the Naqada II period, before 3100 B.C. Yet the vast number of reed ships, many with masts and sails, coming to light in recent years in the long dried-up *wadi* between the Nile and the Red Sea, take us back to the same pre-dynastic period and may well compete in antiquity with those in the early ceramic art of both Egypt and Iraq.

The early transition from compact, bundle-built reed ships to hollow, vested plank ships has generally been credited to the Phoenicians, but this popular belief is contrary to archaeological evidence. The Phoenicians as a people cannot be differentiated from the general mass of Canaanites until sometime in the second half of the second millennium B.C.,[1] and the Hittites, with access to the same cedar forests, had built elaborate wooden ships before that, as shown by two realistic Hittite ship reliefs, one *in situ* at Karatepe in southern Turkey and another from Tell Halaf in the British Museum. In Egypt, however, Pharaoh Cheops had built himself a luxurious wooden ship by about 2800 B.C., which in perfect elegance of maritime lines equals the best Viking vessel, yet in size greatly exceeds the largest of those known and makes them, and even the Phoenician ships, seem almost new. The surprising fact about this, the earliest of all known wooden ships, is that it is sewn together, without proper ribs, from imported Lebanese planks, and although imitating the earlier reed ships in streamlining and decor, its fragile construction shows that it was only intended for use on the calm waters of the Nile.

The sudden jump from bundle ship built from local reed to plank ship built from imported timber is so abrupt in Egypt that it clearly reflects an outside inspiration. It seems natural to look to Asia Minor, from where the pharaoh had received his cedar planks. A clear transition from bundle boat to ribbed hull can be traced in Mesopotamia. Early local temple reliefs abound in realistic representations of reed boats involved in naval battle or in the transport of men and women, but also show cargo transport by log rafts or large *guffa* of the coracle type. These round *guffa* and properly boat-shaped *jillabie* are still in use on the Euphrates today and correspond in every detail to the archaeological models in the Baghdad Museum which were built along the same river some five thousand years ago. Their hull is made from reed matting coated inside and out with bitumen, just as the biblical patriarch Noah built his large ship, according to the very early local authors of the Old Testament. Noah's method was to carve ribs of cypress and reduce the use of reeds from compact bundles to an outer mantle made watertight with pitch. For the early coastal dwellers on the Mediterranean shore of Asia Minor, where reeds were scarce and cedar forests plentiful, the timber being exceptionally suitable for easy splitting into thin, hardwood boards, the substitution of reed mats by a wooden mantle would seem a logical step. Yet even the original population of Mesopotamia had overland access to the eastern limits of the once enormous cedar forests, and wooden ships seem to have been used since very early times in Iraq and the Arabian Gulf. This more durable type of hulled vessel would rapidly spread to Egypt where the pharaohs had been importing cedar planks for temple building since the very earliest local dynasties.

Reed boats had their advantages, however, and have survived until the present day on inland lakes of western Asia, Africa, Mexico, and South America, from where they spread to Easter Island. They are in use, or were so until the beginning of this century, on the Mediterranean islands of Corfu and Sardinia and on the Atlantic coast of Morocco, in the Arabian Gulf, and as far east as the island of Ceylon. It is noteworthy how they tend to survive in waters adjacent to outstanding early centers of civilization: in South America on Lake Titicaca, close beside the ruins of Tiahuanaco; in Africa, where the Lucus River enters the Atlantic beside the colossal ruins of the megalithic city of Lixus, and on Lake Tana, where the Nile begins its flow through Egypt; in Asia on the rivers Euphrates and Tigris, flanked by Sumerian sites; on Bahrain island from where Sumerian civilization is suspected to have derived; and in the swamplands of the Helmand River, which shares its headwaters with the Indus River, the site of India's famous ruined cities of Arappa and Mohenjo Daro. Apart from being among the dominant features in early illustrations from Mesopotamia and Egypt, reed boats are known also from the art of early Cyprus and Crete; they are incised on coastal burial caves in Israel, on seals in the Hittite territory of southern Turkey, and on the megalithic slabs of the ancient temples of Malta, which recent adjustments of carbon datings imply to antedate the rise of civilization in Egypt.

Egypt and Mesopotamia have long been competing for the honor of being considered the oldest source of civilization. It has therefore caused a stir among scholars to be confronted of recent years with radiocarbon evidence to the effect that advanced culture was established on the insignificant island of Malta before it appeared in the large and fertile Nile valley. Matters got still more confused when recently Danish archaeologists, working on the sand-covered offshore island of Bahrain in the Arabian Gulf, found extensive remains of a local civilization antedating that of Mesopotamia.[2]

The long cherished beliefs that culture spread from Egypt both westward and northward through the Mediterranean, and from Mesopotamia southward and eastward through the Arabian Gulf can for chronological reasons no longer be maintained. With mature island cultures in Malta and Bahrain antedating the hitherto assumed birth of civilization in Egypt and Mesopotamia, some isolationists have seen an argument for multiple origins rather than the hitherto supposed spread of culture from the two continental river valleys. This isolationist argument has seemingly been strengthened by the fact that the same adjustment of carbon dates now also brings the Mediterranean-like stone towers and associated vestiges of advanced culture in coastal areas of the British islands and adjacent archipelagoes back to correspondingly early prehistoric dates.

Indeed, archaeology may be confronted with considerable adjustments, and even face a revolution against long-established thinking, but these recent discoveries can hardly be taken as favorable to the isolationist standpoint. Malta and Bahrain, like Great Britain, are islands, and the mere fact that they were peopled is in itself evidence of previous boatbuilding, deep-sea navigation, and accordingly some degree of diffusion. It is not unreasonable to suspect that the impressive knowledge of elaborate megalithic architecture on Malta, and the many other vestiges of organized societies and true civilization left there and on the island of Bahrain, were not developed locally but brought with settlers who must at any rate have acquired their maritime art and navigational skill elsewhere. This seems the more apparent since the ruins from bygone civilizations on Malta and Bahrain, as well as the prehistoric stone towers in the British Isles, all date back to the initial local periods, and certainly not to later centuries, which would have left time for local evolution.

Science has always maintained, and evidently with good reason, that large population groups organized by a common leadership and with a solid economy based on the harvesting of crops from considerable tracts of fertile land would be the requisites for the rise of true civilization with all its complex arts, particularly megalithic temple building with no practical function and yet requiring organized mass labor. Nothing has been found to invalidate this logical reasoning. As to the bulk of the islands under consideration, not least Malta and Bahrain, they lack all those requisites; even before their restricted island surfaces were reduced to their present barrenness they had nothing of economic value to stimulate the growth of civilization that was not present also on the mainland coast. When we find impressive remains of former civilization on just about every inhabitable island in the Mediterranean Sea and the Arabian Gulf, it is unquestionably due to diffusion and not to independent evolution along parallel lines. History shows that all the major islands in the eastern Mediterranean paid taxes to Egypt, which they would never have consented to do to a landlocked nation that could not enforce these overseas obligations, and Egyptian artifacts had diffused as far west as beyond the Straits of Gibraltar, having been found recently in the Phoenician port of Cadiz on the Atlantic coast of Spain. The Phoenicians themselves established colonies and spread their knowledge and artifacts to every corner of the Mediterranean and to the north and south beyond Gibraltar. In the opposite direction, beyond Asia Minor, the ocean similarly served as an early highway. From the chief librarian of the Egyptian papyrus library in Alexandria we learn that Egyptian papyrus ships sailed to such distant regions as Ceylon and the River Ganges. The Sumerians and other early voyagers traded with Bahrain and even with Arappa and Mohenjo Daro in the Indus Valley. The early Arabs showed Vasco de Gama the correct monsoon season and sailing direction for voyaging to India, yet they themselves had been preceded by the Phoenicians, who had explored Asia at least as far east as Indonesia.

It was, indeed, well before all these historic and protohistoric voyages that civilization was established on the islands of Malta and Bahrain. The motives of mariners to visit these islands and settle ashore were probably the same as those which brought Egyptians and Sumerians to India or Phoenicians outside their own Mediterranean Sea. The stimuli for travel have hardly changed from prehistoric to historic times. Man as we know him has been driven by an urge for exploration of the unknown and a search for better pastures; he has been lured by a desire to bring home treasures and establish wealth through new trade routes; he has wanted to convert foreigners to worship his own gods; he has been pushed ahead by religious fanaticism, but also by fear. Since primitive man took the first steps along the road to an organized society he has lived in a never-ending fear of hostile armies that would fall upon him, his family, and his own community to take their property and land. The reason why so many islands became the home of very early civilization might logically be explained by hostile pressure prior to embarkation. There was a threat of unexpected attack from forests, mountains, and endless tracts of wilderness everywhere on the mainland. An island was a secure fortress, at least in the initial periods of civilization, until coastal nations had mustered powerful fleets and sailors who could go raiding anywhere.

The fact that islands like Malta and Bahrain show earlier vestiges of civilization than Egypt and Mesopotamia merely reverses, geographically speaking, the time sequence. It indicates that early culture might perhaps have spread eastward in the Mediterranean Sea and northward in the Arabian Gulf rather than in opposite directions, as has so long been assumed. This should stimulate archaeological attention to areas hitherto unexplored, probably because they are covered by sand or by water, as we have no right to assume that today's extent of desert and salt water concurs in detail to that dominating the Afro-Asiatic world prior to the rise of Egyptian and Mesopotamian civilization. Indeed, we do know that the desert has been creeping up on fertile jungle and pastures, and still does so in northern Africa at a speed measurable in miles per year, with immense mounds of sand obliterating former river beds and settlements. The petroglyphs on the canyon walls of the bone-dry Wadi Abu Subeira in Upper Egypt are over a hundred miles from the Red Sea, and the rock paintings on outcrops in the Tassili desert of southern Algeria are nearly a thousand miles from the Mediterranean coast, yet both depict reed boats surrounded by Egyptian-style bird-men, crocodiles, hippopotamuses, water buffaloes, giraffes, deer, lions, and a number of other river and forest animals which today are unknown in all nearby regions of Africa now buried by the desert sand. In these present barren wastes early man paddled reed boats through what must have been wooded areas with rivers, lakes, and swamps prior to 3000 B.C. Mesopotamia, too, and the whole of Asia Minor to the Mediterranean shores of Lebanon were forest-covered and green when civilized man began his first clearings. The deep sand dunes which have buried countless cities and even lofty pyramids and temples from Ur to Nineveh, and also those which cover the still earlier quarried-stone ruins and a hundred thousand burial mounds, plundered long since, on the island of Bahrain, still conceal untold secrets of man's earliest prehistory.

So much for the sand. And what about the limits of land and sea? A few coastlines are known to have changed. Some of the islands, bays, and ports known to the early navigators were not at all those we recognize today. Geological disturbances have caused some early sites to disappear into the sea; others are hidden under silt, lava, and ashes. Silt and mud from all major rivers in Africa and Mesopotamia have slowly but steadily concealed former delta plains, bays, and landing areas. Most harbor areas of the Afro-Asiatic world have changed since Sumerian, Pharaonic and Phoenician times. An inspection of the tiny port of Byblos today shows remains of the pavements of its former cargo wharfs under the water outside the present medieval entrance. Along the Afro-Asiatic coasts much has changed even since about 600 B.C., when Pharaoh Necho's joint Egyptian-Phoenician expedition set sail from the Red Sea and circumnavigated the African continent. Lost to sight are the six ports down the Atlantic coast of Morocco where Hanno, in about 450 B.C., anchored his fleet from Carthage when he sailed in the opposite direction to explore the west coast of Africa with his sixty galleys packed with 30,000 prospective settlers. Indeed, some of these ports have become inland fields even since the Romans sailed out through the Straits of Gibraltar and conquered Berber and Phoenician settlements.

The main Roman discovery on the Atlantic coast of Africa was the island city of Lixus, then known as Maqom Semes, "City of the Sun." Its impressive sun-oriented, megalithic structures were already then so ancient that the Romans considered Lixus "The Eternal City," older than any settlement inside the Mediterranean; in fact, the Romans associated the place with the demi-gods who preceded men on the earth, and ascribed the grave of Hercules to this island of Lixus which overlooked the Atlantic Ocean. Today Lixus is no longer an island, and ships cannot get near the former wharfs. The impressive ruins are now to be seen half-buried topping a headland, on a ridge surrounded on all sides by flat fields through which the Lucus River undulates toward the Atlantic shore, now barely visible in the distance. Ships that were undoubtedly in proportion to the colossal structures ashore once docked at what was then an island coast; today not even the tiny four-to six-man reed boats, which have survived among local fishermen, are able to approach the foot of the landlocked hill. A large Roman mosaic of Neptune bears witness to former links with the ocean, while the ruins of Arab mosques and Roman temples cover earlier Berber and Phoenician structures, refitted in turn from gigantic blocks hauled from far away by the unknown sun worshipers who first chose the site. At the foot of the hill their former landing area is buried at an untold depth, whereas the vaulted roofs of the much later Roman merchant shops emerge in a row above the green grass where galleys formerly moored.

With known coastal sites drowned in silt and inland cities buried in sand, we still have to take geological disturbances into account to realize how much of the past is still hidden from our eyes. The cities of Pompeii and Herculaneum were lost in A.D. 79 and were not rediscovered until the last century; the Bronze Age city of Akrotiri on the Greek island of Santorini (Thera) was lost, even to traditions, until discovered by excavations in 1956 by the Greek archaeologist Spyridon Marinatos. His discoveries, coupled with geological and oceanographic research, won new terrain for our incomplete knowledge of early Mediterranean history.

We have in Chapter 3 seen how, according to L. Pomerance, the volcanic explosion of Santorini sent tidal waves far and wide across the Mediterranean with devastating effects on surrounding settlements. We know that about 1200 B.C. the dismal record of catastrophe is almost universal in the eastern Mediterranean. Pomerance believes to be able to demonstrate that a cataclysm took place at that time which put an end to existing civilizations and created a horizon of waste land. This disruption spread so far, he argues, that it cannot have been due merely to the violent act of the harassing survivors, the Sea People, but could more logically have resulted from the volcanic explosion and devastating flood waves. It has been generally believed that the volcanic explosion of Santorini took place about 1400 B.C., i.e., about two hundred years before the all-embracing collapse of the East Mediterranean civilizations which according to the consensus happened about 1200 B.C. If future research should prove Pomerance to be right, and the chaos in the surrounding area, including the islands, Egypt and all of Asia Minor, directly or indirectly was triggered by volcanic disaster and tidal waves, then we would indeed have a better reason for the total turmoil than the localized raids of the Sea People alone.

It is remarkable that the escape of the Jews from Egypt and their migration back to Israel is generally considered to have taken place in that very same chaotic period. Since they put their memories of the event on written record, there might indeed be some collective recollection of a contemporary tidal wave behind the Hebrew claim that they were able to escape from Egypt because the Egyptian armies, their chariots and cavalry were drowned in a flood while the refugees fled into the mountains of Sinai. This Hebrew belief, made famous through the account in the book of Exodus, is even more dramatically described in Psalm 114: "When Israel came out of Egypt . . . The sea looked and ran away; Jordan turned back. The mountains skipped like rams, the hills like young sheep. What was it, sea? Why did you run? Jordan, why did you turn back? Why, mountains, did you skip like rams, and you, hills, like young sheep? Dance, O earth, at the presence of the Lord, at the presence of the God of Jacob, who turned the rock into a pool of water, the granite cliff into a fountain."

Undoubtedly it is the same event David sang about in his praise to the God of Israel (2 Samuel 22:4–20): ". . . I will call on the Lord to whom all praise is due, and I shall be delivered from my enemies. When the waves of death swept round me, and torrents of destruction overtook me . . . I called for help to my God, he heard me from his temple, and my cry rang in his ears. The earth heaved and quaked, heaven's foundations shook; they heaved, because he was angry. Smoke rose from his nostrils, devouring fire came out of his mouth, glowing coals and searing heat. He swept the skies aside as he descended, thick darkness lay under his feet. . . . He curtained himself in darkness and made dense vapour his canopy. Thick clouds came out of the radiance before him; glowing coals burned brightly. The Lord thundered from the heavens and the voice of the Most High spoke out. He loosed his arrows, he sped them far and wide, his lightning shafts, and sent them echoing. The channels of the sea-bed were revealed, the foundations of earth laid bare at the Lord's rebuke, at the blast of the breath of his nostrils. He reached down from the height and took me, he drew me out of mighty waters, he rescued me from my enemies, strong as they were . . . He brought me out into an open place, he rescued me because he delighted in me."

Psalm 77, too, stresses that Moses and Aaron led their people out of Egypt when the ocean was troubled to its depths, there were cloudbursts, whirlwinds, and thunder, and they escaped through mighty waters while lightning lit up the world and the earth shook and quaked.

Whether the catastrophe of Santorini took place about 1400 B.C. or occurred about 1200 B.C., it must have had a great effect on the lowlands of Egypt, and it is hard to avoid the conclusion that the very early Hebrew records stem from eyewitness accounts of this geological catastrophe. The Bible might therefore contain the only written records describing the tidal waves which are now suspected to have caused the collapse of Minoan civilization on Crete, put an end to the old Hittite and Egyptian empires, stimulated the continental raids of the unidentified "Sea Peoples," and perhaps ultimately triggered the Phoenician push beyond Gibraltar—population disturbances, all of which appear to have taken place in the critical period around or immediately prior to 1200 B.C.

The city of Santorini was left high and dry, but buried by an enormous depth of lava and ash. As the archaeologists penetrated the volcanic layers and the roofs and walls of city houses came to light, the early importance of ships immediately became apparent. Upstairs in a house on the public square were found mural paintings in gay colors illustrating Santorini's former port. A fleet of streamlined sailing ships, ornamented with flower garlands and with their sails reefed, are shown being paddled into the harbor, while elegant men and women await their return on roofs and balconies of houses towering behind each other against a background of red mountains. Other decorative frescoes represent exotic plants and animals, and a picturesque landscape with a winding river is thought by archaeologists to represent the Nile. Whether or not the Bronze Age mariners of Santorini are shown returning triumphantly from a visit to Africa almost three-and-a-half millennia ago does not prevent the harbor scene from testifying that the sea was not a barrier but a highway to those who had chosen the island as their habitat.

The recent discovery of the lost island civilization of Santorini has brought new life to the old legend of Atlantis. Serious scientists are trying to identify Santorini with Atlantis. Plato's story of Atlantis has until recently been considered almost universally as a fable invented by scholars and used freely by science fiction writers and enthusiasts of the kind that want to bring supermen in from outer space or up from the depths of the ocean. The very legend that for so long had been scorned or passed over in silence by professional scholars apparently lay dormant in the minds of quite a few of them, because what had been considered as a fable if located outside the Straits of Gibraltar seemed plausible if located inside.

With due respect for the many competent anthropologists and geographers who now attempt to identify Santorini with Atlantis, and in full appreciation of the fact that the eruption of Santorini probably had effects on cultural history unmatched by subsequent catastrophes, it would still be tempting to play the devil's advocate: those who look for a kernel of truth in the story of Atlantis ought to follow Plato's version recorded with ample details in two of his dialogues (*Timaeus* and *Cri-*

tias) as there are no other sources to consult. In Plato's writings Atlantis is placed emphatically in the Atlantic Ocean, the main world ocean of which the Mediterranean was said to be but a harbor inside the Pillars of Hercules. The Greek author states that his predecessor Solon had learned of an island named Atlantis, lost in the ocean of the same name, which was described at length in an old papyrus text in the possession of the priests of Sais of Lower Egypt, where Solon had actually been. The essence of the original text as to locality, event, and time can be summarized in three points: Atlantis was beyond Gibraltar; it sank into the ocean and disappeared; this happened in times so remote that it preceded Egyptian history.

Santorini, in contrast, is not beyond Gibraltar, but within Greek home waters, better known to Solon than to his Egyptian informants; the island never sank, but is where it always was; and the local disaster was not so early that it antedates Eyyptian history, but so late that it concurs in time with the end of the pharaonic lines.

Until better reasons to revive the Atlantis legend emerge, it would seem best to let Plato's records rest in the realm of mythology and traditional history. Dry land has sunk into the Atlantic, as can be judged from underwater canyons extending along the ocean floor outside African river mouths; round boulders are found below the sea on the mid-Atlantic ridge and testify to former land; so do sediments of freshwater plankton drilled from the bottom in mid-ocean areas which must once have contained landlocked lakes. But there is as yet nothing to prove that any of these geological changes have taken place in human times. Ocean floors, like continental masses, have never ceased to move. Thus Stone Age man once hunted forest animals where today the North Sea lies: arrowheads are found by trawling the bottom. And one may wonder at the extent of the geological disaster that disturbed the Atlantic and split the countryside of Iceland, creating the impressive rift canyon that runs across it and beyond it, along the ocean floor. Radiocarbon datings of a tree embedded in the lava of the rift shows that this Atlantic catastrophe had occurred in the centuries immediately around 3000 B.C. This coincides with the centuries around 3100 and 3000 B.C., when cultures everywhere in the Mediterranean seem to have taken a new departure, an interlude in the slow evolution of civilization when everything seems to have taken a new and different road as a result of disturbances and displacements of unparalleled dimensions. In many respects the period around 3100 to 3000 B.C.

brings to mind the restless and chaotic time around 1200 B.C., which followed immediately after the disastrous explosion of the island of Santorini. Islands and continental coasts contain clear vestiges of this early disruption of cultures too.

On the strategically placed island of Malta a central date around 3000 B.C. marks the end of the neolithic phase, and there is a distinct break in the continuous cultural development at this point, when a new major period begins.[3] Archaeologists have similarly documented signs of widespread dislocation and upheaval throughout the island of Crete at about 3000 B.C.[4] Many people seem to have taken refuge in caves on the island then, to settle subsequently on high hills. Also around 3000 B.C. the occupation of neolithic sites on Cyprus came to an end, probably as a result of a natural disaster, and a completely new period began.[5] Since these radiocarbon dates are all within a margin of plus or minus 100 years, they match well with the period around 3100 B.C., when true civilization was established both in Egypt and in Mesopotamia with the founding of the first local dynasties.

Seen in relation to the now recognized enormous antiquity of man's presence on earth, does it seem likely to be mere coincidence that the independent dynasties of Mesopotamia and Egypt were founded at the same time and so near each other with only the Arabian peninsula between? A time concurrence within the same century seemed reasonable in the early days of science when the human species was assumed to have existed only for thousands or tens of thousands of years, but a single century about 3000 B.C. becomes like a flash in the human time span actually known to comprise millions of years. Palaeolithic people had roamed across thousands of miles of Afro-Asiatic territory for untold ages, and their descendants had developed a variety of living patterns and primitive cultures throughout all continents, when the river banks of Egypt and Mesopotamia within the same approximate century were occupied by hierarchs with absolute power who claimed descent from the gods, were ancestor worshipers, counted bird-men among their progenitors, navigated reed ships, built enormous pyramids to the sun, incised cylinder seals, and erected giant stele inscribed with the earliest types of hieroglyphics archaeologists have so far found. In short, two dynasties which had already acquired a strikingly similar level of civilization, and whose heirs later ruled these two Middle East river valleys for numerous generations, were founded amid earlier archaic cultures chronologically speaking at the same time and within territories separated merely by a traveling distance of weeks or months.

If these two pioneering civilizations had had independent roots, script might well have been invented on each side of the Arabian peninsula with a time discrepancy of tens of thousands of years. It would be an insult to the developing nations today to suggest that after millions of years of gradual maturing, mankind was just ripe for literacy around 3000 B.C. Let us admit that if it were not for marginal contact and traveling teachers and missionaries, literacy would not have reached Europe from the Middle East, as it gradually did, and if we were to await independent evolution most nations would very likely have remained illiterate until today.

In view of the obvious proximity in time and space, the burden of proof in this case rests clearly on those who sustain the idea of independent origins for the two great civilizations of the Middle East. No scholar would deny that the original hieroglyphic signs of the earliest Sumerian period were later replaced by the completely different cuneiform symbols and next gave inspiration, directly or indirectly, to the large variety of quite dissimilar writings of Asia Minor, from Hittite ideograms to Hebrew and Phoenician letters. Could there not be a similar link between the two seemingly dissimilar scripts of the earliest Sumerians and their contemporaries in the Nile Valley? In fact, we have seen in Chapter 1 that Falkenstein's and Amiet's studies of the earliest known Sumerian script revealed that the hieroglyphic sign for "ship" in the archaic texts from Uruk, prior to the introduction of cuneiform writing, was identical with the ideogram for "marine" in ancient Egypt: a sickle-shaped reed boat which in addition to cross lashings had peculiar Egyptian-style double bends on top of the elevated bow and stern, a stylistic detail with no known practical function and unknown on watercraft anywhere else in the world.

The scribes of the first dynasties of Mesopotamia and Egypt must thus have had some kind of contact or a common source prior to the establishment of separate cultures on each side of the Arabian peninsula. It is significant that the common glyph pertains to ship and navigation.

It is generally accepted that the ancient Sumerians must have been a seafaring people from the time of their first appearance when they established the cities of Ur and Uruk, which around 3000 B.C. were important ports on the Arabian Gulf. The numerous inscriptions from the first period clearly testify to this. The Egyptians, however, have generally been considered a landlocked river people, inept in marine matters. This, on closer examination, is a view which requires modification. Such a judgment is unfair to a nation whose impressive remains testify to their having been true masters of the other early arts and techniques which were diffused to Europe and formed the backbone of European culture into the Middle Ages. All the details in the rigging of the Spanish caravels of the fifteenth century had been inherited from the original designers in the Middle East, as early Egyptian models and illustrations show. These marine designers are lost in the shadow of the all-powerful pharaoh, and the pharaohs were no seafarers. They were so concerned about their own glory and large-scale preparations for their afterlife that nearly all their attention was focused on the two banks of the Nile. To them the rest of the world was definitely of secondary importance. In this respect they contrasted with the roving and extrovert Phoenicians whose merchant colonizers never tired of searching for new lands and trading routes. Yet there is ample evidence that the Egyptian communities, even in pharaonic times, comprised marine architects, shipbuilders, and expert sailors. The ships they designed for the pharaohs abound in the frescoes and bas-reliefs illustrating daily life and special events in ancient Egypt. That the bulk of them served Nile navigation just as the multitude of local vessels do today is quite apparent. Yet the extremely elevated bow and stern, the special details of sail and rigging, as well as the peculiar "bowstring" astern and "fuse" for the rudder oar, clearly show that the prototype was originally designed for, and these vessels also occasionally used for, navigation in the open sea. Why else the bowstring and other details serving only in surf and breaking seas?

Outside sources testify to this. The Hebrew prophet Isaiah refers to the Egypt of his day as the land that sends ambassadors across the sea in ships of reeds. The earliest pre-Christian text of Isaiah, preserved in the Shrine of the Book in Jerusalem, mentions the reeds of these ships as *gomeh,* meaning papyrus. Although frequently translated merely as "reed" today, the term "papyrus" was expressly used in the second century B.C. when Isaiah was translated into Greek by Hellenistic Jews in *Septo Aginta.* One of the duties of these seafaring Egyptian ambassadors was undoubtedly to collect taxes from foreign people. Long after the pharaohs had established themselves as riverside dynasties, they continued to claim taxes from far-off islands in the eastern Mediterranean, islands which could not have come under their dependence unless the Egyptians themselves had navigated beyond the mouth of the Nile.

An exceptionally expansive pharaoh was Rameses II, who personally traveled in Asia Minor and let his portrait be carved in full figure on the coastal cliffs of Lebanon, and whose alliance with the Hittite king can still be seen incised with Egyptian hieroglyphics as far away as Bagazköy in distant Turkey. Queen Hatchepsut's artists immortalized her Red Sea expedition to foreign lands with detailed reliefs of wooden ships where accessories which later appeared on the sailing vessels of Columbus' time were not wanting. The same can be said about the many other highly sophisticated pharaonic sailing ships of both wood and papyrus bundles as depicted in the temple of Edfu, at Karnak, in the Valley of Kings, or on the walls of the tombs of the nobles at Sakara. And the Greek historians preserved in written words the record of Pharaoh Necho, who financed a joint Egyptian-Phoenician fleet for the specific purpose of sailing down the Red Sea, all around Africa, and back through Gibraltar. The Egyptian knowledge of the Atlantic is testified by their accounts to the early Greeks, giving the present name of that ocean, placing its position outside Gibraltar, and describing its size as dwarfing that of the Mediterranean Sea.

Moreover, the Indian Ocean was known to the ancient Egyptians who crossed its full length in their papyrus ships. This knowledge we have from no less an authority than Eratosthenes, the chief librarian of the Egyptian papyrus library in Alexandria before it was burned. He was not only the leading geographer of his time, but the real father of projective maps. He knew very well, like Greek scholars before him, that the earth was a globe and figured out its correct size from its surface curvature two centuries B.C. whereas Columbus gave it a fraction of its real circumference more than a millennium and a half later. In describing the geographical layout on the other side of the Indian Ocean, Eratosthenes rendered distances in traveling time and reported that papyrus ships, with the same sails and rigging as on the Nile, required twenty days to sail from the mouth of the River Ganges to the island of Ceylon. We could have had no better source for the information that Egyptian papyrus ships by-passed all of India and navigated in the distant Bay of Bengal.

The early Sumerians also had trade and contact with India, notably with the Indus Valley civilization, which from the second millennium

B.C. flourished for several centuries along the banks of the River Indus and eastward from its mouth as far as the Gulf of Cambay, where an Arabian Gulf seal was found in the ancient harbor town of Lothal.[6] So many Indus seals with Indus pictographs have been excavated archaeologically from ancient Sumeria that Kramer found good reason to assume that Indus traders were settled more or less permanently in several of the Sumerian cities.[7]

References to ships, overseas trade, and other maritime activities are extremely common on the large number of inscribed tablets excavated from early Sumer. Many texts specify the cargo, and we learn of vessels as large as 300 *gur*, i.e., 96 tons. Other texts show that taxes were imposed on importing ships, and some tablets contain contracts between the merchant navigators and the enterprising capitalists. Shipwrecks are referred to in the earliest inscriptions, so it was reasonable to find a clause in a legal document stating, "the well-preserved ship and its fittings he will return to its owner in the harbor of Ur intact . . ."[8] The importance of navigation is even reflected in Sumerian proverbs, one of which states that a ship intent on honest pursuits will sail off with the wind and the sun god finds honest ports for it, whereas a ship sailing off with evil intentions he will wreck on the beaches.[9]

The very existence of the Sumerians and their culture were unknown to the modern world until archaeological excavations in southern Iraq uncovered their colossal pyramids and found their buried store of tens of thousands of inscribed tablets. Once deciphered these brought back to life the daily conduct and trade activities of the individuals behind this long-lost civilization, whose influence from its earliest period reached up the Mesopotamian rivers to Mari and Brak on the threshold of the Mediterranean world,[10] and out through the Arabian Gulf into the lands of the Indian Ocean.[11]

Of the many geographical names referred to in the Sumerian tablets those of local origin are commonly recognizable, whereas names for foreign lands are not translatable into modern place names. The one most commonly appearing in tablets recording maritime trade is "Dilmun" or "Telmun," identified by most modern scholars as today's Bahrain, the Arabian Gulf island which is littered with the archaeological remains of aqueducts, tombs, and temples that the Danish expeditions under P. Glob and G. Bibby have found to antedate the civilization of Sumer itself. Dilmun plays a central role in the earliest

Sumerian myths and continued to be referred to in legal documents and trade reports of Mesopotamia long after the Sumerians had ceased to exist. One of the Assyrian rulers used the title "King of Dilmun and Meluhha." Professor Kramer, one of the leading authorities on the Sumerians, tentatively identifies Meluhha with Ethiopia, and Magan, another distant land from where ships docked in Mesopotamian ports, he assumes to be Egypt.[12] Unidentified remain other distant countries such as "Hazmani" and "Kuppi," located beyond Dilmun and involving long journeys over sea and land. An inscription at Nineveh expressly states that these regions were so far away that when messengers came from Kuppi, "they had to travel six months to bring their gifts and to greet the king."[13] Assuming that Sumerian reed vessels traveled no slower than the Egyptian papyrus ships which sailed from the River Ganges to Ceylon in twenty days, according to Eratosthenes, the messengers from Kuppi might easily have come from any part of Indonesia or even China during a traveling time of six months.

One of my traveling companions on the two *Ra* voyages, Carlo Mauri, after crossing the Atlantic in our reed boat the second time, traveled by foot and by horse in the footsteps of Marco Polo and reached the borders of China overland from Mesopotamia in not much more than six months. The messengers from Kuppi arrived from across the sea. If we assume that they traveled piecemeal with unfavorable winds and came, say, from one of the great maritime kingdoms in Sumatra or Java, we must be aware of the fact that on other occasions they could easily have sailed just as far in the opposite direction, more than needed to reach China.

Historic records and archaeology show that the great civilizations of Indonesia and China, like those of the Indus Valley, are secondary in time to the flourishing of Sumerian civilization in Mesopotamia. Although some kind of local culture undoubtedly had started to evolve along independent lines in most of these areas, there is nothing to suggest that casual merchant explorers, or "messengers" of the kind recorded by contemporary scribes, could not have transmitted certain attractive ideas over long distances where there was otherwise no regular contact. In view of written records from Alexandria and Nineveh, India had contact with both Egypt and Sumer in the early days of reed boat navigation, and if we want to be cautious in our approaches to the problem, no part of coastal Asia can be considered out of reach for relaying cultural impulses in the second millennium B.C., when so many hitherto modest cultures took on the aspect of full civilization in coastal Asiatic waters. Indeed, the seasonal reversal of wind and current directions in the monsoon area would favor all sorts of maritime communications in the Indian Ocean, whereas the permanent trade-winds and forceful companion currents of the enormous Pacific hemisphere would force early mariners from the Middle East and the Indus Valley, even those from Indonesia, to limit their eastward explorations to strictly coastal Asiatic waters.

The importance of Dilmun (Bahrain) as a market place and trading center for surrounding civilizations in Sumerian times is clearly documented by archaeology and written texts. The predominant role of the same island in Sumerian mythology is at least remarkable and merits some attention. Kramer has rightly pointed out that the Sumerians originated the spiritual concepts and the pantheon which influenced profoundly all the peoples of the Near East. The Assyrians and Babylonians took them over *in toto;* the Hittites translated them into their own language, and they were assimilated by the ancient Greeks. Even Judaism, Christianity, and Mohammedanism have helped some former Sumerian concepts to permeate the modern world.[14] According to the biblical records, Abraham, the first patriarch of all these three modern religions, came from the Sumerian capital of Ur. Together with his father and the whole accompanying tribe, he emigrated from this port on the Arabian Gulf at the beginning of the second millennium B.C., walking northward through Mesopotamia and across the Mediterranean land of the Canaanites. The Sumerians gradually disappeared as a political entity with the destruction of Ur about 2050 B.C. But with Abraham, the recorded founder of Hebrew, Christian, and Moslem faiths, some of the teachings from Ur were carried as literary heritage until entering the printed scriptures. Among these surviving beliefs which must have come, like Abraham himself, from Ur, is the account of the deluge which was supposed to have drowned the majority of mankind.

On the opposite side of Asia Minor the early Greeks had been told by Egyptian scribes of a similar horrifying disaster. Their version was that the earliest known center of civilization had been wiped out when an island sank into the Atlantic Ocean and its total population drowned. The Greeks later also received the Hebrew version brought to the Mediterranean world by Abraham's tribe and hence originating from the Asiatic side of the Arabian peninsula. No sunken island was known to the peoples of Mesopotamia, but a universal flood in which the majority of their own ancestors had perished as a punishment from God.

Only during the last century have archaeologists succeeded to uncover written Mesopotamian texts which antedate the Old Testament and its records of the universal deluge. In 1872 one of the tens of thousands of cuneiform clay tablets from the library of the Assyrian King Assurbanipal was found to contain a detailed version which, although older than the Hebrew version, was so similar to it that there could be no doubt that the two were but variants with a common origin. In the Assyrian version an old man named Utu-nipishtim takes the place of the biblical Noah, and the joint Sumerian-Assyrian water god, Enki, takes the place of the Hebrew god Jahve. The water god, Enki, revealed to Utu-nipishtim that the other gods had decided to drown mankind, and told him to build a large ship and take on board his family and livestock. For six days and nights the tempestuous flood raged, and on the seventh day the ship grounded on a mountaintop in upper Kurdistan, i.e., in the general area where the Hebrews also believed Noah landed on Mount Ararat. A dove and a swallow were in turn sent out, but they returned, and only when next a raven was let loose without coming back did Utu-nipishtim understand that the waters had abated. He disembarked and offered sacrifices to the gods who promised never again to punish all of mankind for the sins of some. The survivors from the ship were told to go and "dwell in the distance, at the mouth of the rivers."[15] To the Assyrians that could only mean the outlet of their twin rivers the former Sumerian habitat.

At the mouth of these rivers, at the turn of our own century, archaeologists from the University of Pennsylvania were excavating the enormous Sumerian ziggurat of Nippur, one of the huge sun-oriented and stepped pyramids with a temple on top which was the chief feature of the early Mesopotamian cities. At the foot of the pyramid was found a collection of 35,000 inscribed tablets, one of them containing the original Sumerian version of the flood story. This is the oldest preserved version of written texts recording the memories of the deluge. The major difference from the younger versions is that the survivors are not remembered as landing on some remote inland mountain peak. They settle Dilmun, the island of Bahrain in the Arabian Gulf. Cities and kingdoms were said to have existed even prior to this universal catastrophe, but again the people apparently displeased the gods, since in this version too they decided to wipe out mankind. As in the Assyrian version so also in the Sumerian text, it was the same water god, Enki, who decided to save mankind. In this case, however, his choice fell on a pious, god-fearing, and humble king named Ziusudra, and the water god "advised him to save himself by building a very large boat." The part of the tablet describing how to build this boat was unfortunately destroyed, but we next learn that the deluge raged over the surface of the earth for seven days and seven nights; "and the huge boat had been tossed about on the great waters," until the sun god, Utu, came forth and shed light on heaven and earth. The king, like Noah, "opened a window of the huge boat," and prostrated himself to the sun god, while he sacrificed an ox and a sheep. He is referred to in the tablet as the preserver of man, and the gods gave him the island of Dilmun where he could begin to repeople the earth.[16]

The same water god, Enki, who in both the Sumerian and Assyrian versions saved certain individuals from the flood, is replaced among the monotheistic Hebrews by the invisible God. Enki, however, was himself visualized by the Sumerians as a navigator, and as such he is frequently illustrated on board his divine reed ship, with its high and gracefully curved bow and stern, sometimes carrying a sacred altar or a sphinx on board, and with an anthropomorphic figurehead helping him move through the water. Enki, identifiable with Poseidon of the ancient Greeks, was also assumed to have lived in, or called at, the island of Dilmum, and it was from here he "set sail" and proceeded to the mainland coast, in fact to Abraham's city of Ur. "To Ur he came, Enki, king of the abyss, decrees the fate: O city, well-supplied, washed by much water . . . green like the mountain, Hashur-forest, wide shade . . ."[17]

This is the oldest known description of Ur, a city today miles from any water, whose shapeless ruins are deeply buried in desert sand, where nothing is green and where no tree gives shade from the scorching sun. This drastic change of scenery since Sumerian time of about 3000 B.C. has to be taken into account in any attempt to reconstruct landscapes and coastlines guiding human preferences and settlement patterns in the days when the first ships sailed the seas. The fact that gods and demi-gods since mythological times were described as and depicted as reed-boat navigators both in Sumer and in Egypt is remarkable. Although wheeled vehicles were known since Sumerian and pharaonic times and used by royalty and warriors, the gods and god-men are never shown traveling by such means but always by small or large reed boats. Not only the water god but the sun god, the bird-men, the lion-headed deities, and the rest of the ancestral supernaturals from which the Egyptian and Sumerian dynasties claimed their descent are all depicted in frescoes, wall reliefs, on papyrus or incised on seals as traveling by boat. Legendary history takes its very beginning from a seagoing ship large enough to rescue its passengers and live-stock from the fury of a deluge. Five thousand years ago the Sumerian scribes, like the ancestors of Abraham, considered shipbuilding as an art not of their own invention. Marine architecture and navigation was clearly then considered as something their ancestors had learned from the gods prior to Sumerian time, prior to the days of Ur and Nimrud, even before man's first arrival on the island of Dilmun.

What brought the deluge story into existence may be open to specu-lation and it may even be dismissed as a myth. But we cannot ignore the fact that, when the Sumerians founded their earliest dynasties in Mesopotamia and their scribes recorded their deeds and beliefs on the tablets at the foot of the ziggurat, they themselves believed that their progenitors were not of local origin but had come from Dilmun far out in the Gulf. Yet Dilmun was not considered the original habitat of their ancestors; King Ziusudra had only landed there with his big ship after the flood.

Since a geological catastrophe took place in the Atlantic in the cen-turies around 3000 B.C. great enough to split Iceland, it is perhaps not entirely out of place to speculate that tidal waves could have caused far-reaching disasters, forcing population groups to search for new land. Such events could well be remembered in early Egypt and Sumer and caused the abrupt superimposition of new civilizations on all major Mediterranean islands as well as in the two major river valleys on each side of the Arabian desert peninsula.

Perhaps flood waves from the Atlantic, that certainly must have reached Gibraltar, caused a stir at that early period corresponding to the chaos resulting from the explosion of Santorini in a much later pe-riod. It is certain that whatever might have been man's initial roads to high culture, the two approximate dates of 3100 and 1200 B.C. represent epochs of major importance in Mediterranean and Middle East his-tory; the first with the cultural disturbances on the Mediterranean is-lands and the births of the first dynasties in Egypt and Mesopotamia, the second with a similar stir that again uprooted established societies, put an end to old dynasties, and sent whole population groups in search of new habitats. Among those who left during the second migration vortex were the untold number of Phoenician families who sailed beyond Gibraltar in organized colonizing expeditions to form major settlements on the Atlantic coasts of Spain and Morocco, even pushing on into the main sweep of the Canary Current to establish bases on the Canary Islands.

The same two mileposts in history, i.e., about 3100 and about 1200 B.C., are crucial also in aboriginal American time reckoning. The zero date in the incredibly exact Maya calendar is 4 *Ahau* 2 *Cumhu,* which converted into our calendar system becomes August 12, 3113 B.C. On the other hand archaeologists have proposed 1200 B.C. as the approximate period when civilization came into bloom in Mexico with the Olmecs founding settlements with pyramid building and colossal stele in the jungles and swamplands along the Mexican Gulf, at the receiving end of the Canary Current.

No satisfactory explanation has ever been found as to why the Maya maintained the early date of 3113 B.C. as their zero year. It has been suggested that they might have calculated back to some special astronomical events at that time, but none are known. Another proposal is that the date was picked at random. This seems equally unlikely. The Maya were so advanced in astronomy and so time-conscious that they had arrived at an astronomical year of 365-2420 days, which is only one day short in every 5,000 years, while our modern calendar is a day and a half too much in every 5,000 years. The Maya year was thus 8.64 seconds closer to the truth than the calendar we use today. We have also seen that a hieroglyphic inscription on the funerary pyramid in Palenque states that 81 months make 2,392 days, giving the local astronomers a month of 29-53086 days, which deviates only 24 seconds from the real length. No wonder that the medieval clergy among the arriving Spaniards for fear of the devil burned all the Mexican paper books and written records they could lay their hands on, considering all that was not narrated in Latin letters to be the work of Satan and savage magic.

Nevertheless, essential details of Mexican history have been conserved together with oral records narrated by observant Spanish chroniclers. Combined with the historic welcome speech given by none less than the Aztec priest-king Montezuma to his guest and later conqueror, Hernando Cortez, we do have adequate information about the most consistent records among these astronomically advanced and historically devoted culture people. Their written and oral texts universally insist that the Spaniards were not the first to have come to Mexico from across the Atlantic. Both the Aztecs of the highlands and the Mayas of the coastal plains claimed descent from a civilized people who had sailed in from the east like the Spaniards, and who had settled ashore and intermarried with an earlier people who were already present. The earlier people had until then lived unorganized in small groups, gathering food in the forest, without agriculture, city communities, temples, script, or astronomical knowledge. The immigrants from across the ocean were not considered foreigners by either the Aztecs or the Mayas, nor by the civilized communities in Central America and Peru, which all shared in the same belief. Although always described as migrant groups of teachers, ministering sun worship and various aspects of culture to local people, and though inferior in number to the illiterate people to whom they brought the blessings of civilization, they were nevertheless considered as an ancestral stock, at least by priestly families and ruling classes. Priests incapable of growing natural beards like these celebrated predecessors often donned artificial ones, both in Mexico and in Peru.

The vivid descriptions in words, script, and art of these early culture bringers as being white and bearded made a profound impression on the Spaniards when they arrived, and thanks to their own physical appearance they were able to take over the two mightiest military empires of the contemporary world: the Aztec and Inca nations. Unlike the Spaniards, however, the culture bringers behind aboriginal American art and memories were illustrated and described from Mexico to Peru as wearing turbans, long loose robes and sandals, and they carried wanderers' staffs and objects resembling breviaries rather than arms. The Spaniards therefore assumed these important predecessors to have been Semitic missionaries, and for a while they formed religious orders in honor of assumed visits by Middle East travelers, St. Thomas in Mexico and St. Bartholomew in Peru.

These all-important memories and hieroglyphic records in the restricted but continuous Central American area from Mexico to Peru long antedate the historic Aztec and Inca dynasties. They can be shown through archaeological art to go back to the very beginnings of Central American high cultures. The earliest human models in former

Peru, both at Tiahuanaco in the highlands and in the Early Chimu area of the northern coast, show statues and ceramic representations of these bearded culture heroes in characteristic attire as described above. Correspondingly, on the shores of the Mexican Gulf the Olmecs, the assumed founders of Mexican civilization, have left self-portraits on colossal monoliths hauled across the local swampland from mountains far away, and they depict in an extremely realistic manner two contrasting physical types. The one has a characteristic Negroid physiognomy, the other has typical Semitic features with long flowing beard. These Olmec personages are depicted in the local rain forest in the same traditional desert fashion with long loose gowns and sandals. Why the founders of Mexican civilizations left such strange reliefs on stele in the swamplands at La Venta, where the current from Morocco washes the shore, has never been properly explained by those who profess a local evolution. There has been no want of theories proposed by those who advocate diffusion. Jungle Indians in Mexico today, as elsewhere in tropical rain forests, prefer to walk barefoot and wear a perineal band, a loincloth or nothing, since a turban and a long gown get hooked up in the thickets of the forest and sandals get stuck in the mud.

Primitive tribes roamed about fishing and hunting in America for tens of thousands of years, and most of them still did so when Europeans reached North and South America. The discoveries of the Leakey family and subsequent archaeologists have pushed the lifetime of early man in the Old World back through time spans of millions rather than tens of thousands of years.[18] Why should the Maya maintain 3113 b.c. as their zero year, concurring with beginnings in Egypt and Mesopotamia, unless this year meant something very special in the religious history of their ancestors, as did the zero year in the Hebrew, Christian, Moslem, and Buddhist calendars? If the date of 3113 b.c. with certainty can be considered too early for any American culture to have started a local time reckoning, could it not be that the zero year was imported from abroad by learned voyagers who might themselves have arrived at any time subsequent to their own zero year? If it is correct, as at present generally assumed, then there was no calendar system in Mexico until the Olmecs evolved the first local civilization. Maya script and astronomy are considered based on a heritage from the earlier Olmecs, who are thought to have begun their spread of culture inland from the Gulf coast about 1200 b.c. Is it not a remarkable coincidence within a human time span of millions of years that the Mayas retained a traditional zero year of 3113 B.C. based on teachings from people who began their astonishing cultural career at the receiving end of the Canary Current about 1200 B.C., the very time in history when Phoenicians pushed entire fleets of colonizers into the Atlantic looking for land in the Canary Current?

Evidence of very early traffic in the Canary Current is found in the pre-European existence of the Guanche, who inhabited the Canary islands before the first Portuguese and Spaniards arrived. The Guanche were a mixed people with a Caucasoid and a Negroid component, varying in dominance from one island to the next. A dark-skinned, clearly Negroid stock lived side by side with a light-skinned people whose men wore long blond or reddish hair and beards. An original water color from Torriani's manuscript of 1590, showing blond and bearded Guanches, is on exhibit in the archaeological museum of Gran Canaria (reproduced by Wölfel in 1940 and Heyerdahl in 1952) together with blond and reddish-brown hair samples from Guanche mummies. A Guanche mummy in the same museum, carbon dated to about A.D. 300, has remains of a red beard.

It is a peculiar characteristic of the Guanche that they were a composite lot, consisting of Caucasoid and Negroid racial elements living as a single people, a characteristic which they fully share with the Berber nation on the nearest coast of Africa, and, to judge from Olmec art, also with the people who started civilization at the other end of the Canary Current.

There is hardly room for doubt that the Guanche were of Berber stock, descending from mariners reaching these islands from the Atlantic coast of Morocco, yet it is difficult to judge to what extent the former Phoenician colonists had also contributed to the mixed blood found by the Europeans on the Canary Islands. The Phoenicians were neither conquerors nor pirates, but peaceful and successful merchants and Middle East culture spreaders. They were as familiar with the stepped pyramids of their neighbors and trading partners in Mesopotamia as with the pharaonic temples and rites of their close collaborators in contemporary Egypt. They brought mixed crews to serve as interpreters and guides on their long voyages, and are in fact recorded to have executed an Egyptian commission when they circumnavigated Africa. They carried Berbers as coastal pilots on Hanno's colonizing expedition down the West African coast. With colonies and trading posts all along the north and northwest coasts of Africa, in numerous localities in Spain, and on all major Mediterranean islands, the Phoenicians themselves had undoubtedly become a mixed lot. Although assumed to have originated in Asia Minor as a blond and bearded branch of the Canaanite people, almost nothing is actually known about the physical appearance of these legendary mariners.[19] The Greek historians gave them the collective name of Phoenicians for lack of anything better, just as today we use the term Olmec to denote the unknown culture spreaders who appeared at the American end of Canary Current just when the Phoenicians entered its African sources.

Hittites, Phoenicians, and Sea People are but a few of the great many names conveniently serving us today for reference to members of a complex group of people, mostly of Canaanite or Semitic origin or affiliations, which roamed the Mediterranean Sea in the centuries between 3000 and 1200 B.C. The Canaanites themselves were overcome by Jews returning from Egypt about 1200 B.C., the period so critical for people all around the Mediterranean shores. In the period between 3000 and 1200 B.C. this diversified and yet interrelated group of early culture people crisscrossed Mediterranean waters and left evidence of their outstanding ceramic art, adobe structures, and exquisitely carved and fitted megalithic blocks in widely separated areas.

That the Guanche on the Canary Islands are in some way linked to this early Afro-Asiatic stock is shown by the presence of such special culture elements as mummification, trepanning, pottery figurines, ceramic stamp seals, and tripod jars. Although no scholar seems to have doubted the validity of these elements as proof that these distant Atlantic islands had received impulses from some unspecified pre-European, Mediterranean culture, yet it seems as if the world ends there, and America is treated as if located on another planet. Nevertheless, the few conformities between early Mediterranean and Canary Island cultures are all as emphatically repeated at the American end of the Canary Current, where they form but a fraction of the total sum of cultural identities and similarities listed in Chapter 3 of this book. And the distance from the Canary Islands to the Mexican Gulf is not measurable in centuries or generations of travel, not even in years, but in a few weeks on board any water vehicle capable of having already reached the Canary Islands.

It is noteworthy that the Guanche on every one of the Canary Islands were ignorant of any kind of boatbuilding when Europeans first arrived there, yet their ancestors must have come by some buoyant craft to reach the islands. Adequate timber was present, as can be judged from the many archaeological remains of very wide pine boards from Guanche sarcophagi. It could be tempting to speculate on whether the Guanche ancestors had ever known how to build plank boats. As we have seen, reed vessels were used in Lixus, the main Berber-Phoenician port on the nearest part of the African mainland, and although the Phoenicians have become renowned for their wooden ships, reed vessels were familiar to them too. In fact, the only known pictorial representation of Phoenician ships left by them west of Gibraltar clearly illustrates reed vessels. A large, three-sided Punic amphora was recently found in the sea at La Caleta, the former Phoenician port on the Atlantic coast of Spain where the Cadiz lighthouse now stands. On each side in relief were depicted sickle-shaped reed boats with incurled bow and stern and bands of transversal rope lashings around the body of the bundle vessel. An Egyptian bronze statuette was found in the same port and is on exhibition in the same Cadiz museum, showing the complex nature or long-range trade of these Atlantic colonists. Why Phoenicians should depict reed vessels in a period when they were long since thoroughly familiar with plank boats is something that can only be conjectured upon; a possible answer could perhaps be found in dramatic experiences with the marine boring worms which abound in the Atlantic and can sink a plank vessel but are harmless to any bundle boat.

The distance from Asia Minor to the Canary Islands is equal in miles to the distance from these islands to Middle America, but this transatlantic leg is infinitely faster and simpler. To traverse the length of the Mediterranean and reach the Canary Islands beyond Gibraltar requires seamanship and a maneuverable craft. To ride along in the Canary Current the rest of the stretch to Middle America requires nothing but a support that will float. Here is something that can never be stressed too much for those who discuss diffusion versus independent evolution: the wide tropic area of sea and air is on a permanent non-stop move westward from Africa to America and again on the further side from America to Asia. History has shown that square-rigged European sailing ships followed these rotations and were trapped in them, being able to return only in higher latitudes.

It is a sound isolationist view that history repeats itself whenever geography is the same or similar. But it is a common mistake to exclude the early Spaniards and other Europeans from consideration. It is frequently argued that if the founders of pre-Columbian culture came from across the Atlantic, why did they not found dynasties and build pyramids on the Caribbean Islands, instead of proceeding to Mexico or even crossing the Isthmus to found a civilization in Ecuador or Peru? This, however, happened to be precisely what the Spaniards did when they arrived with the Canary Current and reached the string of Caribbean islands. Encouraged by this discovery they pushed on to explore the compact jungle coasts of the mainland behind, and within a few decades had chosen to establish their own two main colonies respectively in Mexico and Peru, precisely as the earlier founders of local civilization had done.

Within one generation the Spaniards had walked across Mexico, Central America, and the whole width of South America, covering with no major difficulties all the terrain which in the course of millennia had been the home of a variety of American high cultures. The jungles, swamps, and mountain ridges were the same then as they had been throughout pre-European times and they, like any other voyagers who cared to explore the impenetrable mangrove coasts southward from the narrow Panama Isthmus, had to travel by sea and thus were forced to build new boats on the Pacific side. Prior to 1200 B.C., however, there was less threat of being stopped and overcome by mighty armies of civilized nations such as confronted the Spaniards.

There is, accordingly, no geographical reason to assume that transatlantic voyagers would have settled Mexico ages before they reached Peru. The Spaniards did not. Pizarro sailed a fragile caravel from the new watercraft to discover and conquer Peru. Chances seem to be equal for early sailing craft entering the Caribbean Sea to land either north or south of Yucatán. If landing was affected in the Isthmus area rather than in the Mexican Gulf, experienced colonizers like the Phoenicians would be bound to do as Pizarro did. They would push on to look for more inviting shores than the mangrove-covered swamps that barred the coastline until opening into the bays and beaches of southern Ecuador and the open river valleys of Peru with the cultivable highlands behind.

If geography alone was a decisive factor, there are ample reasons to suspect that the choice of exploring colonizers from the Afro-Asiatic world would be the transition area between southern Ecuador and northern Peru. Here a verdant jungle landscape with deep harbors slowly opens into wide, semi-arid, but irrigable river plains, an inviting coast washed by upwellings where the cold Humboldt Current meets the warm Niño Current, forming the richest fishing grounds known anywhere in the world. The local shell mounds testify to the great antiquity of local settlements and the paramount importance of the sea as a local source of economy. Archaeology and history combine to show that from the earliest prehistoric time well into the historic period, this was a major center of maritime activity. From here large balsa rafts with sail and rigging as on the Spanish caravels, but maneuvered with a local system of *guara,* carried commerce nearly two thousand miles down the open Inca coast and far up into Meso-America. The balsa raft encountered by Pizarro while making its way up to Panama with over thirty tons of cargo had come from this coast.

It should accordingly cause no great surprise if this should be the area where early radiocarbon dates began unexpectedly to emerge from local excavations initiated by the Ecuadorian amateur archaeologist E. Estrada and his professional tutors C. M. Evans and B. J. Meggers of the United States National Museum. Yet their discoveries and conclusions caused more stir in isolationist circles than any other event since the demonstration that a raft of the local type could cross to Polynesia. Long established views began to waver and dogma were disproven. After a generation of twentieth-century archaeologists, who were so accustomed to modern transport that they could not visualize aboriginal Americans walking or paddling beyond their own tribal territories, modern investigators have begun to find that early man traveled too. They have been able to demonstrate that the Olmecs were active from the Atlantic side of Mexico to the Pacific shores of Guatemala, establishing jungle and mountain settlements a thousand miles apart. And in quite recent years even ardent isolationists have yielded to accumulating evidence indicating that diffusion and not independent evolution has caused an almost simultaneous growth of high cultures of related character throughout the area on each side of the Central American isthmus. D. Collier in 1976 made himself a spokesman for this new trend of thought among Americanists who formerly thought otherwise: "The cultural achievements in Peru and Mexico—and elsewhere in Meso-America—were based on diffusion from a common source: Ecuador. . . . Clearly the generally accepted view of cultural history in Nuclear America, stretching from Mexico to Peru, needs extensive revision."[20]

Undaunted by often bitter attacks from colleagues who accused them of being wild theorists, the archaeological pioneers Dr. Betty Meggers and her husband Dr. Clifford Evans continued to defend what to them seemed to be the most logical explanation for the very early and abrupt appearance of sophisticated ceramic effigy vessels at Valdivia on the jungle coast of Ecuador. In their opinion this earliest known forerunner of American civilization was not born on the hot and damp tropical coast where they had discovered its remains, and they suspected that it might have arrived fully developed with voyagers from across the ocean. Like Heine-Geldern, Ekholm, and other colleagues who began searching outside the Arctic area of Siberia for some of the elements composing the complex picture of culture in aboriginal America, they fastened their attention on some of the civilized nations on the other side of the Pacific hemisphere: in southern Japan and China.

There is no reason to disregard and still less to ridicule such theories of transpacific contacts. Manned balsa rafts have sailed from both Ecuador and Peru to Australia during recent decades, and Southeast Asia could be reached with the same kind of vessel from any part of Mexico, Ecuador, or Peru. A return voyage would require a far more complicated maneuver but would be feasible if the route subsequently discovered by the captains of the square-rigged European caravels were followed north of Hawaii.

In an issue of *American Anthropologist* in 1975, Meggers suggested an extra-American source for Mexican high culture too, just as she had previously done for her own discoveries in Ecuador. She points out that most authorities agree that civilizations began in Meso-America about 1200 B.C., with the appearance of Olmec culture, and that there also seems to be a consensus that Olmec culture had a significant impact on subsequent Meso-American civilizations. She quotes a whole list of leading authorities on Mexico using phrases like the "sudden appearance of Olmec civilisation in full flower," "all known major art styles of lowland Mesoamerica have a single origin in the Olmec style," and "the world of the Olmecs and Olmecoids formed Mesoamerica and set patterns of civilization that were to distinguish this area from all other parts of the Americas." Meggers proposes a possible arrival in Meso-America about 1200 B.C. of immigrants from the Shang civilization which had been imposed on a neolithic Chinese population about 1750 B.C. She lists six basic cultural correspondences to bolster her hypothesis and challenges her colleagues to take a less biased attitude toward the possibility of early sea voyages.[21]

In an effort to rebut this diffusion theory, D. C. Grove replied with a counterproposition. He stressed that, although his reply was not a denial of the possibility that transpacific contacts may have taken place in prehistoric time, he has his own viewpoint: "Both Lathrap . . . and I . . . have suggested that some of the basics of the Olmec belief system probably derive from an ancestral South American tropical forest belief system which diffused northward to southern Meso-America. . . . the possibility of South American contacts seems a far more fertile and productive ground for research than do transpacific contacts."

In fairness to Meggers, he says, it must be noted that she is herself a specialist in Ecuadorian and not Mexican archaeology, and must therefore be forgiven for relying upon published data rather than the duplicated manuscripts that were circulating only between himself and other Mexican field researchers. Literature published prior to the early 1970s, he says, does not necessarily reflect the most recent "thinking" on the Olmecs by him and others. He marvels at how Meggers, as a specialist on Ecuadorian archaeology, can have failed to discuss the strong similarity between early Ecuadorian ceramics and those of the formative period in Mexico, "Yet in these instances a far stronger case can be made that diffusion was real and significant."[22]

An outsider may wonder how deep a specialist must dig his hole before he realizes that he has lost sight of the horizon; and how Grove, declaring Meggers to be incompetent on matters inside his own Mexican hole, can permit himself to peep into hers in Ecuador and tell her that *this* was the evolutionary center whence *his* Mexican civilization derived. When specialization becomes so narrow that an archaeologist digging in tropic Ecuador is deemed incompetent on archaeology in tropic Mexico, then the reverse must also be the case, and it seems apparent that specialists are not the best people to draw broad conclusions. Unfortunately, too few universities are so far prepared to educate students to become specialists in horizontal research, i.e., train them to acquire an academic ability to piece together the fragments that vertical research brings forth from its deep trenches.

If unpublished copies of manuscripts can invalidate what Mexican experts have thought and argued about prior to the early 1970s, and there is no reason to doubt that perhaps they may succeed, then diffusionists have won a major battle and the maritime center around

Guayaquil Bay in Ecuador takes a central place in the spread of American impulses. It then assumes additional importance that the specialists in the archaeology of Ecuador are themselves convinced that civilization had not evolved here but was imported from some other area.

Collier, as the earlier quoted spokesman for the new school of thought that makes Ecuador the diffusion center for aboriginal American civilizations, says that by 3000 B.C. early farmers were well established on the Ecuadorian seacoast and along river plains, traveling by dugout canoes and reed boats.[23] He forgets that this was also the very center of balsa raft navigation, but what really matters seems to be overlooked by all: from the assumed evolution areas of American high cultures at Valdivia, Machalilla and Chorrera no traveler can reach Meso-America except by watercraft. Not even the most ardent diffusionist can find a path to walk northward through the coastal mangrove swamps or cut his way through the world's densest inland jungles that make the 2,000-mile stretch between Ecuador and Mexico an isolationist's paradise. In other words, diffusion from Ecuador to Mexico would have to go by boat, either in a straight line off the Gulf of Panama or by hugging the coast against the southbound Niño Current. In either case the distance between the widely separated cultures now thought to have a common source, as pointed out by Collier, is some 2,000 miles, or equal to the distance from West Africa to South America!

Meggers' calm reply to her opponents had the heading: "Yes if by Land, No if by Sea: the Double Standard in Interpreting Cultural Similarities."[24]

It is remarkable that the very center of American maritime activity as witnessed and recorded by the early Spaniards—Ecuador and North Peru—is now suspected of being also the area from where early culture diffused. There seem to be some who believe that this South American area was accessible only to Pizarro and his men who knew how to build caravels after crossing the Isthmus of Panama. It may be worthwhile to recall that reed-boat building had a major world center in these waters, and empiric tests have shown that such readily built vessels could bridge the gaps. Simultaneously with my own experiments with the reed ships *Ra I* and *Ra II*, showing that the Atlantic could be crossed from North Africa to Middle America, passing the Canary Islands on the way, another reed ship, tested by G. Savoy, sailed from the central coast of Peru past Ecuador to Panama.

With modern science beginning to see aboriginal American civilization as one coherent block, a considerable revolution has taken place in a long-stagnant field of thought. Once a common trunk is accepted it might be simpler to look for common roots than to see the genesis of individual branches. Valdivia, Mochica, Tiahuanaco, Nazca, Chavín, San Agustín, Coclé, Olmec, Toltec, Mixtec, Aztec, Maya, Chibcha, Inca and many other extinct as well as historic cultures then become like the complex of limbs and twigs of a tree, whereas previously they were thought to have bred like scattered mushrooms in the tropical American jungle.

New World archaeology is on the move. Long cherished dogma and generally accepted chronologies are distrusted by an increasing number of field workers who search early sites in tropic America for more concrete evidence than assumptions based on schools of thought. Most recently a joint archaeological project by the British Museum and the University of Cambridge is casting doubt on the hitherto accepted beginnings and antiquity of Maya culture. Reporting on their result so far, N. Hammond claims that continuing work in Belize, formerly British Honduras, "has pushed the beginnings of the Maya Formative (or Preclassic) period back by more than 1,500 years, from about 900 B.C. perhaps as long ago as 2600 B.C." This is no speculation; the conclusion is based on controlled excavations and many concurrent carbon datings from sites facing the Caribbean side of the Yucatán peninsula. The earliest dates found ranged from 2450 to 2750 B.C. This in one stroke pushes us closer to the zero Maya year of 3113 B.C. than to the approximate date of 900 B.C. hitherto accepted by scholars. Hammond makes it clear that these Belize excavations have not yet located the real beginnings. He shows that the ceramic complex encountered is one considerably advanced in both color and decor: "The vessels are indisputably the produce of a mature technology rather than an emerging one. Yet these are the earliest ceramics from the Maya lowlands and among the earliest in all Meso-America. Where did this technology evolve?"

Although Hammond says that he leaves to future archaeology the question of where its creators came from, and when, he does state that his colleague D. Lathrap maintains that there are "close resemblances" between this 4,500-year-old Belize pottery and 4,500-year-old pottery which Lathrap recently had excavated from Real Alto, a site in southern Ecuador.[25] Again, then, American chronology is fluid; Olmec and Maya civilizations may have completely different beginnings. If it remains firm that Olmec civilization started on the shores of the Mexican Gulf about 1200 B.C., and if Maya beginnings continue to be pushed back to concur with Ecuadorian beginnings of about 3000 B.C., then the two crucial dates in Old World cultural evolution are reflected also on the other side of the Atlantic.

The steadily emerging discoveries in New World archaeology are evaluated by specialists within each geographical region who disagree in their judgments and conclusions, but they all look for unidentified beginnings. At this point it is important to bear in mind that vertical specialization makes it easier to see the local variations and differences between all these neighboring cultures than the broad common lines. Secondary growths and artistic preferences have such distinctive local stamps that an expert usually has little difficulty in identifying ethnographic or archaeologic artifacts. It requires a different skill, and a horizontal approach, to detect and extract from behind the surface decoration the essentials which join in a once common but now lost root: i.e., to reduce, assemble and compare the least common denominator such as is now being done increasingly by modern Americanists. What they have so far achieved, however, is mainly to point out a whole series of basic concepts assumed to be inherited throughout Meso-America from migrants whose influence directly or indirectly spanned the strip of land, two thousand miles long, from Mexico to Peru. These basic concurrences are indeed many and complex, as they range from social and architectural structures to cylinder seals, tripod vessels, flat ceramic figurines and specialized effigy jars, involving customs and techniques as well as the basic religious concepts. The snake, the feline, and the plumed serpent were symbols for a hierarchy claiming solar descent in all of this coherent area, and there was no discrepancy in time level. However, although these specialized features unite the American high cultures and separate them from the aboriginal Indians throughout the rest of pre-Columbian America, none of these elements distinguish them from the Afro-Asiatic civilizations that sent diffuse branches as far as the Canary Islands. There is in fact not one of the hitherto specified elements on the joint Mexican-Peruvian list that does not also form part of the transatlantic parallels listed at the end of Chapter 3. In several cases specific concurrences can be shown between one restricted culture area in America and one in the Mediterranean world without being present everywhere in these two areas, either because they were lost or never full diffused within both localities.

A continental area in the Old World which seems to have more than its reasonable share in such conformities to New World civilization is the former Hittite region of Asia Minor, where a number of truly specific conformities seem to cluster. Among these is an important Hittite stele with the relief of a bearded culture hero raising his hand to kill a monstrous snake with two horns, standing vertically before him on the tip of its tail. A stele with a relief illustrating this precise motif was also left by the earliest Olmecs at their coastal site of La Venta in the Gulf of Mexico. Equally remarkable conformities can be found in the motifs and technique of the highly specialized ceramic effigy jars of this same area; the stone statues with inlaid shell and obsidian eyes; the huge eroded adobe mounds; the symbolic representation of their solar hierarch with a feather crown and with his body as half bird and half snake (a plumed serpent); and not least the peculiar outward appearance of the hieroglyphics left in low relief on local stele. They are utterly different from Sumerian cuneiform script, Egyptian ideograms or Phoenician letters, but most of all resemble the undeciphered hieroglyphics left on Olmec, Mixtec, and other early Mexican stele. Since it is recognized that, in spite of outward differences, the idea behind these diversified Afro-Asiatic script systems is interrelated, it is noteworthy that no two of them so closely approach each other in signs, style, execution, and application as do the Hittite and earliest Mexican hieroglyphics. It is remarkable that the Hittites, whose mere existence was unknown to archaeologists until recent centuries, preceded the Phoenicians and yet had great ships of both wood and reeds, as can be judged from their early art. What is more, this focus area of Hittite correspondences to Meso-America is also the geographical bridge and short cut between the fertile valleys of Mesopotamia and the Mediterranean coast, i.e., the once rich plains around Aleppo in Syria, where the caravan route has passed since earliest prehistoric time. Here the distance from the River Euphrates to the Mediterranean Sea is less than two hundred miles. It is and always was a focal point of trade and diffusion between the three Old World continents which here met and blended. Phoenicians, later plying the local coast, carried their overland trade between Egypt and Mesopotamia across these former Hittite fields, and the Jews passed here on their migration from Ur to the land of Canaan. Other localities, rich in specific and sometimes unique parallels to Meso-American cultures, are the chain of Mediterranean islands from Cyprus, Crete, and Malta to the Phoenician settlement on Ibiza. In the New World such focusing areas of concentrated correspondences seem to be the Vera Cruz and Tabasco jungles adjacent to the Gulf of Mexico, and the aforesaid transition area from jungle to desert coast of Ecuador and North Peru.

In a broader sense, however, it is the elements shared by, and special to, the pre-European civilizations of the Afro-Asiatic corner and offshore islands, which are correspondingly shared by, and equally characteristic of, the restricted section of America stretching between Mexico and Peru. In other words, the basic complex of elements which distinguishes a restricted Afro-Asiatic area and has been considered as a valid indicator of a fundamental cultural unity within that area, is duplicated only in one other equally clearly confined geographical area separated by, or rather tied to, the first by the waters of the Canary Current.

Only future archaeology may be able to demonstrate conclusively whether seeds for a common Meso-American culture took root in Ecuador or on the Gulf of Mexico, or both. As the Maya began their time reckoning with 3113 B.C., perhaps the recent suspicion by archaeologists may prove correct: that the earliest branch of Meso-American culture began in Ecuador at a time around 3000 B.C., conforming with the Maya zero year. The Canary Current, accompanied by the perpetual trade winds, never stopped rotating in the millennia under discussion, and perhaps more than one group of colonists affected the lives of local American people. The Maya themselves, as quoted in Chapter 4, claimed to descend from two waves of immigration: the Great Arrival, led by the first legendary civilizer, Itzamná, and the subsequent Lesser Arrival under the celebrated solar hierarch, Kukulcan, the Plumed Serpent.

If the balsa forests of coastal Ecuador played an important part in the Meso-American diffusion of culture, it is easier to understand the great importance this shoreline played in the beliefs and memories of the historically minded highland Incas. It was upon Pizarro's arrival here, at the northern extremities of the Inca Empire, that coastal messengers from the port of Tumbez ran in relay to the Inca headquarters in the Andes bringing the news that made the powerful Inca Empire collapse without a battle: the white and bearded men who had previously brought civilization to the country had now come back to Peru. Throughout the vast territories of Peru and present Bolivia it was firmly believed that the white and bearded men from Tiahuanaco, whose blood ran in the veins of the ruling Inca, had finally set sail from the Ecuadorian port of Manta into the open Pacific Ocean under the leadership of their solar hierarch Con-Tici-Viracocha. Later, only three generations before the arrival of Pizarro, an Inca conqueror named Tupac had set sail from the same Manta coast because, when he visited this place with his army, local merchants had come back on sailing rafts to tell him of inhabited islands in the open Pacific.

The voyages of the legendary Inca civilizers Con-Tici-Viracocha, known in Tiahuanaco only as Tici or Ticci, and that of the protohistoric Inca Tupac, also known in Peru as Tupa, did not pass unnoticed elsewhere, for both figure prominently in the memories of the historically minded Polynesians. Tiki, also known as Tisi and Ti'i, was a pan-Polynesian hero-god widely celebrated throughout most of the East Pacific. In the Marquesas group nearest Ecuador Tiki was the man-god who had brought the earliest settlers to their present habitat; elsewhere his mythical relative Mauri-Tiki-Tiki was symbolically credited with having fished the islands out of the ocean in a futile attempt to haul them ashore at *Hilo* in the mythical fatherland. Ilo happens to be the Inca name of one of the best aboriginal harbors on the Pacific coast directly below Lake Titicaca and Tiahuanaco.[26]

Tupa, contrary to Tiki, figured only as the leading personage of Mangarevan tradition, where he was remembered as an important king who had come to the island on a simple visit with a whole fleet of sailing rafts, arriving from the east. He had told the Mangarevans of his mighty kingdom in the direction of the sunrise to which he returned after his visit. Tiki settled in Polynesia, but Tupa went back, in each case in full concurrence with Inca traditions.

Sailing directions to islands two months raft voyage westward from Ica and Arica in southern Peru were also given to the arriving conquistadors, and combined with the pan-Peruvian memories of Tici's and Tupac's voyages in tempting the Europeans to continue their explorations westward. These Inca reports made such an impression on the Spaniards of Pizarro's generation, who had seen the sailing abilities of the local rafts and witnessed the great seamanship of the local coastal population, that they finally assembled the sailing directions and set off into the Pacific, intent on locating the reported islands. The immediate result was the European discovery of Melanesia and Polynesia. No sooner had the Europeans secured a foothold on the

Pacific coasts of America before they ventured into this ocean with their square-rigged caravels and successively discovered all the islands in a complete hemisphere which for three centuries had been inaccessible to other Europeans with a foothold in coastal Asia, and which continued to be inaccessible for them for another two hundred years until modern sailing ships replaced the square-rigged caravels of medieval times. For five centuries of documented history man could reach Oceania from Asia only in a roundabout way by sailing north and east into the westerlies between Hawaii and the Aleutian Islands and coming back to Polynesia and the other islands from the American side. The same trans-Pacific rotation routes have been found decisive in the movements of replicas of prehistoric rafts and junks tested in modern times. The best of the coastal vessels existing in South America and Southeast Asia in pre-European time could enter the mid-Pacific only along the routes subsequently utilized by the Spaniards.

When the Europeans had circumnavigated the world they found the distance to Asia to be five times longer than estimated by Columbus, who had calculated only the width of the Atlantic (but to perfection); and they found that the global circumference derived by Greek astronomers from astronomical observations in Egypt proved amazingly correct after all. Wherever these Europeans advanced around the world they found they had been preceded by others; on the Canary Islands, in the Caribbean archipelago, in America, and on every habitable island in the Pacific. Plank ships like their own were not encountered anywhere in this hitherto hidden area, yet people were always on the shores welcoming the new visitors, who conquered and sacked and were hailed in Europe as the true discoverers of the land.

The encounter with these new overseas sources of wealth had such an effect on global history and left such an impression on contemporary and subsequent generations of Europeans that we have never quite calmed down to consider those we conquered as legitimate equals; they and what they possessed, from monuments to golden treasures, were our property with room for no rival discoverer. Until our own time we have been so possessive of this New World, so strongly influenced by the almost religious dogma that none could lay claim to this land before Columbus, that we have refused to consider the possibility of any earlier arrivals except by the Norsemen, who were Europeans anyway. And none could have left the other side of America until we came and showed the way into the open Pacific.

This attitude has had an equally firm grip on most scientists. Isolationists accept extreme diffusion as long as it leaves America alone. The same scholars who have refused to believe that the large Galápagos group could have been reached by aboriginal Americans on a 600-mile downwind drift from Ecuador have postulated an 8,000-mile head wind and countercurrent expedition to tiny Easter Island by aboriginal Indonesians, so long as this voyage stopped there and did not involve America. The isolation of America has indeed gone so far that Polynesia is considered the Old World, though it was discovered by the Europeans after America, and is even recognized by all anthropologists as the last major area on earth to have been settled by man as such. If Polynesia were to be distinguished from the New World it had to be denominated the Newest World.

Those who judged Galápagos inaccessible to American rafts but Easter Island within the reach of Asiatic canoes overlook the lessons of history. Only two years had passed after Pizarro's conquest of Peru when Bishop de Berlanga came from Europe and ran into the Galápagos group because he was caught by the invisible current that dragged him into the Pacific while he tried to hug the coast of Ecuador. At a corresponding proximity to continental Asia, Indonesia, and Japan lies the even more extensive group of the Marianas with Guam. This group, however, remained unknown to the nearby oriental civilizations and the long established European colonies in the Philippines until Magellan sailed his three square-riggers from South America and found Guam even before Pizarro had reached Peru. Magellan himself had previously spent five years in Indonesia, but had to go to South America to discover Guam.

Those who have not personally seen the Pacific hemisphere from small craft and experienced how the world is reduced to endless horizons of trackless ocean, where isles and atolls seem non-existent unless chance happens to put one just at the bow, are thoroughly misled by easy island hopping along a chain of names compressed on a lifeless, minute map. Nothing can be less representative of the vast rotating Pacific hemisphere, which equals all the rest of the world's oceans and continents put together. On the paper ocean the bulk of the Pacific islands seems large and clustered on the Asiatic side, leaving empty spaces on the American side where island hopping seems to peter out naturally with Easter Island. The living ocean, in complete contrast, is traversed by a wide marine conveyer belt, embracing all these islands, pulling them away from Asia, and placing them right at the doorsteps of Mexico and South America, as history clearly reflects.

The Galápagos, on paper seemingly far from Ecuador, are so close in reality that the group was immediately stumbled upon by caravels not looking for new land but intending to sail along the Ecuadorian coast. Arid and deprived of water, the group was never settled by the Spaniards who, like the coastal aborigines, preferred the richer coasts and inland areas of Ecuador and Peru. The first archaeological survey of this cactus-covered group, however, had no difficulty in establishing that very extensive use had been made of these islands in pre-Spanish times. Mariners from the coasts of Ecuador and Peru had probably come for fishing and catching tortoises and iguana, perhaps even for cotton cultivation. The frequency of the many independent visits can be judged by the numerous shards of identifiable pottery types with origins ranging at least from the Guayaquil area of Ecuador down to Casma some 500 miles south on the Peruvian coast. The time span of the visits appears from the fact that the ceramic types are identifiable with various periods on the continent dating as far back as Coastal Tiahuanaco time. A chalk stone spinning whorl was also excavated and may explain why the wild cotton of the Galápagos was found by botanists to be of the twenty-six-chromosome species produced by the aboriginal American civilizations through artificial hybridization.

Cocos Island would seem equally accessible and serviceable to early navigators who frequented the waters between Ecuador and Meso-America prior to Pizarro's arrival. The island got its name because arriving Europeans were pleasantly surprised to find the landing areas and high inland plateau cleared and densely covered by coconut groves. So sure were we Europeans that nobody could have come there before us that anthropologists and botanists alike theorized that the coconuts must have drifted there by sea either from tropical America or from Polynesia, according to what view one held as to the original homeland of that useful palm, unknown in a truly wild state. None, until our visit in 1956, thought of checking the island to learn that hardly any coconut palms are left today. The jungle has recaptured the whole island, and those few palms that struggle to survive on the inland plateau could not have reached there unless transported up the high cliffs by man after he had first cleared the inland area of its original jungle. The prodigious task of converting this high and moist jungle island to a coconut plantation obviously exceeded the local needs of those who had been responsible for this temporary transformation, and can only have served to supply aboriginal vessels trafficking this area off Panama with much required supplies of fresh drink and food.

Easter Island was the next island nearest to South America, famous since the time of its discovery for its giant statues in human form. When first reached by Europeans the statues stood on masonry platforms of large cut blocks dressed and fitted with an astonishing technique otherwise unknown except in association with similar giant stone statues in pre-Inca South America. Stratigraphic excavations had never been attempted on this island until our expedition arrived in 1955. In spite of its surface remains, which were unique in the entire Pacific area, it had been assumed that the island, being nearest Peru, was the one last reached by voyagers from Asia: accordingly its surface could have nothing man-made old enough to be covered by age and erosion. Excavations, however, pushed the date of its earliest known settlement a thousand years back beyond that hitherto assumed and, combined with dates others later found from the Marquesas Islands, brought the settlements of these two Polynesian regions nearest South America back to centuries greatly antedating anything so far found from the Society Islands or any adjacent part of Central Polynesia.

The geographical position of Easter Island nearest South America does not in itself argue that this must necessarily have been the first Pacific island encountered by voyagers from the New World. The Spaniards, expressly looking for islands when sailing on their own first expeditions from Peru, discovered Melanesia in 1568, then the Marquesas group in 1595, and not until 1722 did a Dutch exploring expedition, also sailing from South America, run into Easter Island. Although the European discoverers sailed in individual ships or in fleets of two or three, the Peruvian explorers are known to have sailed large numbers of rafts in fan formation and thus had far better chances of sighting small islands. Nevertheless, it is more than likely that aboriginal voyagers from Peru, like the subsequent Europeans and some of the twentieth-century balsa raft voyagers, missed the tiny and widely separated isles of Polynesia and first ran into the large, semi-continental and closely packed groups of Melanesia, where Negroid peoples from Asia were already present. The early choice of tiny and insignificant Easter Island as a cultural nucleus, which the local presence of script shows to be the remnants of civilization, may still have a clear geographical significance. Among the hundreds of larger and more fertile islands, none was closer to Peru than Easter Island, and if Peru was the spreading center and ancestral abode, this island would be chosen for its mere proximity. As a geographical link this island among the myriad would logically get its Polynesian name, which is Te-Pito-o-te-Henua, "The Navel of the World."

Throughout Polynesia there is evidence of a complex stock of people and a blend of aboriginal cultures. Physically and culturally the historic population of these East Pacific islands show the closest affinities to aboriginal America, linguistically to present Indonesia. Admitting a basic proto-Indonesia or early Southeast Asiatic element in the Polynesian stock, we still cannot violate all other facts and barriers by bringing them through a false short cut thousands of miles straight eastward over a paper ocean. As history and recent junk experiments have shown, we must bring these prehistoric voyagers from Southeast Asia northward and across to Northwest America before they can sail or drift straight down upon Hawaii and on to the rest of Polynesia and New Zealand. Historic traditions throughout Polynesia—except in Hawaii—specifically record that an island group variously recalled as Hawai'i and Hawaiki was the spreading center from which the ancestors reached their many scattered islands. The Maori of New Zealand give a list of legendary kings and their respectives wives, who according to historic traditions had ruled in Hawaiki prior to any migration to New Zealand. These names prove to concur with a sequence of kings and queens in Hawaiian genealogies, but in Hawaii they are remembered as local rulers.

Except for vestiges of a root relationship in an estimated one per cent of the total vocabulary,[27] traces of Polynesian ties of any sort to any region in the west Pacific have never been found. The contrasts in physical types between Polynesians and Indonesians have become even more apparent since the recent development of blood testing, which clearly groups the Polynesians with the aboriginal people of America. Over a century of concentrated search in the West Pacific has indeed failed to disclose a single center where Polynesian culture could have been at home before its spread over the far-flung islands next to America. It was early assumed that more than one migration must have reached Polynesia, not merely because this is stated in the historic traditions of all the tribes, but because of the uneven blend of physical and cultural components in different groups of Polynesia.

To break down and analyze the diversified and yet clearly interrelated cultures within the Polynesian triangle would have been impossible but for the fact that throughout the area historically minded ancestor worshipers had been religiously tied to old cultural traditions and made little effort to alter inherited customs and techniques. The cultural blend seems most complete in the densest island area of western and central Polynesia, where interisland trade and marginal contact with Melanesia continued until historical time. Easter Island and New Zealand, including the Chatham group, were excluded from this continued communication because contact with the rest of Polynesia ceased soon after the arrivals at these islands from the other groups in the early centuries of the present millennium. Easter Island, New Zealand, and the Chatham Islands therefore offer better possibilities than any other areas for a breakdown of the racial and cultural blend.

Easter Island's historical traditions and genealogical lines recount that the ancestors of the now dominant component in their mixed island population came from the west in the days of Tuu-ko-iho. This would infer their arrival from somewhere in Polynesia some twenty-two generations ago, or during the busiest pan-Polynesian migratory period. The same early traditions expressly state that another people were already present then, people who extended their ear lobes and erected stone statues. These original settlers had come from the east under the leadership of King Hotu Matua. This would infer a previous arrival from the direction of South America. A modern analysis of Easter Island culture shows that none of its elements are typically Polynesian except the wood-cutting tools. All other traits in the material culture as well as in the customs and belief systems reappear as well in South America and are generally alien to the rest of Oceania but characteristic of South America in the pre-Inca period.

Turning to New Zealand we find that historical traditions insist that in this territory, too, another and foreign people were found in possession of the land when the Maori ancestors arrived from Hawaiki. Some of these fled, to take refuge in the Chatham Islands, evidently using the reed boats of the *mokihi* type formerly used on New Zealand and being the only type of water vehicle found by the Europeans when they discovered the Moriois of the Chatham Islands. Nothing has made the Chatham Islanders more interesting than their own physical appearance: they were commonly found to have Arabic–Semitic countenances, often with hooked noses of portentous dimensions and reddish hair.

The Maori themselves also differed from the Polynesian norm. They were ignorant of the outrigger, the chicken, and the pig, cultural treasures which in the meantime had diffused to most of the other islands through close contact with Fiji. Their dominant physical features and cultural characteristics were those which, among all Polynesian tribes, showed the closest affinity to the maritime tribes along the Northwest American archipelago. In fact, from the time of the early European explorers until modern ethnologists began to investigate New Zealand culture, the full complex of often highly specialized Maori traits have found direct counterparts on the continental American islands beyond Hawaii. The Hawaiians themselves are recorded as having built their big canoes from pine that had drifted to their islands from this Northwest American coast.

Combining all presently known evidence, and excluding no known facts from consideration, a logical solution to the Polynesian problem would seem to be that the historically known population has roots somewhere in Southeast Asia, but that they did not come directly to Polynesia on an oversea voyage from that area. Nor did they pass through or stop over in the 4,000-mile-wide alien Micronesian–Melanesian buffer territory that barred the road to the East Pacific. They must have followed the natural maritime route northward rather than eastward and reached Polynesia as a sub-division of the immigrants from East Asia who since neolithic times had occupied the island area along the Northwest American coast. When this Maori–Polynesian ancestry, after an absence from Asia of two millennia or more, finally reached the East Pacific islands at the beginning of the present millennium, still as a strictly neolithic people and ignorant of both loom and pottery, they found an earlier population there. All available evidence indicates that these original discoverers of Polynesia and marginal Melanesia had descended from voyagers from pre-Inca South America. The newcomers, during the interisland migratory vortex in the earliest centuries of the present millennium, partly expelled and partly absorbed the original settlers. Evidence of this culturally advanced sub-stratum, other than in the historical traditions of the present population, is seen in the non-Polynesian ruins of circular stone houses and *tupa* towers, the remains of Peruvian-type megalithic masonry and the abandoned stone statues on the fringe of islands facing

South America, the growth on widely separated Polynesian islands of artificially produced aboriginal American cotton, the sparse but enduring shards of non-Polynesian earthenware, the local breed of dog absent on the islands westward but corresponding to the dog of aboriginal America, the survival until European arrival of *kumara* or sweet potato cultivation, the pre-European presence also of gourd, pineapple, husk tomato, coconut, *Argemone, Polygonum, Pepsicum, totora,* papaya, and a number of other useful plants of American origins that could only have reached Polynesia through human agency. Evidence of inheritance from this cultural sub-stratum is present in various degrees everywhere within the Polynesian triangle, and not only in the archaeology. On most Polynesian islands the custom was adopted of masticating roots in preparation for kava-drinking ceremonies in characteristic South American fashion. In all corners of the Polynesian triangle the practice of building reed boats survived or was remembered. Almost universal was the preservation of royal genealogies attached to legendary culture heroes or deities, with dynasties venerated as demigods. Sporadically appearing throughout Polynesia were also brother and sister marriage in royal families, the royal use of feather cloaks and feather headdresses, mummification, circumcision rites, the difficult surgical operation of trepannation, an advanced calendar system with the new year starting with the first annual appearance of the Pleiades, local appearance of special traits like the idea of incising ideograms in boustrophedon on wooden boards used for ritual singing, or of preserving memories through an intricate composition of knotted strings, the *coups de poing* for stone quarrying and some of the rich Polynesian variety of adz and fishhook types, the angular slab-lined Easter Island oven, polished stone bowls, and perforated sewing needles, the Society Islands poncho, the Hawaiian wickerwork mummy container and slate mirrors, the Marquesan stilts and *pavahina* head ornament, and the Pitcairn arrowheads, merely to list some of the more apparent examples pointing toward ancient Peru.

The great pan-Peruvian civilizations of South America lived in a treeless world of rock and sand, flanked by a straight and open coastline inviting navigation by shallow, sturdy, wash-through rafts. The fishing cultures of the fiords and island-dotted coast of Northwest America, in contrast, lived in the richest forest region of the entire Pacific, with unrestricted access to giant and easily split timber.

It is accordingly only natural that students of Polynesian watercraft have found a sub-stratum of raft navigation everywhere and concluded that some at least of the early migration into the Pacific must have come on wash-through vessels. The newcomers who reached Hawaii from the forest area of the North Pacific, however, did not come by raft; they came in large dugout canoes, carved and inlaid with abalone shell and lashed together as double canoes to be sturdy in the ocean waves. They knew nothing about the quarrying of stone, but were expert wood carvers, who built their gabled houses of split planks whenever the climate permitted; they erected totem poles and carved wooden images and bowls, they ignored pottery and baked their food in round earth ovens, they overlooked the local access to spinnable cotton and searched for bark that could serve for clothmaking when beaten with grooved mallets. Their traditional weapons were not the sling and long wooden clubs previously brought to these islands in conformity with fighting traditions in Peru, but the conventionalized Northwest American one-hand whalebone and stone clubs of the *patu* and *mere* types. They also brought the principal household implement of all the Northwest Coast tribes, the beautifully carved and polished bell-shaped and T-shaped stone pestles which can be archaeologically demonstrated on Hawaii to have been slightly modified to pounders that spread over Polynesia with the newcomers as the principal kitchen implement of nearly all these islands.

The artifact complex of Polynesia, other than perishable items, is extremely poor, and besides certain forms of tanged stone adz blades, clubs, and pounders, few novelties could have been brought from Northwest America that would noticeably differ much from nonperishable tools and implements already present among island settlers from South America. Fishhook types, basic adz forms, scrapers, files, stone saws, mortars, and other durable items already familiar to the newcomers overlapped and blended with those of their predecessors from farther south on the same continent and left little to mark an abrupt transition in local archaeology other than what has been listed above. Although, for instance, fishhooks of any form were unknown in Indonesia and Southeast Asia, the highly specialized archaeological forms of composite stone-shank bone-barb hook of the American Northwest Coast are almost identical to those of Chile and southern Peru.

The blend of the overlapping cultures within Polynesia is so complete that the supreme pan-Polynesian hero-gods Tiki and Kane conflict and compete from island to island in leadership in the genealogical lines. The solar deity and supreme man-god Kane is thus to the Hawaiians what Tiki is to the Marquesans. We have to go back to the continental area of the New World to see them clearly separated. In South America, Tici was celebrated as the pan-Peruvian hero-god and culture bringer who claimed descent from the sun, erected the giant statues at Tiahuanaco, and instructed the Inca in extending their ear lobes before he left for Manta on the coast of Ecuador and sailed with his white and bearded followers into the Pacific Ocean. In Northwest America, Kane was remembered in traditional history as the solar hero-god who came by foot to the local people, did marvelous things, and stayed with them for a while before he married a woman of the sea and set out into the Pacific Ocean, leaving only his brother behind.

The two hero-gods were as real to all the Polynesian islanders as they were to the people of the Inca nation and to the tribes of Vancouver Island on the Northwest Coast. If their names, qualities, and itineraries were myths concocted on the American mainland, at least someone brought them as such to the scattered East Pacific Islands, indicating that a transfer of some sort did take place. If so, why ignore the very essence of these traditions, which claim that the two celebrated American hierarchs voyaged into the Pacific themselves. There are no historic traditions about departures into the open Pacific anywhere else in the Americas but among the historically oriented ancestor worshipers in Peru and the Kwakiutl in the area around Vancouver Island on the Northwest American Coast, and these are indeed the very two areas where we have every reason to suspect geographical, physical, and cultural sources for the composite East Pacific stock.

We are critical of the priests who burned the paper books of the Aztecs because contemporary Europe looked down upon the non-Christian Americans and wanted to destroy their heathen beliefs. But we ourselves have so little esteem for these same beliefs that although the most important ones were recorded by the early Spaniards, we reject them as the fables of primitive nations. We deny their historic value simply because we refuse to believe that any hierarch could have moved to or from his fixed place inside the Americas until Europeans came and set things in motion on the other side of the Atlantic.

The oceans on both sides of America were busy with rafts, canoes, and large reed ships long before Europeans were civilized by voyagers from the Middle East, who taught Europe how to write, whom to worship, and introduced the many skills and arts of civilization on land and at sea. What Europeans took to America in the age of discovery was only what we ourselves had inherited through diffusion from the Middle East at a time when the greatest of the Afro-Asiatic civilizations had long since flourished, declined, and vanished. In traveling time northern Europe was farther away from the pioneers who had brought Afro-Asiatic civilization into being than were the peoples at the receiving end of the Canary Current. The Olmecs were familiar with script before the art of writing had diffused from Asia Minor to Spain, and yet the Spaniards burned the Mexican hieroglyphics in contempt in order to introduce the Semitic scriptures which were written with Phoenician characters.

Perhaps the culture of coastal Ecuador antedates that of the Gulf of Mexico. Perhaps one inspired the other, and perhaps they have different origins. Maybe a fleet of prospective settlers reached Meso-America with the Canary Current. Maybe they even came the longer way, around southern Africa with the winter monsoon from Asia and with the southeast trade winds of the South Atlantic at their backs. Perhaps both these Atlantic routes brought early mariners to tropical America. None of them required centuries, only months, to carry families of mariners with wash-through reed ships and fishing gear from home waters to the tropical regions of the New World. If they came they were certainly preceded by tribes of jungle dwellers whose ancestry had come millennia before on a long trek through the Arctic regions from Siberia to Alaska. Only future archaeology may give the full answer to the major questions which remain unsolved concerning the complex and certainly multiple origins of aboriginal tribes and cultures in the world opened to us by Columbus.

In the meantime, the only certain way to err in our speculations is to ignore the marine clockwork which moves steadier over the deep ocean than any river over dry land. The only approach more incautious than extreme diffusionism against the clockwork of the sea is to affirm dogmatically that man only began to travel once we from Europe had set the pace.

NOTES

CHAPTER 1

1 Resch 1967
2 Lhote 1958, Pls. 26, 32
3 Oppenheim 1954, pp. 6–17; see also Kramer 1963, p. 112
4 Rao 1963, p. 99 and map p. 97
5 Amiet 1961, pp. 121–22; Falkenstein 1936; p. 56, glyphs nos. 216–19
6 Oppenheim 1954, p. 8; Salonen 1939, pp. 5, 160; see also Salonen 1942
7 Kramer 1944, pp. 54, 60, 97–98
8 Plinius 77, Vol. 2, Bk. 6, pp. 399–401

CHAPTER 2

1 Bisschop 1939, p. 57
2 Sharp 1898, p. 204
3 Levison, Ward & Webb 1973, p. 44
4 Ibid., p. 42
5 Ibid., p. 40
6 Ibid., p. 61
7 Ibid., p. 46
8 Stokes 1934, pp. 2791–92; Handy
9 Greenman 1962
   1930a, p. 102; Sayce 1933, p. 261
10 Glas 1764, p. iv

CHAPTER 3

1 Fraser 1965
2 Rowe 1966
3 Hutchinson, Silow & Stephens 1947, p. 79
4 Stonor & Anderson 1949, p. 392
5 Sauer 1950, p. 499
6 Rowe 1966, p. 335
7 Hutchinson, Silow & Stephens 1947
8 Prescott 1847, p. 147
9 Rochebrune 1879, pp. 346, 348
10 Harms 1922, p. 166
11 Merrill 1946, p. 300
12 Sauer 1950, p. 527
13 Pomerance 1970, pp. 2, 14, 16, 26

CHAPTER 4

1 Behrens 1722, pp. 134–36
2 Thomson 1889, pp. 526–32
3 Wilson 1862, Vol. 2, pp. 228, 232, 235, 246
4 Stewart 1943, p. 59
5 Kroeber 1944, p. 56
6 Chervin 1908, p. 139
7 Trotter 1943, pp. 69, 70, 72, 75
8 Letter to author dated June 22, 1951, from M. Trotter, Professor of Gross Anatomy, Washington School of Medicine
9 Letter to author dated May 21,

1951, from W. R. Dawson; see
also Dawson 1928
10 Pizarro 1571, p. 380
11 Relación Anónyma 1615, p. 148
12 Garcilasso 1609, p. 71
13 Ibid.; Karsten 1938, p. 200
14 Cieza de León 1553, Chap. 87, p.
309
15 Valcárcel, *viva voce*
16 Cieza de León 1553, Chap. 105, p.
379
17 Ibid.
18 Bandelier 1910, p. 294
19 Garcilasso 1609, Pt. 3, p. 62
20 Cieza de León 1560, Chap. 5, pp.
5–6

21 Betanzos 1551, Chap. 2
22 Andagoya 1541–46, p. 55
23 Zárate 1555, p. 44
24 Gómara 1553 (as translated by
Bandelier 1910, p. 304)
25 Stevenson 1825, Vol. I, p. 394;
Bandelier 1910, p. 305
26 Stout 1948, p. 267
27 Brinton 1882, pp. 73, 82, 89, 140,
145, 159, 163, 210, 212, 218
28 Bennett 1934, pp. 441, 482
29 Heyerdahl 1952, pp. 295–303
30 Morris, Charlot, and Morris 1931,
Vol. 2, Pl. 146

CHAPTER 5

1 Holtsmark and Seip 1942, pp. 1–4
2 Wilson 1970, pp. 8–9
3 Gray 1930, pp. 35–36
4 Ibid., p. 37
5 Ibid., p. 65

6 Enterline 1972, p. 85
7 Holtsmark & Seip 1942, pp. 426–27
8 Ibid., p. 549
9 Kolsrud 1913, no. 527
10 Caddeo (n.d.) p. 10

CHAPTER 6

1 Heyerdahl 1952, p. 77
2 Gregory 1927, p. 56
3 Sullivan 1922, p. 232
4 Simmons, et al. 1955
5 Murdock 1949; Buck 1938a, p. 17
6 Buck 1938a, pp. 45, 307, 309–11
7 Christian 1910, p. 246
8 Petri 1936, pp. 551 & 553
9 Cook 1910–12, p. 317
10 Friederici 929, pp. 461–62
11 Moerenhout 1837, Vol. 2, p. 244
12 Brown 1924, p. 264
13 Brown 1927, Vol. II, p. 46
14 St. Johnston 1921, p. 244
15 Beyer 1948, pp. 81–82
16 Heine-Geldern 1932, p. 584
17 Buck 1949, p. 181
18 Cook 1784, Vol. 2, p. 373
19 Dixon 1789, p. 244
20 Jacobsen 1891, p. 162
21 Holmes 1919, p. 29
22 Olson 1927–29, p. 30
23 Boas 1895, p. 376

24 Shapiro 1940, p. 28
25 Hrdlička 1944
26 Cook 1784, Vol. 2, p. 301
27 Vancouver 1798, Vol. 2, p. 262
28 Jacobsen 1891, p. 162
29 Hill-Tout 1898
30 Matson, et al. 1946, p. 22
31 Graydon 1952, p. 338
32 Mourant 1954
33 Simmons, et al. 1955, p. 687
34 Thorsby, et al. 1973, p. 294
35 Campbell 1897–98
36 Hill-Tout 1898
37 Goddard 1924
38 Niblack 1888
39 Dreyer 1898, p. 137
40 Voss 1926
41 Olson 1927–29
42 Brown 1927, Vol. 2, p. 68
43 Best 1925, p. 173; Swanton 1905
44 Bancroft 1875
45 Best 1925
46 Gudger 1927, p. 342

47 Cook 1784, Vol. 2, p. 280
48 Jacobsen 1891, p. 162
49 Schurmann 1927, pp. 12–18
50 Petri 1936, p. 550
51 Dreyer 1898, pp. 128, 132
52 Stokes 1932, p. 599
53 Brown 1924, p. 265
54 Jacobsen 1891, p. 162
55 Imbelloni 1928, p. 327; 1930, p. 336
56 Skinner 1931
57 Dixon 1933, p. 315
58 Polack 1838, Vol. 1, p. 92
59 Barbeau 1929
60 Dreyer 1898, p. 131; Bachmann

1931
61 Niblack 1888
62 Drucker 1943, p. 33
63 Dawson 1888, p. 81
64 Boas 1935, Pt. 1, pp. 1, 5
65 Fornander 1878, Vol. 1, pp. 25, 60
66 Malo 1898, p. 180
67 Heyerdahl 1952, pp. 71–158
68 Buck 1933
69 Fornander 1878
70 Shortland 1856, p. 2
71 Fornander 1878, Vol. 1, p. 203
72 Smith 1910, p. 125

CHAPTER 7

1 Ibid., pp. 131–33
2 Handy 1927, p. 105
3 Cook 1784, Vol. III, p. 159
4 Amherst and Thomson 1901, Vol. I, p. XVII
5 Sáamanos 1526, p. 196
6 Andagoya 1541–46, p. 36
7 Oviedo 1535–48, Vol. 4, Bk. 46, Chap. VI
8 Zárate 1555, Bk. 1, Chap. VI
9 Pizarro 1571, p. 157
10 Zárate 1555, Bk. 1, Chap. VI; Cieza de León 1553, LIV, p. 196
11 Garcilasso 1609, p. 432
12 Cobo 1653, Bk. 12, Chap. XXXII
13 Garcilasso 1609, Vol. 1, Bk. 3, Chap. XVI
14 Sarmiento 1572, p. 135
15 Balboa 1576–86, p. 501; 1586, p. 81
16 Betanzos 1551, Chap. III
17 Sarmiento 1572, pp. 32, 186
18 Balboa 1576–86

19 Stevenson 1825, Vol. 1, p. 394
20 Oliva 1631, p. 325
21 Acosta 1590, Vol. 1, p. 56
22 Heyerdahl 1952, pp. 550–55; Eisleb 1963
23 Amherst and Thomson 1901, Vol. 2, pp. 463–68
24 Agüera 1770, p. 109
25 Amherst and Thomson 1901, Vol. 1, pp. IV–VI
26 Gonzalez 1770–71, p. XLVI
27 Amherst and Thomson 1901, Vol. 1, pp. 8, 67, 83–85, 97–98, 161–62, 217–18, 461
28 Christian 1924, p. 525
29 Rivet 1928, pp. 583, 603; 1943, p. 124
30 Buck 1938, pp. 22–23, 453
31 Heyerdahl and Skjölsvold 1956; Heyerdahl 1961
32 Beechey 1831, Vol. 1, pp. 186–88

CHAPTER 8

1 Haddon and Hornell 1936, Vol. 1, pp. 144, 219
2 Hornell 1931, p. 353
3 Beechey 1831, p. 135
4 Knudsen 1963, pp. 43–44
5 Polack 1838, Vol. 2, p. 221
6 Best 1925
7 Hornell 1931, p. 354

8 Heyerdahl 1941
9 Hutchinson 1875, pp. 426, 454
10 Lothrop 1932, pp. 229–56
11 Means 1942
12 Hornell 1945, pp. 167–91
13 Sáamanos 1526
14 Xeres 1534
15 Murphy 1941, p. 17

16 Sáamanos 1526, p. 196
17 Pizarro 1571, p. 138
18 Las Casas 1559, Chap. XLI, pp. 78–79
19 Oviedo 1535–48, Vol. 4, Bk. 45, Chap. 17; Andagoya 1541–46, p. 41; Zárate 1555, Bk. 1, Chap. 6
20 Benzoni 1565, p. 242
21 Garcilasso 1609, Vol. 1, Bk. 3, Chap. XVI
22 Lizarraga 1560–1602, pp. 32–33
23 Balboa 1586, p. 81
24 Sarmiento 1572, p. 135
25 Cobo 1653, Chap. XIV, p. 218
26 Spilbergen 1619, p. 83
27 Juan and Ulloa 1748, Vol. 1, p. 189
28 Lescallier 1791, Vol. 1, pp. 458–63
29 Charnock 1801, Vol. 1, p. 12
30 Humboldt 1810, p. 295
31 Stevenson 1825, pp. 222–23
32 Blaxland 1840
33 Paris 1841–43, p. 148
34 Lothrop 1932, p. 240
35 Bennett 1954, Figs, 89, 90
36 For illustrations and descriptions see Bird 1943; and Heyerdahl 1952, pp. 553–55, Pl. LXXVI
37 Uhle 1922, p. 49

38 Nordenskiöld 1931, p. 265
39 Valverde 1879, p. 179
40 Lothrop 1932, p. 238
41 Byam 1850, p. 200
42 Means 1942, pp. 15, 18
43 Hornell 1946, p. 54
44 Dixon 1932
45 Dixon 1934, p. 173
46 Emory 1933, p. 48; 1942, p. 129
47 Morgan 1946, p. 80
48 Buck 1945, p. 11
49 Weckler 1943, p. 35
50 Heyerdahl 1941
51 Garcilasso 1609, Vol. 1, p. 261
52 Gretzer 1914, p. 7
53 Cobo 1653, Chap. XIV, p. 218
54 Eisleb 1963
55 Lothrop 1932, p. 240
56 Spilbergen 1619, p. 83
57 Juan and Ulloa 1748, pp. 189ff.
58 Humboldt 1810, p. 295; Stevenson 1825, p. 223
59 Morell 1832, p. 120
60 Paris 1841–43, p. 148
61 Skogman 1854, Vol. 1, p. 164
62 Heyerdahl 1954

CHAPTER 9

1 Byron 1764–66, p. 102
2 Forster 1777, Vol. II, Bk. 3, Chap. I, p. 226
3 White 1889, Vol. 1 p. 173
4 Candolle 1884, p. 461
5 Cook and Cook 1918; Cook 1901, 1903, 1910–12, 1916a, 1916b and 1925
6 Merrill 1920, p. 195
7 Heyerdahl 1952, pp. 429–30
8 Dixon 1932
9 Merrill 1954, p. 213
10 Martius 1823
11 Candolle 1884, p. 433
12 Guppy 1906, p. 413
13 Edmondson 1941
14 Merrill 1954, pp. 195, 267
15 Nordenskiöld 1931, p. 269
16 Buck 1938a, p. 315; 1945, p. 11
17 Eames and St. John 1943, p. 256
18 Merrill 1950, p. 9
19 Bird 1948; Whitaker & Bird 1949

20 Merrill 1954, p. 242
21 Hutchinson, Silow & Stephens 1947, p. 79
22 Sauer 1950, p. 537
23 Carter 1950, p. 169
24 Merrill 1954, pp. 190, 242, 338
25 Brown 1935, p. 174
26 Cook and Cook 1918, pp. 156, 169
27 Merrill 1920, p. 195
28 Carter 1950, pp. 164, 181
29 Roggeveen 1722, p. 21; Behrens 1722, p. 135
30 Forster 1778, p. 236
31 Eyraud 1864, pp. 126–27
32 Hervé 1770, p. 123
33 Thomson 1889, pp. 456, 535
34 Hervé 1770, p. 121
35 Thomson 1889, p. 456
36 Knoche 1925, p. 122
37 Thomson 1889, p. 456

38 La Pérouse 1797, Vol. II, p. 335
39 Hervé 1770, p. 123; Agüera 1770, p. 102
40 Smith 1961, p. 193
41 Skottsberg 1956, pp. 407, 412
42 From Polynesia *Chenopodium* and *Solanum insulaepaschalis;* from America *Scirpus riparius* (principal building material), *Sophora toromiro* (only wild local tree, most treasured for wood carving), *Lycium carolineanum* (only wild shrub, edible berries), *Cyperus vegetus* (edible roots), and *Polygonum acumenatum* (medical plant)
43 Skottsberg 1934, p. 278; 1957, p. 3
44 Brown 1931, Vol. i, p. 137
45 Heyerdahl 1952, p. 467; 1974, Chap. 9
46 Porter 1815, Vol. II, p. 134
47 Brown 1931, p. 137
48 Brown 1935, p. 190
49 Ibid., p. 49
50 Hillebrand 1888, p. 14
51 Bertoni 1919, p. 280
52 Degener 1930, p. 88
53 Collins 1949
54 Hutchinson, Silow & Stephens 1947, p. 79
55 Hillebrand 1888, p. 310
56 Carter 1950, pp. 172–74
57 Prain 1895, p. 325
58 Fedde 1909, p. 280
59 Yacovleff & Herrera 1935, p. 41
60 Stokes 1932, p. 599
61 Carter 1950, pp. 172, 179
62 Buck 1938b, pp. 20, 23
63 Seemann 1865–73, p. xvi
64 Merrill 1946, p. 339
65 Baker 1893, p. 192
66 Cook 1903, p. 490
67 Heyerdahl 1961, Pl. 2c
68 Sauer 1950, p. 511
69 Carter 1950, p. 165
70 Brown 1931, p. 158
71 Jakeman 1950, p. 32
72 Yacovleff and Herrera 1934, p. 283
73 Clausen 1944, pp. 3, 7, 29, 31
74 Guppy 1906, p. 413
75 Cook 1903, pp. 483, 496
76 Quiros 1609, p. 23
77 Barrau 1963, pp. 1–2

CHAPTER 10

1 Heyerdahl and Skjölsvold 1965, pp. 3–7
2 Orcutt 1953, p. 270
3 Sharp 1704, pp. 58, 64
4 Cowley 1684
5 Skogman 1854, Vol. i, p. 164
6 Hutchinson 1875, pp. 426, 454
7 Means 1942, p. 15
8 Lothrop 1932, p. 238
9 Hornell 1946, p. 60
10 Hagen 1949, p. 178

CHAPTER 11

1 Coe 1960, pp. 384–86, 390
2 Dampier 1729, Vol. I, p. iii
3 Wafer 1699, pp. 379–81
4 Candolle 1884, pp. 434–35
5 Kerchove 1878, p. 147; Cook 1910–12, pp. 283–84; Candolle 1884, p. 431
6 Candolle 1884, pp. 429–35
7 Cook 1910–12, pp. 293, 304, 318, 340
8 Porter 1815, Vol. 2, p. 139
9 Chubb 1933, p. 26

CHAPTER 12

1 Heyerdahl 1974
2 For more detailed reports on observations by the various European visitors see Heyerdahl 1961, pp. 45–89
3 Ibid., pp. 33–43

4 Routledge 1919
5 Ibid., pp. 186–87
6 Métraux 1940, p. 293
7 Buck 1938a, p. 234
8 Skjölsvold 1961, Rpt. 14
9 Mulloy 1961, Rpt. 1; Smith 1961, Rpt. 2
10 Routledge 1919, pp. 171–72; Métraux 1940, pp. 414–16; Lavachery 1936, p. 393
11 Ferdon 1961, Rpts. 13 & 10; Skjölsvold 961, Rpt. 9
12 Skottsberg 1920, Fig. 2; Métraux 1940, p. 157
13 Ferdon 1961, p. 338
14 Ibid., pp. 230–40
15 Reproduced in Heyerdahl 1976, Pl. 156i
16 Métraux 1940, p. 344
17 Heyerdahl 1976, Pl. 304 a & b
18 Bennett 1934, pp. 460–75

19 Skjölsvold 1961, p. 362
20 Routledge 1919, pp. 295–99
21 Knoche 1925, pp. 313–14
22 Lavachery 1936, p. 392; Métraux 1940, pp. 88–94
23 Englert 1948, p. 156
24 Chubb 1933, p. 33
25 Métraux 1940, p. 7; Lavachery 1935, pp. 346–47
26 Smith 1961, p. 391
27 Englert 1948, p. 157
28 Smith 1961, Rpt. 16
29 Skjölsvold 1961, pp. 291–92, 343–45
30 Smith 1961, pp. 218–19
31 Heyerdahl and Ferdon 1965, Pls. lc, 26–31
32 Buck 1938a, p. 232
33 Heyerdahl 1965, Pls. 35–45
34 Ferdon 1965, p. 121; Heyerdahl 1965, pp. 136–38
35 Heyerdahl 1958, Chap. 5

CHAPTER 13

1 Shand 1894, p. 77
2 Poirier 1953
3 Buck 1922, pp. 38, 40
4 Sullivan 1924a, p. 22; 1924b, p. 25
5 Linton 1923, p. 447
6 Handy 1930b, p. 4
7 Behrens 1737, pp. 134, 136
8 Agüera 1770, p. 96; Corney 1908, p. XIV
9 Cook 1777, Vol. 2, p. 296
10 Thomson 1889, p. 532
11 Knoche 1912, pp. 876–77; 1925, pp. 309–12
12 Balfour 1917, pp. 377–78
13 Haddon 1918, pp. 161–62
14 Routledge 1919, pp. 221, 295–96
15 Shapiro 1940, pp. 24–30
16 Métraux 1940, pp. 414–15
17 Lavachery 1935, pp. 324–25; 1936, p. 393
18 Heyerdahl 1941, pp. 18, 21–22
19 Englert 1948, pp. 88, 101, 156–57
20 Ibid., pp. 121–22
21 Agüera 1770, pp. 109–11
22 Ross 1936; Métraux 1940, p. 31
23 Englert 1948, pp. 139–47; see also Heyerdahl & Ferdon 1961, pp. 30, 39–40

24 Cook 1777, Vol. 1, p. 290; Forster 1777, Vol. 1, pp. 564, 584–85
25 Cook 1777, Vol. 2, p. 364; Forster 1778, p. 284
26 Cook 1777, Vol. 1, p. 278
27 Roussel 1908
28 Palmer 1870, p. 109
29 Pinart 1878, p. 238
30 Churchill 1912, p. 5
31 Englert 1948, p. 327
32 Bergsland and Vogt 1962
33 Métraux 1940, pp. 309, 315
34 Geiseler 1883, p. 131; Ferdon 1961, pp. 250–53
35 Ferdon 1961, pp. 250–54
36 Roggeveen 1722, p. 15; Behrens 1722, p. 133; Ferdon 1961, p. 534
37 Smith 1940; Debenedetti & Casanova 1933–35, Figs. 1–3
38 Métraux 1940, pp. 340–41
39 Ferdon 1961, p. 534
40 Ibid., p. 535
41 Thomson 1889, pp. 537–38
42 Heyerdahl 1965, Colour Pl. XIV & Pl. 320
43 Geiseler 1883, Fig. 7; Thomson 1889, Pl. 23; Lavachery 1939,

Figs. 315 & 398; Ferdon 1961, Figs. 65b & f

44 Ferdon 1961, pp. 254–55; Means 1931, pp. 424–25; Joyce 1913; Heyerdahl 1976, pp. 59, 63, 75, 85, 201, 202, 216, 248, 327, Pl. 183

45 Thomson 1889, pp. 481–82

46 Jaussen 1894, p. 261

47 Buck 1938a, p. 232

48 Mulloy 1961, pp. 100, 128, 130, 133–35

49 Ferdon 1961, p. 535

50 Geiseler 1883, p. 31; Ferdon 1961, pp. 381–83, Fig. 12b

51 Ferdon 1961, p. 329

52 Skjölsvold 1961, pp. 295–303; Ferdon 1961, pp. 305–11

53 Ferdon 1961, p. 338; Bruayn 1963

54 Thomson 1889, p. 486; Ferdon 1961, pp. 329–331

55 Mulloy 1961, pp. 138–45; Smith 1961, pp. 287–89; Skjölsvold 1961, pp. 291–93; Heyerdahl 1961, pp. 449–50

56 Heyerdahl 1976, Pl. 307d

57 Heyerdahl and Ferdon 1961, Pl. 40d; Izumi & Sono 1963, Pls. 24c–e

58 Tautain 1897, p. 674

59 Behrens 1737, p. 136

60 Beechey 1831, p. 38

61 Markham 1911, p. 67

62 Pizarro 1571, p. 275

63 Bandelier 1910, pp. 304–5; Oliva 1631, p. 37

64 Betanzos 1551, Chap. III

65 Eyraud 1864, pp. 71, 124; Roussel 1869, p. 464; Zumbohm 1880, p. 232

66 Croft 1874, pp. 318–20

67 Jaussen 1893

68 Barthel 1958

69 Carroll 1892, pp. 103–6, 233–53

70 *American Anthropologist,* Vol. 66, pp. 148–49

71 *E.g.,* José Quintela de Melo in *O Cruzeiró Internacional,* Brazil, 11.4.1973

72 Métraux 1938, p. 238

73 Hornbostel 1930

74 Heine-Geldern 1938, p. 890

75 Routledge 1919, pp. 279, 281

76 Knorozov 1964, p. 4

77 Montesinos 1642, pp. 18, 32, 58, 62

78 Métraux 1940, p. 390; Englert 1948, p. 316

79 Englert 1948, pp. 222, 316

80 Molina 1570–84, p. 4

81 Sarmiento 1572, p. 200

82 Lavachery 1939; 1965

83 Heyerdahl 1976

84 Geiseler 1883, pp. 31–32

85 Thomson 1889, p. 470

86 Lavachery 1965, p. 159

87 Aichel 1925; Ortiz 1964; Letter to the author from Dr. Hernan San Martim of Concepción, Chile, dated 6 December 1966

88 Métraux 1940, p. 201

89 Ibid., p. 215

90 Heyerdahl 1961, pp. 412–13; Izumi & Sono 1963, Pl. 164

CHAPTER 14

1 Harden 1962, p. 32

2 Bibby 1969, p. VIII

3 Evans 1971, pp. 212–14

4 Hood 1971, p. 29

5 Karageorgis 1969, p. 37

6 Rao 1963

7 Kramer 1963, p. 114

8 Oppenheim 1954, p. 10

9 Gordon 1954, p. 84

10 Mallowan 1965, p. 17

11 Oppenheim 1954, p. 12

12 Kramer 1963, p. 112

13 Oppenheim 1954, p. 17

14 Kramer 1944, p. vii

15 Bibby 1969, pp. 75–76

16 Kramer 1944, pp. 97–98

17 Ibid., 54–60

18 Johanson 1976

19 Harden 1962, pp. 19–24

20 Collier 1976, pp. 16–17

21 Meggers 1975

22 Grove 1976, pp. 635–36

23 Collier 1976, p. 17

24 Meggers 1976, p. 637

25 Hammond 1977, pp. 116, 121, 130, 133
26 Fornander 1878, Vol. I, p. 199
27 As already pointed out by Dixon (1921, p. 79), only some 250 Polynesian words either were similar to or probably had the same roots as in Malay tongues.

He stressed that since known Polynesian words at least exceed 25,000, "this would give us a percentage of only one per cent—not, we submit, a sufficient percentage on which to base a racial connection."

BIBLIOGRAPHY

ACOSTA, J. DE (1590): *Historia natural y moral de las Indias.*—Seville.

AGÜERA Y INFANZON, F. A. DE (1770): Journal of the principal occurrences during the Voyage of the Frigate "Santa Rosalia" in the year 1770.—*Hakluyt Soc.,* 2nd ser. no. 13. Cambridge, 1908.

AICHEL, O. (1925): Osterinselpaleolithen in prähistorischen Gräbern Chiles.— *Congr. Int. Américanistes,* Vol. XXI, No. 2. Gothenburg.

AMHERST, LORD, and THOMSON, B. (1901): *The Discovery of the Solomon Islands by Alvaro de Mendaña in 1568.*—2 vols. London.

AMIET, P. (1961): *La Glyptique Mesopotamienne Archaique.*—Paris.

ANDAGOYA, P. DE (1541–46): *Narrative of the Proceedings of Pedrarias Davila . . . 1541–46.*—Hakluyt Soc., Vol. XXXIV. London, 1865.

BACHMANN, K. W. (1931): *Die Besiedlung des alten Neuseeland.*—Leipzig.

BAKER, J. G. (1893): A Synopsis of the genera and species of Museae.—*Ann. of Bot.,* Vol. VII. London.

BALBOA, M. C. DE (1576–86): *Miscelanea antartica.*—Manuscript in New York Public Library.

————(1586): *Histoire du Pérou.*—In: Ternaux-Compans: Voyages, Relations et Mémoires originaux pour servir a l'histoire de la découverte de l'Amerique. Paris, 1840.

BALFOUR, H. (1917): Some Ethnological Suggestions in Regard to Easter Island, or Rapanui.—*Folklore,* Vol. XXVIII, pp. 356–81. London.

BANCROFT, H. H. (1875): *The Native Races of the Pacific States of North America.*—5 vols. London.

BANDELIER, A. F. (1910): *The Islands of Titicaca and Koati.*—New York.

BARBEAU, M. (1929): Totem Poles of the Gitksan, Upper Skenna River, Br. Columbia.—*Nat. Mus. Canada Bull.* No. 61, Anthrop. Ser., No. 12. Ottawa.

BARRAU, J., ed. (1963): *Plants and the Migrations of Pacific Peoples.*—Bishop Museum Press, Honolulu.

BARTHEL, T. S. (1958): The "Talking Boards" of Easter Island.—*Scientific American,* Vol. 198, No. 6, June 1958, pp. 61–68. New York.

BEECHEY, F. W. (1831): *Narrative of a Voyage to the Pacific and Bering's Strait.* —Philadelphia.

BEHRENS, C. F. (1722): Der Wohlversüchte Süd-Länder, das ist: ausführliche Reise-Beschreibung um die Welt.—English translation: *Hakluyt Soc.,* 2nd ser., no. 13. Cambridge, 1908.

————(1737): Reise durch die Süd-Länder und um die Welt.—*Hakluyt Soc.,* 2nd ser., no. 13, Appendix I. Cambridge, 1908.

BENNETT, W. C. (1934): *Excavations at Tiahuanaco.*—Anthrop. Papers Amer. Mus. Nat. Hist., Vol. 34, Pt. 3. New York.

————(1954): *Ancient Arts of the Andes.*—New York.

BENZONI, G. (1565): *Historie of the New World.*—Transl. by W. H. Smyth. Hakluyt Society, No. 21. London, 1857. (Orig. ed. *La Historia del Mundo Nuevo.* Venice, 1565).

BERGSLAND, K., and VOGT, H. (1962): On the validity of glottochronology.—*Current Anthropology,* Vol. 5, No. 12. New Haven, Conn.

BERTONI, M. S. (1919): Essai d'une monographie du genre Ananas.—*Anal. Ci. Paraguayos,* Vol. II, No. 4. Asuncion.

BEST, E. (1925): The Maori Canoe, An Account of Various Types of Vessels used by the Maori of New Zealand in Former Times . . .—*Dominion Mus. Bull.* No. 7. Wellington, N.Z.

BETANZOS, E. DE (1551): *Suma y narración de los Incas.*—Madrid, 1880.

BEYER, H. O. (1948): Philippine and East Asian Archaeology, and Its Relation to the Origin of the Pacific Islands Population.—*National Research Council of the Philippines, Bull.* 29. Quezon City.

BIBBY, G. (1969): *Looking for Dilmun.*—New York.

BIRD, J. B. (1943): Excavations in Northern Chile.—*Anthrop. Papers Amer. Mus. Nat. Hist.,* Vol. 38, Pt. 4. New York.

———(1948): America's Oldest Farmers.—*Nat. Hist.,* Vol. LVII, No. 7. New York.

BISSCHOP, E. DE (1939): *Kaimiloa. D'Honolulu à Cannes par l'Australie et le Cap à Bord d'Une Double Pirogue Polynésienne.*—Paris.

BLAXLAND, G. (1840): *Treatise on the Aboriginal Inhabitants of Polynesia with Evidences of their Origin and Antiquity.*—MS No. B760, Mitchell Library. Sydney.

BOAS, F. (1895): Mitteilung zur Anthropologie der Nordamerikanischen Indianer.— *Zeitschrift Ethn.,* Vol. XXVII. Berlin.

———(1935): *Kwakiutl Tales.*—New Series, Pt. 1–2. New York.

BRINTON, D. G. (1882): *American Hero-Myths. A Study in the Native Religions of the Western Continent.*—Philadelphia.

BROWN, F. B. H. (1931): *Flora of Southeastern Polynesia.* Vol. I, *Monocotyledons.* B. P. Bishop Mus. Bull. 84. Honolulu.

———(1935): *Flora of Southeastern Polynesia.* Vol. III, *Dicotyledons.*—B. P. Bishop Mus. Bull. 130. Honolulu.

BROWN, J. M. (1924): *The Riddle of the Pacific.*—London.

———(1927): *Peoples and Problems of the Pacific.*—Vols. I–II. London.

BRUAYN, E. DE (1963): Informe sobre el descubrimiento de un area arqueologica.—*Museo Nacional de Historia Natural Publicación Ocasional,* No. 2, pp. 1–16. Santiago de Chile.

BRYAN, E. H., Jr. (1935): *Hawaiian Nature Notes.*—Honolulu.

BUCK, P. H. (1922): Maori Somatology: Racial Averages.—*Journ. Polynesian Soc.,* Vol. XXXI, Nos. 1, 3, 4. New Plymouth, N.Z.

———(1933): Polynesian voyages.—*Man,* Vol. XXXIII, No. 136. London.

———(1938a): *Vikings of the Sunrise.*—New York.

———(1938b): *Ethnology of Mangareva.*—B. P. Bishop Mus. Bull. 157. Honolulu.

———(1945): *An Introduction to Polynesian Anthropology.*—B. P. Bishop Mus. Bull. 187. Honolulu.

———(1949): *The Coming of the Maori.*—Wellington, N.Z.

BYAM, G. (1850): *Wanderings in some of the Western Republics of America,* . . .—London. (German edition: *Wanderungen durch Südamerikanische Republiken.* Dresden, 1851.)

BRYON, L. G. A. (1764–66): *Bryon's Journal of his Circumnavigation, 1764–1766.*—Ed. R. E. Gallagher. Hakluyt Society, 2nd ser. No. 122. Cambridge, 1964.

CADDEO, E., ed. (n.d.): *Giornale di Bordo di Cristoforo Columbo 1492–1493.*—(Danish ed. transl. by C. V. Östergaard) Copenhagen, 1942.

CAMPBELL, J. (1897–98): The Origin of the Haidahs of the Queen Charlotte Islands.—*Trans. Royal Soc. of Canada,* 2nd ser. Vol. III, Sec. 2.

CANDOLLE, A. DE (1884): *Origin of Cultivated Plants.*—London. (Eng. transl. of: *Origine des plantes cultivées,* 1883.)

CARROLL, A. (1892): The Easter Island Inscriptions, and the Translation and Interpretation of them.—*Jour. Polynesian Soc.,* Vol. I, No. 4, pp. 103–106, 233–253. London.

CARTER, G. F. (1950): Plant Evidence for Early Contacts with America.—*Southwestern Journ. Anthrop.,* Vol. VI, No. 2. Albuquerque, N.M.

CHARNOCK, J. (1801): *A History of Marine Architecture.*—London.

CHERVIN, A. (1908): *Craniologie,* Vol. III *of Anthropologie Bolivienne.*—Paris.

CHRISTIAN, F. W. (1910): *Eastern Pacific Lands: Tahiti and the Marquesas Islands.*—London.

———(1924): Early Maori Migrations as Evidenced by Physical Geography and Language.—*Report Sixteenth Meeting Australas. Ass. Adv. Sci.,* Wellington, N.Z.

CHUBB, L. J. (1933): *Geology of Galápagos, Cocos, and Easter Island.*—B. P. Bishop Mus. Bull. 110. Honolulu.

CHURCHILL, W. (1912): *Easter Island. The Rapanui Speech and the Peopling of Southeast Polynesia.*—Carnegie Inst. Wash. Publ. no. 174. Washington, D.C.

CIEZA DE LEÓN, P. DE (1553): *The Travels of Pedro de Cieza de León, A.D. 1532–50, Contained in his First Part of his Chronicle of Peru.*—Hakluyt Soc. London, 1864.

———(1560): *The Second Part of the Chronicle of Peru.*—Hakluyt Soc. London, 1883.

CLAUSEN, R. T. (1944): *A Botanical Study of the Yam Beans (Pachyrrhizus).*—Cornell Univ. Mem. 264. Ithaca, N.Y.

COBO, B. (1653): *Historia del Nuevo Mundo . . .*—Ed. Marcos Jiménex de la Espada. Seville, 1890–95.

COE, M. D. (1960): Archaeological Linkages with North and South America at la Victoria, Guatemala.—*American Anthropologist,* Vol. LXII, No. 3.

COLLIER, D. (1976): Ecuadorian Roots.—*The Univ. of Chicago Magazine,* Vol. LXIX, No. 1, Autumn, pp. 16–18.

COLLINS, J. L. (1949): History, Taxonomy and Culture of the Pineapple.—*Econ. Bot.,* Vol. III, No. 4. Lancaster, Pa.

COOK, J. (1777): *Second Voyage Towards the South Pole and Round the World, Performed in the "Resolution" and "Adventure," 1772–75.*—2 vols. London.

———(1784): *A voyage to the Pacific Ocean . . . In the years 1776–80.*—3 vols. Dublin.

COOK, O. F. (1901): The Origin and Distribution of the Cocoa Palm.—*Contr. U.S. Nat. Herb.,* Vol. VII, No. 2. Washington, D.C.

———(1903): Food Plants of Ancient America.—*Ann. Rept. Smithsonian Inst.* Washington, D.C.

———(1910–12): History of the Coconut Palm in America.—*Contr. U.S. Nat. Herb.,* Vol. 14. Washington, D.C.

————(1916a): Quichua Names of Sweet Potatoes.—*Jour. Wash. Acad. Sci.,* Vol. VI, No. 4.

————(1916b): Agriculture and Native Vegetation in Peru.—*Jour. Wash. Acad. Sci.,* Vol. VI, No. 10.

————(1925): Peru as a center of domestication.—*Jour. Heredity,* Vol. XVI, Nos. 2 & 3. Washington, D.C.

COOK, O. F., and COOK, R. C. (1918): The Maho, or Mahugua, as a Trans-Pacific Plant.— *Journ. Wash. Acad. Science,* Vol. VIII.

CORNEY, B. G. (1908): Introduction to *The Voyage of Captain Don Felipe Gonzalez to Easter Island in 1770.*—Hakluyt Soc., 2nd Series, No. 12. London.

COWLEY, W. A. (1684): Manuscript in the British Museum, *B.M. Sloane MS 54.* London.

CROFT, T. (1874): Letter of April 30, 1874 from Thomas Croft, Papeete, Tahiti, to the President of California Academy of Sciences.—*California Acad. Sciences. Proc.,* Vol. 5, pp. 317–323. San Francisco, 1875.

DALES, G. F. (1962): Harappen Outposts on the Makran Coast.—*Antiquity,* Vol. XXXVI, No. 142, pp. 86–92.

DAMPIER, W. (1729): *Captain William Dampier's Voyage round the Terrestrial Globe.*—A Collection of Voyages, 4 vols. London.

DAWSON, G. M. (1888): Notes and Observations on the Kwakiool People of the Northern Part of Vancouver Island and Adjacent Coasts, . . . with a Vocabulary of About Seven Hundred Words.—*Proc. Trans. Royal Soc. Canada,* Vol. V, Sec. II. Montreal.

DAWSON, W. R. (1928): Mummification in Australia and in America.—*Journal of the Royal Anthropological Institute,* Vol. LVIII. London.

DEBENEDETTI, S., and CASANOVA, E. (1933–35): Titiconte.—*Museo Antropologico y Ethnografico,* Publicaciones, Ser. A., Vol. 3, pp. 7–36. Buenos Aires.

DEGENER, O. (1930): *Ferns and Flowering Plants of Hawaii National Park.*— (2nd photolithoprint ed.: Ann Abor, Mich., 1945.) Honolulu.

DIXON, G. (1789): *A Voyage Round the World, but more particularly to the North West Coast of America Performed in 1785–88.*—London.

DIXON, R. B. (1921): A New Theory of Polynesian Origins. A Review.—*Jour. Polynes. Soc.,* Vol. XXX, No. 2, New Plymouth, N.Z.

————(1932): The Problem of the Sweet Potato in Polynesia.—*American Anthropology,* Vol. XXXIV.

————(1933): Contacts with America Across the Southern Pacific.—In: *The American Aborigines Their Origin and Antiquity.* A Collection of Papers, by Ten Authors. Assembled by D. Jenness. Toronto.

————(1934): The long voyages of the Polynesians.—*Proc. Amer. Philos. Soc.,* Vol. LXXIV, No. 3.

DREYER, W. (1898): *Naturfolkenes Liv.*—Copenhagen.

DRUCKER, P. (1943): Archaeological Survey on the Northern Northwest Coast. —*Bur. Amer. Ethn. Bull.* No. 133, Anthrop. Papers, No. 20. Washington, D.C.

EAMES, A. J. and ST. JOHN, H. (1943): The Botanical Identity of the Hawaiian Ipu Nui or Large Gourd.—*Amer. Journ. Bot.,* Vol. XXX, No. 3.

EDMCNDSON, C. H. (1941): Viability of Coconut Seeds After Floating in Sea.— B. P. Bishop Mus. Occ. Papers, Vol. XVI, No. 12. Honolulu.

EISLEB, D. (1963): Beitrag zur Systematrik der Altperuanischen "Ruder" aus der Gegend von Ica.—*Baessler-Archiv,* N.F., Band 10, pp. 105–28. Berlin.

EMORY, K. P. (1933): *Stone Remains in the Society Islands.*—B. P. Bishop Mus. Bull. 116. Honolulu.

——(1942): Oceanian Influence on American Indian Culture. Nordenskiöld's View.—*Journ. Polynesian Soc.*, Vol. LI.

ENGLERT, P. S. (1948): *La Tierra de Hotu Matu'a. Historia, Etnologia y Lengua de Isla de Pascua.*—Imprenta y edit. "San Francisco" Padre las Casas, Chile.

ENTERLINE, J. R. (1972): *Viking America.*—New York.

EVANS, J. D. (1971): *The Prehistoric Antiquities of the Maltese Islands: A Survey.*—London.

EYRAUD, E. (1864): Lettre au T. R. P. Supérieur général de la Congrégation des Sacrés-Coeurs de Jesus et de Marie.—Valparaiso décembre 1864.—*Ann. Assoc. Propagation de la Foi.* Vol. 38, pp. 52–71, pp. 124–38. Lyon, 1866.

FALKENSTEIN, A. (1936): *Archaische Texte aus Uruk.*—Berlin.

FEDDE, F. (1909): Papaveraceae-Hypecoideae et Papaveraceae-Papaveroideae.— A. Engler, *Das Pflanzenreich,* Hft. 49. Leipzig.

FERDON, JR., E. N. (1961): The Ceremonial Site of Orongo.—Sites E-4 and E-5. —Stone Houses in the Terraces of Site E-21.—Easter Island House Types. —Site E-6, an Easter Island *Hare Moa.*—A Summary of the Excavated Record of Easter Island Prehistory.—6 papers in: Heyerdahl and Ferdon (1961), pp. 221–55, 305–11, 313–21, 329–38, 381–83, 527–35.

——(1965): Surface Architecture of the Site of Paeke, Taipi Valley, Nukuhiva.—Report 9 in: Heyerdahl and Ferdon (1965).

FORNANDER, A. (1878): *An Account of The Polynesian Race, Its Origin and Migrations,* 4 vols. London.

FORSTER, G. (1777): *A Voyage Round the World, in His Britannic Majesty's Sloop, Resolution, Commanded by Capt. James Cook, During the Years 1772, 3, 4, and 5.*—2 vols. London.

FORSTER, J. R. (1778): *Observations made during a Voyage Round the World . . .*—London.

FRASER, D. (1965): Theoretical Issues in the Trans-Pacific Diffusion Controversy. —*Social Research,* Vol. 32, No. 4.

FRIEDERICI, G. (1929): Die vorkolumbischen Verbindungen der Südsee-Völker mit Amerika.—*Anthropos,* Vol. XXIV. Vienna.

GARCILASSO DE LA VEGA, INCA (1609): *First Part of the Royal Commentaries of the Yncas.*—Hakluyt Soc., Vols. XLI–XLV. London, 1869–71.

GEISELER, Kapitänlieutenant (1883): *Die Oster-Insel. Eine Stätte prähistorischer Kultur in der Südsee.*—Berlin.

GLAS, G. (1764): *The History of the Discovery and Conquest of the Canary Islands: Translated from a Spanish Manuscript Lately Found in the Island of Palma.*—London.

GODDARD, P. E. (1924): *Indians of the N.W. Coast.*—Amer. Mus. Nat. Hist. Handbook Ser., No. 10. New York.

GÓMARA, F. L. DE (1533): *Primera y Segunda Parte de la Historia general de la Indias hasta el año de 1551.*—Madrid, 1858.

GONZALEZ, F. (1770–71): *The Voyage of Captain Don Felipe Gonzalez in the Ship of the San Lorenzo, with the Frigate Santa Rosalia in Company, to Easter Island in 1770–1771.*—Hakluyt Soc., 2nd ser. no. 13. Cambridge, 1908.

GORDON, E. J. (1954): The Sumerian Proverb Collections: A Preliminary Report.—*Journ. Amer. Oriental Soc.,* Vol. 74, No. 2, pp. 82–85.

GRAY, E. F. (1930): *Leif Eriksson Discoverer of America A.D. 1003.*—London.

GRAYDON, J. J. (1952): Blood Groups and the Polynesians.—*Mankind,* Vol. IV, No. 8, pp. 329–39. Sydney.

GREENMAN, E. F. (1962): The Upper Palaeolithic and the New World.—*Current Anthropology,* Vol. III. Chicago.

GREGORY, H. E. (1927): The Geography of the Pacific.—*Problems of the Pacific,* Proc. 2nd Conf. Ist. Pac. Rel. Honolulu, Chicago.

GRETZER, W. (1914): *Die Schiffahrt im alten Peru vor der Entdeckung . . .*—Mitteil. Roemer-Museum, Hildesheim, No. 24. Hannover.

GROVE, D. C. (1976): Answer to B. J. Meggers in *American Anthropologist,* Vol. 78, pp. 634–37.

GUDGER, E. W. (1927): Wooden hooks used for catching sharks and *Ruvettus* in the South Seas; a study of their variation and distribution.—*Anthrop. Papers American Mus. Nat. Hist.,* Vol. XXVIII, Pt. 3.

GUPPY, H. B. (1906): *Observations of a Naturalist in the Pacific Between 1896 and 1899.* Vol. II of *Plant-Dispersal.*—London.

HADDON, A. C. (1918): Melanesian Influence in Easter Island.—*Folk-lore,* Vol. LXXX, No. 1, pp. 161–62. London.

HADDON, A. C., and HORNELL, J. (1936): *Canoes of Oceania.*—Vol. I of *The Canoes of Polynesia, Fiji, and Micronesia* by J. Hornell. B. P. Bishop Mus. Spec. Publ. No. 29. Honolulu.

HAGEN, V. W. VON (1939): *The Tsàtchela Indians of Western Ecuador.*—New York. Mus. Amer. Ind., Heye Foundation, Indian Notes and Monographs, No. 51. New York.

——(1949): *Ecuador and the Galápagos Islands.*—Oklahoma.

HAMMOND, N. (1977): The Earliest Maya.—*Scientific American,* March, pp. 116–133.

HANDY, E. S. C. (1927): Polynesian Religion.—*B. P. Bishop Mus. Bull.,* 34. Honolulu

——(1930a): Sources of Polynesian Culture.—*Hawaiian Annual for 1931.* Honolulu.

——(1930b): The problem of Polynesian origins.—*Occ. Papers B. P. Bishop Mus.,* Vol. IX, No. 8. Honolulu.

HARDEN, D. (1962): *The Phoenicians.*—Vol. 26 in *Ancient People and Places,* ed. by Dr G. Daniel. London.

HARMS, H. (1922): Übersicht der bisher in alt-peruanischen Gräbern gefundenen Pflanzenreste.—*Festschrift Eduard Seler . . . herausgegeben von W. Lehmann.* Stuttgart.

HEINE-GELDERN, R. VON (1932): Urheimat und früheste Wanderungen der Austroneisier.—*Anthropos,* Vol. XXVII.

——(1938): Die Osterinselschrift.—*Anthropos,* Vol. XXXIII.

HERVÉ, J. (1770): Narrative of the Expedition undertaken by order of His Excellency Don Manuel de Amat, Viceroy of Peru . . . to the Island of David in 1770.—*Hakluyt Soc.,* 2nd ser., no. 13. Cambridge, 1908.

HEYERDAHL, T. (1941): Did Polynesian Culture Originate in America?—*International Science,* Vol. I. New York.

——(1952): *American Indians in the Pacific: The theory behind the Kon-Tiki expedition.*—London.

——(1954): En Gjenoppdaget Inka-kunst. Guara-metoden som lar flåter krysse og jibbe uten ror eller styreåre.—*Teknisk Ukeblad,* Vol. 48. Oslo.

————(1958): *Aku-Aku. The Secret of Easter Island.*—(Orig. ed.: Oslo, 1957) Chicago.

————(1961): An Introduction to Easter Island.—Surface Artifacts.—General Discussion.—3 papers in: Heyerdahl and Ferdon (1961), pp. 21–90, 397–489, 493–526.

————(1965): The Statues of the Oipona *Me'ae,* with a Comparative Analysis of Possibly Related Stone Monuments. In: Heyerdahl and Ferdon (1965), pp. 123–51.

————(1974): *Fatu-Hiva: Back to Nature.*—London.

————(1976): *The Art of Easter Island.*—London.

HEYERDAHL, T., and FERDON, JR., E. N. (1961): *Archaeology of Easter Island. Reports of the Norwegian Archaeological Expedition to Easter Island and the East Pacific,* Vol. I.—Monogr. School American Research and Mus. New Mexico, no. 24, pt. 1, 1961. Santa Fe, N.M.

————(1965): *Miscellaneous Papers. Reports of the Norwegian Archaeological Expedition to Easter Island and the East Pacific,* Vol. II.—Monogr. School American Research and the Kon-Tiki Mus., no. 24, pt. 2, 1965. Santa Fe, N.M.

HEYERDAHL, T., and SKJÖLSVOLD, A. (1956): Archaeological Evidence of Pre-Spanish Visits to the Galápagos Islands.—*Mem. Soc. Amer. Arch.,* no. 12. Salt Lake City.

————(1965): Notes on the Archaeology of Pitcairn.—In: Heyerdahl and Ferdon (1965), pp. 3–7.

HILL-TOUT, C. (1898): Oceanic Origin of the Kwakiutl-Nootka and Salish Stocks of British Columbia and Fundamental Unity of Same, with Additional Notes on the Déné.—*Proc. Transact. Royal Soc. Canada,* 2nd ser., Vol. IV.

HILLERBRAND, W. (1888): *Flora of the Hawaiian Islands.*—Heidelberg.

HOLMES, W. H. (1919): *Handbook of Aboriginal American Antiquities,* pt. 1.—Smithsonian Inst. Bur. American Ethn. Bull. 60. Washington, D.C.

HOLTSMARK, A., and SEIP, D. A., translators (1942): *Snorres Kongesagaer.*—Oslo.

HOOD, S. (1971): *The Minoans: Crete in the Bronze Age.*—London.

HORNBOSTEL, E. VON (1930): Chinesische Ideogramme in America.—*Anthropos,* Vol. XXV.

HORNELL, J. (1931): South American Balsas: The Problem of their Origin.—*Mariner's Mirror,* Vol. XVII. Cambridge.

————(1945): Was there a pre-Columbian contact between the peoples of Oceania and S. America?—*Journ. Polynesian Soc.,* Vol. LIV.

————(1946): How Did the Sweet Potato Reach Oceania?—*Journ. Linnean Soc. of London, Botany,* Vol. LIII, no. 348. London.

HRDLIČKA, A. (1944): *Catalog of Human Crania in the U.S. National Museum Collections: Non-Eskimo People of the Northwest Coast, Alaska, and Siberia.*—Proc. U.S. National Mus. Vol. XCIV. Washington, D.C.

HUMBOLDT, A. DE (1810): *Vues des Cordillères et monuments des peuples indigènes de l'Amérique.*—Paris.

HUTCHINSON, J. B., SILOW, R. A., and STEPHENS, S. G. (1947): *The Evolution of Gossypium and Differentiation of the Cultivated Cottons.*—London, New York, Toronto.

HUTCHINSON, T. J. (1875): Anthropology of Prehistoric Peru.—*Jour. Roy. Anthrop. Inst.,* Vol. IV. London.

IMBELLONI, J. (1928): Einige kondrete Beweise für die ausserkontinentalen Beziehungen der Indianer Amerikas.—*Mitteil. Anthrop. Ges. Wien,* Vol. LVIII. Vienna.

———(1930): On the Diffusion in America of Patu Onewa, Okewa, Patu Paraoa, Miti, and Other Relatives of the Mere Family.—*Jour. Polynesian Soc.,* Vol. XXXIX, no. 4. New Plymouth, N.Z.

Izumi, S. and Sono, T. (1963): *Excavations at Kotosh, Peru 1960.*—Andes Report 2, The Univ. of Tokyo Scientific Expedition to the Andes, 1960. Tokyo.

Jacobsen, A. (1891): Nordwestamerikanischpolynesische Analogien.—*Globus,* Vol. LIX, No. II. Braunchweig.

Jakeman, M. W. (1950): The XXIX International Congress of Americanists.— *Bull. Brigham Young Univ.,* March. Salt Lake City.

Jaussen, T. (1893): *L'Île de Pâques. Historique—Ecriture et Répertoire des signes des tablettes ou bois d'Hibiscus Intellegents.*—Paris.

———(1894): L'Île de Paques. Historique et écriture.—Mémoire posthume rédigé par Ildefonse Alazard D'après les notes laissés par le prélat.—*Bull. Géogr. Hist. et Descriptive,* no. 2, pp. 240–270. Paris.

Johanson, D. C. (1976): Ethiopia Yields First "Family" of Early Man.—*The National Geographic Magazine,* Vol. 150, No. 6, Dec.

Joyce, T. A. (1912): *South American Archaeology.*—New York.

———(1913): The Weeping God.—In: *Essays and Studies presented to William Riedgway . . . ,* pp. 365–75. Cambridge.

Juan, G., and Ulloa, A. de (1748): *Relación histórica del viaje a la América Meridional.*—4 vols. Madrid.

Karageorgis, V. (1969): *The Ancient Civilization of Cyprus.*—New York.

Karsten, R. (1938): *Inkariket och dess kultur i det forna Peru.*—Helsinki.

Kerchove de Denerghem, O. de (1878): *Les Palmiers: histoire iconographique, géographie, paléontologie, botanique, description, culture, emploi, etc.*— Paris.

Knoche, W. (1912): Vorläufige Bemerkung über die Entstehung der Standbilder auf der Osterinsel.—*Zeitschrift f. Ethnologie,* Vol. 44, pp. 873–77. Berlin.

———(1925): *Die Osterinsel. Eine Zusammenfassung der chilenischen Osterinselexpedition des Jahres 1911.*—Conception.

Knorozov, J. V. (1964b): Recorded statements at Izvestija's Round Table Conference, August 10, 1964, in "Kon-Tiki plyl ne zrja."—*Izvestija,* Aug. 12, 1964, p. 4. Moscow.

Knudsen, K. (1963): Traces of Reed Boats in the Pacific.—*The American Neptune,* Vol. XXIII, No. 1. Salem, Mass.

Kolsrud, O., ed. (1913): *Diplomatarium Norvegicum,* Oldbreve til Kundskab om Norges indre og ydre forhold . . . i Middelalderen.—Christiania [Oslo].

Kramer, S. N. (1944): *Sumerian Mythology; A Study of Spiritual and Literary Achievements in the Third Millennium B.C.*—Philadelphia.

———(1963): Dilmun; Quest for Paradise.—*Antiquity,* Vol. 37, No. 146, pp. 111–115.

Kroeber, A. L. (1944): Peruvian Archaeology in 1942.—*Viking Fund. Publ. Anthrop.,* 4. New York.

La Pérouse, J. F. G. de (1797): *A Voyage Round the World Performed In the Years 1785, 1786, 1787, and 1788 . . .*—2 vols. and atlas. (Orig. ed.: Paris, 1797.) London, 1798.

LAS CASAS, B. DE (1559): *Historia de las Indias.*—Colección de Documentos In-
éditos para la Historia de España. Madrid, 1876.
LAVACHERY, H. (1935): La Mission Franco-Belge dans l'Île de Pâques.—*Bull.
Soc. Royale de Géogr. d'Anvers,* Vol. LV, pp. 313–61. Antwerp.
———(1936): Easter Island, Polynesia.—*Ann. Rpt. Bd. of Regents Smithsonian
Inst.,* pp. 391–96. Washington, D.C.
———(1939): *Les Petroglyphes de l'Île de Pâques.*—2 vols. Antwerp.
———(1965): Thor Heyerdahl et le Pacifique.—*Journ. Soc. Océanistes,* Vol.
XXI, No. 21, pp. 151–59. Paris.
LEICHT, H. (1944): *Indianische Kunst und Kultur. Ein Jahrtausend im Reiche
der Chimu.*—Zurich.
LESCALLIER, M. (1791): *Traité pratique du gréement des vaisseaux et autres
bâtiments de mer.*—Vol. I. Paris.
LEVISION, M., WARD, R. G., and DEBB, J. W. (1973): *The Settlement of Polyne-
sia: A Computer Simulation.*—Canberra.
LHOTE, H. (1958): *Die Felsbilder Der Sahara.*—(Orig. title: A la découverte
des fresques du Tassili.) Würzburg, Wien.
LINTON, R. (1923): *The Material Culture of the Marquesas Islands.*—B. P.
Bishop Mus. Memoirs, Vol. VIII, No. 5, Honolulu.
LIZARRAGA, R. DE (1560–1602): *Descripción de las Indias: Crónica sobre el An-
tiguo Perú* . . .—Los Pequeños Grandes Libros de Historia Americana,
Ser. 1, Vol. 12. Lima, 1946.
LOTHROP, S. K. (1932): Aboriginal navigation off the west coast of South Amer-
ica.—*Journ. Royal Anthrop. Inst.,* Vol. LXII, July–Dec., pp. 229–56. Lon-
don.
LUTZ, H. F. (1927): Neo-Babylonian Administrative Documents from Erech.—
Univ. California Publ. Semitic Philol., Vol. 9, No. 1, pp. 1–115.
MALLOWAN, M. E. L. (1965): *Early Mesopotamia and Iran.*—London.
MALO, D. (1898): *Hawaiian Antiquities.*—B. P. Bishop Mus. Spec. Publ. No. 2.
Honolulu, 1951. (Transl. from Hawaiian by Dr N. B. Emerson 1808. 1st ed.
Wellington 1903.)
MARKHAM, C. R. (1911): *The Incas of Peru.*—London.
MARTIUS, C. F. P. DE (1823–50): *Historia Naturalis Palmarum.* 3 Vols. Munich.
MATSON, G. A., LEVINE, P., and SCHRADER, H. F. (1946): *Anthropological Ap-
plication of the Blood Groups.*—Dept. Bacteriology, Univ. Utah Medical
School. Salt Lake City.
MEANS, P. A. (1931): *Ancient Civilizations of the Andes.*—New York, London.
———(1942): Pre-Spanish Navigation Off the Andean Coast.—*American Nep-
tune,* Vol. II, No. 2.
MEGGERS, B. J. (1975): The Transpacific Origin of Mesoamerican Civilization:
A Preliminary Review of the Evidence and Its Theoretical Implications.—
American Anthropologist, Vol. 77, No. 1, March.
———(1976): Yes if by Land, No if by Sea: The Double Standard in Interpreting Cultural Similarities.—Answer to D. C. Grove in *American Anthropologist,* Vol. 78, pp. 637–39.
MERRILL, E. D. (1920): Comments on Cook's Theory as to the American Origin and prehistoric Polynesian Distribution of certain economic Plants, especially Hibiscus tiliaceus Linnaeus.—*Philippine Journ. Science,* Vol. XVII.
Manila. (Reprinted in: Merrill 1946.)
———(1937): Domesticated Plants in relation to the diffusion of culture.—
In: *Early Man.*—Philadelphia.

————(1946) Merrilleana: A selection from the general writings of Elmer Drew Merrill.—*Chronica Botanica*, Vol. X, Nos. 3–4.

————(1950): Observations on Cultivated Plants with Reference to Certain American Problems.—*Ceiba*, Vol. I, No. 1. Tegucigalpa, Honduras.

————(1954): *The Botany of Cook's Voyages and Its Unexpected Significance in Relation to Anthropology, Biography and History.*—Waltham.

MÉTRAUX, A. (1938): The proto-Indian script and the Easter Island tablets.—*Anthropos,* Vol. XXXIII.

————(1940): *Ethnology of Easter Island.*—B. P. Bishop Mus. Bull. 160. Honolulu.

MOERENHOUT, J. A. (1837): *Voyagers aux îles du Grand Océan.* 2 vols. Paris.

MOLINA, CHRISTÓVAL DE (ca. 1570–84): *The Fables and Rites of the Yncas.*—Hakluyt Soc., Vol. LXVIII. London, 1873.

MONTELL, G. (1929): *Dress and Ornaments in Ancient Peru. Archaeological and Historical Studies.* Diss, Gothenburg.

MONTESINOS, FERNANDO (1642): *Memorias antiquas historiales del Perú.*—Ed.: P. A. Means. London, 1920.

MORELL, B., JR. (1832): *A Narrative of Four Voyages to the South Sea, . . .*—New York.

MORGAN, A. E. (1946): *Nowhere was Somewhere.*—New York.

MORRIS, E. H., CHARLOT, J., and MORRIS, A. A. (1931): *The Temple of the Warriors at Chitzen Itza, Yucatan.*—Carnegie Inst. Wash. Publ. No. 406, 2 vols. Washington, D.C.

MOURANT, A. E. (1954): *The Distribution of Human Blood Groups.*—Blackwell Scientific Publ. Oxford.

MULLOY, W. (1961): The Ceremonial Center of Vinapu.—The *Tupa* of Hiramoko.—2 papers in: Heyerdahl and Ferdon (1961), pp. 93–180, 323–28.

MURDOCK, G. P. (1949): Report on the Seventh Pacific Science Congress [1st Special Issue].—*New Zealand Science Rev.,* Vol. VII, Nos. 1–2.

MURPHY, R. C. (1941): The earliest Spanish advances southward from Panama along the West Coast of South America.—*Hispanic Amer. Hist. Rev.,* Vol. XXI. Durham, N.C.

NIBLACK, A. P. (1888): The Coast Indians of Southern Alaska and Northern British Columbia.—*Report of the National Museum of British Columbia 1888.*

NORDENSKIÖLD, E. (1931): Origin of the Indian Civilizations in South America. —*Comp. Ethnogr. Stud.* Vol. IX. Gothenburg.

OLIVIA, P. ANELLO (1631): *Histoire de Pérou.*—Paris 1857.

OLSON, R. L. (1927–29): *Adze, Canoe, and House Types of the Northwest Coast.*—Univ. Washington Publ. Anthrop. 2. Seattle.

OPPENHEIM, A. L. (1954): The Seafaring Merchants of Ur.—*Journ. Amer. Oriental Soc.* Vol. 74, No. 1, pp. 6–17.

ORCUTT, P. D. (1953): A Stone Carving on the Galápagos.—*American Antiquity,* Vol. XVIII, No. 3, January, p. 270. Salt Lake City.

ORTIZ, O. (1964): El Matá: Un Instrumento Litico Pascuense y Sus Problemas. —*Apartado del Boletín de la Universidad de Chile,* Nos. 53–54, Nov.–Dec., pp. 101–7.

OVIEDO, G. F. DE (1535–48): *Historia general y natural de las Indias, islas y tierra-firme del mar océano.*—4 vols. Madrid, 1855.

PACHACUTI YAMQUI SALCAMAYHUA, J. (1620): *An Account of the Antiquities of Piru.*—Hakluyt Soc., Vol. XLVIII. London, 1873.

PALMER, J. L. (1870): A Visit to Easter Island, or Rapa Nui, in 1868.—*Royal Geogr. Soc. Journ.*, Vol. XIV, pp. 108–119. London.

PARIS, F. E. (1841–43): *Essai sur la construction navale des peuples Extra-Européens.*—Paris.

PETRI, H. (1936): Die Geldformen der Südsee, 1–2.—*Anthropos,* Vol. XXXI. Vienna.

PINART, A. (1878): Voyage à l'Île de Paques.—*Le Tour du Monde,* Vol. XXXVI, pp. 225–240. Paris.

PIZARRO, P. (1571): *Relación del Descubrimiento y Conquista de los Reinos del Peru.*—Colección de Documentos ineditos para la Historia de España, Vol. V. Madrid, 1844. Translated into English and annotated by P. A. Means: *Relation of the Discovery and Conquest of the Kingdoms of Peru.* 2 vols. New York, 1921.

PLINUS GAIUS SECUNDUS (77): *Historia naturalis.*—37 books. (Various transl. from Latin incl. *Natural History,* ed. and transl. by H. Rackham *et al.,* Loeb Classical Library, London & Cambridge, Mass. 1969.)

POIRIER, J. (1953): L'élémend blond en Ploynésie et les migrations nordiques en Océanie et en Amérique.—*Société des Océanistes.* Paris.

POLACK, J. S. (1838): *New Zealand. Being a narrative of Travels and Adventures during a residence . . . 1831 and 1837.*—2 vols. London.

POMERANCE, L. (1970): *The Final Collapse of Santorini (Thera).*—*Studies in Mediterranean Archaeology,* Vol. XXVI. Gothenburg.

PORTER, D. (1815): *Journal of a Cruise made to the Pacific Ocean.*—Philadelphia.

PRAIN, D. (1895): An Account of the genus Argemone.—*Jour. Bot.,* Vol. XXXIII.

PRESCOTT, W. H. (1847): *History of the Conquest of Peru.*—2 vols. London.

QUIROS, P. F. DE (1609): *Narrative of the Second Voyage of the Adelantado Alvaro de Mendaña.*—Hakluyt Soc., 2nd ser., No. 14, Vol. I. London, 1904.

RAO, S. R. (1963): A "Persian Gulf" Seal from Lothal.—*Antiquity,* Vol. 37, No. 146, pp. 96–99.

REISCHEK, A. (1924): *Sterbende Welt.*—Leipzig.

RELACIÓN ANÓNYMA (1615): *Relación Anónyma, de los Costumbres Antiguos de los Naturales del Piru.*—Madrid, 1879.

RESCH, W. F. E. (1967): *Die Felsbilder Nubiens.*—Graz.

RIVET, P. (1928): Relations commerciales précolombiennes entre l'Océanie et Amérique.—*Festschrift P. W. Schmidt.* Vienna.

——— (1943): *Les origines de l'homme américain.*—Montreal.

ROCHEBRUNE, A. T. DE (1879): Recherches d'ethnographie botanique sur la flore des sépultures péruviennes d'Ancon.—*Actes Soc. Linn. Bordeaux,* 4th ser. Vol. III. Bordeaux.

ROGGEVEEN, M. J. (1722): *Extract from the Official Log of the Voyage of Mynheer Jacob Roggeveen, in the Ships Den Arend, Thienhove, and De Afrikannische Galey in 1721–22, in so far as it relates to the Discovery of Easter Island.*—Hakluyt Soc., 2nd ser. no. 13. Cambridge, 1908.

ROSS, A. S. C. (1936): Preliminary notice of some late eighteenth-century numerals from Easter Island.—*Man,* Vol. XXXVI, No. 120.

ROUSSEL, H. (1908): *Vocabulaire de la Langue de l'Ile-de-Paques ou Rapanui.*—Extract from Muséon, Nos. 2–3, pp. 159–254. Louvain.

ROUTLEDGE, K. S. (1919): *The Mystery of Easter Island.*—London.

ROWE, J. H. (1966): Diffusionism and Archaeology.—*American Antiquity*, Vol. XXXI, no. 3, pt. 1, January, pp. 334–37.

SÁAMANOS, J. DE (1526): *Relación de los primeros descubrimientos de Francisco Pizarro y Diego Almagro . . .*—Colección de Documentos Inéditos para la Historia de España, Vol. V. Madrid, 1844.

ST. JOHNSTON, T. R. (1921): *The Islanders of the Pacific Or The Children of the Sun.*—New York.

SALONEN, A. (1939): Die Wasserfahrzeuge in Babylonien nach sumerischak-kadishen Quellen.—*Studia Orientalia Edidit Societas Orientalis Fennica*, Vol. VIII, pp. 1–199. Helsinki.

————(1942): Nautica Babyloniaca.—*Studia Orientalia Edidit Societas Orientalis Fennica*, Vol. XI, pp. 1–118. Helsinki.

SARMIENTO DE GAMBOA, P. (1572): *History of the Incas.*—Hakluyt Soc., 2nd ser., Vol. XXII. Cambridge, 1907.

SAUER, C. O. (1950): Cultivated Plants of South and Central America.—In: *Handbook of South American Indians.* Vol. VI. Smithsonian Inst. Bur. Amer. Ethn., Bull. 143. Washington, D.C.

SAYCE, R. U. (1933): *Primitive Arts and Crafts. An Introduction to the Study of Material Culture.*—Cambridge.

SCHURMANN, E. (1927): *Samoa.*—Konstanz.

SEEMANN, B. (1865–73): *Flora Vitiensis.*—London.

SHAND, A. (1894): The Moriori people of Chatham Islands.—*Journ. Polynesian Soc.,* Vol. III. New Plymouth, N.Z.

SHAPIRO, H. L. (1940): The Physical Relationships of the Easter Islanders. In: Métraux (1940).

SHARP, B. (1704): *The dangerous Voyage, and bold Attempts of Capt. Bartholomew Sharp . . . , The History of the Buccaneers of America,* Vol. 2, T. 4. London.

SHARP, B. (1898): Rock Inscriptions in Kauai, Hawaiian Islands.—*Proc. Acad. Natural Science,* 1898. Philadelphia.

SHORTLAND, E. (1856): *Traditions and Superstitions of the New Zealanders.*—London.

SIMMONS, R. T., GRAYDON, J. J., SEMPLE, N. M., and FRY, E. I. (1955): A blood group genetical survey in Cook Islanders, Polynesia, and comparisons with American Indians.—*American Journ. Anthrop.* New Series, Vol. XIII, No. 4, Dec. Philadelphia.

SKINNER, H. D. (1931): On the Patu Family and its occurrence beyond New Zealand.—*Journ. Polynesian Soc.,* Vol. XL, No. 4. New Plymouth, N.Z.

SKJÖLSVOLD, A. (1961): Dwellings of Hotu Matua.—House Foundations (*Hare Paenga*) in Rano Raraku.—Site E-2, a Circular Stone Dwelling, Anakena. —The Stone Statues and Quarries of Rano Raraku.—4 papers in: Heyerdahl and Ferdon (1961), pp. 273–86, 291–93, 295–303, 339–79.

SKOGMAN, C. (1854): *Fregatten Eugenies Resa Omkring Jorden Aren 1851–53.* —2 vols. Stockholm.

SKOTTSBERG, C. (1920): Notes on a Visit to Easter Island.—*The Natural History of Juan Fernandez and Easter Island,* Vol. I. Uppsala.

————(1934): Le peuplement des iles pacifiques du Chili.—*Soc. de Biogéogr.,* Vol. IV. Paris.

————(1956): Derivation of the Flora and Fauna of Juan Fernandez and Easter Island.—*The Natural History of Juan Fernandez and Easter Island,* Vol. I, pp. 193–438. Uppsala, 1920–56.

——(1957): Påskön.—*Göteborgs Handels- och Sjöfarts- Tidning,* Oct. 7. Gothenburg.

SMITH, A. L. (1940): The Corbeled Arch in the New World.—*The Maya and Their Neighbors,* pp. 202–21. New York.

SMITH, C. S. (1961): A Temporal Sequence Derived from Certain Ahu.—Two Habitation Caves.—The Maunga Ahuhepa House Site.—Tuu-ko-ihu Village.—The Poike Ditch.—Radio Carbon Dates from Easter Island.—6 papers in: Heyerdahl and Ferdon (1961), pp. 181–219, 257–71, 277–86, 287–89, 385–91, 393–96.

SMITH, S. P. (1910): *Hawaiki: The Original Home of the Maori.*—Wellington, N.Z.

SPILBERGEN, J. VAN (1619): *Speculum Orientalis Occidentalis que Indiae navigation 1614–18.*—Leiden.

STEVENSON, W. B. (1825): *A Historical and Descriptive Narrative of Twenty Years' Residence in South America.*—3 vols. London.

STEWARD, J. H., ed. (1949): The Comparative Ethnology of South American Indians.—*Handbook of South American Indians,* Vol. V. Smithsonian Inst. Bur. Amer. Ethn., Bull. 143. Washington, D.C.

STEWART, T. D. (1943): Skeletal Remains from Paracas, Peru.—*American Journ. Phys. Anthrop.,* Vol. I.

STOKES, J. F. G. (1932): Spaniards and the sweet potato in Hawaii and Hawaiian-American Contacts.—*American Anthrop.,* Vol. XXXIV, No. 4.

——(1934): Japanese cultural influences in Hawaii.—*Proc. Fifth Pacific Congr. Canada 1933,* Vol. IV. Toronto.

STONOR, C. R., and ANDERSON, E. (1949): Maize among the Hill Peoples of Assam.—*Ann. Missouri Bot. Gard.,* Vol. XXXVI, No. 3.

STOUT, D. B. (1948): *Handbook of South American Indians,* Vol. IV.—Smithsonian Inst. Bur. Amer. Ethn., Bull, 143, ed. J. H. Steward. Washington, D.C.

SULLIVAN, L. R. (1922): A Contribution to Tongan Somatology.—*B. P. Bishop Mus Mem.,* Vol. IX, No. 2. Honolulu.

——(1924a): Race Types in Polynesia.—*American Anthrop.,* Vol. XXVI, No. 1.

——(1924b): The Racial Diversity of the Polynesian Peoples.—*Rept. Australas. Ass. Adv. Science,* Wellington Meeting 1923. Wellington, N.Z.

SWANTON, J. R. (1905): *Haida Texts and Myths.*—Washington, D.C.

TAUTAIN, DR. (1897): Notes sur les constructions et monuments des Marquises. —*L'Anthropologie,* Vol. VIII. Paris.

TESSMANN, G. (1930): *Die Indianer Nordost-Perus.*—Hamburg.

THOMSON, W. J. (1899): *Te Pito te Henua, or Easter Island.*—Rept. U.S. National Mus. for year ending June 30, 1889.—Washington, D.C.

THORSBY, E., COLOMBANI, J., DAUSSETT, J., FIGUEROA, J., and THORSBY, A. (1973): HL-A, Blood Group and Serum Type Polymorphism of Natives on Easter Island.—*Histocompatibility Testing 1972.* Copenhagen.

TROTTER, M. (1943): Hair from Paracas Indian Mummies.—*American Journ. Phys. Anthrop.,* Vol. I.

UHLE, M. (1922): *Fundamentos étnicos y arqueología de Arica y Tacna.*—Quito.

VALVERDE, V. (1879): *Relación del sitio del Cuzco y principio de las guerras civiles del Perú . . . 1535 a 1539.*—Colección de Libros Españoles Raros o Curiosos, Vol. XIII. Madrid.

VANCOUVER, G. (1798): *A Voyage of Discovery to the North Pacific Ocean and Round the World . . . in the Years 1790–95.*—3 vols. London.

VOSS, J. C. (1926): *The Venturesome Voyages of Capt. Voss.*—London.

WAFER, L. (1699): A New Voyage and Description of the Isthmus of America.—In: Dampier 1729. Vol. III.

WECKLER, J. E. (1943): *Polynesian Explorers of the Pacific.*—Smithsonian Inst. War. Background Stud., no. 6. Washington, D.C.

WHITAKER, T. W. and BIRD, J. B. (1949): Identification and Significance of the Cucurbit Materials from Huaca Prieta, Peru.—*Amer. Mus. Novitates,* No. 1426. New York.

WHITE, J. (1889): *The Ancient History of the Maori, His Mythology and Traditions.*—4 vols. London.

WILSON, D. (1862): *Prehistoric Man. Researches into the Origin of Civilization in the Old and New Worlds,* 2 vols. London.

———(1970): *The Vikings and Their Origins.*—London.

WILSON, J. (1799): A Missionary Voyage to the Southern Pacific Ocean, 1796–1798. London.

XERES, F. DE (1534): A True Account of the Province of Cuzco.—Part I of *Reports on the Discovery of Peru.* Hakluyt Soc. London, 1872.

YACOVLEFF, E. and HERRERA, F. L. (1934); El mundo vegetal de los antiguos peruanos.—*Rev. Mus. Nacional,* Vol. III, No. 3. Lima.

———(1935): El mundo vegetal de los antiguos peruanos, (Continuación).—*Rev. Mus. Nacional,* Vol. IV, No. 1, Lima.

ZÁRATE, A. DE (1555): *A History of the Discovery and Conquest of Peru: Books I–IV Translated out of the Spanish by Thomas Nicholas Anno 1581.*—London, 1933.

INDEX

Abraham (patriarch), 367, 369, 370
Adam of Bremen: *Geography of the Northern Lands,* 143
Africa, 29, 66, 76, 237, 352; Central, 14; desert, 355; migrations, 27; North, 28, 50, 65, 66; West, 67
Afro-Asiatic civilizations, 375, 384, 397
Age Unlimited, voyage, 40, *ill.* 42–43
Agriculture, 86, 88, 110, 161–62; America–Polynesia, 214–15, 232; botanists' theories, 241. *See* Culture plants
Ahmed Joseph, 11
Aku-Aku, v
Alaska, 44, 45, 54, 397; Asia land bridge, 59, 60
Alcohol, 161–62
Aleutians, 38, 48, 54
Alexander III, Pope, 141–42
Algeria, 6, 8, 20
Alonso de Mesa, 189
Alsar, Vitale, 40, 42–43, 53, 55
Amazon River, 28, 79–80
America: aboriginal, 5–6, 59–60, 70, 71, 73–74, 153ff., 382, common trunk theory, 382, milestones, 371; area nearest Polynesia, 215; civilizations: aboriginal, 70, chronology, 382–83, first, 119 (*see* Olmecs), two main sources, 69; culture "bringers," 372 (*see* Culture "spreaders"): discovery, 4 (*see* Columbus, Christopher); evolution, 63; first people, 59ff., 63, 129; high culture, 80, 378,
383, areas, 89, 162, 214, 341; Indians, 25, 51, 62, 70, 78ff., 93, name, 145, origin, ix; influence, spread of, 77; islands nearest, settling, 257ff.; isolation, 388 (*see* Isolation); Northwest Coast, 165, 174, 176, 319–20, 395; Polynesia, 162ff.–83, 395, watercraft, 31; Oceanian parallels, 174; oceans as barrier, 64 (*see* Isolation); Pacific navigation, 37ff.; Polynesia, contact, 229ff., 238ff., 281; pre-Columbian, 59ff.–75, 128ff., 138, Mediterranean, 61, stimulators, 69, use of sail, 223 (*see also* Pre-Columbian entries); sea routes to/from, 48–55, *ill.* 49; steppingstones to, 48ff.; Viking sites, 137. *See also* New World, Pre-Columbian entries, Spain *and* South America
American Anthropologist, 379
American Indians in the Pacific, 153
Americanists, 213, 214, 215, 257, 378, 383
American Museum of Natural History, The, 170, 259, 345
Amiet, P., 9, 362
Anastasius IV, Pope, 140–41
Anderson, E., 75, 232
Andes, 23, 53, 80
Animals, 73–74, 181, 331, 393, *ill.* 72; ceramic, 89–90; dogs, 160, 394; felines, 331; origin evidence, 159–60; royal symbols, 90

Antarctic: Current, 275; -globe, *ill.* 339

Anthropology(ists), 4, 6, 28–29, 41, 47, 59, 99, 164, 204ff., 229, 233; American standards, 61; biases, 213–16, disproving (*see Kon-Tiki*); -botany, 279; branches, 30; doctrines, 241; exact science, growth, 61; genetics, 157ff., 247; isolationism-diffusionism controversy, 74; navigation, primitive (*see under* Navigation); Pacific, 214, 215; physical, 96, 100, 155–56, 157, 322–23; problem, most controversial, 152–53; turning point (1492), 64

Antipodes, 34–35, 151

Arabian Gulf, 352, 354

Arabian Peninsula, 8, 9

Arabs, 51, 84, 123, 354; marsh (Iraq), 3, 24

Arappa, 352, 354

Arca, Carlos Caravedo, 40, 42–43

Archaeology(ists), 8, 11, 29, 45, 50, 53, 63–64, 82, 100, 105, 118, 119, 122, 137, 158–59, 211, 215, 226, 258–59, 270, 287, 292, 327, 357, 365–66; dating (radiocarbon), 80–81, 100, 137, 302, 312, 332, 347, 352, 360, 361; "Diffusionism and . . . ," 54ff.; evidence, 98, of Pre-Columbian use of sail, 223; future, 397; Galápagos, 259ff.; Heyerdahl Easter Island expedition, 292ff.; New World, 382ff.; purpose, 383; riddles, 290; stratified, 297ff., 311, 323, 347, 390; underwater, 29

Architecture, v, 29, 86, 114, 163, 327; marine, 4, 66, 209; megalithic, 80, 81, 105, 353

Arctic, 48, 54, 133, 344, 397

Argentina, 63

Aristophanes, 74

Art, 5, 6, 8, 10, 20, 118, 119, 122–23, 328, 330–31, 341–44, 347, 353, 355; aboriginal, 29; archaeological, 372–73; ceramic 89–90, 172–73, 183, 218, 265ff.–76, 350; frescoes, 122; historians, 342; iconographic, 30, 218; mnemonic, 9; parallels, 34; pre-Columbian, 93, 117–18; prehistoric, 350, 352; religious, 9, 90, 331, 343; rock carvings, 6, 8; symbolic, 90, 331, 341–42. *See also* Easter Island *and under* country

Artifacts, 71–73, 170ff., 219ff., 344–46, 395; *ill.* 72, 221

Art of Easter Island, The, 292

Asia, 27, 31, 54, 161–62, 352, 367; –Alaska, land bridge, 59, 60; culture elements, 155; –Easter Island migration theory, 310ff.; Europe: expansion to, 145, parallels, 162–63; migration routes, 44, 153ff.; Pacific explorations, 37ff.; plants, 279; Polynesia, 151–84: migration routes, 153ff., steppingstones, 164–65; South America, 34; Southeast, 54, 162, 164, 242, –Central America cultures, theories, 53

Asia Minor, 10, 65–66, 70, 84ff., 351

Assyria(ns), 10, 67–68, 366, 367, 368; version of the flood, 368–69

Astronomy(ers), 66, 68, 81–82, 91, 129, 144–45, 300, 371, 373, 387; Easter Island, 304, 309, 327

Aswan Dam, 8

Atlantic Ocean, v, 4, 22, 84–92, 364; castastrophe, 360–61; crossings, 71, 364, 397 (*see Ra I and II*); dogma, ix; Europeans' belief about, 66; Heyerdahl experiments, 12 (*see* crossings); meaning, 71, 120; problem: 57–148: Columbus-Vikings, 127–48, isolationists vs. diffusionists, 59–92,

pre-Columbus bearded gods,
93–125
Atlantis, 81, 359–60, 367–68
Australia, 38, 39, 40, 41, 52, 94, 157,
210; settlement, 152
Aymara Indians, 14–16, 92, 97
Aztecs, v, 64, 68, 71, 93, 102,
110–12, 128, 371, 396; Conquest,
93, 110, 372; culture hero, ill.
121; empire, size, 110; origin, 67,
70, 372; tradition, 114. See
Montezuma and Quetzalcoatl

Babylonians, 9–10, 367
Bachelor's Delight, 263–64
Baffin Island, 48
Baghdad Museum, 9, 351
Bahrain (Dilmun), 8, 21, 352,
368–70; civilization, 352–55, 365;
importance, 367
Baker, J. C., 251
Balboa, Father Miguel Cabello de,
35, 191–93, 206, 208, 218, 260
Baleares (islands), 72
Balfour, H., 322
Balsa rafts, v, 55, 211, 254, 269ff.,
378; aboriginal, 263, 275; balsa
forests, 192, 213; building
principles, 217, ill. 212;
characteristics, 204–18, 260, 269;
drawings, 223–24; experiments,
39–41, Heyerdahl, 216–18; guara,
55, 188ff., 210–11, 218–28, 260,
267, 287, ill. 221; Inca type, 46,
188; judgments of, 213ff., (see
Kon-Tiki); migrations, 192ff.;
navigation, 201–28, 323, secret,
226, ill. 227; range, 245, 269–70,
322. See Kon-Tiki and
Watercraft
Banana (plantain). See Culture
plants
Bancroft, H. H., 169
Bandelier, A. F., 106
Banks, Sir Joseph, 282
Barbados, 14
Barbeau, M., 175–76

Barrau, J., 230, 254
Basra, 24
Beauchesne-Gouin, M. de, 264–65
Belgium, 290, 296
Bella Coola Indians, 168
Bennett, W. C., 118, 211, 307–8
Benzoni, Girolamo, 207, 218
Berbers, 84, 374
Berlanga, Bishop Tomás de, 79–80,
260–62, 265, 272, 388
Bernice P. Bishop Museum, 246,
249
Bertoni, M. S., 248
Best, E., 94, 169; The Maori Canoe,
203
Betanzos, Juan de, 192, 335
Betel chewing, 182
Beyer, H. O., 163
Bibby, G., 265
Bible, the, 20–21, 357–58; the flood,
367–69
Bird, Junius, 236
Blacks, 198, 199–200
Blaxland, George, 210
Boas, Franz, ix, 165; Kwakiutl
Tales, 178
Boats. See Ships
Bochica (or Xue), 109–10
Bolivia, 80, 213, 328
Botany(ists), 22, 30, 74ff., 161,
229–30, 232ff., 239, 246, 279, 281,
302; America–Polynesia contact
evidence, 229ff., 242ff.; ethno-,
74, 78, 232, 236, 238–40, 241ff.,
252, 254, founder, 231, 279–80; as
evidence of origin, 74–76, 159;
isolationists, 79, 231; Pacific, 241,
279
Bounty (ship), 258
Brazil, 28, 29, 54, 226
Brinton, 111, 112, 113ff.
British Columbia, 44, 46–47, 170
British Museum, 263, 304, 309, 350,
351, 382
Bronze, 161; Age, 82, 89
Brown, F. B. H., 239, 246–48
Brown, J. M., 162, 169, 173

Buck, Sir Peter, ix, 159–60, 163, 179, 199, 236, 241, 313; "Introduction to Polynesian Anthropology," 215; reputation, 298; *Vikings of the Sunrise,* 298
Buduma boatbuilders, 14
Bugge, Alexander, 141
Burial customs, 10–11, 25, 29, 71–73, 85–86, 89–90, 103, 179, 310, *ill.* 72; cremation, 300–1, 309, 316, 332; Easter Island, 332–33. *See* Mummification
Byam, G., 213
Byblos, 20, 81

Cacaxtla, 120, 122
Cadiz, 6, 354; Museum, 6, 71, 376
Cairo, papyrus plantation, 22
Calendars, 66, 70, 81–82, 91, 94, 113, 115, 371, 394; zero year, 373
California, 116, 345
Cambridge University, 382
Canaanites, 351, 367, 375
Canary Current, 28, 50, 69, 74, 83, 103–4, 124, 128, 371, 374, 385; ends, 71, 84ff.; traffic evidence, 374
Canary Islands, 51, 103, 319, 371; Caribbean route, 51; discovery, 123, 124; Guanches, 51, 103, 123–25; Mediterranean parallels, 375–76
Cannibalism, 176
Canoes, 4–5, 10, 44, 47, 155ff., 168–69, 174, 179, 350, 393, 395; dugout, 25, 163; Polynesian, 32, 41, 55, 168; seagoing, 31, 168
Cape Verde Islands, 79
Caravels, 31, 35, 38, 51, 205; routes, 41, 54
Caribbean Islands, 14, 28, 145
Carolines (islands), 37, 54
Carroll, Dr. A., 337
Carter, G. F., 229, 232, 238, 241, 249–50, 252
Carthage, 67
Cartographers, 262–63. *See* Maps

Castro, W., 203
Catastrophes, 82–83, 357ff., 367, 370
Catholic Church (Vatican), 138, 140ff. *See* Christianity
Celeusta, voyage, 40, *ill.* 42–43
Central America, 53, 63, 80
Ceylon, 23, 352, 354
Chad, 14, 15
Charles III, King of Spain, 265
Charles V, King of Spain, 205, 219
Charlot, J., 122
Chatham Islands, 31, 160, 202, 320, 345, 392–93
Chavín culture, 63, 70
Chervin, A., 101
Chichén Itzá, 91, 114, 122–23
Chile, 6, 37, 41, 63, 162, 262, 272, 295
Chimu Indians, 70, 101, 108, 193
China, 35, 41, 47, 131, 279, 366; Sea, 41; Silk Road, 131
Christian, F. W., 161, 199, 258
Christianity, 127, 187, 313, 325, 326, 343, 367; concept of earth, 144; spread, 130ff.
Chubb, L. J., 283
Circumcision, 86, 122, 394
Cities, 355, 357; oldest, 81
Civilization(s), 6, 9, 27–28, 54, 60, 67–68, 352, 361; concepts, transmission of, 66–67; evolution, 360–61, 370ff.; first, 8; growth, requisites, 353–54; lost, 116; milestones, 370–71; on islands, reasons for, 354–55; oldest source, 352; pre-European, 67ff., 84–92; true, sign of, 337. *See also* Mediterranean *and* Pre-Columbian entries
Climate, 63, 64, 98
Coasts: changes, 355–57; water, fear of, 31–33
Cobo, Bernabe, 208, 218
Coconuts: Heyerdahl experiment, 281. *See under* Culture plants
Cocos Island, 275ff., 389–90; discovery, 277; geography,

276–77, 286–87; name, 278, 389;
settlement, 257, 258, 285
Coe, M. D., 276–77, 287
Collier, D., 378, 381
Collins, J. L., 248
Colnett, James, 265–66
Colombani, J., 167
Colombia, 80, 109–10, 283
Colonization, 66–67, 71, 108, 120,
182, 243, 266–68, 354, 363, 374;
European, pre-Columbian, 145;
Norse, 136–38
Columbus, Christopher, 4, 35, 38,
48, 51–52, 65, 66, 123, 144–48,
206, 231; accomplishments,
128ff.; America, 66, discovery,
144, 145; beliefs, 144–47, 364;
characteristics, 135, 144ff.; price,
146–47; rivals, 129–30; route,
50–52, 61, 68, 71, 84, 95, 145ff.,
ill. 49; son, 144, 147; and
Vikings, 127–48; voyages, 252,
279
Commonwealth Serum
Laboratories, 157
Concepts, transmission of, 66–67
Congressional Record, 128
Conquistadors, 61, 63, 70, 93,
104–6, 110, 118, 129, 188, 189,
190, 386
Constantinople, 140
Cook, Captain James, 3, 38, 39,
155–56, 164–66, 171, 174, 185,
186, 202, 230, 242, 248; aides,
281–82; "first" botanist, 253;
death, 186; Easter Island, 294;
theories, 251
Cook, E. I., 308, 321, 324
Cook, O. F., 161–62, 232, 239, 241,
280, 287
Cook, R. C., 232, 239, 241
Cook Islands, 37, 179
Coral atolls, 151, 159–60
Corfu, 6, 22, 352
Cortez, Hernando, 37, 65, 66, 71,
93, 110–11, 119, 372; Carta
Segunda, 110

Costa Rica, 283, 285, 286
Cotton (plant). See under Culture
plants
Couffer, J. D., 270
Crete, 6, 70, 81, 82, 84ff., ill. 10; art,
22, 29, 352; collapse, 358, 361
Croft, T., 336
Cuba, 113, 279
Cultural parallels, 54, 61–63, 64ff.,
76, 80, 92, 94ff., 122, 123, 128,
176, 251, 277ff., 282–83, 301ff.,
376–77, 383–85, 392; expansion
period (dates), 84; explanations,
64, 69 (see Diffusion); list,
84–92; as proof of contact, 83–84.
See also under Mediterranean,
Old World and Polynesia
Culture, 60ff., 84, 175, 360–61, 375,
381; bearers, 104ff., 116, 120 (see
also heroes); diffusion (see
Diffusion); elements, 163, 205,
215, 375, 392; environment
relationship, 68–69; heroes,
104ff., 109, 113, 114–16, 124,
177–78, 190, 192, 372–73, 384,
394, ill. 118–19, 121; isolation
(see Isolation); "retrogression,"
161; spread, 84, 355ff.;
"spreaders," 374, 375, 391, 396
(see Olmecs); origins, v, 353
Culture plants, 172, 181–82, 233ff.,
242ff.; banana, 78–80, 237;
coconuts, 234ff., 246, 250, 275–87,
389–90, 394; contact evidence,
73ff., 229ff., 242ff.; cotton, 76–78,
88, 109, 128, 181, 183, 237–38,
246ff., 275–76, 389, 394; early
navigators, 229–54; gourd,
235–46 passim; hibiscus, 239–41,
249; natural spread, 83, 283, 284;
origin evidence, 159; poppy,
249–50; reeds (see Reeds); rice,
242, 254; sweet potato (kumara),
230–51 passim, 394; taro, 251–52;
tobacco, 243–44
Cuna Indians, 110, 338
Currents, 28, 32, 34, 37–38, 39, 40,

44, 47–48, 50, 52, 60, 174, 215,
219, 241, 252–53, 261, 276, 279;
contemporary position on, 64;
marine life, 276. *See under* name
Cuzco, 104, 105, 107, 109, 191, 340
Cyprus, 6, 22, 84ff., 352, 361, *ill.* 7,
10

Dales, G. F., 8
Dampier, Captain, 277
Danube River, 28
Dausset, J., 167
Dawson, W. R., 103, 178
De Bisschop, Eric, 40, 41, 42–43,
53, 55
De Cadres, Captain, 193–94
De Candolle, A., 231, 234–35,
379–80: *Origin of Cultivated
Plants,* 231; thesis, 232, 236
Defoe, Daniel, 258
Degener, O., 248
De León, Cieza, 105–7, 189
Denmark, 127, 132, 137, 253, 265
Desert, spread of, 355
Dialogue (magazine), 3
Diffusion(ists), 70, 78, 80, 120, 250,
353, 354, 381, 388, 397;
archaeology, 64ff.; defined, 64ff.;
evidence of, 378; Isolationists,
59–92; "Theoretical Issues in the
Trans-Pacific Diffusion
Controversy," 62ff.; theories, 47,
94, 239, 373, 379–81, 385; Vienna
School, 41, 61; vs. independent
evolution, 376
Dixon, R. B., 155, 164, 165, 214–15,
320; "Contacts with America
Across the Southern Pacific,"
174, 175; "Problem of the Sweet
Potato in Polynesia," 233
Dogs, 73, 74, 210, 230, *ill.* 72
Dreyer, W., 171
Drift voyages, 45–47, 123
Dulcie Island, 258

Earth, 34, 47, 361; concepts of, 144,
146, 147, 364; circumnavigation,

38; seen from Antarctic, *ill.* 339
Easter Island, 35, 45, 52, 80, 94ff.,
172, 181–83, 195–98, 202, 245,
258, 259, 290ff., 319–48, 390–92;
America, contact evidence,
242–46, 254, 328–45; archaeology,
290, 295ff., 323, 337; art, 330,
341–45 (*see statues*); culture,
297, 301–2, 311–12, 321ff., high,
292ff., parallels, 392, sub-stratum,
322–23; discovery, 37, 97, 185,
187, 194, 198, 242, 292, 293, 296,
321; ethnology, 298, 302, 308,
323; fame, 305, 310, 390; flora,
245, 247, 328; genealogies, 317,
322, 347; Heyerdahl expedition,
276, 291ff.; kings, 310, 312–17,
338, 348; language, 323ff.,
335–40; legends, 312, 334;
location, 95, 290, 291–92, 335;
migration, theories, 310ff., 322ff.;
mystery, 293–95; name, 199, 291,
391; Polynesia, 201, 296, 316–17,
321, 326ff., 345–47; religion,
309–10, 314, 326ff., 347, *ill.* 329;
settlement, 94–97, 103, 295,
336–37, 388, 392, theories, 290ff.,
310–14; statues, 215, 289–317,
332, 334, 390; watercraft, 31,
202ff., 327ff., 352
Ecuador, 40, 41, 80, 109, 188, 192,
207, 213, 225, 257–58, 266,
378–81; art, 270–73; diffusion
center, 381, 385; Galápagos,
266–68, 276; Japan, 34
Egypt, 3, 6, 8, 9, 20, 22, 25, 29, 68,
70, 80, 81, 84ff., 91, 94ff., 124,
363–64; Alexandria library, 23,
210, 354, 364, 366; art, 6, 8, 9,
19–20, 25, 71, 123, 350;
civilization, 66, 352ff., 361, 362;
collapse, 82; cotton, 76ff. (*see
under* Culture plants); Hebrews,
357–58; Karnak, 103; papyrus,
22, 23–25; Pharaohs, 103, 124,
351, 363–64; pyramids, v, 10, 25,
ill. 87; ships, 6ff., 10ff., 16, 19–20,

24, 350–52, 363–64, *ill.* 5, 13; tombs, 10–11, 25, 103; Valley of the Kings, 85

Egyptologists, 14

Eirikson, Leif, 129ff., 136, 141, 145; discovery, 135ff.; route, 48–50, *ill.* 49

Eirik the Red, 132–38

Enchanted Islands, 262, 276

England, 48, 140, 174, 185, 213, 225, 235, 258, 290, 294; Galápagos, 262–64; Norway, 48, 144; Oxford, 258; pirates, 142–44, 262–66, 272; prehistoric, 353; Royal Geographical Society, 296; Royal Navy, 265; U.S., 266. *See* British Museum

Englert, Father Sebastian, 290, 311, 323ff., 340

Environment-culture relationship, 68–69

Equator, 38, 164, 235, 276; concept, 34; navigation, 228

Equatorial Counter Current, 34, 39, 40, 41, 53–55, 276

Eratosthenes, 23, 364, 366

Eskimos, 133, 319

Estrada, Emilio, 226, 378

"Eternal City, The," 67, 356. *See* Lixus

Ethiopia, 22, 23

Ethno-botany. *See under* Botany

Ethnology(ists), 29, 155, 158, 174, 175, 232, 249, 259, 290; bias, 254; founders, 173

Euphrates River, 21, 24, 27, 91, 351, 352

Europe(ans), 27, 35, 48, 64, 66, 131, 185–86, 209, 224–25, 387; Atlantic, beliefs about, 66; civilization, 70, 396–97; culture, backbone of, 363; expansion, 35, 37, 130, 145; Polynesians, 165–66

Evans, C., 271, 272, 378, 379

Evolution, 59; in America, 63; cultural-isolationist interpretation, 231; independent, 62, 229, 273,

337, 354, 362, probability, 83–84, 91–92, vs. diffusion, 376, 378; local, 373; "micro-," 158–59

Explorations, 3, 8, 37ff., 53, 66, 123, 187; oceanic, 37; stimuli, 354. *See* Heyerdahl *and Ra I and Ra II*

Explorers, 35, 37ff., 40ff., 52–53, 55, 65, 70–71, 79, 93, 95, 97, 116, 130, 132–33, 135ff., 164ff., 193, 199, 205, 207, 260ff., 388, 390; primitive, 39. *See also under* name

Eyraud, Eugène, 292, 294–95, 325

Faeroes (islands), 48, 50

Falkenstein, A., 9, 362

Far East, European arrival, 35. *See* Asia

Fatuhiva (island), 289–90

Fedde, F., 249, 250

Ferdinand, King, and Isabella, Queen, 138; Columbus, 146–47

Ferdon, E. N., 229, 236–37, 287, 302–4, 313, 328, 330, 333

Fiji, 152, 159, 160, 168, 171, 198, 237, 250, 393; America, plant contact evidence, 251; cultural interisland diffusion, 241–42

Flood, the (biblical), 367–69

Floods, primal, 21

Floreana Island, 259, 266–70

Food-gatherers, 63, 129, 275

Forests: balsa, 213; cedar, 19, 20, 351, 352; rain, 99, 284, 373

Fornander, A., 94, 178, 179, 180

Forster, G., 230, 324

France, 264–65, 290, 294, 296

Galápagos Islands, 39, 40, 52, 183, 199, 225, 237, 259ff., 265–66, 388–89; archaeology, 258ff., 270, *ill.* 270; art, 265ff., 270–73, 276; characteristics, 257–58, 262ff., 268, 272, 275; discovery, 262, 265, 272; Ecuador, 389; Europeans, 260ff.; Incas, 199; location, 275; maps, 265; name, 262–63;

settlement, 266ff., 276; Spain, 260ff., 265ff., pre-Spanish visits, 257–73, *Archaeological Evidence,* 260

Gamboa, Sarmiento de, 187ff., 208, 218, 260, 340–41

Ganges River, 23, 354

Garcilasso, Inca, 78, 80, 105, 107, 189, 207, 211, 218

Genealogy, 160, 177, 179, 180

Genetics, 157–58, 166–67, 229; America–Polynesia contact evidence, 245, 247–48; indicators of human movement, 230

Geography(ers), 144, 155, 364, 376–77

Geology, 355, 357, 370

Germany, 143, 268; Berlin-Dahlem Museum, 222, 223

Gibraltar, 6, 50, 81; Straits of, 6, 71

Gilbert Island, 37

Gods, 94, 108, 111, 112, 127, 132, 178, 179, 182; bearded, pre-Columbian, 93–125; -culture, 115; -hero, 114, 395–96. *See* Viracocha

Gonzalez, Felipe, 199, 293

Graydon, J. J., 157, 166–67

Greece, 22, 70, 81, 84, 357, 359–60, 364; astronomy, 144–45; Egypt, 364; origins, 70

Greenland, 29, 48, 50, 129, 131, 135ff., 145, 319; decline, 142–44; discovery, 132–33; religion, 134, 141–42; settlement, 48, 50, 136–37

Gregory, H. E.: *Geography of the Pacific,* 155

Gretzer, W., 221–23

Grove, D. C., 380

Guam, 54; discovery, 37, 52–53, 388

Guanche, 374, 375–76

Guatemala, 116, 262, 272, 287

Gulf of Mexico, 64, 67, 71, 120

Gulf Stream, 52

Haddon, A. C., 322; *Canoes of Oceania,* 202

Handy, E. S. C., 47, 320; *Polynesian Religion,* 186

Harappans (early people), 8–9

Hawaii, 38, 39, 41, 47, 52, 98–99, 172, 175, 178, 180–81, 202, 215, 237, 248, 249, 281, 391, 395; America, 44, 242, 248–50; canoes, 44, 174, 393; discovery, 185, 186, 248, 249; museums, 246, 249; Polynesia, 165; settlement, 178, 179; steppingstone, 172, 180

Hebrews, 20, 21, 362, 363; flight from Egypt, 357–58; God, 368, 369; the flood, 367, 368

Heine-Geldern, R. von, 41, 163, 338, 345, 379

Henderson Island, 258

Herculaneum, 357

Heyerdahl, Thor, 12, 42–43, 204, 289, 366, 374; *American Indians in the Pacific,* 153; Asia-Polynesia migration route, 153; balsa raft voyage: South America–Polynesia, 290; Easter Island, 291ff., 323ff., *Art of,* 321, expedition, 336, 343, 347, 390; Galápagos, 270ff.; lectures, 154, 204, 292, 321. *See Kon-Tiki and Ra* voyages

Hieroglyphics, 9, 70, 84, 85, 94, 115, 128, 361, 362, 372; pre-Columbian, 93

Hillebrand, W., 249; *Flora of the Hawaiian Islands,* 248

Hill-Tout, Prof. C., 166, 167

History(ians), 12, 23, 37, 39, 48, 50, 78, 82, 112, 127, 131, 138, 141, 143, 208, 364; art confirmation of, 117–18; chroniclers, 104ff., 146, 206, 208, 371; Inca, 35, 106; lessons of, 388; milestones, 370–71; Norse sagas, 127, 132, 136; oral records, 371; recorded, 128; repeating, 376–77; traditional, 67; written, 67

Hittites, 20, 67–68, 83, 88, 306, 351, 352, 358, 367, 375, 384; art, 73, 85, *ill.* 72
Holland, 97, 185, 187, 292–93, 321
Holy Land, 127, 132, 139–40
Hornell, J., 202ff., 214, 269
Human contact-cultural parallels, 64. *See* Diffusion
Human movements, 279. *See* Migrations
Human nature, 117, 123
Humboldt, Alexander, 209, 225, 229, 280–81
Humboldt Current, 28, 33, 219, 261, 263, 276, 378; birthplace, 41
Hutchinson, J. B., 76–77, 237–38, 248

Ibiza, 72, 73, 90, 385
Iceland, 48, 50, 127, 129, 319, 360, 370; Christianity, 134
Imbelloni, J., 173–74
Incas, v, 35, 68, 70, 102, 104–7, 128, 162, 192, 193, 214. 268–69, 275, 347, 385–86; civilization, 63–64, 67, 88; descendants, 73; economy, 189–90; god, 112; historians, 35, 187, 190, 208, 268–69, 322, 340–41; language, 108; last, 187; mariners. 188–90, 218ff.; Pacific exploration, 187ff., *map* 197; Polynesia, 185–200; pre-Inca period, 63–64, 76, 109, 211, 339–40; rise (date), 347–48; route, 52 (*see* Mendaña route); watercraft, 46, 188ff., 269. *See* Viracocha
India, 8, 162, 279, 354; Columbus, 145; famous cities, 352; Mediterranean contact, 364–65
Indian Ocean, 94, 364
Indo-Americans, 165
Indonesia, 35, 38, 39, 41, 54, 96, 97, 98, 101, 145, 153, 165, 242, 254, 366: America, 54; ancestry, 174; coconut. 250, 279. 280: language, 156; Mexico, route from, 53–54,

ill. 49; Peru, 34–35; Spain, 37ff.; watercraft, 168. *See* Polynesia
Indo-Pacific route, 95
Indus Valley, 8, 337–38, 354; civilization, 364–65; Easter Island hypothetic migration, *ill.* 339
Ingris, Eduard, 39, 40, 42–43, 53, 55
Inland seas, 22
International Congress for Anthropology and Ethnology: 7th, 321
International Congress of Americanists: 33rd, 204; 35th, 28; 36th, 187
Inventions, spread of, 84
Iraq, 3, 9, 10, 24, 350, 352, 365; Arabs, 3, 24
Ireland, 48, 50, 139
Isabela Island, 266, 267, 268
Isolation(ists), 120, 237, 238, 239, 353, 378, 388; basic law, 68; cultural revolution, 231; -Diffusionists, 59–92, 378, anthropological controversy, 74; genetics, 79; premise, 376–77; theory, 257ff.
Israel, 6, 20, 352, 357, *ill.* 7; Lost Tribe, 120
Italy, 6, 145, 207
Itzamná, 113

Jacobsen, Captain A., 164, 166, 171, 173
Jakeman, M. W., 252
Japan, 38, 47; Current, 34, 38, 47, 54, 96, 164, 248; Ecuador, parallels, 34
Jaussen, Bishop T., 331, 336
Jerusalem, 139–40, 363
Jesuits, 193
Jews, 375. *See* Hebrews
John XXI, Pope, 142
Juan, G., 209, 224–25
Juan Fernandez Islands, 257, 258, 275

Judaism, 367

Junks, 31, 39, 41, 55, 391

Kava drinking, 162, 163, 182, 345, 346

Knöbl, Kuno, 41, 55

Knoche, W., 243, 311, 322

Knorozov, J. V., 339

Knudsen, R.: *Traces of Reed Boats in the Pacific,* 202

Kon-Tiki (book), v

Kon-Tiki (raft), v, 201; experiments, 217–19, 226–28, 245, 281; model for, 39, 216; name, 216; Pacific dogma prior to voyage, ix; voyage (1947), 32–33, 39, 40, 41, 153, 198, 216–18, 229, 234, 236, 270, 291, *ill.* 42–43, accomplishments, 41, 236, objective, 215–16, route, *ill.* 197, success, 257

Kramer, Prof., 365, 366, 367

Kukulcan, 113–14

Kuroshiwo Current, 54, 154. *See* Japan Current

Kuviqu, voyage, *ill.* 42–43

Kwakiutl people, 165, 168, 176, 177–78; *Tales,* 178

La Aztlán, voyage, 40

La Balsa, voyage, 40, *ill.* 42–43

Labrador, 48; Current, 52

Lacandones (civilization), 69, 73

La Cantuta I, voyage, 39, *ill.* 42–43

La Cantuta II, voyage, 40, *ill.* 42–43

La Guayaquil, voyage, 40

Lake Chad, 22, 24, 91

Lake Tana, 23, 352

Lake Titicaca, 14, 70, 91–92, 95, 105–6, 108, 118, 211, 245, 307; reed boats, 22, 23, 328, 352

La Mooloolaba, voyage, 40

Landström, Björn, 12, 14, 19

Language (linguistics), 45, 127, 158, 167, 178, 239, 337–38; biblical, 139; contact evidence, 240–41, 243–44, 247; cultural

parallels, 167; hibiscus, 239–40; ideograms, 335–36, 338, 341–42, 362; -racial kinship, 155, 156, 157. *See under* Easter Island *and* Polynesia

La Pérouse, 244, 254, 294, 308

Laplanders, 319

Las Casas, 146, 206, 218

Las 3 Balsas, voyage, *ill.* 42–43

Lavachery, H., 290, 296, 298, 301, 311, 312, 323, 342, 343

La Venta, 69, 70, 73, 85, 121

Leakey family, 373

Lebanon, 6, 19, 22, 124, 140; cedar, 19, 20, 351

Leeward Islands, 31

Legends, 108ff., 114–16, 177, 178, 180, 186; Atlantis, 359–60

Leif Eirikson route, 48–50, *ill.* 49

Lescallier, M., 209, 225

Libraries. *See* Alexandria *under* Egypt

Libya, 6

Literature, 127, 131, 258, 359; pre-Columbian, 134–35

Lixus ("Eternal City"), 22, 67, 68, 81, 123, 352, 356, 376

Lothrop, S. K., 100, 205, 211, 213–15, 223, 269; "Aboriginal Navigation off the West Coast of South America," 213

Magdalena River, 28

Magellan, 3, 37, 52–53, 388

Malays (and archipelago), 54, 94, 96, 153–54, 156

Malaysia, 162

Malta, 6, 81, 352ff., 361, *ill.* 10

Man: timespan, 373–74

Mangareva, 31, 199, 202, 250, 289

Maoris, 160, 169, 171, 173ff., 180, 203, 230, 251, 319–20, 391; cultural parallels, 393; Polynesians, v, 174, 175, 233. *See* New Zealand

Maps(makers), 34, 155, 265, 364; Mercator, 34, 48

Marco Polo, 35, 38; retracing route, 366

Marianas, 37, 54

Markham, C. R., 238–69, 322, 323, 335

Marquesas (islands), 31, 45, 165, 183, 215, 237, 246, 247, 281, 282, 307, 346; America, contact evidence, 242ff.; art, 313, 332, 344, 347; discovery, 37, 185, 198, 254, 390; Heyerdahl, 289; Peru, 33–34

Marriage, 84, 94, 141, 394

Marshall Islands, 37

Martius, C. V. P. de, 235–36, 279, 280

Mayas, v, 64, 67, 68, 70, 73, 113–14, 116, 119, 128, 382, 383; ancestry, 372, 373, 385; calendar, 81, 371, 373–74, 385; pyramids, 122 (*see* Chichén Itzá)

Means, P. A., 205, 214, 268–69, 331

Medicine, 129, 250. *See under* Plants

Mediterranean, 20, 81–82, 354, 357, 375; Afro-Asiatic area, 120; America, shared culture traits, 61, 84ff.; catastrophes, 82–83, 357ff.; civilization(s), vi, 6, 8, 352–54, 370ff.; culture, 70, 360–61, evolution, 383, high areas, 94, 319, parallels: Peru, 65, 68, 76, 118, Polynesia, 94ff.; important dates (milestones), 370ff.; watercraft, 6, 10, 31, 81

Meggers, B. J., 271, 272, 378–81

Melanesia, 37, 40, 45, 52–53, 94, 184, 250–51, 291, 320; America, contact evidence, 251; discovery, 35, 38, 386, 390, 393

Mendaña Alvaro de, 52, 95, 185, 187; expeditions, 35, 37, 38, 187ff., 200, 208, 254, 260; route, 52–55, 95, *ill.* 49

Mendel's law of inheritance, 157

Mercator's world map, 34, 48

Merrill, E. D., 79, 231ff., 241, 251

Meso-American culture, 378, 379, 385

Mesopotamia, 6, 8–9, 21, 22, 29, 76, 91, 94ff., 368; art, 20, 123, 350; civilization, 66, 352ff., 361ff.; Egypt, 8, 61; pyramids, 85–86, *ill.* 87; watercraft, 8, 10, 21, 24–26, 351–52. *See* Sumer *and* Ur

Métraux, Alfred, 259, 290ff., 311, 312, 324, 326, 327, 337–38, 340; Easter Island, 302, 323

Mexico, 28, 29, 37, 38, 53, 60, 65, 72, 80, 81, 85, 87, 99, 110, 114ff., 129, 185, 306, 338, 352, 371–72; civilization, 64, 119, 371, 373; culture, 66ff., 84ff., pre-Columbian, 73, 306; empire, 61; Indonesia: route, 53–54, *ill.* 49; Peru, 61, 378; plants, 74ff., 249; pyramids, *ill.* 87; Spain, 37ff., 377ff. *See also* Aztecs *and* Olmecs

Micronesia, 39, 41, 45, 53, 54, 94, 152, 158–59, 184; as buffer, 241, 393; discovery, 37, 53; size, 151

Middle East, 8, 25, 182, 367, 396–97; civilizations, 71, 80ff.; dates, 370ff.; watercraft, 26, 31

Migrations, 27, 81–82, 127, 133, 192ff., 254, 287, 319, 376; America–Polynesia, 391; Asia–Easter Island, 290, 310ff., Polynesia, 164, routes, 44, 153ff., 164; to Easter Island, 322ff.; eastward from Indonesia, 158ff., 161; Heyerdahl theories, 289ff.; hypotheses, 29ff., 94, 95; Mediterranean, 370–71; Pacific, 345, 395, –America, 232, interisland, 393; Polynesia, 168ff., apex, 392; routes, v, 34, 35, 397; steppingstones from South America, 255–397; theories, 60, 80, 152ff., 180, 254ff., 310ff., 345; transoceanic, 34, 245, 345. *See* Isolation *and* Diffusion

Minoan civilization, 82. *See* Crete

Missionaries, 244, 254, 290, 292, 295, 303, 306, 310, 325, 335, 372
Mixtecs, 70
Mochica culture, 63, 68, 70
Mohammedanism, 367
Mohenjo Daro, 352, 354
Monetary systems, 161, 171
Montesinos, Father, 339–40
Montezuma, 71, 110–11, 117, 129, 371–72
Morocco, 6, 14, 22, 51, 67, 120, 352; Berbers, 51, 123–24
Moses, 20
Moslems, 139, 140, 367
Mount Ararat, 21, 368
Movement (human), freedom of, 27
Mulloy, W., 292, 299–300, 313, 337
Mummification, 76, 86, 94, 98ff., 117, 182, 375, 394
Museums, 6, 9, 71, 85, 87, 154, 217, 220, 222, 242, 246, 249, 258, 259, 263, 271, 292, 296, 304, 309, 336, 343, 345, 350, 351, 363, 374, 376, 378. See under name
Musical instruments, 178–79
Mycenaean civilization, 82
Mythology, 114–16, 160, 177, 326–28, 335, 360

Navigation, ix, 37ff., 100, 131, 193–94, 225, 364, 366, 370, 394–95; aboriginal, 188, 260, ". . . off the West Coast of South America," 213; Asia, 44, 161; centerboard, 209, 224; culture transmission, 53, 366; Diffusionist theory, 41: early, 3–26, 353; evolution, 349ff.; guara (see under Balsa rafts); importance, 365; ocean, 4, 10, 12, 20, 25, 66, 363; prehistoric, 34, 232; primitive, 28ff., 41; sailing, 218ff. See also under Balsa rafts and Pacific problem
Navigators, 8, 39, 44, 55, 130, 134, 187, 190, 208, 231, 275, 282;

early: -culture plants, 229–54; gods as, 368–70
Nazca culture, 63, 70
Newfoundland, 50, 137
New Guinea, 38, 52, 53, 161
New Hebrides, 37
New World, vi, 5–6, 48–50, 116–17, 135–37, 232; culture, geographical pattern, 69; discovery, 135; Homo Sapiens, 59ff.; -Old, 60ff., isolationists vs. diffusionists, 59–92
New Zealand, 31, 45, 165, 175–76, 179, 332, 344, 392–93; discovery, 39. See also Maori
Niblack, A. P., 168, 176
Nicaragua, 338
Nicholas III, Pope, 142
Nicholas V, Pope, 143
Nile River, 8, 11–12, 15, 16, 27, 28, 350, 351, 352; Blue, 22; Valley, 8
Nineveh, 10, 123, 366
Niño Current, 218, 219, 261, 276, 378
Noah, 20–21, 351, 368, 369
Nordenskiöld, E., 211, 236, 338
Norsemen, 48, 50, 124, 127ff., 137, 148, 387; route, ill. 49; sagas, 127, 132, 136
North Equatorial Current, 37, 50, 52, 54. See Canary Current
Norway, 48, 50, 127ff., 139ff., 217, 257–58, 268, 292; Oslo, 91, 92, 259, 289
Norwegian Archaeological Expedition to Easter Island and the East Pacific (1965), 276–92
Nubian Desert, rock carvings, 6, 8

Oceania, 156, 175, 185–86, 344–45, 387; America, pre-Columbian contact, proof, 236; exploration-drift theory, 45–46; rafts, 202ff., voyages, 39–41, ill. 42–43
Oceanography, 48
Oceans, 31, 145, 367, 396–97 as

barriers, 232, 239; clockwork, 397; as culture highways, 354, 359; currents (*see* Currents *and under* name); danger areas, 32; distances, determinants, 33–34; drifts, 152, 247, 284; isolationists vs. diffusionists, 60, 78; liners, 61; marine conveyers, 61, 67, 95, 290, 388–89; navigation, 4, 10, 12, 20, 25, 66, 363; paths across, 27–55 (*see under* name)

Odin, 132, 133

Oeno Island, 258

Olav, King, 133–35

Old Testament: the flood, 368

Old World, 4, 162–63, 231ff.; civilizations, direction of movement, 81; -New, 64ff., contact evidence, 73ff., 231–32; Polynesia, 155ff., 162ff., 241–42

Oliva, Anello, 193

Olmecs, 68–70, 71ff., 80, 81, 83, 90, 91, 119–20, 124–25, 128, 371, 378, *ill.* 121; art, 73, 85, 119, 373, *ill.* 72; civilization, 64, 66–67, 69, influence, 379; culture, 373–74, hero, *ill.* 121

Olson, R. L., 164, 168–69

Oppenheim, A. L., 8, 9

Orellana (explorer), 79, 116

Orkney Islands, 134

Ortelius, Abraham, 263

Oviedo, 189, 207, 218, 279

Pacific Ocean, v, 4, 30, 38, 155, 187ff., 253, 389; America, 38ff., 47; Asia, 35ff., 44, 53; currents, 28, 252–53; diffusion, 160; dogma, ix; East, 96, 168, 181, 183, 276; exploration: determinants, 52, drift theory, 45–46; hemisphere, 34, 35, 38, *ill.* 36 (*see* size); islands, naming, 185; Micronesia, size, 151; migrations, 393, 395, routes, 35, 37, 38ff., 41, 54, 159 (*see* America *and* Asia); natural

conveyers, 54, 388–89 (*see also* routes); peoples, origins, 161–62; problem (*see* Pacific problem); size, 38, 145, 151, 164–65, 388; South, 53; steppingstones (*see* Hawaii); trans-Pacific theories, 241; West, 96, 162. *See* Kon-Tiki *and* Oceania

Pacific problem, 149–254: Asia–Polynesia (easy way), 151–84; balsa raft navigation, 152, 201–28; culture plants/early navigators, 229–54; Incas as guides to Polynesia, 185–200; island-hopping theory, 155. *See* Migration theories

Pacifica, voyage, 40, *ill.* 42–43

Pacific Science Congress: 5th, 47; 10th, 230, 254, 260; 13th, 28, 154

Palenque, 115

Panama, 79, 110, 206, 272, 276, 283, 338; Isthmus, 35, 65, 68, 80, 95

Pan-Polynesian cultures, 163, 169–71, 172ff., 317, 345–46, 391, 393ff.; gods, 326, 386, 395–96; migrations, apex, 392; roots, 393

Papua-Melanesia, 39, 96, 152

Papyrus, 14, 22, 23, 24. *See under* Ships

Parchesi-patolli relationship, 62–63

Paris, F. E., 210–11, 212, 225, 226

Parrots, 229–30

Penal colonies, 267–68, 284–86

Persian Gulf, 8, 22

Peru, v, 6, 29, 33–34, 37, 74, 98, 104, 107ff., 182, 185, 208, 211–12, 229–30; Ancon, 74, 79; art, 29, 80, 270ff., 327; burial customs, 25, 76–80, 98–103, 220, 221; culture, 60ff., 66, 84, 106, 109, 211, 328ff., 339–41, 391, 394, hero, 216; discovery, 104, 107; Easter Island, 291; empire, 61; Galápagos, 273, 276; Mediterranean, 68, 76; Mexico, 378; navigation, 204–18, 228; plants, 74, 76, 243; Polynesia, 41,

182ff., 204ff.; population, 100;
pre-Inca, 97, 98, 100–1; pyramids,
101, 118, *ill.* 87; sailings from,
37ff., 41, 46; Spain, 68, 377,
Conquest, 78, 104, 106;
watercraft, 15, 22, 24, 25, 32,
202ff., 208, 214, 222, 390. *See also*
Incas

Peru Current, 52, 194, 229, 246,
258, 272, 276

Petri, H., 161, 171

Petroglyphs, 5, 8, 10, 29, 44

Philip II, King of Spain, 187

Philippines, 35, 37, 38, 161

Philippine Sea, 54, 164

Philology, 156

Phoenicians, 6, 20, 51, 67–68,
70–71, 81, 82, 84, 89–90, 124, 319,
362, 363, 374–75, *ill.* 72;
civilization, 66, 354; origin, 375;
ports, 6, 14, 70–71, 354;
watercraft, 31, 350–51, 376

Piracy, 48, 131, 142–44, 258, 262ff.,
272

Pitcairn Island, 258, 307, 313, 394

Pitt Rivers Museum (Oxford), 258

Pizarro, Francisco, 65, 66, 68, 71,
93, 104, 110, 188, 192, 228, 262,
335, 377, 388; expeditions, 205–7

Pizarro, Hernando, 213

Pizarro, Pedro, 104, 189, 206, 335

Place names, 94–95, 179, 365

Plant geographers, 79, 229, 232, 252

Plants: as contact evidence (*see*
Culture plants); medicinal 245,
249–50, 253, 297, 314

Plato, 359–60

Pliny, 23

Polack, J. S., 175, 203

Polynesia, ix, 33, 39, 40, 41, 49, 52,
96ff., 154ff., 165–66, 176, 186,
201–2, 230, 237, 282, 289, 326,
393ff.; America, 242, plant
contact evidence, 229ff., 246ff.
(*see* Easter Island, Hawaii *and*
Marquesas); ancestry, 41, 45–46,
160ff., 174, 181; area, 183; from

Asia (easy way), 151–84;
cultural parallels, 94ff., 103,
155ff., 162ff.; culture, 96, 163ff.,
201–2, 346, authority, 298 (*see*
Buck, Sir Peter), sub-stratum,
181–83, 237, 393ff.; discovery, 35,
37, 38, 198, 387, 393; East, 168ff.,
344; Incas as guides, 185–200;
Indonesia, 156ff.; location, 152;
Malays, 154, 174; Old World
links, 155, 241; origins, 152,
155ff., 174, 175, 183–84, 204ff.;
Peru, 214–15, 233 (*see*
Kon-Tiki); Philippine Sea,
steppingstone area, 47; plants, 77,
241 (*see* Culture plants); routes
to, 45–47, 165; settling, 94, 96,
258, 319–20, 388, theory, 41;
triangle, 181, 182, 202, 233, 321,
392, 394; *uru-keu*, 96, 99, 103;
watercraft, 25, 31, 168, 201ff.,
394ff. *See also* Easter Island,
Kon-Tiki voyage *and* Maori

Poma, Guaman, 78

Pomerance, L., 82, 357

Pompeii, 357

Popes, 140–42

Population, 64, 82

Porter, David, 266, 282

Ports, 6, 8–9, 14, 20, 35, 356, 376

Portugal, 35, 38, 79, 140, 145

Prain, D., 249

Pre-Columbian civilizations,
116–18, 231ff.; bearded gods,
93–125; determinants, 70;
founders, 102ff., 377; Old
World-New contact, 60–92, 387

Prescott, W. H., 78

Primitive Navigation, 154

Proas, 31, 47, 168

"Projekt Pazifik," 41

Ptolemy, 144

Puna Island, 188, 189, 206, 207

Pyramids, 10, 11, 25, 66, 85–86, 94,
109, 114, 115, 120, 122–23, 179,
218, 355, 365, 368, *ill.* 87;

pre-Inca, 101. *See under* country *or* culture

Quechua Indians, 15–16, 73, 97
Queen Charlotte Islands, 165, 168, 173
Quest for America, The, 60, 94
Quetzalcoatl, 110, 111ff., 129; pyramid, 120
Quiros expedition, 37

Ra (sun god), 94
Ra voyages: Atlantic dogma prior to voyages, ix; expeditions, 23–24, book, v. *See Ra I and Ra II*
Ra I, 10, 14ff., 33, 68, 366, 381
Ra II, 7, 8, 10, 14ff., 24, 33, 68, 91–92, 366, 381, *ill.* 18; Columbus route, 52
Rafts 5–6, 31, 32, 40, 41, 55, 193–94, 210ff., 211, 390; balsa (*see* Balsa rafts); evolution, 349ff.; modern voyages, 39–41, 46; navigation sub-stratum, 395
Raivavae Island, 307, 313
Rao, S. R., 8
Raroia, 39, 40, 201, 216
Red Sea, 6, 8, 22
Reed, E. K., 226, 270
Reed boats, 3, 6–8, 9, 10, 22, 23, 25, 31, 55, 68, 122–23, 182, 202ff., 244, 327, 328, 352, 355, 356, 376, 394, *ill.* 5, 6–7, 17, 329; building, 15–16, 95, 203, center, 381; cultural parallels, 91, 92. *See also Ra I and Ra II*
Reeds, 22, 24–25, 244–45; sources, 22. *See* Papyrus
Religion(s), 84, 85, 86, 111, 138–39, 326–28; modern, 367; orders, 372
Resch, Walther, 6
Rivadeneira, Capt. Diego de, 262, 272
Robinson Crusoe, 258
Rochebrune, A. T. de, 78–79
Roggeveen, Jacob, 37, 97, 185, 187, 194, 199, 293, 317, 334
Rome (ancient), 22, 23, 48, 67, 68, 70, 81, 84, 132, 140, 356
Ross, A. S. C., 324
Routledge, Katherine Scoresby, 290, 296, 347; expedition, 301ff., 317, 322, misinterpretation, 298
Rowse, J. H., 64ff.; "Diffusionism and Archaeology," 64
Ruins, megalithic, 85, 94, 95, 105, 116, 181
Ruiz, Bartolomeo, 205, 206
Rulers, 84, 94, 104, 111, 113, 310ff., 338, 348, 368, 371. *See also under* name *and/or* culture
Russia, 133, 294, 339

Sáamanos, Juan de, 205, 206, 218, 219
Saavedra (explorer), 38, 53; route, 53–55, *ill.* 49
Sahara, 6, 8, 350, *ill.* 13
St. Brendan, 50
St. John, H., 236
St. Johnston, T. R., 162–63
Sala-y-Gómez, 194–95, 258
Salmon, A. P., 322
Salmon, Tati, 295
Salonen, A., 9–10
Samoa, 39, 40, 45, 158, 159, 171, 181, 183, 198; Polynesia, 165; -Tonga-Fiji triangle, 251
San Cristobal, 267–68
Sanskrit, 156
Santa Cruz Island, 259, 268, 270
Santiago Island, 259, 264, 266, 270
Santo Domingo (Hispañola), 79
Santorini (Thera), 357–59; Atlantis, 359; volcanic explosion (1200 B.C.), 82, 357, 358, 361, 370
Sardinia, 6, 22, 352
Sauer, C. O., 75, 79, 232, 238, 251, 252
Savoy, Gene, 42–43, 68, 381
Sayce, R. U., 47
Scandinavia, 124, 127
Schurmann, E. S., 171

Science, 353, 361, 388
Scotland, 134
Seafaring, vi, 31, 32, 54
"Sea Peoples," 82, 88, 104, 375
Sea Routes to Polynesia (lecture), 154
Seemann, B., 161, 251
Selkirk, Alexander, 258
Selling, O. H., 296, 297
Semitic peoples, 51
Semple, N. M., 167
Serologists, 166
Seven Sisters, voyage, 39, *ill.* 42–43
Severin, T., 50
Shafat (reed boats), 22
Shapiro, H. L., 165, 320, 322–23
Sharp, Bartholomew, 263
Shetlands, 48
Shipbuilding, 6, 24, 204, 209, 225–26, 363, 370, 375–76; buoyancy, 4, 31; evolution, 10ff., 20, 22, 25–26; first, 350; principles, 350
Ships, v, 4, 6, 10, 11–12, 22, 31, 39, 50, 205, 350–52, *ill.* 13; Bible references, 20–21; early, and the sea, 1–55, importance, 359, navigation, beginning, 3–26, paths across the oceans, 27–55 (*see* Pacific routes); first, theory of, 4; hieroglyphic sign, 9; papyrus, v, 10–12, 14, 20, 24, 25, 91–92, *ill.* 13 (*see Ra I and Ra II*); rafts (*see* Rafts); reed (*see* Reed boats); sailing, 3, 4, 8, 16, 26, 35ff., 54, 55, 61, 223, 364. *See also* Watercraft, *under* culture *or* civilization, *and under* type of ship
Shortland, E., 179
Siberia, 59, 62, 397
Sicily, 140
Silow, R. A., 75–77, 232, 237–38
Simmons, R. T., 157, 167
Skinner, H. D., 174
Skjölsvold, A., 226, 259, 260, 276, 292, 299, 302, 308, 313, 337

Skogman, C., 225, 267, 270
Skottsberg, Carl, 244–45, 247, 302, 328
Smith, C. S., 292, 311–12, 337
Smith, S. Percy, 94, 180, 186
Smithsonian Institution, 271
Society for American Archaeology, 260
Society Islands, 37, 172, 198, 202, 215, 237, 250, 284
Solomon Islands, 37, 187
Soto, Captain, 189
South America, 14, 15, 31, 34, 37, 352, 393ff.; drift theory, 46; high-culture area, 347; Indians, ix, 15–16, 91, 97 (*see under* name); Oceania, raft voyages, 39–43, *ill.* 42–43; overseas contact, 287; Pacific, explorations from, 37ff.; steppingstones from, 255–397. *See* Balsa rafts
Southeast Asia. *See under* Asia
South Equatorial Current, 50, 52
South Pole, 130
South Seas, 174
Southwest Journal of Anthropology, 204
Spain, 6, 37ff., 140, 145, 192, 205, 209, 224, 264, 279; caravels (*see* Caravels); Cocos Island, 277ff.; Columbus, 146–47; Conquest, 93, 95, 106, 108, 110–11, 185, 189, 335, 372; Easter Island, 293, 294, 323; Galápagos, 260ff., 272–73; Indonesia, 35; New World, 68, 71, 93ff., 116–17, 377; Pacific, 185, 187ff., routes, 38. *See* Conquistadors
Spilbergen, Joris van, 208–9, 223
Stephens, S. G., 75–77, 232, 237–38
Stevenson, W. B., 209–10, 225
Stewart, T. D., 100–1, 102
Stine, Anne, 137
Stokes, J. F. G., 47, 172, 249
Stone Age, 3, 129, 360; people, 151, 152, 161, 200
Stone masonry (statues), 85, 90, 94,

109, 215, 276, 313; Easter Island, 301ff.
Stonor, C. R., 75, 232
Sturlasson, Snorre, 127, 132, 135, 139, 140, 141
Sullivan, L. R., 157, 320
Sumatra, 161
Sumer(ian) civilization, 25, 67–68, 352, 354, 362ff., 370; art, 9, 10, 25, 73, 365, *ill.* 72; excavations, 365, 368; founding, 21; influence, 365, 367; version of the flood, 368–69
Sun: personification, 108; worshipers, 67–68, 84, 94, 109, 117, 192, 314–15, 327, 347, 356, 372
Survival (at sea), 31, 32, 54
Sweden, 127, 132, 267, 292, 296, 302
Syria, 6, 8

Taboos, 167, 179
Tahiti, 41, 175, 179–80, 295, 320, 325, 326; discovery, 37; pyramids, *ill.* 87
Tahiti Nui II, voyage, 40, *ill.* 42–43
Tai Ki, voyage, 41ff., 44, 47
Tangaroa, voyage, 40, *ill.* 42–43
Tasmania, 38–39, 152
Tax, crusader's, 138, 142
Tello, J. C., 100
Thomas, W. J., 242–43, 244, 306, 320, 343
Thorsky, E. and Anne, 167
Tiahuanaco, 63, 69, 70, 95, 101, 105–6, 118, 307–8, 328, 331ff., 341, 347, 396; builders, 108; Easter Island parallels, 314ff.; importance, 109; ruins, 352
Tidal waves, 357, 358–59, 370
Tierra del Fuego, 60, 172, 195
Tigris River, 21, 24, 27, 91, 352
Tilikum (canoe), 44
Toltecs, 64, 70
Tombs. *See* Burial customs
Tonga Islands, 37, 39, 159, 160, 165, 215

Totem poles, 175–76, 395
Trade, 8–9, 20, 37, 67, 70, 159–60, 354, 364–65; Dilmun (Bahrain), importance, 365–67; importance, 20; posts, 37, 67, 70, 145, 287; routes, 38, 131, 137–38, 276, 354; winds, 33, 37, 46–48, 50, 52, 174, 194, 367, 397
Traditions, 160, 396
Transatlantic parallels, 92, 383
Transoceanic voyages, 3, 4, 34, 124–25
Trans-Pacific contacts, 241, 379–80
Treasure hunters, 285–86
Trepanation, 86, 94, 182
Tres Zapotes, 121
Trotter, M., 101–2
Tuamotu Islands, 32, 33, 37, 39, 40, 198, 199, 201, 216
Tundar, 59, 60, 61
Tupac Inca, 190–92, 198–200
Tupia of Ulitea, 281–82
Turkey, 8, 10, 351
Tzendals (Indians), 114–15

Uhle, M., 211
Ulloa, A. de, 209, 224–25
Universities: Cambridge, 382; Heidelberg, v; Kansas, 292; New Mexico, 204; Oslo, 289; Pennsylvania, 368, Museum, 154; Wyoming, 292
Ur, 8, 9, 10, 21, 72, 73, 80, 95, 369, 370; importance, 367; Jews' migration from, 384
Urdaneta, 38; route, 54–55, *ill.* 49
Uru Indians, 15–16, 95, 97
Uruk, 10, 24
United States, 63, 225, 259, 266, 271; National Museum, 242, 378

Vaca, Caboza de, 116
Valcárcel, Dr. L., 105
Valli, Mario, 40, 42–43
Vancouver, Captain, 44, 155, 165, 166, 174

Vancouver Island, 165, 177, 396.
    See Kwakiutl people
Vargas, Juan de, 106
Vasco de Gama, 354
Vatican, 48, 138
Venezuela, 110
Vikings, 127ff., 136, 231, 319;
    Columbus, 127–48; defined, 131;
    watercraft, 11–12, 31, 131, 351
Villamil, General, 266–67
Vinaque, 105
Vinland, 139ff., 143, 146
Viracocha, Con-Tici, 104ff., 116,
    190, 192, 275, 331, 386; statues,
    118, 307
Volcanoes, 199, 258, 296, 297, 303,
    314, 357
Volga River, 27
Von Hagen, V. W., 269
Von Hornbostel, E., 338
Voss, Captain J. C., 44, 168

Wafer, Captain, 278–79, 283, 284
Ward, R. G., 45, 46
Watercraft, 3, 4, 9–10, 23, 25, 29ff.,
    39–41, 192ff., 225, 350, *ill.* 10;

evolution, 349ff.; cultural
    parallels, 91. *See also under* Ships
    and type
Weapons, 173–74, 182, 301, 344,
    395
Webb, J. W., 45, 46
Weckler, J. E., "Polynesian
    Explorers of the Pacific," 215
West Indies, 234
Wheel, 71–73, 89, 161, *ill.* 72
White, J.: *Ancient History of
    Maori,* 230
Willis, William, 39, 40, 42–43
Wilson, David, 99–100, 131
World War I, 24
World War II, 41, 153, 268
Writing, 337–41, 366, 397; script,
    337–38, 362

Xeres, Francisco de, 205, 218

Yanglinge Saga, 127
Yucatán, 113–14. *See* Chichén Itzá

Zárate, 189, 207, 218
Zoologists, 30

ASIA

NORTH PACIFIC OCEAN

JAPAN

"URDANETA ROUTE"
from the Philippines to
northwestern North America
and Mexico

NORT

Hawaiian Is.

PHILIPPINES

Johnston I.

"SAAVEDRA ROUTE"
from Mexico to Micronesia
and Indonesia

M I C R O N E S I A

*Marshall
Is.*

Christmas I.

Caroline Is.
M E L A N E S I A

*Gilbert
Is.*

P O L Y N E S I A

INDONESIA

*New
Guinea*

Solomon Is.

PAPUA

*Ellice
Is.*

Samoa

*Marquesas
Is.* **KON-TIKI** 1947

Raroia

*Society
Is.* *Tahiti*

*Tuamotu
Archipelago*

*Fiji
Is.*

*Cook
Is.*

AUSTRALIA

*New
Caledonia*

Raivavae

Rapa *Pitcairn*

Easter I.

SOUTH PACIFIC OCEAN

Sala-y-Góm

NEW
ZEALAND

| 0 | 1000 | 2000 | 3000 | 4000 |

MILES

| 0 | 1000 | 2000 | 3000 | 4000 |

KILOMETERS

KON-TIKI